MEMORIAL STADIUM 1948

LOWELL,, MASSACHUSETTS

LATER CHANGED TO CAWLEY STADIUM

TITUS

TITUS PLOMARITIS

To Tony & Pam

Best Wishes

Titus Plomaritis

author**HOUSE®**

AuthorHouse™
1663 Liberty Drive
Bloomington, IN 47403
www.authorhouse.com
Phone: 1-800-839-8640

Published by AuthorHouse   11/8/2012

ISBN: 978-1-4772-7137-7 (sc)
ISBN: 978-1-4772-7139-1 (hc)
ISBN: 978-1-4772-7138-4 (e)

Library of Congress Control Number: 2012917764

CONTENTS

SECTION ONE

Section Two

SECTION THREE

SECTION FOUR

SECTION FIVE

SECTION SIX

DEDICATION

The dedication of this book, over seven years in the making, is to my wife of the past sixty years, Claire. We were married December 1, 1951. For our four children, she has been the most dedicated mother on this planet and she is my very best friend.

She stands 4'10" and weighs ninety-eight pounds. An expert seamstress; she alters all her own clothing and even made her wedding gown with the help of Mrs. Casaubon, a French-SPEAKING woman, from Canada, that always called me Tyrus. You will read more about Claire, in several parts of this book, but what you won't read about is this little incident that occurred prior to the nuptials.

She asked me to give her "another" driving lesson on a beautiful Sunday afternoon. At that time, I was driving a sixteen-year-old,1934, 4-door Ambassador Nash sedan, when automatic transmissions were not in existence. I felt a drive to Jamaica Plain to meet my cousins, would be reasonable, especially with the rather light traffic on Sundays. She did fairly well driving from Lowell to Boston, however when we arrived at the four-way intersection in Jamaica Plain, Washington and Green Streets, under the overhead subway tracks, she panicked and was painfully grinding the transmission gears, bucking the car like a bronco, in the dead center of the intersection. I tried to tell her what to do, in a rather loud tone, and at that instant she pulled the emergency brake, opened the door, jumped out of the car, in the middle of the intersection she said, "drive your own fucking car." Throughout our sixty years of marriage, I remind her that she was the first female I ever heard swear. (her Dad was a professional boxer, had over 100 bouts, was the **FLY WEIGHT CHAMPION** of New England and pulled no punches when he spoke to his four daughters).

For Claire (Hebert) Plomaritis, my wife and best friend for over sixty years, I created and wrote the following as an anniversary card a few years ago. I keep it in an area close to my desk and whenever we have a quarrel (yes, we do too) I read it slowly to myself, and quickly realize how precious she is. This prompts me to apologize immediately, whether I'm right or wrong.

Claire you are the **LOVE OF MY LIFE**

64 years ago (1948)   Our first kiss
61 years ago (1951)   Our first love session

With some great memories down memory lane leading up to our 61st Anniversary

i.   Our dates at Hampton and Salisbury Beach with a picnic basket full of your personally packed sandwiches

ii.   Our date at the South Common with you wearing my All Star Football Sweater and my Lowell High Football Pendant around your neck, which was my first indication that you would be my **WIFE FOR LIFE** and the **MOTHER OF OUR CHILDREN**

iii.   My Senior Prom date, when you told your dad "I'm only going to the prom, not marrying him"

iv.   December 1,1951 **OUR WEDDING DAY**, at the Rex Ballroom with the Boston University Football team in attendance

v.   Our first apartment on Liberty Street in Lowell

vi.   When you drove to BU's football camp for a little back seat love session (a coach Buff Donelli no-no)

vii.   Our first home on South Loring Street in Lowell

viii.   Our drive across the United States to California, pulling a thirty-eight foot house trailer with our ford sedan, with Titus Jr. in the back seat of our home made playpen

ix.   Our no frills grind of four additional years of Chiropractic Schooling in New York, which included the births of both Lyn and Steven

x.   Imagine eight years of college without financial assistance from anyone!!

xi.   1959, building our home-office combination and the start of a very successful private practice, also the arrival of little Di (Diane)

xii.   Our vacations with Marvin Weisberg and Warner Davis to Portugal, Spain, London, France, Italy, Belgium and Denmark

xiii. The creation of the Plomaritis Professional Center

xiv. Our lunches at Bishops and those great matinees when the kids were in school

xv. Our trip to Okinawa, (giant bubble bath) Japan **"WOVE YOUR BWOO EYES"**

xvi. Our trip to Greece, driving on the narrow mountain roads, cruise and island shopping and the funny airport departure with inability to pay for our overweight luggage

xvii. Our trip to Stuttgart, Germany to pick up our 1984 M/B from the factory and drive 1,000 miles through Switzerland and Germany enjoying Octoberfest

xviii. Our political involvement with Governor Gallen, President Carter and of course, the three time elected Representative Claire Plomaritis

xix. Our purchase and winterizing of the ski house in Bethlehem, N.H.

xx. Our twenty year involvement with the National Board of Chiropractic Examiners which included business meetings to every major city in the USA as well as Australia, New Zealand, Mexico, Bermuda and the Virgin Islands

xxi. Our diligent joint efforts and sacrifices in the growth and development of our **FOUR OUTSTANDING COLLEGE GRADUATES.**

LOVE YOU DEARLY—UNTIL DEATH DO US PART

"TITUS"

FORWARD

THIS BRIEF INTRODUCTION IS MEANT TO GIVE THE READER AN INSIGHT INTO THE LIFE OF A MAN WHO WENT FROM FARMER TO DINING WITH THE PRESIDENT OF THE UNITED STATES AND BEYOND, TO HIS MANY ACCOMPLISHMENTS AND FINALLY AS AN AUTHOR.

READ ON AS YOU TRAVEL THROUGH THE PAGES FILLED WITH ACHIEVEMENTS ACCOMPLISHED BY TITUS PLOMARITIS.

TITUS PLOMARITIS (quite a mouthful, isn't it?) LIKE MOST YOUNGSTERS IN GRAMMAR SCHOOL, THAT NAME BROUGHT FORTH A CHUCKLE FROM ME. IN FACT, AS HIS CLASSMATES, WE ACTUALLY MADE FUN OF HIM BECAUSE HE WAS A SMALL BOY AND THE NAME HE CARRIED SEEMED TOO BIG FOR HIM. WE SOON CHANGED OUR RUDE ATTITUDES! INSTEAD OF CHANTING HIS NAME, WE SPOKE IT WITH RESPECT.

GRADUATION DAY PROVED TO BE A DAY OF HAND SHAKES AND MANY PATS ON THE BACK FOR MANY OF US BUT THE OUTSTANDING STUDENT WAS TITUS PLOMARITIS...... NOT FOR HIS GRADES (he was not a disciplined scholar) BUT FOR HIS RIVETING PERSONALITY.

HIGH SCHOOL BROUGHT ABOUT MANY CHANGES AS WE EMBARKED ON OUR FUTURE. THE FRIENDSHIP BECAME MORE DISTANT DUE TO DIFFERENT ACTIVITIES BUT THE NAME TITUS PLOMARITIS WAS HEARD IN THE CORRIDORS AND

ON THE FOOTBALL FIELD. ESPECIALLY ON THE FOOTBALL FIELD.

IT WAS WARTIME IN THE EARLY 1940'S AND MEN WERE MEN. THEY WANTED TO SERVE THEIR COUNTRY AND TITUS WAS NO EXCEPTION. HE PUT HIS EDUCATION ASIDE IN HIS JUNIOR YEAR AND JOINED THE PARATROOPERS. AFTER HIS "HITCH", HE RESUMED HIS EDUCATION AND LAUNCHED A FOOTBALL CAREER THAT BROUGHT HIS FELLOW STUDENTS TO NEW HEIGHTS. THE SHORT HALFBACK CREATED A FUROR ON THE FIELD THAT HAD THE SPECTATORS ON THEIR FEET THROUGHOUT THE GAMES. HE MADE UP FOR THE LACK OF BEING TALL BY BEING FAST, SHIFTY AND DIRECT. HE GAVE US REASON TO BE PROUD AND AS HIS LIFE PROGRESSED, HE MADE US PROUDER STILL.

BECOMING A CHIROPRACTOR PUT THE FROSTING ON HIS CAKE. SUCCESSFUL IN HIS SPECIALIZED FIELD HE BECAME PRESIDENT OF THE NATIONAL CHIROPRACTIC EXAMINING BOARD AND INSTRUMENTAL IN LAUNCHING THE CAREERS OF UPCOMING CHIROPRACTORS BY EMPLOYING THEM IN HIS OWN OFFICE UNTIL THEY TOO PRACTICED IN THEIR OWN BUSINESSES.

I HAVE ONLY TOUCHED THE TIP OF THE ICEBERG IN THE ILLUSTRIOUS CAREER OF TITUS PLOMARITIS. THE BOOK THAT YOU ARE ABOUT TO READ IS HEARTWARMING AND ACCURATE IN EVERY DETAIL AND IS WRITTEN BY A POPULAR ATHLETE, A LOVING HUSBAND, A DEVOTED FATHER BUT MOST OF ALL, BY A BIG MAN.

HOW FORTUNATE I AM TO KNOW THIS MAN, HIS WIFE AND THEIR FAMILY AND TO BE GIVEN THE HONOR OF WRITING THIS SHORT FORWARD TO INTRODUCE YOU TO THEM. READ ON AND ENJOY THE LIFE AND TIMES OF TITUS PLOMARITIS, A DEAR FRIEND, WHOSE FRIENDSHIP I WILL TREASURE AS LONG AS I LIVE.

CLAIRE IGNACIO
CLASS OF 1949—LOWELL HIGH SCHOOL

INTRODUCTION

It all started about seven years ago when my children encouraged me to buy a new Macintosh computer. They convinced me that it was learner-friendly and even at my age I would quickly catch up to the children in the first grade.

They continued to feed me quips and comments that they knew would get me to the **APPLE STORE** in a hurry. The two lines that jump off the top of my head were: "Dad, you will be able to transfer the thousands of photos and negatives that you have been saving in boxes in the basement into your personal Apple iPhoto Library?", also "You will be able to preserve the hundreds of stories you've been telling us over the past fifty years, for our children and grandchildren".

My oldest daughter, Lyn, literally took me by the hand (after all she is a retired school teacher and knows how to handle children) to the Apple Store in Salem, New Hampshire, where I purchased my first iMac. She was extremely helpful in setting up my one-to-one program, which I have faithfully attended weekly, from day one.

In November, 2006 I went to Michigan to have shoulder surgery, resulting from a slip and fall with arm extended accident. There are plenty of excellent orthopedic surgeons in the Lowell community, however I opted for Michigan, where my youngest son, Steven, an Orthopedic Surgeon, specializing in shoulder and knee reconstruction could supervise my surgery and rehabilitation.

Not wanting to miss my weekly one-to-one sessions, I located and called an apple store forty-five miles from my son's residence. When I explained my situation, the customer service person, graciously set me up with a one-to-one schedule, gave me directions and when I got to the apple store, it was like I never left home.

Here I am, seven years later, on my second iMac and third MacBook Pro, continuing to attend my weekly sessions as well as attending the personal projects and never seeming to learn enough to keep up with the advancement of the new Apple programs or products.

The big difference now is that with all my photographs properly indexed in my Aperture library, I'm spending all my time writing stories (typing that is). You see, I would be remiss if I didn't tell you about my exceptional experiences with the entire Apple team, including the greeters, trainers, genius bar experts and the managers.

It was a little over two years ago that I decided I didn't want to one-finger type anymore and asked for guidance from my tutors. They not only recommended, but even pitched in and gifted me with a Mavis Beacon Teaches Typing program. I'm so excited to have gone from a one finger (eyes glued to the keyboard) to typing at twenty-five words a minute in Mavis Beacon advanced typing program.

As I continued to type story after story, my trainers began to encourage me to consider having them published. At first I thought they were blowing smoke, but after a while I could see that they were sincere.

Then my children started on the same theme, saying that as I journeyed on into my past, they not only were reading what they had heard over the past fifty years, but it was in more detail and interesting to read, in its chronological order.

At eighty-one years of age, I felt it would take me several years to complete this project without some assistance. I initially entertained asking my youngest daughter, Diane, who teaches English, for help however, she is also working toward a Doctorate at Northeastern University in Boston and did not have a spare minute in her extremely busy schedule to help me with my project.

In March of 2011, I read an article in the Lowell Sun daily newspaper, written by Sam Weisberg, as a guest writer. He was reminiscing about several outstanding sporting events that he had witnessed throughout his career as a reporter at the Lowell Sun and Lowell Sunday Sun. In that article, he mentioned the 1948 Lowell Lawrence football game, as the most exciting high school football game that he has ever seen in his lifetime.

After reading the article, I decided to contact Sam and arranged a luncheon meeting to find out if he was available to help me with my project.

We had a leisurely lunch as I explained my project in detail, which seemed to interest him. I was not aware that Sam had seen all of my high school and college football games. Considering his knowledge of my background at

Lowell High and Boston University, I felt he would be a good fit to assist me with my project.

Sam then related that he was retired and was only doing special events for the Lowell Sun, and in addition he was covering only one football game per weekend during the football season. Therefore he would be available to edit my stories and assist me in any other way that I could use his assistance to complete my project.

There were two concerns that created some hesitation on my part to make a quick decision. He explained that he wrote his stories in pencil and that the newspaper then retyped his articles for publication. Secondly, that he was computer illiterate.

Looking for quick answers to my concerns, I turned to my three favorite trainers at the Apple store and, as usual, they again came to my rescue. Knowing that I had already discussed purchasing a new MacBook Pro, they suggested that I could program the old MacBook Pro for Sam's use and bring him with me for weekly sessions until he got up to speed.

For the next three months we worked side by side at the Apple store, with the trainer working with me and me working with Sam for a three-hour session once a week. We had a one-to-one trainer for one full hour then we worked at the project table for two hours, sharing a trainer with a few other Apple students.

Once Sam became familiar with the Dropbox application, we developed a simple, smooth procedure, with me typing a story, sending it to Sam via the Dropbox, Sam editing the story and sending it back to me via the Dropbox. I then selected the proper photos from my Aperture photo library and inserted them into the predetermined locations.

Once each story was completed the above process, I would then send it to my six critics for review and honest to goodness critiques.

I couldn't have found a better source than these six, all emotionally close to home, however not geographically.

Lyn Plomaritis, my older daughter, and Charlie O'Neil, reside six months in Alaska and six months in New Zealand. Lyn is a retired Talented and Gifted teacher who loves to read and still talks to me like I'm her third grade student. Charlie, her husband is an inveterate reader, with an active library card, reading two to three novels weekly.

Diane Hartley, my younger daughter and high school English teacher, spends fifty percent of her time correcting students' reading assignments. Angela Hartley, my granddaughter, is an English teacher in South Korea.

Dr. Titus Plomaritis Jr., Eden, North Carolina and Dr. Steven Plomaritis,

Grosse Pointe, Michigan are both Orthopedic Surgeons, who are excellent proofreaders for wildlife and medical publications.

When the critiques were returned with some minor typos or suggestions that did not change the intent of the story, we addressed them and put it into the **VAULT**. If two or more of the critiques came back with negative comments, we pulled the story and re-wrote it until five of the critics give it a passing grade.

Soon after my decision to have a total hip replacement, Sam and I started meeting once weekly at my home in Pelham, NH. My lovely wife of sixty years, Claire, set up a great work area for us to continue our work sessions. The once weekly meetings become twice weekly and Sam no longer needed to go to the Apple store. I continued with my one-to-one and workshops once weekly as soon as I could resume driving. Usually, I arrived with a minor problem or a list of "HOW TOs", that I needed some refreshing.

Finally, I sat down with Brain Nagel who displayed the utmost patience in sorting out the last minute details of reducing file sizes, inserting photos and rearranging stories. Writing this book has been a story in itself and I owe a lot of thanks to these main characters.

ACKNOWLEDGMENTS

To my wife, Claire, for the many days and nights that I was engrossed in this mammoth project, that started as a little project, saving storage boxes full of family photographs and negatives, about seven years ago.

To my children, Titus Jr., Lyn, Steven and Diane for their constant encouragement, to put on paper, the multitude of stories that I've been repeating year after year, that they never seem to get tired of hearing.

Yours truly, Titus Plomaritis, (sitting) with my friend, Sam Weisberg, who was also my "side-by-side editor"

To my side-by-side editor, Sam Weisberg, who has personally seen all of my high school and college football games, has a great memory and is a stickler for details. He has more than fulfilled his role as my side by side editor. Sam researched, composed and wrote most of the football related stories over the span of the last sixty or so years. After he thought he'd retired, Sam graciously accepted my offer to edit this book, working tireless hours to write, rewrite and arrange these stories. Even in our eighties, we still have a lot to learn from one another.

To my proofreaders, Charles O'Neil, from Alaska and New Zealand, an inveterate reader who has more punch holes in his library card in one week, than most people have in a lifetime. Titus Jr., from Eden, North Carolina, and Steven Plomaritis from Grosse Pointe, Michigan who have proof read hundreds, if not thousands, of medical and sports journals over the past twenty years.

To my two daughters, Lyn and Diane who have been performing the second level editing as well as critiquing, story by story with outstanding commentary in between. Lyn is a retired teacher from Alaska, while Diane from Bourne, Massachusetts, is an English teacher at Plymouth South High School with a recent PHD in Education from Northeastern University in Boston, Massachusetts.

A very special thanks to Angela C. Hartley, working as an English teacher in South Korea. I have given her the title of "**SUPER EDITOR**", responsible for editing my editors' editing. She is not working alone however, as she has an assistant in Adam Hogue, also an English teacher in South Korea.

Angela C. Hartley, "SUPER EDITOR" of the book, Titus. Responsible for the third tier of the editing process, with her associate editor Adam Hogue, who also doubles as a proof reader.

I also want to thank these editors' family members who supported them while reading my work, Jan Plomaritis, Erica Plomaritis, and Robert Hartley. They are all part of a great critique system which received my rough, unedited stories. I instructed them all to be honest and unsympathetic toward my eighty-two-year-old self. On many instances, I got nosebleeds from their critical comments and on many occasions, stories required total rewrites.

To members of my Lowell High School Class of 1949, especially Claire Ignacio, who has authored several books and is presently getting ready to launch another. Claire has been very encouraging and a major contributing factor in convincing me to put on paper my long list of stories, memories and accomplishments.

To the Raymond A. Sullivan family, for their assistance in filling in the blank spaces in my memory from time to time.

To Patrick "Paddy" Sullivan, Tappan, New York, in helping me relive my pleasant experiences of sharing his living quarters, in the mid 1950's, at the Sullivan Tappan Inn.

To the Riddick family, especially Raymond Riddick Jr., for providing me with precious family photos of his dad, my coach, my patient and my friend, until the day of his passing.

To the staff at the National Board of Chiropractic Examiners, especially Mr. Horace Elliott, Executive Vice President, Lynn Stugart, Exec. Senior Administrative Assistant and her assistant Kay Leff who provided me with authenticating documentation of my twenty year tenure with the NBCE.

To Bill Gardner, New Hampshire Secretary of State, Anthony Stevens, Assistant Secretary of State and Karen Ladd, Assistant Secretary of State, for their assistance and direction at the State Capitol.

To Mike Welcome, who was my extra set of wheels, during my total left hip replacement, exemplifying what true friendship is all about.

To Art Ramalho, West Side Gym, Lowell, Massachusetts, for his assistance in locating documentation and photos of Frankie Hebert's boxing career.

To my brothers Joseph, Anthony, David and my sister Priscilla for their assistance in locating old family photos and refreshing my memory with dates of significance.

To my favorite cousins from Miami, Florida, all formerly from Jamaica Plain, Massachusetts: Tarky Varkas, Mary (Varkas) Lymneos, Percy (Varkas) Peppas, and Electra (Varkas) Spillas, for providing me with memorable family history and outstanding family photos

I ALSO WANT TO THANK THE APPLE STORE GENIUS BAR, ESPECIALLY COREY COOPER, GREG CRISP, LINDSEY TISHLER.

WHO REPEATEDLY PUT MY MIND AT EASE, EVERY TIME I WAS IN A STATE OF PANIC IN FEAR OF LOOSING MY DOCUMENTS AND PHOTOGRAPHS. ALSO TO THE PROFESSIONAL TRAINERS WHOM I REFER TO AS MY "PROFESSORS", I'VE BEEN GOING TO THE ONE-TO-ONE CLASSES FOR THE PAST SEVEN YEARS CONTINUOUSLY, SO IT'S UNDERSTANDABLE THAT MANY OF THEM HAVE MOVED ON OR TO OTHER NEWLY OPENED STORES.

SPECIAL THANKS TO THESE CURRENT "PROFESSORS" WHO ALWAYS SHOWED PATIENCE WHEN I WAS HAVING DIFFICULTY UNDERSTANDING THEIR PROFESSIONAL TERMINOLOGY: BRIAN NAGEL, MIKE PARSONS, JOE PROVENZANO, JAY COLANTUONI, NATHAN SOUSA, , KEN McKENZIE, RUBIN , JON, CHRIS — AND TO KATRINA, WHO HAS SINCE DEPARTED TO DISPLAY HER TALENTS AT VICTORIA SECRET. AS WELL AS, **VICTOR HUOT** WHO WAS MY VERY FIRST CONTACT AND TRAINER AT APPLE, WHO **FED ME THE INTRODUCTORY PHASES WITH A BABY SPOON.**

SECTION ONE

This biography follows in his own words, plus excerpts from well known journalists and from newspaper clippings.

TITUS—A MAN OF MANY NAMES
By Sam Weisberg, (my editor)

It's safe to say that **TITUS PLOMARITIS** has undergone more aliases than Whitey Bulger during his stellar athletic, military and personal careers.

Very few people, living or dead, has had their first or last names misspelled or misquoted more than the Good Doctor.

It all started the day that he was born—September 6,1929—when Doctor Vurgaropulos jotted down on his birth certificate: **TITUS PLOUMARITIS**. (Brother George earlier also had his name misspelled).

The **PLOU** spelling continued to plague Titus throughout his military career, appearing on all his U.S. Army certificates—including the Paratrooper graduation document and eventually the final honorable discharge paper, signed on January 14, 1948.

Even his own father called him **TITOS**, which is Greek for Titus.

A MAJORITY of the time over his all-star football career his name in the newspapers was spelled **PLOMARITUS**, both in the numerous bold headlines and in the story contents.

Titus' hometown newspaper—**THE LOWELL SUN**—spelled his name correctly only some of the time, in addition to printing it with the **"US"** ending, depending who the writer or the editor was at the time. They couldn't make up their minds.

However, as mentioned above, the majority of his press clippings showed **PLOMARITUS** in bold type headlines—including football write-ups at Lowell High School, Boston University, the Bogalusa bowl game and All-State stories.

DOWN SOUTH he was called **TARTUS,** by Mississippi State University head football coach **SLICK MORTON**. "We want you here,

Tartus," the coach said immediately after the prospect from Lowell dazzled during a preview of his gridiron skills.

Famed country comedian, **JERRY CLOWER**, during a Jerry Clower Day ceremony at Mississippi State, yelled out "Stand up Tartus!" That came as a result of Clower's 1976 **"THE AMBASSADOR OF GOODWILL"** best-selling country album, which contained a comical football story about Titus entitled **"TITUS PLUMMERITIS"**.

AMONG OTHER memorable items which dotted Titus' football career:

The Lowell-Lawrence game program listed him as five-foot eight and 170 pounds, when he was actually 5'5" and 155......Famed announcer **CURT GOWDY,** during pre-game lineup announcements of Boston University grid games at Fenway Park, would bellow **"AN-HERE-COMES-TY-TUS-PLOM-A-RITE-US!!"**...Even Titus would have fun with his own name. When as a youngster in Lowell, trying out for the mostly Irish St. Peter's Cadets baseball team, he answered a roll call by **BISHOP MARKHAM** as **"O'PLOMARITIS"**...Another baseball misspelling took place in the 1944 cutline of the photo of the Pawtucket Junior High diamond squad, as Titus' name was spelled **PLUMARITES**.

HOWEVER, the most famous printed miscue of his name occurred in a Boston newspaper the day after he starred for Lowell High in the 1948 Cambridge Jamboree. It read: "Lowell, which looms as a powerhouse this coming season, sent the fans home talking about left halfback, **TIM LOMERITUS.**

GORHAM STREET CHILDHOOD

I was born on September 6, 1929, the third of seven children of Greek immigrants and then resided at 191 Gorham Street in Lowell, Massachusetts, for 10 years during the Depression years, 1929 to 1939.

My parents were born in Greece. My mother, Niki, came to America at the age of one, while my father, Demosthenis, came here when he was 35. They were married on July 26, 1926, when she was 18 and he was 35 in an arranged marriage.

My Parents and Siblings
Left to right: My brother Joseph, myself, my father Demosthenis, my mother Niki and my brothers George & Timothy (photo taken in 1935)

My oldest brother, Timothy, was born in 1927, followed by brothers George in 1928 and Joseph on December 25th, 1930—my Christmas present.

After we moved to 29 Johnson Street—at the very end of the bus stop on

Varnum Avenue—my parents had three more children—brothers Anthony (1943), David (1946), and sister Priscilla (1947) as my mother finally got her wish with a girl, she was the end of the production line.

My mother (maiden name Niki Mantis) was born on August 14, 1908, and passed away on May 18, 1990. My father, born on May 26,1892 and died on August 15, 1980. We lost my brothers Timothy on January 28, 2011, and George on May 5, 1993.

My father's occupation was a barber, owning his own shop on Gorham Street. He hardly spoke English. However, he had another barber working for him who spoke English and Greek and more or less doubled as my father's interpreter. My father only read the Greek bible and the Greek newspaper.

My father was very religious and he conducted Greek bible meetings one evening a week in our living room.

The barber shop was located at 111 Gorham Street, only a short distance from our three bedroom cold water flat, which was over the Pioneer Market. The market was owned and operated by the owner of the building.

Pioneer Market
Titus Plomarltis Birthplace Sep. 6, 1929
Gorham Street
Lowell, Massachusetts

The window directly above the "P" in the Pioneer Market sign was my bedroom window. Directly across the street from that window there was a Portuguese bakery. Early every morning I watched the baker working from that window and eventually drifted down, told him who I was and that I had been watching him from across the street and asked if I could help because someday I would like to be a baker just like him (age 8-9). My payment for helping was a loaf of fresh Portuguese bread to bring home for breakfast.

Needless to say, my father was a strict disciplinarian and with his temperament—he would use his barber shop strap quite often—causing my mother to intervene, at times crying, telling him to stop.

The memories of my mother remain with me, with her genuine loving kindness, always with a smile on her face and protecting me and my brothers from my father's temperament.

Another memory is when my father came in the front door I would jump out the back window, run down the back stairs, up Union Street and wouldn't stop running until I got to the South Common playground.

SOUTH COMMON BASEBALL

The South Common hosted the prize sports event of the city of Lowell— the TwiLight Baseball League, which attracted huge crowds, especially during the playoffs—which usually featured arch rivals, the Lincoln Square Associates and The Gates Theater teams.

The players were not paid, but the familiar little old man in the straw hat would pass the hat around the wooden bleachers and the standing room only crowd, collecting a bountiful of loose change while chanting "Something for the boys!" The money would be distributed to the players at the postseason banquet.

Many outstanding baseball players came out of the Twi League before World War ll, including future Major League stars Tony "Cookie" Lupien, Al "Skippy" Roberge, Frank Skaff and Johnny Barrett.

Lupien would succeed the great Jimmy Foxx at first base for the Red Sox, Roberge would play four seasons as an infielder for the Boston Braves, Skaff would eventually be the manager of the Detroit Tigers and the speedy Barrett would lead the National League in triples and stolen bases in 1944 with the Pittsburgh Pirates.

Another familiar Twi League veteran was the fabulous Fronko Purtell, who was still playing third base at the Common in his 70's.

While watching a baseball game at the Common I would chase a foul ball, pick it up and run down Union Street like the whole police department was chasing me and hide under our porch for a few minutes. That baseball would last for about a week before the cover would peel off and then I would have to repeat the procedure.

MY FATHER, MEAN BUT HONEST

Sometimes I reflect back on those early years and realize that my father was mean spirited, old fashioned and not fun to be with. He was not educationally oriented, but he did have some good qualities—such as he was a non-smoker, a non-drinker except for an occasional glass of wine, was not a womanizer nor a gambler and he didn't hang around the Greek coffee houses and was extremely honest.

An example of his honesty occurred when I was eight years old and my father heard a ticking noise coming from my jacket. Following about 10 minutes of intense questioning of where the watch came from, I finally admitted that I took it from a local merchant on Gorham Street. That prompted a severe tongue lashing followed by a battery of barber shop straps on my butt until I couldn't sit for a week. The next day he took me to the merchant, had me return the watch, apologize and say I would not do it again.

Routinely, the punishment for being bad was that I had to sit in the barber shop and read the bible, sometimes for a whole week.

Another example of my father's honesty took place on a Saturday at the barber shop, when he sent me to the Washington Savings Bank with a paper bag and a note to the teller, relative to getting change for the barber shop's cash register. When I got back to the barber shop my father counted the change and noticed a mistake with an extra roll of quarters. He immediately sent me back to the bank with another note and the money, which remains in my memory like it was yesterday.

My mother was a stitcher and she worked full time when not having children. She worked at one of the factories on Thorndike Street and she walked to work, crossing the south common twice daily.

I vividly remember her coming home some cold wintry late afternoons, sitting in front of our kerosene stove, opening the oven door and sticking her feet in until she thawed out.

We lived on the middle floor, directly over the market. The structures on both sides of our tenement were also three story tenement buildings that formed a semi-circle which created a fairly large opening in back of the buildings that became a backyard play area, designed with clothes lines on every back porch.

Our tenement was located about 200 yards from the barber shop. It's funny how distance over the years make a difference. When I was five years old 200 yards would have been about 20 10-yard field goals. At 15 years old, about five 40-yard field goals, in college about four 50-yarders, and now at 82 it would take my very best T-Shot.

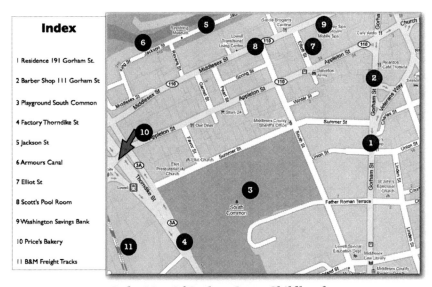

Index

1 Residence 191 Gorham St.

2 Barber Shop 111 Gorham St

3 Playground South Common

4 Factory Thorndike St

5 Jackson St

6 Armours Canal

7 Elliot St

8 Scott's Pool Room

9 Washington Savings Bank

10 Price's Bakery

11 B&M Freight Tracks

Index Map Of Gorham Street Childhood

I have drafted the attached Map of the Gorham Street and South Common areas, to show where I spent 95% of my time while residing on 191 Gorham Street. Notice the closeness of numbers 1, where our residence was located and Number 2, the location of my father's barber shop, that was 111 Gorham Street. Then you can see the two farthest distances, were No. 6, Armours Canal, where I learned to swim, and No.10, Price's Bakery, where we picked up our day old bread. As a guess I'd estimate that 50% of my time was at Number 3, THE SOUTH COMMON.

CLOSE CALLS SIX TIMES

As I reflect over the past eighty plus years, it seems someone was looking over me because I can envision six times that I was fortunate to survive close calls without suffering tragedy.

FIRST INCIDENT

My first close call occurred on a hot summer day when I was five to seven years old and again unsupervised and walking from Gorham Street to the Shedd Park Playground and pool area.

View of the Concord River rapids from Rogers Street Bridge

As we walked over the Rogers Street Bridge, with the extremely fast rapids of the Concord River about fifty feet below where we were walking, I climbed up on the wall with one of my friends to get a better look at the fast-moving water rapids below. I lost my footing and started to tumble headfirst into the Concord River, which would have been certain—or very close to—death, but luckily a passing pedestrian grabbed one of my legs and held on tightly, until a second adult assisted him in pulling me up and over the wall to safety.

NOTE:—The remaining five Close Calls incidents will follow in chronological order

MORNING LINEUP

We had a family morning ritual, with my father at the helm. He held a bottle of **COD LIVER OIL** in one hand and a tablespoon in the other and lined up the four boys, by seniority, with Tim, George, myself and Joe standing in a straight line like ducks in a pond.

With our mouths wide open to haul in the cod liver oil, and with a quarter slice of an orange in our hands to act as a chaser, we had to use the Paratrooper Shuffle to quickly get back in line. We had to repeat this procedure three times each morning.

OATMEAL BREAKFAST

Our gourmet breakfast started immediately following our cod liver oil delight.

In order to explain this breakfast procedure, I'll bring you up to date on the preliminaries in such a manner that you can envision all the details involved.

1— One of my father's barber shop customers operated a dairy product concession on Market Street. It was a normal practice in those days to have milk delivered to your front door. We had a five gallon container delivered to our residence on 191 Gorham Street twice weekly. My father gave the milkman a key to the ground level front door that gave him entry to the stairway and he would leave the full container of milk at the top of the stairs and remove the empty one.

2— Another one of my father's customers owned a mini grocery store only a couple of doors away from the barber shop. He would sell my father oatmeal by the case.

3—The night before, one of the boys would go to the cellar to fetch a couple of loaves of bread from the burlap bags. The bread, which was usually hard as a rock and at times had a little mold and rat bites which would be trimmed off before soaking it in warm water for about an half hour. The timing was quite good in that there was very little wasted time as this part transpired while we were doing our morning "cod liver oil shuffle". We would squeeze most of the water out of the two loaves of bread and put them in the oven for about 30 minutes while my father made the oatmeal

Remember, my mother had left the house early for work, therefore my father usually prepared breakfast.

"Titos" (which is Greek for Titus), bring the **KART-SAH-RHO-LAR** (Greek for large pot)', he would say.

We would pour four or five quarts of milk into the large pot and it would take two of us to pick it up and place it on the flat surface of the stove. My father would then pour an entire box of oatmeal into the pot of milk and stir it with a huge ladle until it was cooked. By this time the bread in the oven was baked and ready to eat.

We each had our favorite bowl and mine was a glass bowl with a picture of Shirley Temple on the bottom. I couldn't wait to get to the bottom of my dish to look at her pretty face as I had somewhat of a crush on her most of my childhood.

My father had the ladle ready with another load of oatmeal and just when you thought you got to the bottom of the dish another healthy portion covered Shirley's pretty face. I can honestly say to this day I still enjoy a good bowl of oatmeal—however, prepared considerably differently.

Let me share with you my favorite recipe, that I call Market Basket Old Fashioned Oats Supreme.

Market Basket
OLD FASHIONED
OATS SUPREME

INGREDIENTS—3 TO 4 SERVINGS

1 cup Market Basket Old Fashioned Oats.
8 oz water.
8 oz 2% milk.
1 teaspoon butter.
1/8 teaspoon sea salt.
1/4 cup craisins.
1/4 cup chopped walnuts.
1/4 cup brown sugar.

COOKING PROCEDURE:

Using a two quart cooking pot

1—Bring milk/water to a boil
2— Add oats and stir slowly until water comes to a boil again
3— turn burner down to simmer for 5 minutes, stirring occasionally.
4— Add the craisins, chopped walnuts and brown sugar.
5— Stir until all ingredients blend in.

Remove from the stove.

ENJOY ! ! !

FREIGHT TRAIN STORY

It was my turn to fill the five gallon kerosene bottle for our kitchen stove. I remember it being a good size that had been converted from a wood burning stove. It was of cast iron construction with an oven, four burners and a flat surface for cooking with large pots on top. It had a five gallon bottle attached to the left side.

It was late fall or early winter because I remember darkness about five P.M., and I was about eight or nine years old at the time of this incident.

The route from the kitchen stove to the kerosene barrel was:

Out the back door.

Down a flight of stairs with a sharp turn at the bottom.

Unlock the cellar door.

Down another flight of stairs, about five or six wooden steps.

Reach out with one hand while carrying the kerosene bottle with the other to find and pull the chain to turn on the light.

Unlock the second padlocked door to enter our section of the cellar.

There was the kerosene barrel and also in that area is where the burlap bags where bread from Price's Bakery were located.

After filling the kerosene bottle and exiting the cellar, I pulled the chain to shut off the light and on my way out I tripped and fell down the stairs and the bottle broke with kerosene spilling all over me and the cellar stairs.

I was so scared and afraid of my father that I decided to run toward the south common playground, as I normally would do when afraid of another "barber shop strap to my butt punishment." Only this time I did not stop running until I ran through the South Common, past the factory where my mother worked and sat down next to the railroad tracks.

I was confused and didn't know what to do or where to go.

A short while later a freight train was going by, slow enough so I could jump on. I remember that my heart was pumping so fast, as if I just ran the marathon.

When I thought I was far enough away, I jumped off the freight train— at that time I thought I was in California. However, I was actually in Billerica, only about five miles up the road from Lowell.

As I was walking along the tracks in total darkness, a spotlight was glaring in my face, coming from a police car just off the tracks and I remember a cop asking me what my name was, where did I come from and what was that kerosene odor?

After telling him my story he took me to the Billerica Police Station, called the Lowell Police, exchanged information, gave me a ride to the Lowell Police Station and eventually I was returned to 191 Gorham St, about three hours after the broken bottle incident.

Note:— Up to that incident in time I remember being disrespectful to policemen. I would toss tomatoes at them, call them "flatfoots" and run so fast they could never catch me.

Those policemen in Billerica made an everlasting impression on me. They were very friendly, comforting and assured me that my father would not hurt me. Thus, to this day I make it a policy to donate to the local Policeman's association.

This time there was no punishment except that the cost of replacing the broken kerosene bottle was deducted from my shoe shine earnings.

SOUTH COMMON WITH JOE

My brother Joe was born with a physical handicap to both lower extremities and spent a great deal of time at the Children's Hospital in Boston.

He underwent several surgical procedures, some we believe were experimental at that time.

I remember several times we went to the south common to play with some of our friends when he was wearing braces on both legs. What he lacked in running skills and speed due to the braces, he made up with his large hands and great grip on the football. That allowed him to throw passes much further than any of us.

I enjoyed it most when we got to the Common before any of the others showed up, so Joe could throw passes to me alone. It gave me many more opportunities and fun chasing his errant passes—he was not too accurate.

I remember running full speed, looking over one shoulder, and Joe's passes going 45 degrees in the opposite direction. I would make quick turns while running full speed with an attempt to catch up to the ball, always with the thought of getting my hands on the football. Even at that age I felt if I could touch it, I should catch it.

When some of the other kids showed up we would split up in teams of four or five, depending on how many we had. I also remember that they quite often would tire out sooner than I and would look for a shady tree to sit under. Then Joe and I would play catch again until they got their second wind and returned for another session.

When I no longer had volunteers to continue playing catch with, I would again drift over to the baseball backstop and practice my placekicking the football, with my ultimate goal and determination to kick the ball over the backstop some day.

IRVING'S FRUIT STAND

Our apartment was always well-stocked with fruits and vegetables. One of my father's customers owned a fruit and vegetable stand on Gorham Street, located only a few doors away from the barber shop going towards our apartment.

Although I do not remember his last name, I do remember his first name was Irving and I also remember he had a son named Herby.

It was one of our weekly rituals that two of us would have to go to the barber shop on Saturday around five o'clock, when it was normal closing time. It was quite normal for my father to still have customers in the barber shop at closing, so he would pull the shades and turn the sign from open to closed which indicated that he and Charlie, the other barber, would take care of the customers that were already in the shop, but no one else was allowed to come in.

Whatever time it was when my father actually closed the barber shop we would go to see Irving and he would be expecting us.

It was quite a circus to watch my father, with his heavy Greek accent, only able to say a few words in English, (specifically the names of the fruits and vegetables he was interested in buying), dealing with another immigrant with his heavy Yiddish accent.

"Denny" he would say—my father's barber shop was called "Denny's"— "that's the best I can do" if it was for a bushel of oranges or grapefruits.

We knew that was not the last of the bargaining because we heard it every week, and my father would say "OK" as he would keep that figure in the back of his head and continue shopping with Irving by his side.

About 30 to 45 minutes later when he had added a bushel of over-ripened tomatoes, a half bushel of over-ripened bananas and several other vegetables he would tell Irving that he would buy the entire order for the original price of the first bushel of fruit. Irving's reply was "I can not sell you all those vegetables and fruits for less than I pay for them at my wholesale price." Most of the time my father would add a dollar or two and Irving would accept. My father's argument was that the fruit stand is closed all day Sunday and with Monday and Tuesday not being good shopping days for the fruit and vegetable business he would have to throw them out and get nothing, so anything is better than nothing. Sometimes Irving would not bend and tell my father to either take it or no deal.

If my father felt like playing hard ball, he would say in Greek, "Let's go boys," and literally walk out and start heading home. 99% of the time Irving would go out on the street and call my father back to consummate the deal.

That's where we would come into play, taking a big container with one of us on each end and carrying it home.

My father's thinking was that he could stop at Saunder's Market (see map of Gorham Street) for a few other items and go back Monday morning and offer Irving even less.

If Irving was busy his son Herby would try to wait on my father, but my father would always say that he would wait for Irving because Herby was very disrespectful, would intentionally squeeze the tomatoes once they were in the bag, or would play the switch game where my father would select certain vegetables and he would replace them with rotten ones.

Herby was what we called a big fat slob, 150 pounds overweight and always making fun of my father, my brothers and I.

Note:—The reason that I stated our weekly order always consisted of a bushel of oranges or grapefruits was because in those days each orange and grapefruit was individually wrapped with a slippery onion skin-type paper to protect the fruit, which we used for toilet paper. When we ran out we used newspapers. Do you wonder why every bathroom in our house today has the double sheet baby-soft toilet tissue?

PRICE'S BAKERY

Price's Bakery was located approximately a half mile from our Gorham Street residence.

Our route of travel (see index map) was as follows:

From Gorham Street residence,
Up Summer Street,
Cross the South Common to Thorndike Street,
Over to Appleton Street,
Onto Chelmsford Street,
To Price's Bakery.

The owners of the bakery—Ben Price and his brothers—were customers of my father and they agreed to sell day-old or older bread for two cents a loaf, provided that we would pick it up.

We—Tim, George, Joe and I—would take turns walking to the bakery with an empty burlap bag. Most of the time we would go alone, however sometimes we would go in pairs, depending how many days expired between trips.

Usually if Mr. Price (Ben) was there he would give me a cupcake or cookie—a day old, of course.

Mr. Price would keep an accounting of the loaves of bread he placed into the burlap bags and he would collect his two cents a loaf in trade for his haircuts. It should be noted that haircuts in that era were 25 cents and shaves were 15 cents.

In the summer months my father would clip all our hair off so we would have bald heads, as a means of preventing us from getting head lice (cooties). This would be after our mother found lice while using an extra fine-toothed comb.

Sometimes in the summer months as we returned crossing the South Common some of the older boys would harass us, then offer us a penny beer barrel candy for a "doughnut"—which was a knuckle on the head. We would lean forward with our heads bowed and our faces facing the ground, and they would make a fist, with the middle knuckle extended, and rap the bald heads. "Ouch!" we yelled as we journeyed the rest of the way home with a lump on our heads and sucking on a penny beer barrel candy.

SHOE SHINE STORY

I started shining shoes when I was six years old in my father's barber shop.

My equipment included a little wooden box with one brush, a can of black shoe polish and a can of brown polish.

To initially clean the shoes before applying polish, I remember having a little brown bottle of soapy water for cleaning brown shoes and a little black bottle with soapy water for cleaning black shoes.

I only had one brush at first, causing the brown shoes to have black stains, but when my business picked up—more than five customers a week—my father got me a second brush for brown shoes.

My father had me give him my earnings and said that he would put the money in the bank for me. He also would take money out to pay for my breaking windows from playing baseball in the back yard and for whatever other damages I was responsible for, including the broken kerosene bottle.

Net result: **ZERO INCOME**

As time moved on—approaching nine years of age—my business moved from out of the barber shop, to some of the merchants on Gorham Street, and to seven bar rooms—three on Gorham Street, one on Charles Street, one on Central Street and two on Middlesex Street.

Recent photo by Titus Plomaritis that has TWO reflections: (1) 111 Gorham Street was the location of my father's barber shop. (2) window reflection shows one of my old shoe shine bar rooms that was then called "Old 99"

The bar room business was mostly on Saturdays, but because of my age I was constantly tossed out of them. However, those customers were the best tippers, especially soldiers from Fort Devens, therefore I would keep going into the bar rooms through the back doors, give a quick shine, collect my money and run like hell, going from one bar room to another until I had a pocket full of coins. That's when I decided to shove a couple of quarters and dimes into my shoes before turning in my receipts.

I eventually had enough coins in my shoes, (making me a half inch taller) to purchase a BB gun (I had an older friend buy it for me) from Lull & Hartford's Sporting Goods Store. My brother George and I would spend hours target practicing in the woods and gravel banks on outer Varnum Avenue.

When I had more coins in my pocket than I normally would turn over to my father I would hightail it over to Elliott's Lunch (see #7 index on map) for their Saturday Special—**"FIVE HOTDOGS & AN ORANGE DRINK FOR 25 CENTS".**

Elliot's Famous Hot Dogs
Photo by Titus Plomaritis on July 4, 2011

Note:

I personally took the photo above and stopped in for a hot dog the next day and did notice that there was a slight increase to $1.50 for one dog. I introduced myself to the owner and related the story of 5 dogs and a drink for two-bits. I sensed that he was trying to embarrass me, as he replied in a rather loud tone— "WOW YOU MUST BE 100 YEARS OLD".

OH by the way, the dog was scrumptious.

I also had a few regular customers that were doctors and lawyers and they expected me in their offices once a week to shine their shoes, tell a little story and snap the shoe shine rag to the tune of Yankee Doodle.

NOTE— Dr. Titus, M.D., of Downtown Lowell approached me after one of my Lowell High School Football games in 1948 and told me he was following my high school football career and wanted to tell me how he remembered me going to his office every week to shine his shoes. "However, in addition to our namesake," he said, he remembered me for my short stories. He pointed to his shoes, smiled and wished me luck for whatever college that would be lucky enough to get me.

ROLLER SKATING ON SUMMER STREET

I remember one bright sunny summer day we, several of my friends and I, were roller skating on Summer Street, directly adjacent to Saunder's market. For the previous two weeks we had been skating practically every day, learning new skills like spinning, jumping up and off the curb stones and jumping over the man hole covers. My recollection is that I was about eight years old at the time.

In that era we had roller skates that were designed with four wheels, a heel support to prevent the back of your shoes from slipping off the back, leather straps were threaded through two slits in the back plate and would wrap around your ankle and fastened. The front flat surface of the skates had a clamp on each side that would be tightened to the soles of your shoes with a metal key. We were playing a game of keep away, using a rubber ball, with three on each team. This particular day the manhole cover had been removed for some kind of repair work related to Saunder's Market. We had been skating around it as well as jumping over it for quite a while until this one time, I reached to retrieve an errant throw by one of my teammates and lost my balance. I was going head first into the upper edge of the open manhole when my instinct was to protect my head which apparently had my shoulder take the brunt of the impact. The result was a trip to the hospital emergency room by one of the Saunder's Market managers.

One of my best friends at that time who lived just a stone's throw from us, on Summer Street went to the hospital with me. When we were on our respective back porches (see Gorham map)

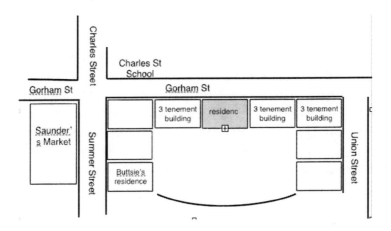

we often conversed with each other, like, let's go to the common or do ya wanna play catch in the back yard or the likes? His real name was Edward Correa but we all were called by our nick names and he was known as "Buttsie". The doctor said I had a broken collar bone and although surgery was unnecessary, I would have to wear a brace for about four to six weeks. The brace consisted of a wooden structure placed between my shoulder blades with bandages wrapped around my upper body, covering the "plank" several times over and under my armpits creating such a brace that more or less forced me to stand up straight with my shoulders thrust backwards. This was my first experience with such an injury, however, not my last. I'm planning on relating that interesting story in detail when I get to that stage of my life.

MARY, ON GORHAM STREET

I have two flashbacks every time I meet someone named Mary. They reflect back to my young growing up experiences while residing at 191 Gorham Street.

The first was a rainy day that involved several of my five to seven- year-old buddies and one gal named Mary.

We were sitting under a porch that was protecting us from the rain and from view of the parents' "lookout tower" (rear porches in our back yards).

At that time in my life we were four brothers and no sisters and we were playing some simple rainy day outdoor games, like a pebble in one hand, showing it and then placing both hands behind your back. When bringing your hands to the front they would try to guess which hand it was in.

We would all have a game to explain and play, and when it got to Mary she said "I'll show you mine if you show me yours."—Her father must have been a bookie because she must have studied the odds and had several to look at compared to our **ONE QUICK LOOK.**

Now, the second flashback came a couple of years later, involving the same Mary.

It was a cloudy, cool afternoon and we were in our back yard's semi-circle playground (see Gorham Street map). We had a larger group of boys and this time there were three girls.

My brother George gathered a pile of debris, that was plentiful in the back yard area, and decided to do what we tell our kids today not to do—play with matches—and he started a mini bonfire. Needless to say, as kids, we were excited because we were doing something our parents wouldn't approve of.

As the fire was weaning down we scavenged the entire back yard area and even went into some of the barrels under the porches to keep the fire going. During my back yard expedition I found a small bullet, which I threw into the fire, and we were all anticipating a loud gunshot noise—but not expecting what developed.

The "BANG" finally came and we were all cheering and laughing, when suddenly we noticed blood coming from Mary's leg. We were scared and did not know what to do. However, we must have done the correct thing because I saw her the next day with a bandage on her leg and a smile on her face.

Again, I feel that her dad must have been a bookie or a member of "Angelo's Army" because **SHE NEVER TOLD ANYONE THAT I WAS THE CULPRIT!!**

SAINT PETER'S CADETS

Saint Peter's School, located somewhat kitty-corner to our tenement at the corner of Union and Gorham streets, was a Catholic Parochial school that most of my friends from the South Common attended.

They were also Christened as Catholics and attended Saint Peter's Church, which was a mammoth building that extended from Gorham Street to South Street, abutting a portion of the South Common.

Saint Peter's Church was a sponsor for the Saint Peter's Cadets baseball team that played in a Catholic league throughout the city of Lowell. I had been the catcher of the team up to this particular day when Bishop Markham strolled from his palace headquarters across Summer Street to the South Common baseball diamond where we were practicing.

This was his first visit to any of our baseball practices or games and in his rather pompous mannerism started addressing each of the team members, like "And what is your name, lad?" with a heavy Irish accent.

Going from player to player with responses like "Driscoll", "O'Malley", "O'Hearn"…and when he got to me —I had been warned that this day was coming—my reply was "O'Plomaritis".

DIDN'T WORK, GOT THE HEAVE-HO!

When the volunteer coach explained that I was the only one that would catch without a catcher's mask, the bishop decided to spring for the cost of a mask—and that was the end of my career playing on the Saint Peter's Cadets baseball team.

OLD ORCHARD BEACH

During the summer months we would go to Old Orchard Beach in Biddeford, Maine at least once and sometimes twice each year as a family. Although we did not have an automobile, my father was able to have one of his friends that was a member of his bible class take us as a family in his Ford station wagon up to Old Orchard Beach.

I remember when we pulled into a gas station that my father payed the attendant for the gas. It was ten gallons of gasoline for one dollar, and that included the attendant checking the oil level, tire pressure for all four wheels and the water supply in the radiator.

Our picnic lunch consisted of a couple loaves of greek bread, a big chunk of cheese, raw carrots, a head of lettuce, small basket of tomatoes and good old ripe bananas for dessert.

We always enjoyed going up to Old Orchard Beach. It was like a day in Wonderland.

We were in and out of the cold water all day. The water always seemed to be much colder the farther you would go up the coastline into Maine. They had an exceptionally long pier and when the tide went out we played in the shady sand area underneath. They also had a famous amusement park close by that you could walk to in a bathing suit and have a lot of fun with only a couple of coins.

RADIO AND SOUTH COMMON

Now I will attempt to relate a short story when I was a young boy, between five and ten years of age.

I was walking from my house on Gorham Street to the South Common playground and while going past a trash can I heard static-like noises coming from it. I reached into the trash can and pulled out a small broken box with batteries attached to it.

My curiosity prompted me to turn the small wheel-like button and POOF!—my first and everlasting impression of Notre Dame football. I honestly don't remember who they were playing, however the cheering noises and excitement in the broadcaster's voice had me sitting on the curb with my ear pressed tightly to the broken-down box [a portable radio], anxiously waiting for each and every word and phrase coming from the announcer's voice.

I continued on my way to the South Common with my football tucked under one arm and the box in my other hand, looking for my friends to share my findings and to play some playground football, that included passing, running and catching the ball.

Quite often I would go the playground only to find none of my chums were there yet, so I would proceed over to the baseball backstop where I would practice placekicking into the backstop, hoping some day I'd kick one over the top.

I enjoyed football so much I can still envision my walking to and from the South Common playground with my football in my hands and as I approached telephone and light poles I would pretend it was someone trying to catch me and I would extend my arm with the ball tucked under my other, make a quick step to either side, pretending I was dodging a player trying to tackle me. Sometimes I would spin to my left or right and continue running like I just dodged another tackler.

Other times as I was walking or jogging with the football under my arm I would come across a hydrant and I would pretend it was trying to tackle me. I would tuck the football under one arm and with the other place it on top of the hydrant to straddle it. Needless to say, many times I was unsuccessful, **"OUCH"**, getting my crotch caught and tearing my trousers.

As I reflect back on that era; I would always have a football under my arm, whether I was going to a movie, school, or the store for my mother.

SNOW SHOVELING GORHAM STREET AND BEYOND

In the winter months we loved to see the snow for several reasons as living so close to the South Common presented typical activities for the Plomaritis family.

We had a Flexible Flyer that our father bought in a second hand shop, and to us, it was the Cadillac of sleds. When my father bought a recreational item such as a sled, it was for the four of us.

We would either take turns going down the somewhat challenging slopes for five to seven year olds or, all four of us would jump on the sled after a good push off and see how many of the other sleds we could tip over on the way down.

Keeping warm in the winter was no problem. You see our father would do all the shopping, being uninterested in styles or sizes, but rather in warmth and quality. Our mother, being an excellent seamstress, would take it from there with her gifted hands and great patience. She would sit by the kerosene stove in her comfy cushioned chair, making all the necessary alterations including added zippers and buttons to be sure that even with our tumbling in the snow we would not get cold. She even knitted us woolen mittens, hats and scarfs.

As for our feet, our father had another barber shop customer who owned an army surplus store where he would buy heavy woolen socks and winter shoes for those of us not requiring special shoes.

Our father was a sucker for a bargain. Quite often he would come home with shoes two to three sizes too big and when we stuffed newspapers into the toe areas he would say in Greek: "A perfect fit".

Another good reason George and I enjoyed the winter snow storms was that after we shoveled our front entrance and the sidewalk in front of the barber shop, which was among our chores, we would go up Gorham Street, onto Central street and all the way up to Kearney Square and shovel snow in front of any storefront that wasn't already cleared. Most of the stores were not open yet. However, we figured we would go back when they opened and inform the owners that we were the ones that shoveled and asked if they would like to be our customer. Usually they would give us 25 to 50 cents, depending how much snow had fallen and how wide of a storefront area that we shoveled.

Recent photo by Titus Plomaritis of one of our best customers 70 years ago located in the middle of Kearney Square.

We did have a few stiffs that would say they did not ask us to shovel their sidewalk and would not even cough up a dime. We would just write them off and not shovel that storefront again. However, my brother George with his temperament didn't feel the same as I. He would go back out on the street and shovel all the snow back in front of the stiffs' stores.

The third reason I enjoyed the winter snow storms was that we would pile the snow up in our back yard, fairly close to our tenement and take turns jumping off our back porch directly into the snow bank below. After each jump we would shovel more snow into the hollow area created by the last jumper.

When we had an exceptionally heavy snow storm we piled the snow bank halfway up to our back porch. With that much snow we then were able to jump off the third story porch— if the tenants were not home. George and I were always the first ones for the challenge.

When we were a little older, between eight and nine years of age, the ultimate goal was to shimmy up to the roof by placing one foot on each side of each tenement in the narrow alley between the tenements and slowly climb to the roof. I remember the excitement of my first jump from the rooftop. It was similar to my first climax.

SWIMMING LESSONS

I remember one day while in the fourth grade, at the Colburn elementary

Colburn School at 136 Lawrence Street in Lowell, Massachusetts is listed in the National Register of Historic Places. Photo by Titus Plomaritis

school, the gym teacher gave me papers to bring home requiring my parents' signatures authorizing me to go to the YMCA for free swimming lessons.

Not being a good student and looking for another opportunity to get out of classroom work, I signed my father's name to authorize me to attend the free group lessons once weekly for six weeks.

We would walk as a group with a teacher to the YMCA for the six weeks' time.

This is a good time to relate that I was already an accomplished swimmer as it was customary in our neighborhood to be thrown into the Armours Canal by the older boys when we were between five or six years of age. The current was strong and the water was filthy with rodents and raw sewage.

We had to dog paddle to the side wall and grip onto some ridges to climb out—only to be thrown back in. We were all naked.

When I first arrived at the YMCA the person in charge said I had to go to the Public Health Clinic and get a physical exam before I could attend the free swim classes. That is when I remember the nurse asking me what my father's occupation was and I said he was a barber. Then she asked me about my mother's occupation and I could only remember her conversations with the neighbors and I said "She works in a slave shop."

It is interesting to note that in that era all the boys in the YMCA swim classes were also naked. If it was for sanitary reasons at the YMCA, I can understand the reasoning, however, Armours Canal **"No Fucking Way"**.

SANDLOT FOOTBALL MEMORIES

I find it amazing how at times I can actually envision myself playing football on the South Common some 70 to 75 years ago.

I can remember two brothers, Joe and Pasquale "Patsy" Depolito, who were volunteer coaches that just liked the game of football and had fun coaching us younger boys. They were fun to be around and we were fortunate to have them as coaches.

They were the oldest of a large family of seven children—five boys and two girls. Three of the boys played football with me on the South End team. They were Albert, Donald and Louie.

I particularly remember this family so well because their mother was such a kind woman, who always made me feel welcome in her home and had me sit down at her table to have dinner with her family.

Mrs. Depolito was an early widow who also had two charming daughters—Rita an Anita—for whom most mothers would kill.

Louie, better known as "Mousy", was more my age and we would quite often play kids' games. With all those kids they had plenty of games to choose from in the house when the weather was too bad to be outdoors.

Joe was the bigger of the two oldest and it was only natural he would be the so-called line coach.

Patsy, with a slender build and great finesse, was a natural coach for the backfield. He just loved to show us his slick movements with the football and would carry out each play like it was a drama on the stage. His emphasis was with the quarterback and my recollection is that it was his only chance to show us how he could throw the football—and believe me he did get our attention.

During that era there was no such thing as football injury insurance. We had 15 to 20 kids on our South End team and when the coach sent in a substitute, the player going out would give his helmet to the player coming in.

Whatever equipment we had was donated, mostly handed down from year to year. Nobody was paid. The coaches, referees and time keepers were all volunteers.

If somebody was injured he had an option to either play injured or sit on the sidelines until he was well enough to play again. If the injury was more of a serious nature it would be the responsibility of the parents to take care of it. In those days it was only about $3.00 for a doctor's visit and most of the General Practitioners wouldn't charge anything, knowing we belonged to one of the park teams.

The coaches would arrange a somewhat organized schedule to play at each of the parks in the city of Lowell.

We practiced every day for an hour or so, sometimes under a street light because in those days we did not have the great lighting that today's playgrounds have.

The South End team from the South Common had a mixture of Irish, Portuguese, Italian and Polish kids with a couple of Greek boys thrown in—George and I.

The North Common had two teams—the Blackhawks and the Acre Shamrocks. The Blackhawks consisted of mostly Greek kids, while the Acre Shamrocks were mostly all Irish.

Some of the other playgrounds that had teams included Pawtucketville, Shedd Park, Highland Park, McPherson Park, Gage Hill Park and one or two other teams that were not too top heavy with a particular nationality.

Our father never knew that George and I played sandlot or any other kind of football. Whenever he asked where the bruises came from we would just say "playing at the common."

As we got older, around the time we moved to Outer Varnum Avenue, I remember playing for three different teams during the same season— South Common, North Common and Pawtucketville.

My main mode of transportation at that time was my bicycle, which had balloon tires and only one gear—**STRICTLY LEG POWER.**

FACTORY WORKER AND COOK

Here is a short story of my working mother, who also was a great cook.

My mother worked as a stitcher at a factory on Thorndike Street. She walked to and from work. Her travel route was as follows: from Gorham Street, up Union Street, across the South Common to the factory "Slave Shop" which was located between the old Keith Academy building and the since removed Commodore Ballroom.

The total distance was about five to six football fields.

The factory building where my mother worked in the 1930's, taken from the South Common, 2011. Photo by Titus Plomaritis

She would leave the house at 6:30 a.m. and return at 5:30 p.m., earning $2.00 per day.

Crossing the South Common in the winter months was brutal, with the area being wide open and the strong winds and swirling snow making extremely unpleasant walking conditions.

My mother was not a complainer. However, I often overheard her many times relating to some of her friends and neighbors that she "worked like a slave".

I remember her getting home from work and taking a short rest. In the winter time it included putting her feet on the oven stove until thawing out, before preparing dinner.

MY MOTHER WAS AN EXCELLENT COOK

Most of her great Greek recipes included fish, chicken, ground beef, eggs, cheese, milk and pasta.

I remember her sending me to the Boston Fish Market on Gorham Street—about one football field from our residence—with two dimes to get four pounds of fish, whichever was five cents a pound.

Chiklis
Yep!, Michael Chiklis, famous for TV shows The Shield & The Commish, Grandson of founder of Chiklis Market."

On other occasions she often would send me to Saunder's Market —about a 40 yard field goal from our residence— with two nickels to get two pounds of hamburg, which was also five cents a pound at that time.

My father would buy the feta (Greek cheese), chickens, eggs and on special occasions a leg of lamb from Chiklis's Greek Market on Market Street, once a week.

MY MOTHER'S RECIPE

The following is a somewhat modified version of my mother's recipe of Greek stuffed meat balls. In Greek they are called **"KIF- THED -DIES"**

Ingredients: 1 pound prime beef (ground)
3/4 pound lamb or pork (ground)
1 large egg
2 slices of whole wheat bread (toasted)
1 medium onion (chopped)
2 tablespoons crushed garlic
6 sprigs of parsley
1/2 teaspoon of black pepper
1/2 cup of graded parmesan
1/4 teaspoon of Greek One Spice

Directions: use an oversized container for mixing.
Place all ingredients into container.
With both hands mix all of the ingredients together, squeezing

and pulling continuously for approximately 10 minutes, until you have one large ball.

Separate and shape into golf ball size meatballs.

Best to use 100% Virgin Olive Oil to slightly cover bottom of the pan.

Using medium heat, turning frequently for 8 to 10 minutes

NOTE;— In the past couple of years I have enjoyed sharing the cooking with my wife, Claire, of 60 years. We were married on December 1, 1951.

MOVE TO VARNUM AVENUE AREA, 1939

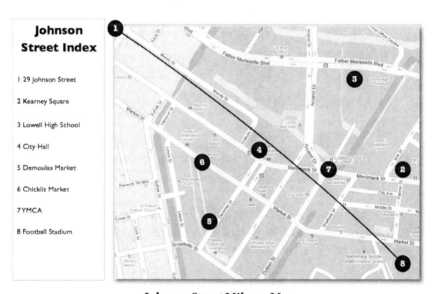

Johnson Street Index

I 29 Johnson Street

2 Kearney Square

3 Lowell High School

4 City Hall

5 Demoulas Market

6 Chicklis Market

7 YMCA

8 Football Stadium

Johnson Street Mileage Map

BICYCLE DISTANCES FROM 29 JOHNS0N STREET

Lowell general Hospital	1.5 miles
Pawtucket School	2.3 miles
Lowell High School	4.5 miles
Kearney Square	4.7 miles
Demoulas Market	4.5 miles
Barber Shop	4.5 miles
North Common	3.5 miles
South Common	4.5 miles
Lowell Alumni football Stadium	7 miles

When my parents bought the house at 29 Johnson Street in 1939 its cost was approximately $1000.

The house was old, with about two to three acres of land and it had a dirt cellar and a wood burning stove. It was located at the end of the street and beyond the house were several acres of woods that ran into a huge gravel pit.

Over the past seven or so decades the property has been greatly improved and several more adjacent homes were constructed, which has extended the street. Our former house has had a major renovation and it probably would be worth hundreds of thousands of dollars more than our original purchase price. **NOTE**—To see how the house looked in 2011 go to the following "Remaining in High School" story.

1938 HURRICANE PROVIDED FUEL

BACK TO THE PAST—The wooded area next to our property had about fifty trees that were uprooted, as a result of the severe hurricane of 1938. That was a blessing in disguise for us because it provided fuel for our wood burning furnace.

You must remember that back in 1938 we did not have televisions or computers, which meant that we had very little advance warning to prepare for that devastating hurricane. Telephone and train services were disrupted for many days.

1938 Hurricane Devastation.
Uprooted trees are shown above, as a result of the powerful hurricane of 1938 that swept through the area, becoming the costliest disaster in Southern New England history.

The hurricane traveled from the coast of North Carolina one morning, and roared as far North as Montreal, Canada, moving at 50 mph. Long Island and Southern New England ended up with the worst damage, with wind gusts of well over 100 mph, knocking down trees onto homes and power lines. The total deaths of the hurricane reached 682. In some areas 10 inches of rain fell, rivaling the levels of the catastrophic floods of just two and a half years earlier.

WORK FOR THE BOYS

My father bought a secondhand two-man crosscut saw from a nearby farmer and we used it to saw the fallen trees into eighteen to twenty-four inch pieces.

The farmer gave us an old wooden pull cart that needed repairs and four wheels, and after repairing it and adding the wheels and a mini harness it was "Hi Ho, Hi Ho, it's off to work we go", for the next two years.

We actually cut up all the fallen trees with that one saw and hauled off all of the pieces to our back yard on that one wooden pull cart.

The front man wore the harness and pulled while the other three would balance and push the load of cut wood from the woods to our back yard, where it would be stockpiled and ready for splitting. We always felt that the work would be done faster if we piled more wood on the wagon, which would allow for more playtime later.

We would have turns wearing a harness with straps around both shoulders and pulling which was instrumental in leg development and power. From there we would turn the sawed pieces of wood end-up and use an axe to split them into sizes that would fit into our furnace. Once the wood was split we carried and stored it into the cellar, where we had two large storage bins. We learned from experience that the longer the wood remained in the cellar, which was a dry place, the better it would burn. Therefore, we developed a system to completely burn the wood that had been stored in the bin the longest before going to the other bin. The ultimate goal was to have both bins stacked from the floor to the ceiling.

CLOSE CALLS—SECOND INCIDENT

This **SECOND CLOSE CALL** in my life relates to the time after our move to the Varnum Avenue area, and it involves playing in and around the gravel pit near our Johnson Street home. At that time there were only a total of three houses on Johnson Street and ours was the last one and the closest to the gravel pit.

We had created a pathway from the upper level of the pit to our backyard, hauling wood in a wagon over a period of time.

Just envision a thirty to forty foot drop from the top to the bottom of the gravel pit. My brother George and I had been digging a tunnel in the pit that was only about three feet below the surface pathway that we had created from hauling the wood back to the house.

WE HAD PENETRATED about six to eight feet, taking turns to carry out the gravel from a tunnel that was just big enough for our ten and twelve year-old bodies to crawl in and out of. We would crawl in with an empty pail, fill it up and then go back out to empty it. We worked on this tunnel day after day and had dug out about two body lengths.

"WELL, AGAIN SOMEONE UP ABOVE WAS LOOKING OVER ME!!"

One day, my brother Joe decided to go to the gravel pit to see what George and I were up to. As he walked over the tunnel while I was inside, a portion of gravel collapsed and I was covered from the waist up.

FORTUNATELY, George happened to be at the tunnel's edge and he saw what was happening. He started pulling me out by my feet, and with Joe's assistance, using every ounce of strength in their bodies, they successfully dragged me out as I was gasping for air.

YEP!! ANOTHER CLOSE CALL.

RIDE TO THE HOSPITAL

This would be the appropriate time to relate my one bad experience related to splitting wood.

It was a hot summer day and I was home alone when I decided to surprise my brothers and split a pile of wood. I was 12 years of age at that time. As I was splitting the wood at a fairly good clip, the axe apparently was getting dull and needed sharpening, but I just ignored the warning and kept chopping away.

This one time the axe got stuck and I was having a difficult time separating it from the block of wood. I pulled real hard on the long handle—and it released suddenly. Losing my balance, I fell to the ground and landed on a broken bottle. Then I noticed blood squirting out of my left upper thigh.

I ran into the house and jumped into the bathtub with a bottle of peroxide and a towel. I kept pouring the peroxide on the wound until the bottle was empty, keeping the towel pressed on the wound. I then took one of my father's neckties and tied it around my leg, ran down the stairs jumped on my bicycle and rode it to Lowell General Hospital, which was located one and a half miles from our house. I ran into someone's office, and that someone in turn took me to the emergency room.

After explaining the details of the accident to the doctor, he cleaned up the messy necktie bandage ensemble, added a few stitches and sent me off.

I don't remember if the hospital ever sent my father a bill, if so, I'm sure it was deducted from my shoe shine account, as was the necktie.

COURTNEY'S FARM

When we first moved to the Varnum Avenue area and were not cutting trees for the wood burning stove, I remember working on a big farm only a short walking distance from the house.

Everyone in the area purchased their vegetables and milk from what was called Courtney's Farm. I can still envision Mr. Courtney wearing the old-time one piece overhauls with several pockets and wide bands that crossed in the back and came over his shoulders and attached to the front, with fastener-like hooks, onto metal buttons. I don't remember his first name because I only called him Mr. Courtney.

He was a tough farmer to work for and only paid me ten cents an hour. I remember several times, especially in the summer months, when my count was fifty hours and he would only pay me $4.00. However, when I look back and think of all the free corn, tomatoes and other vegetables he gave me to take home, I guess he wasn't the cheapskate after all.

His farm included a large barn to house his cows, and that is where I learned the technique of milking cows. We purchased our milk from him daily in two half gallon glass containers. The milk was raw, unpasteurized, right from the cows.

Within a couple of years we had our own vegetable farm and two cows, and that ended my career on Courtney's Farm. We also had a few apple trees, so it is needless to say that Irving's Fruit and Vegetable Market gradually lost a good customer too, but I'm sure Irving missed my father's Saturday night dialogue.

VARNUM AVENUE BUS TRANSPORTATION

My mother continued to work as a seamstress at different factories in the City of Lowell after we moved to the Varnum Avenue area. She did take the bus early every morning and return at around 6 p.m. She did take brief vacations in order to give birth to my brothers, Tony (in 1943), David (1946), and my sister, Priscilla (1947).

My father also traveled by way of the bus system to Kearney Square. The bus schedule to all areas of the city of Lowell was directed through the Square, which was downtown in the heart of the city. He would walk between Kearney Square and the barber shop in order to save the transfer fee. If the weather was inclement he would spend the extra dime and transfer to a bus that would get him to the corner of Appleton and Gorham streets, only a short walk to the barber shop.

Just recently I drove out to the end of the Varnum Avenue bus line and followed the bus to its final destination, extended about one mile to Greater Lowell Technical High School, Tyngsboro, MA.

Recent photo in 2011 depicting a newer modern
bus with a newer revised Pawtucketville route
Photo by Titus Plomaritis

Eddie Martinez, the bus driver in the attached photo, informed me that several years ago they changed the Varnum Avenue route to the **PAWTUCKETVILLE ROUTE.**

FOOTBALL AT VARNUM AVENUE

Varnum Avenue did not have a football team. However, we had several kids, including one of the coaches, from our area that played for the Pawtucketville team.

We played on a field called the "Cow Pasture", located directly across the street from the Pawtucket School, which became our newly transferred school from the Colburn School.

The Pawtucket School went up to the eighth grade. Physical education classes three times a week would be held across the street at the same "Cow Pasture" on which the Pawtucketville football team played and practiced.

CALLING US TRAITORS

With our own bicycles, purchased from the second hand shops, my brother, George, and I, would quite often peddle between venues to play in two games on the same day. We were always committed to the South End team, but when another team such as the Blackhawks was playing on the North Common and it didn't conflict with the South End squad that had already played that day on the South Common, we would hightail it over to the North Common and play with our newly acquired friends.

When the South and North Common rivals played each other, we were always loyal to our creators and played for the South Common even though some of the Blackhawk players (speaking Greek) would swear at us and call us "**TRAITORS**".

INTEREST IN FOOTBALL STARTS

My interest and desire to practice and play football increased, whereas my brother George's decreased as he found other interests. That is perhaps when we started spending less time together.

Although it was against the rules for anyone on the Lowell High School team to play football elsewhere like sandlots, I got to know that quite a few of the underclassmen at the school (the freshmen and sophomore players who didn't play in the varsity games), continued to play sandlot football, irrespective of the school rules.

When I was in the eighth grade I was permitted to attend football practices a couple of days a week with the Lowell High School team, partaking mostly in the exercise and skill drills, but no contact. It would allow me to learn the plays and prepare for my freshman year.

On those days I would take my bicycle to the Pawtucket School and, as soon as school got out, I would fast-pedal through the city and out to Alumni Field. My main concern was to get home before my father, who was usually on the 6 o'clock bus from Kearney Square. The bus ride from Kearney Square to the end of the line was only four miles however, it would take between 25 to 30 minutes due to the number of stops it had to make.

My bike ride from Alumni Field to 29 Johnson Street was seven miles, but I had no trouble beating my father home while I was in the eighth grade because I could leave practice early. However, when I was a freshman and sophomore at LHS I did not want to miss one minute of practice, so I would stay until the end of it. All the coaches knew of my dilemma and they would come over to me at times, when practice was running late, and tell me, IT WAS TIME, meaning, "Go in and change, don't shower and see if you can beat the bus home".

Even the bus drivers were aware of my racing the 6 o'clock bus headed for Varnum Avenue—especially Red Walmsley and Ray Riddick's father. Sometimes when the bus wasn't very crowded, the bus driver would look in the rearview mirror, checking on my whereabouts, and he would make several unnecessary stops, even if no one was exiting the bus, to give me a chance to get ahead of the bus and beat my father home.

PAWTUCKET SCHOOL DAYS

As I reflect back on history, I can see that there was definitely a change, for the better, in my growth and development once we moved to the Varnum Avenue area and when I attended the Pawtucket School, now the McAvinnue School, on Mammoth Road.

I actually remember looking forward to attending school as the classroom teachers and physical education instructor were actually playing the role of my parents. However, homework was still somewhat of a problem.

I met new friends, one in particular, Bea Dean, who lived fairly close to the school on West Meadow Road. I would walk her home from school on occasion and she would show me the horses she always talked about in class. She and her family also had a good sized pond that we skated on during the winter months.

During that era I had three options of transportation: my "footmobile", my bicycle and the bus. Our house at 29 Johnson Street was only about one fourth of a mile beyond the last bus stop on the Varnum Avenue route, which in turn was five miles to Kearney Square in downtown Lowell.

As for the bus, the students were issued a bus ticket at the beginning of each month, with two allowance trips per day. The bus driver would punch a hole into the ticket each time you got on.

I remember that we would either walk or take our bikes to the Pawtucket School most of the time to preserve the bus ticket punches for the longer trip to downtown Lowell. Some of the bus drivers that got to know us and were egg customers would just click the puncher next to the ticket and wink their eyes (like don't mention it). It was explained to me later that the bus company has what they call spotters that ride the buses to observe the bus drivers for the prevention of free riders and theft.

The physical education instructor at the Pawtucket School, Mr. Duffy, took a special interest in me from day one. I think because he noticed that I was always up in front and anxious to learn a new skill that he was introducing to our class. When he got to the football part of his physical education program he also realized that I had already had some previous coaching, so he used me as his assistant in demonstrating whichever skill he had planned for that particular day like passing, catching or kicking the football.

By that time I had advanced to the seventh grade and, believe me, it wasn't easy. You see, I never had the parental discipline to be a good student and therefore I had very poor study habits.

When living on Johnson Street I also played baseball as several of my classmates in the seventh and eighth grades were on the school's team, as well as playing sandlot football. **NOTICE** in the team photo, all

1944 Pawtucket Junior High Ball Club
Coach Joe Duffy's Pawtucket school team is competing in the Junior high league this season. The squad includes, front, left to right: Dick Fadden, Bob Heslin, Titus Plumarites, Dennis Callahan, Donald Edwards, Clayton Stoddard; rear—Raymond Roy, Phil Chamberlain, Bob Andreoli, Captain Walter Burns, Dan Carneville, Jim Chandler and George Hughes. Sun staff photo

the protective gear I'm wearing, compared to O'Plomaritis who caught for the St. Peter's Cadets, and was mask-less.

On occasion, Mr. Duffy would take me and a couple of the eighth graders to Lowell High School football practices and introduce us to the coaches and we would watch the team practice. I think his motive was for stimulation and to prepare us for high school football, similar to a high school player attending a college practice facility. Pawtucket School only went up to the eighth grade so students there would go to Lowell High as Freshmen.

GRADUATION PROGRAM

1944 Pawtucket School Graduation Class
With Principal Joseph McAvenue 4th row left end.
Titus back row 2nd from right on tip toes.

Tuesday, June 13, 1944

****

1. a. The Pledge of Allegiance
   b. Excerpt from Declaration of Independence
      i. Chorus—"Be Thou Their Master, Pilot, Friend"—Terry
2. "Buckingham Palace"   Reading Choir
3. "America is Worth Fighting For"
   Walter Burns

Elinor Reilly
Virginia Taylor
George Scagos
4. "The Old Refrain" Girls Glee Club
5. Reading of Honor Roll
6. "Pirate Don Durk of Dowdee"
7. Distribution of Diplomas
   Mr. Gerald Cronin, School Committee Member
8. Finale—"Star Spangled Banner"

****

Miss Mary Wallace, Director of Music
Miss Mary Casey, Director of Reading Choir
Miss Christine McPherson, Pianist

LIST OF GRADUATES

BOYS

Robert Francis Andreoli, Thomas Charles Ballos, Walter S. Burns, Dennis Francis Callahan, Daniel C. Carnevale, Phillippe M. Chamberland, James Richard Chandler, John Roger Clement, Donald I. Edwards, Raymond G. Edwards, Robert Graham Edwards, Richard Robert Fadden, Robert Rene Gaudette, John Joseph Harrington, Robert Rene Heslin, George Joseph Hughes, William Francis Kappler, William Nison Lamarre, Richard Paul Lebel, Paul Lois LaBourdais, Charles F. Lefebvre, Roland Lupien, Vincent Michael Mahoney, Harold Joseph McGrail, Donat Edward Noel, William Panagiotou, Frederick D. Peterson, **TITUS D. PLOMARITIS**, George Scagos, Norman Wesley Silcox, Richard James Smith, Clayton Bartlett Stoddard.

GIRLS

Mary Rita Ainsley, Claire Pauline Bisson, Elizabeth Ann Brosnan, Phyllis Ann Corcoran, Mary Louise Cram, Mary Rita Furlong, Phyllis Margaret Howard, Christina Ann Kelly, Effie Koukias, Evanthea Koukias, Dolores Carmen Bernadette La Fleur, Stavroula Lallas, Lorraine Evelyn Levasseur,

Theresa Pauline Maher, Emma Mary Mailloux, Ann Louise McArdle, Elizabeth Louise McHugh, Marilyn Mildred Martini Malloy, Helen Frances Mullin, Ann Elizabeth O'Connor, Marguerite Monica O'Neil, Jeannine Beatrice Poirier, Ruth Dorothy Proulx, Mary Elinor Reilly, Cynthia Scagos, Patricia Elizabeth Silk, Margaret Ann Snee, Virginia Viola Taylor, Mona Mary Wise.

BICYCLE STORY

Oh yes, there is a bicycle story that I just have to share with you. It occurred when I was 13 years of age. I remember it was late August, because we were getting ready for school.

Sitting—my father Demosthenes Plomaritis with his only sister Irene and her husband George Varkas. Family photo of 1920's

I must first explain that my father had one sister. Her name was Irene and she was married to George Varkas, who was also a barber.

They lived in Jamaica Plain, Massachusetts, which was about 40 miles from our home on Johnson Street. They had three daughters, Mary, Percy and Electra, and one son, George, better known as Tarky.

Aunt Irene was a kind and loving person, just like my mother. Her husband, Uncle George, had the same temperament. When in his company he would make you feel like you were one of his own.

My uncle George was fun to be around. He played the mandolin and would partake

My one speed balloon tired bicycle.

in Greek dances in the living room with his children while my Aunt Irene would make me a plate of pancakes. When I woofed them down, she would make me a second plate.

Now, back to Johnson Street. At about six on a Sunday morning everybody was still in bed, when I decided to go for a bike ride. I was dressed in summer clothing, short pants, a lightweight shirt and sneakers.

I started riding towards Kearney Square, which by this time was just a short joy ride, if you will. When I arrived at the Square, where all the buses were lined up ready for departure to just about everywhere, I noticed a bus with a sign that said "WILMINGTON", and I made a quick decision to follow that bus on my bike and see if I could find my way to visit my favorite cousins in Jamaica Plain.

By now, I considered myself an experienced distance traveler—remember my **FREIGHT TRAIN STORY?**

Anyway, I followed the bus through Tewksbury and noticed signs along the way that read, "Route 38" about every couple of miles. I did have trouble keeping up with the bus when it was on the straightaway. However, I figured that the bus was following the Route 38 signs, so I did likewise.

I continued on, with no fear or panic of getting lost until I got to Medford!! Then doubt began to settle in when I looked for the Route 38 sign and could only see signs with arrows pointing in all directions and showing cities I never heard of before.

Just about then I noticed a bus that read **"NORTH STATION"**, and I quickly remounted my bike and followed that bus, never letting it get out of my sight. Traveling at the speed of sound, I patted my bike on the forehead and said, "HI HO, SILVER", and followed that bus. I knew that if I reached the North Station I could get to Jamaica Plain.

I had been to my aunt's and uncle's house on two occasions and both times they took me on subway rides back and forth, to and from North Station to the end of the Jamaica Plain run, where it would turn around and go back to North Station in Boston. For one token you could ride all day long without getting off the subway. The subway would travel both below ground at accelerated speed and above ground at slower speeds, which was very exciting as a kid, like on the rides at an amusement park.

The walk from the Jamaica Plain station was only a few blocks to their house, which had been implanted in my memory bank so I had no trouble finding it. I did get to my destination after a few corrections from wrong turns and a couple of extra miles. My legs had been conditioned over the past three years and showed no signs of fatigue.

When I walked up the stairs and knocked on the door, they were so happy to see me they showered me with hugs and kisses. I felt as if I had just scored the winning touchdown!!

After just a few minutes, expecting to see my parents follow me up the stairs, came the question, "where are they?" When I explained that I was alone, they laughed and thought I was kidding. I told them of my journey from Johnson Street in Lowell, and they still didn't believe me until they looked out the window and saw my balloon-tired bicycle taking a much deserved nap as it rested on its side on the grass.

My Aunt Irene went directly to the telephone and called my father, speaking Greek so quickly that I had difficulty understanding her.

Her main concern was that she wanted him to know that I was with her and not to worry. She explained that I had gotten there on my bicycle and that they had plans of going to Cohasset Beach in the afternoon for a picnic and swim and that they would drive me back home the next day.

Cohasset Beach is a great place to go for a family picnic because it has an outstanding sandy beach for kids to play on and build castles. It also has a lengthy oceanfront, and most of all, the water is warmer than the water in Hampton Beach, New Hampshire, and considerably warmer than the water on the Maine coastline.

It is interesting that as I reflect on some of my experiences of so many years ago such as this one, how all the names of places and people keep flashing back into my head as I remember the occasion.

PLOMARITIS CHICKEN
& EGG BUSINESS

We had a working farm on Johnson Street which eventually turned into a large chicken and egg business. The farm included one double-decker coop, divided into four sections that housed over one thousand chickens, and one smaller coop where we started with baby chicks and with a progressive schedule we would caponize them so they would grow into bigger eating chickens for market and retail.

Marketing was considerably different in those days. I remember for about three years we would dress the chickens on Fridays, and on Saturdays we would carry two double shopping bags full of chickens on the bus from Varnum Avenue to individuals who had ordered them the week before.

I also remember getting off the bus in front of the Lowell City Hall with the two shopping bags full of chickens and walking about one eighth of a mile to the first Demoulas Market, in the early 1940's, on Dummer Street.

Tony delivering two more slaughtered chickens to the boiling pot to be dressed for tomorrow's bus ride for delivery to customers and Demoulas Market on Dummer Street.

Telemachus, better known as "MIKE", would dump the chickens onto a huge scale hanging from the ceiling. He would read the weight indicator, write it on a piece of paper and hand it to me without wasting any time as he told me to give it to my father, who in turn would walk to the Demoulas Market, from the barber shop on Mondays, to collect payment.

Our egg business was with Rhode Island Red hens, most popular in this part of the country. They only lay brown eggs. It was our responsibility to keep the stalls clean so the next feathered "boarder" would recognize our Motel 6 invitation sign, we'll leave light on, "Come On In And Have A Lay".

We also had to be sure to pick up the eggs at least twice daily otherwise the hens would either peck at the eggs, causing them to break or sit on them and try to hatch them.

By the time I was twelve years old the house's cellar had a poured concrete floor and the boiler was converted to coal. A portion was designated to dress the chickens for market. This is not the same as dressing for school. It's actually undressing the chickens by first killing them and dipping them into a large container of boiling water, then removing their feathers.

Another portion of the cellar was reserved for candling the eggs, which is a fairly simple process of testing them for freshness or fertility by holding them to a special light. Eggs that failed the candle test went directly into our home refrigerator for our personal use.

CAPONS, CHICKEN FARM

I feel that it is imperative for me to give you, readers that are not familiar with caponized chickens, a little capon education based on my early life hands-on experience.

Poultry is the catch-all term for domesticated birds that are meaty enough to eat. Poultry tends to be lower in saturated fat than any other meat, so it is a good choice if you are worried about your health or weight. You can lower the fat still more by removing the skin and by using light meat from the breast instead of the darker meat from the thighs and legs.

Younger birds are more tender than older ones, so they are best for grilling, roasting and frying. Older, tougher birds do better if they are cooked in stews or soups.

Now, let's get on with a brief education of caponized chickens, from birth to consumption. The first task was to build a smaller chicken coop to house about ten dozen baby chicks. We then purchased the baby chicks from the wholesaler. The chicks did require a little more watching when they were still babies so as not to get trampled, and they needed to have clean water containers, changed daily.

At first, we would make an appointment with an experienced farmer just up the road, who we called the "Capon Doctor". You see, it did require a skillful pair of hands, since it is a serious operation. We always scheduled the "Capon Party" on a Sunday so we would all be at home to help.

The male birds were usually about three to four weeks old at the time they were about to lose their "manhood". The testes of a male chicken are located in the abdominal cavity. The cockerel, better known as a cock, is a male chicken, whereas a hen is a female chicken. The males were taken off feed and water for twelve to twenty-four hours prior to surgery and post-operative antibiotics are given to reduce the possible chances of infection.

We would place a divider inside the coop to make it easier for us to catch the cocks and then hold them steady on a block, by holding both wings with one hand and their legs with the other. The "Doctor" would then make a one-inch surgical incision with a sharp scalpel between the two posterior ribs and remove both testicles. The testes were usually yellowish in color and about the size of a large piece of grain.

I remember that we had to pay special attention to the birds for the next two to three days, as some of them would develop large air bubbles at the place of the surgery. We would gently puncture the bubbles with a sterilized needle and then turn them loose. Luckily, our fatality rate was minimal, and at ten weeks they would weigh anywhere from seven to nine pounds.

It has been sixty-five years since I've worked in the chicken coops or shoveled the chicken droppings, which was the most devastating of all my country farming chores. We actually wore moistened cloth masks over our noses and mouths to avoid inhaling the gassy fumes.

CHICKEN EVERY SUNDAY

We had chicken almost every Sunday, cooked in every which way you can imagine. My mother did not have the convenience of a convection oven such as we have today, but let me share with you one of my favorite recipes cooked in our convection oven.

ROASTING CHICKEN WITH CONVECTION OVEN

Pre-heat oven to 350 degrees.
Place chicken in a large roasting pan, breast up.
Add two quarts of water.

PREPARE A MIXTURE OF:
2 tablespoons of olive oil,
1 teaspoon of black pepper,
1/2 teaspoon of sea salt.

BRUSH THE ENTIRE MIXTURE ON THE CHICKEN

CUT UP THE FOLLOWING VEGGIES INTO 2" PIECES:

4 to 6 medium red potatoes,
4 to 6 carrots,
1 onion,
1 pepper.

PLACE VEGGIES INTO ROASTING PAN ALL AROUND THE CHICKEN
PLACE ROASTING PAN INTO OVEN, USING MIDDLE RACK

SET OVEN TIMER TO COOK AT 20 MINUTES PER POUND
—Example: 2 hours for a 6-pound roaster.

NOTE—Basting every 15 to 20 minutes enhances external crispness while preserving internal moisture of the chicken.

ENJOY!!!

REMAINING IN HIGH SCHOOL

When I turned fifteen years of age and was a Freshman at Lowell High School, my father related the traditional custom in the Old Country, for the older children to go to work and help out with the household expenses. At that time, I was the only Plomaritis playing football and I made the varsity team. I went to Mr. Sullivan, the LHS headmaster, and told him my disappointment that I had to leave school. His wheels went into action immediately. He called and spoke to Mr.Vincent McCartin, the superintendent of schools and athletic director. They arranged to take me me in a police car to my father's barber shop. They proceeded to scare the living shit out of my father, telling him, through Charlie the barber, who worked for my father, that it was against the law to take me out of school before age sixteen and that he would go to jail if he didn't allow me to stay in school. My father agreed as long as "Titos" would take care of the farm duties like milking the two cows and attending to the chickens. I was then allowed to continue in high school, however even more determined to attend football practice every day and beat the six o'clock bus home.

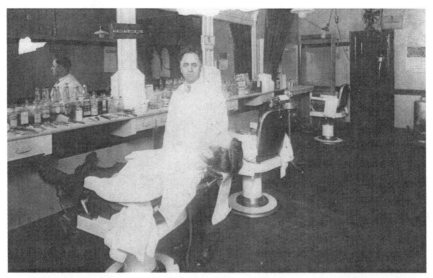

My father Demosthenes startled by the Police car with me in it accompanied with uniformed Police Officers.

Recent photo by Titus Plomaritis of 29 Johnson Street, outer Varnum Avenue, Lowell MA. The window directly above the front entrance was my escape hatch on Sundays— the bedroom window.

All of Lowell High School's football games were played at one p.m. on Sundays. That created somewhat of a problem for me because my father was home and he would put on his work clothes and expect us to work beside him either in the chicken coops or in the vegetable garden.

Sometimes I would fake sickness and my mother would cover for me, saying she gave me some hot soup and told me to go to bed. At eleven a.m. I would go out of my bedroom window, which was above the roof of the front porch of the house, jump off the roof, which was about eight to ten feet high, sneak into the garage, which was our storage area, as we did not have an automobile, and get my bicycle. Off I would go like a speeding bullet and get to the stadium in about twenty-five to thirty minutes.

On other occasions my father would send me in the house or cellar to get something, and that little opening was all I needed to run up to my bedroom, make a quick change and scoot to the stadium. The games were usually over by three p.m., so I would get home about an hour later, only to expect a tongue-lashing.

DUTCH TEA ROOM

During those years I was working on Saturdays at the Dutch Tea Room in Kearney Square, which was located on Merrimack Street.

The Dutch Tea Room was a famous high-scale sandwich shop with fancy pastries made on the premises. It also featured a quality soda fountain. It was owned by two Kaknes brothers, Bill and Ernie, who were loyal LHS boosters and who always encouraged me to continue on my journey to succeed, saying that I could get a college scholarship playing football and get a free college education.

I started work as a dishwasher, bussed tables and gradually was promoted to the soda fountain where I washed glasses and kept the fruit and ice cream containers full. I eventually learned how to make all kinds of fancy sundaes and banana splits.

They paid me fifty cents an hour, plus meals, and gave me pastries that were not sold that day to take home. Bill was the brother who drove me home most of the time.

Sometimes I would go home very late, close to midnight. On those days they asked me if I wanted to stay and clean the oven. We had to wait for the oven to cool down because I would have to go head-first into it while they held my feet.

After those late Saturdays, I would stay in my bedroom on Sundays until everybody was engrossed in their work in the chicken coops, telling my father I was too tired to work. BUT, when the clock struck eleven a.m., I was on my way to the stadium.

NOTE—see the bicycle mileage indicator and just imagine how many miles I traveled in those seven years on the Varnum Avenue area.

THE PARATROOPER STORY

The following story exemplifies what I would consider the most important fifteen months of my life. In that time some phase of the following seven components of my U.S. Paratrooper training took place. These, engrained into my mind and body through repetition have also guided me throughout the remainder of my life:

DISCIPLINE
DIRECTION
DEVELOPMENT
RESPONSIBILITY
RESPECT
LEADERSHIP
SPORTSMANSHIP

FROM THE BEGINNING—

My father was not receptive of my decision to enter into the Army and I needed his permission and signature to enlist.

TWO REASONS WHY MY FATHER AGREED—

1—I told him that the Army would pay me twenty-five dollars a month and I would sign a payroll statement, sending the money directly to him.

2—To prevent my brother George from going to jail.

EXPLANATION—George, who was quick tempered, was in trouble with the law for striking a bus driver in the back of the head while the bus was in motion.

(NOTE)—Because my mother left for work considerably earlier in the morning, it was our (George's and my) responsibility to drop off our younger brother Tony at the day care center, on our way to Lowell High School.

One morning the bus was overcrowded with standing-room-only (long before the era of school buses) and George couldn't get out of the rear door soon enough with Tony on his shoulders. He yelled at the top of his lungs for the bus to stop, however it did not stop and continued going to the next bus stop.

George then pushed his way through the crowd and punched the bus driver on the back of his head, prompting the driver to accelerate, skipping the next few bus stops, until he arrived at Kearney Square and quickly flagged a police officer. The bus driver related the incident and then the policeman took George to the police station.

With the threat of George going to jail, the Chief of Police gave him an ultimatum to enlist in the Army in order to have the charges dropped. George refused unless I went in with him.

At that time I was a first stringer on the LHS football team. Herb Cochran was our head coach and he was a great physical conditioning coach. However, historically he turned out to be one of the worst win-loss football coaches in Lowell High School history—**WE LOST EVERY GAME. EXCEPT THE LAWRENCE CONTEST ON THANKSGIVING!** I was also a member of the school's baseball team.

The LHS Headmaster, Athletic Director and coaches, having already experienced my father's anti-educational mentality, encouraged me to enlist into the United States Army, because the Army recruiters were at the high school at that time recruiting seventeen and eighteen-year-old students. They were guaranteeing the "G.I. Bill of Rights", with an opportunity to get a free college education. We were told that it would be only an eighteen month commitment, and if we were sent to Japan to relieve the troops it would only be for fifteen months.

LHS Headmaster, Raymond Sullivan, was a very kind person and apparently took a personal fondness to me. I remember on several occasions sitting in his office for a sundry of disciplinary reasons, receiving his fatherly advice and guidance. Prior to leaving school in 1946 for my basic training, Mr. Sullivan gave me the necessary study courses to complete my junior year. He also gave me a pep talk relative to the importance of secondary and college education, and in departing he informed me how to keep in touch with Lowell High School.

U.S. ARMY ENLISTMENT DATE: October 2, 1946

My brother George and I reported to Fort Dix, New Jersey for orientation and were then sent to Fort Bragg, North Carolina for our Army Basic Training.

Upon completion of our eight week Basic Training we were informed that the U.S. Army Paratroopers were accepting volunteers to attend a six week vigorous physical training program at Fort Benning, Georgia, to ultimately become paratroopers. Those who survived would be sent to Japan to relieve combat troops.

I was quick to volunteer for two reasons:

1—It paid an extra twenty-five dollars per month, which I did not have to send to my father.

2—The memory of the climactic experience of jumping off the Gorham Street roof.

My brother George failed the required physical exam and we were separated for the first time, as I departed for Fort Benning.

The U.S. Army Paratroopers historically are trained to become the most conditioned soldiers in the entire U.S. Military. For six weeks our morning schedule consisted of a five a.m. wakeup call, our drill sergeant, shouting the following phrase: "Drop your cocks and grab your socks!!".

We had to quickly make our beds and within fifteen minutes conduct our morning hygiene, including a mandatory shave. We then lined up in front of our respective barracks in drill formation, answered roll call and were off for our routine pre-breakfast five mile run, followed by a fifteen minute cool down session, consisting of push-ups, side straddle hops and more push-ups. We then had our seven a.m. breakfast, followed by barracks and ground detail.

We had physical training (PT) during the first period each day, followed by seven hours of demanding, vigorous training. Failure to complete the five mile run (two times) within the forty-five minutes of allotted time, resulted in dismissal from the program. The physically weak were more likely to either not complete the course because of an injury, or fail the course due to an inability to qualify on the training apparatuses.

OUR DAILY SCHEDULE

8:a.m—We made double time (jog) over to the obstacle course for motor fitness training, including speed, agility and related skills.

These skills were essential for planning strategy, making split-second decisions, learning teamwork and demonstrating leadership. Physical performance and success in combat depended on a soldier's ability to perform skills like those required on the obstacle course. For this reason, and because they helped develop and test basic motor skills, obstacle courses were valuable for physical training.

The PT morning session also included one hour of calisthenics, consisting of chin-ups, sit-ups, rope climbing, extensive grass drills and stop-and-go sprints.

Rope climbing from a sitting position.

11:30:a.m.—We lined up in formation and double-timed back to our barracks.

12:00 noon—We had lunch.

1:00:p.m—We double-timed it to the firing range for weapons training, first aid training and individual and team shooting practice.

3:00:p.m.—We double-timed over to the platform and tower training areas. Although this area emphasized lower extremity strength and agility, we learned all the techniques and skills of jumping and landing from various heights, starting at a **STOOL LEVEL UP TO A 250 FOOT TOWER.**

4:30:p.m.—We double-timed back to our respective barracks.

5:00:p.m.—We had supper.

6:00:p.m.—K.P. or latrine duty.

9:00:p.m.—**LIGHTS OUT!!**

EARLY SURVIVOR DAYS

The first day was a survivor day as several of the recruits and volunteers could not keep up, and were dropped from the program.

My conditioning at Lowell High School under coach Herb Cochran was paramount to my survival. Push-ups and running were the emphasized physical activities and when our drill sergeant felt like being a hard nose, for the slightest reason or no reason at all, he would say, "Gimme ten!!" I would hit the deck and do ten push-ups. If that didn't satisfy him he'd say, "Gimme another ten!!"

34 foot training tower.

I remember one day in particular, he got down next to me, just to show the group how good he was. After two sets of ten, he said to me, "Had enough?" Stupid me replied, "Only if you're tired, Sergeant." One hundred push-ups later we got up and for being insubordinate he angrily ordered me to return to the drill area with my rifle at 1900 hours (7:00 p.m.).

I had to jog up and down the street in front of all the barracks, with my rifle extended over my head, for one solid hour, singing repeatedly, **"I'M A BIG ASS BIRD WITH A BROKEN WING."**

Our drill sergeant informed us after our first week that our platoon would have a competition during the final week of training, which gave me an added incentive to excel in each category, including the firing range.

INTRODUCED TO THE PARACHUTE

One morning, while jogging, we heard an extremely high-toned screeching sound—like **"EEEEEEEE"**—and the drill sergeant said, "Another chute didn't open!!" He was quick to say, "Soon you'll be introduced to your best friend, **YOUR PARACHUTE!!"**

It was stated that we would receive training to know everything about the parachute—how to wear it, adjust it, use it—all the works. We would also learn all the techniques needed to accomplish our mission with absolute confidence, how to stay loose, get ready for impact, let our legs absorb the shock, roll and collapse our chute quickly, release our harness, unsling our weapon, and deploy into position.

During the first two weeks we encountered daily physical fitness and basic parachutist training. We were taught how to wear the parachute harness and how to use special training apparatuses.

Being an Army parachutist was very often an incredibly demanding job, and being physically fit was of high importance. Development of strength, flexibility, agility and cardiovascular and muscular endurance were constantly emphasized, along with the safe and proper ways to exercise.

AGILITY EXERCISES

1. All fours run- Place your hands in front of you and run, using your hands and feet.
2. Broad jump- Jump forward on both feet in a series of jumps. Swing the arms vigorously to help with the jumps.
3. Crab walk- Place your hands and feet on the ground, hands behind you and stomach facing the sky. Walk on your hands and feet from this position.
4. Three line shuffle drill- Mark three parallel lines on the floor, four feet apart. Straddle the center line. Begin by shuffling to the far left, then to the far right, then left, etc. for the allotted time, crossing each line with the foot.
5. Bench jump- From a standing position, bend your knees slightly and jump to the side (laterally), pushing off both feet and landing up on a low bench/step. Come to a full stop, then jump off the other side of the bench, and repeat.

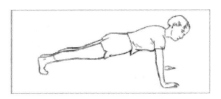
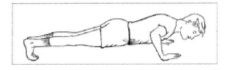

PUSH-UPS

Push-ups measure the endurance of the chest, shoulder and triceps muscles, as well as core strength, and are emphasized so much that I will describe how a legitimate push-up is performed and evaluated by the scorer during competition.

EXPLANATION

The event supervisor read the following:

"The push-up event measures the endurance of the chest, shoulder and triceps muscles. On the command, 'get set', assume the front-leaning rest position by placing your hands where they are comfortable to you. Your feet may be together or up to 12 inches apart."

When viewed from the side, your body should form a generally straight line from shoulders to your ankles. Begin the push-up by bending your elbows and lowering your entire body as a single unit your upper arms are at least parallel to the ground. Then, return to the starting position by raising your entire body until your arms are fully extended. Your body must remain rigid in a generally straight line and move as a unit while performing each repetition.

At the end of each repetition the scorer stated the number of repetitions completed correctly. If one failed to keep his body generally straight, to lower the whole body until the upper arms are at least parallel to the ground, or to extend the arms completely, that repetition was not counted and the scorer repeated the number of the correctly performed repetitions.

If we failed to perform the first ten push-ups correctly the scorer would tell you to go to our knees and explained what the mistakes were. We were then sent to the end of the line to be retested. After the first ten push-ups were performed and counted however, no restarts were allowed. The test continued and any incorrectly performed push-ups were not counted.

An altered, front-leaning rest position was the only authorized rest position. That is, one could sag in the middle or flex his back. When flexing the back, one could bend his knees, but not to such an extent that he was supporting most of his body weight with his legs. If this occurred, his performance was terminated. One had to return to, and pause in, the correct starting position before continuing. If he rested on the ground or raised either hand or foot from the ground, his performance was terminated.

Repositioning of the hands and/or feet during the event was allowed as long as they remained in contact with the ground at all times. Correct performance was important. We had two minutes in which to do as many push-ups as we could.

The event supervisor was the timer. He called out the time remaining every thirty seconds and every second for the last ten of the two minutes. He ended the event after two minutes by the command, "HALT!!"

SCORER'S DUTIES

The scorer allowed for the differences in body shape and structure of each soldier. The scorer used each soldier's starting position as a guide throughout the event to evaluate each repetition. The scorer also talked to the soldier before the event began and had him do a few repetitions as a warm-up and reference to ensure he was doing the exercise correctly.

The scorer either sat or kneeled about three feet from the test-takers' shoulders at a 45-degree angle in front of them. The scorer's head was about even with the soldier's shoulder when in the front-leaning rest position. Each scorer determined for himself if he would sit or kneel when scoring. He could not lie down or stand while scoring. He counted out loud the number of correct repetitions completed and repeated the number of the correct push-ups if an incorrect one was made.

Scorers tell the test-takers what they did wrong as it occurs during the event. A critique of the performance was done following the test, and when the soldier completed the event, the scorer recorded the number of correctly performed repetitions, initialed the scorecard, and returned it to the soldier.

BATTLING MOSKOWITZ

As the weeks flew by, it became apparent that one of our recruits, W.W. Moskowitz, similar to the attached photo, from New York City and had his picture on the cover of Mr. America Magazine, excelled in every phase of the physical fitness component of the competition. It was apparent that he was the one to beat; his only weaknesses were running the sprints and the obstacle course.

When the competition began, Moskowitz took the early lead, easily winning the strength events consisting of chin-ups, push-ups, sit-ups and the rope climbing. On the second day I gained ground on him at the firing range as I had achieved sharpshooter status thanks to my BB gun days in the Johnson Street gravel pit. I gained more ground on him in the obstacle courses competition, and with the sprints coming up

Moskowitz look alike

on the final day, drama was building with Moskowitz leading and me in second place, which meant we were in the final pairing.

THE SPRINTS

1—Sprints consisted of two roped off lanes, 30 yards long.

2—We sprinted to the end, touched a stationary post, pivoted and return, making a total of six trips (180 yards).

3—Two contestants, head-to-head, would sprint within their lanes.

4—Stopwatches were also used for individual times against the entire field.

5—Pairings were decided by total points going into the sprints.

6—Points were gained from head-to-head, as well as against the field.

SPRINTING TO THE CHAMPIONSHIP

The sergeant blew the whistle and off we went. I was ahead by one step at the end of the first 30 yards, made a quick pivot, like my straight-arm telephone pivots on Gorham Street, and was ahead by five yards as I made my second pivot, gaining a few yards with each pivot.

As I approached the finish line, all my little people classmates were cheering me on and I was still running at full speed, while Moskowitz had not completed his fifth leg. I ended up winning by a full thirty yards.

My overall time was second best, compared to Moskowitz's twenty-fifth place finish, which leap-frogged me into **THE WINNER'S CIRCLE!!**

Throughout my life, whenever I would get down on myself, I'd see flashbacks of that day and tell myself, **"DETERMINATION AND HARD WORK CAN ACCOMPLISH EVEN WHAT SEEMS ALMOST IMPOSSIBLE".**

THE FINAL WEEK

The sixth and final week of our Paratrooper School was what we had prepared for over the previous five weeks.

We had to employ all of the physical and psychological training techniques and skills for our **FIVE LIVE JUMPS** (one daily) from a C-54 or C-47 cargo transport plane in order to graduate and receive our Paratrooper Wings.

Notice the Photos

This picture (left) shows more realistically how we looked making our first jumps. As much as I felt confident that I would not need my reserve parachute, I was prepared to pull the cord if I didn't feel the jolt of the rip cord opening the main parachute by the time I counted to "three thousand"

The outstanding picture (left) shows the perfect posture of this parachutist as he leaves one of our C-54 cargo planes. He has his legs together, knees slightly flexed and his chin is tucked and touching his chest.

His upper arms are tightly pressing against his body, elbows bent forty-five degrees and both hands to the front of his body wrapping around his reserve parachute. His right hand is gripping the release in the event the main chute does not open after the count of **ONE THOUSAND, TWO THOUSAND, THREE THOUSAND**.

Perfect Jump Posture.

A Copy of My Hard Earned Paratrooper Wings

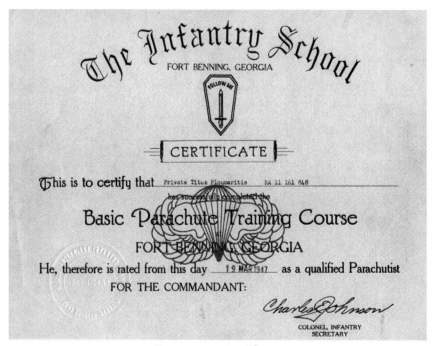

Paratrooper Certificate

PATROLIA AND FOOTBALL IN JAPAN

This is also a good time to mention a fellow named Jack Patrolia, who I thought was my shadow for week after week until I realized we were sorted out alphabetically. He followed me from day one at Fort Dix, on to Fort Bragg and then to Fort Benning.

The only differences between us were our height and weight, me at five feet, five inches and 150 pounds and Jack at six-foot, five and 250. We became very good friends, and at times he thought I was a toy, picking me up and carrying me on his shoulders, just for the hell of it.

Jack was a humble, gentle giant that wouldn't hurt a fly, unless it was an opposing lineman with me in his sights, and I eventually found out how great a football player Jack was as the season progressed. I also later learned of his outstanding football career at Cohasset High School in Cohasset, Massachusetts.

NOW, BACK TO OUR FIRST DAY OF TRIALS.

With close to 200 candidates and a high percentage of those being college and professional football players fulfilling their military obligations, it is reasonable to presume that the coaches were not interested in a five foot, five, 150 pound nobody. Well, this presumption is correct!! Within thirty minutes, one of the assistant coaches tapped me on the shoulder and told me to turn in my shoes and uniform. Jack survived the first three days with no problem, and I felt as long as he was still alive that I would go and watch them practice.

NOW COMES THE JUICE OF THIS STORY.

They were having special team practice, with the emphasis on punting and placekicking. It seemed like every tackle on the team thought he was Lou Groza, with one after another running to the ball and kicking with no thump. The very best I saw was about fifty yards, and that was with no trajectory.

I decided to go over to the retrieving area, and although I was wearing fatigues and paratrooper boots I felt that I may recover a loose ball and just boot it back to the kickers. Well, even without a tee or wearing my football cleats, only taking a three step delivery, I made about five of my South Common kicks with the thump and high trajectory, each boot going about fifty-five to sixty yards. You could see the heads turn with each thump following the ball high up into the sky.

When the coach was told that he had cut me the first day, he said, **"GIVE IT BACK TO HIM, HE'S OUR KICKER!!."**

As the season progressed, with injuries to several of the regulars, I was allowed some playing time at left halfback. I was scheduled to start in a game against a Navy team in Hakodate, Japan, and as I was on the field warming up, an MP (Military Police) approached me with one of my coaches and asked if I had a brother named George Plomaritis. I answered in the affirmative, and then the MP stated that my brother was in the **"BRIG"** (military jail) and he said that he hadn't seen me since basic training and requested permission to watch me play.

George was on the sidelines and was as loud as ever. With just a two yard gain he'd scream and yell as if it was a TD. After the game they allowed us fifteen minutes to chat. As usual, he said it wasn't his fault that he had, "slugged a sergeant for picking on him." It was great just seeing him alive and I didn't see him again until we were discharged.

Stanley Stoklosa wrote to me about once monthly, to keep me posted on the goings on at Lowell High School. I, in turn, told him about making the football team as a kicker and eventually starting a game at left halfback.

My Friend and Protector, Jack Patrolia

Now, we were warming up on the field, preparing to play our last game, and the Captain (two times-a military captain as well as our team captain and left halfback) twisted his ankle in a mud hole. We had rain all night and it was still raining cats and dogs. The coach told me of the Captain's condition and said I was starting in his place at left halfback.

The conditions couldn't have been any worse, and there was no score with about five minutes to play. I carried the ball on three consecutive plays, just going straight ahead following Jack Patrolia's butt, and on the third carry he led me into the end zone for the only score of the game. The PAT never got off the ground.

A picture of me totally covered with mud, my feet in mud up to my ankles, and wearing the bullet helmet with the football tucked under my arm, appeared on the front page of Stars & Stripes, a military overseas newspaper. I sent the paper along with my next letter of correspondence to Stan Stoklosa, and he must have been so proud of me that he made copies for just about everybody at Lowell High School.

Note: First let me explain that it was mandatory to jump once monthly to maintain paratrooper status and to qualify for the extra $25.00 monthly stipend.

If a paratrooper were to become injured making a jump and require a stay in the infirmary, his stateside trip would be cancelled.

Our purpose of going to Japan, in the first place, was to relieve the actual combat troops when they were scheduled to return stateside. If a paratrooper were scheduled to jump within that same timeframe, I became a jumper for hire. We would swap dog tags; I would jump in the paratrooper's place for an easy twenty-five bucks. I ended up making a total of twenty jumps, half of which were for hire. I enjoyed jumping so much that I would have jumped for nothing; however, the cash came in handy.

THE GENERAL OMAR BUNDY

The General Omar Bundy transport vessel was the ship that transported me from Seattle, Washington, on July 18, 1947, and arrived at Yokohama, Japan, on August 1st.

The General Omar Bundy

The trip took fourteen days, and believe me it was "sea sick heaven" for the over 3800 troops. We all had some type of bullshit chores to keep us occupied as a means of offsetting the sea sickness syndrome.

After a couple of days I managed to follow a few of the experienced goof-offs and quickly learned the skills of "hide and seek". The best one, that seemed to work often, was to carry a wet mop with you all the time. When a sergeant or someone with authority was on the horizon, we'd place it on the deck and look busy

Now to carry this scenario out one step better, which I never shared with the tutored goof-offs, was to gradually mop my way to the lowest level of the sleeping quarters, then find a vacant cot, climb into it with the mop by my side, close my eyes and think of something pleasant. It was the only cure for my sea sickness, so I convinced myself that it was a prescription and that I was not really goofing off. To break the monotony, I managed to mop my way to the mess hall three times daily.

My return to the United States, by coincidence or whatever, was via the same General Omar Bundy troopship and it took eleven days, leaving Yokohama on December 23, 1947, and arriving in Seattle on January 3, 1948. My first and last order of business for the journey home was to find me a mop!!

FOLLOWING IS SOME INFORMATION ON
THE USS GENERAL OMAR BUNDY:

The ship was a General G.O. Squire-class transport ship for the U.S. Navy in World War ll, and was named in honor of U.S. Army General Omar Bundy. It was transferred to the U.S. Army as USAT General Omar Bundy in 1946, and was later sold for commercial operation under several names before being declared missing and presumed sunk.

The ship's displacement was 9950 tons, light, and 17,250 tons, full. Its length was 522 feet 10 inches, or 59.36 m., and its beam was 71 feet, 6 inches, or 21.79 m. Its capacity was 3823 troops.

SECTION TWO

CLOSE CALLS—THIRD INCIDENT

I was discharged from the U.S. Army Paratroopers on January 14, 1948, in Seattle, Washington, and my brother George was being discharged at that time in San Francisco, California. We had made arrangements in Japan to meet in San Francisco, buy an automobile and drive back to Lowell together.

Although I had my monthly Army pay of twenty-five dollars going directly home to my father as agreed prior to my enlistment, I had my

1938 Buick 4 door sedan

twenty-five dollars of Paratrooper pay deposited into a special account. We used the money from our military insurance discharge to purchase a 1938 Buick four-door sedan.

Although I was inclined to go straight home, George had different ideas. He wanted to visit Hollywood, go to Santa Anita Race Track and dance at The Palladium Ballroom. It seemed that at every stopover we would accumulate more baggage or additional weight for us to carry home.

Now, with that said, after fulfilling our fix of movie stars, race tracks and Gene Krupa at The Palladium, we were headed home when **THE INEVITABLE HAPPENED!!**

We were driving through Texas, already overloaded with a roof rack and trunk full of clothing and souvenirs. George was at the wheel and he decided to stop and give three hitchhikers, including one being a female, a lift. We tied some of their baggage on the roof and the remainder on their laps in the back seat. (It should be noted that there were no seat belts in that era.)

About an hour later we were in a happy sing-a-long mood and traveling at a fairly good clip when George attempted to pass a truck, while going uphill. And then it happened.

BANG!!—a blowout.

George quickly turned the wheel to avoid an oncoming vehicle, causing our "tank-like-built" Buick to roll over and off the road. We continued rolling over and over for some 200 feet and it looked like a war zone with clothing and people all along our path.

The female passenger required hospitalization and George had one of his ears 3/4 detached and it had to be sewn back on. I came out of the accident unscathed except for a few bruises and a runaway heart beat.

The car was absolutely demolished, and being young and inexperienced, we had no insurance on it. I can't remember all the particulars, however we were detained for a week due to police and hospital reports.

I used the balance of my savings to purchase a 1934 Nash four door sedan and invited George to a no-nonsense, no excuse direct drive back to 29 Johnson Street, Lowell.

RETURNING TO LOWELL

I returned to Lowell, Massachusetts, in the spring of 1948, driving a 1934 Nash four-door sedan. I had difficulty trying to live with my parents on 29 Johnson Street, so I decided to reside in a rooming house on Appleton Street, just a few doors away from the Salvation Army building and a long field goal from Elliott's Famous Hot Dog Stand.

I got a few part time jobs that enabled me to pay for my room, put gas in the car and survive with bare essentials. One of my jobs was selling Watkins Products door to door. This required salesmanship and personality, which came quite easily for me, just referring back to my Shoe Shine and Dutch Tea Room days.

I returned to Lowell High School and met with Mr. Sullivan to prepare for my senior year. I also met my new football coach, **RAYMOND E. RIDDICK,** at spring practice in time to prepare for the Spring Jamboree.

MEETING CLAIRE AT THE HOODSIE HOP

With my friend, Buttsie Correa, I attended a local teenage dance that most of the high school kids frequented on Friday nights. It was there where I was mesmerized by this slightly built, well-groomed, teenage girl named Claire, who was better known as "Smokey" by her classmates and friends at Lowell High School.

Buttsie was a walking encyclopedia when it came to who's who, and he was quick to give me her name, nick name, where she lived and that her father was a retired professional boxer and currently owned a pool room on Aiken Avenue.

I watched her dance with several of her friends from Lowell High and it was obvious that she had rhythm and liked to jitterbug. I figured it would be my best bet to practice up on my jitterbug steps and come back the following week and see if Buttsie could arrange an introduction so I could make a good impression.

I learned to dance at the USO's, my source of entertainment at practically every base I was on during my fifteen months in the military. The big bands featuring Gene Krupa's "Boogie Woogie" for the jitterbug and Glen Miller's "In the Mood" provided a unique beat that was ideal for great fox trotting. My brother George and I had the pleasure of dancing to both of those great bands, and I figured that if I could fine tune my dance steps I'd make a good impression with **LITTLE SMOKEY.**

NO, NO!! To answer your inquisitive minds, she was not a smoker, but she was given a proper nickname. You see, she had no regular in her tank, only high-test and was such a bundle of energy. The best I can describe her would be like a ten-foot giant trying to get out of a 4'10" frame.

It was two weeks later before I felt that I was ready to go in and dazzle her with my zoot suit, peg pants et all and win her over with my fancy footwork.—**NO DICE, DIDN'T WORK!!**

So, I tried the next best thing I could think of and that was to go to her house with my little case of Watkins Products and see if I could make an

Claire Hebert, summer of 1949
Photo by Titus Plomaritis.

impression as a hard working door-to-door salesman.

I remember the incident as if it was yesterday. Wearing my only shirt and tie and sparkling shoes from military training, I was ready to display my salesmanship to make a sale. It was a sunny Saturday morning about ten o'clock. I walked up to her home porch steps on 89 Aiken Avenue, noticed some commotion in the kitchen and gently rapped on the screen door. Claire's dad came to the door and asked my business.

I told him that I was the local representative for Watkins Products, which included personal hygiene products and home goods. I politely asked if I could come in and show him some of our specials. He was gracious and had me come to the kitchen table with my case of goodies.

Sporting the archway leading to the stairway was a 24"x36" picture of Claire's dad in his boxing pose with a decorated Diamond Belt attached to the bottom of the photo.

It was the prize for winning the **FLYWEIGHT CHAMPIONSHIP OF NEW ENGLAND!!**—I believe it was an intended message to those of us who had desires of dating his daughters to "keep your hands in your pockets."

Now would you believe that Claire, with her three sisters, Laurie, Dolores and Lucille, surrounding the kitchen table, gave me her attention as I skillfully demonstrated and sold two bottles of coconut oil shampoo to her dad who was bald as a cue ball, with only about a dozen hairs on his head. His reasoning was that if someone had the ambition to go door-to-door, he deserved a sale.

It was kind of a **DOUBLE WHAMMY,** as it opened the door, actually two doors counting the screen, to a great barrage of jitterbug dancing at the Friday Hoodsie Hops that her LHS classmates had never seen before.

NOW—you'll have to wait for the second part of the **DOUBLE WHAMMY.** Remember, now this is still the spring of 1948. Wait until you hear what she told her father!!

INTRODUCTION TO COACH RIDDICK

Titus Plomaritis's first day of practice after returning to Lowell High School from the U.S. Army Paratroopers. Photo by Sun Staff.

After my orientation with Mr. Sullivan, the headmaster, and Tom McIntyre, the athletic director, I was introduced to football coach, Ray Riddick, who stood 6'4" and weighed 265 pounds with a barrel chest and mitts like bear paws. His hand shake just about stopped the circulation in my right hand.

Coach Riddick played college football at Fordham University with Vince Lombardi and pro ball with the Green Bay Packers, being the opposite end with Hall of Famer, Don Hutson.

The Coach related that baseball coach,

Stan Stoklosa, had kept him informed of my football activity with the 11th Airborne in Japan, and he was anxious for me to join the Red and Gray team.

I met a few of the team members in the cafeteria who kind of guided me as to what to expect at practice. When I got off the bus at the practice field I was told that the Lowell Sun had a photographer waiting to take a couple of pictures of me, so I kind of rushed and dressed into my practice uniform and football cleats. After satisfying the Sun photographer I rushed over to join my teammates doing calisthenic drills and started to learn the Ray Riddick playbook.

STARTING OFF WITH A BANG

Coach Riddick would stand in front of the offensive team holding large cards with the players' assignments as a simple method of viewing the blocking or running assignments. I stood in back of the offensive unit just watching for about fifteen or twenty minutes. Then the coach told me to jump in at left halfback to run the play he was holding up, an off-tackle right play. My first touch of the football under the Coach Riddick regime went for a forty-yard touchdown, and although I tried to make it look like I wasn't exhausted I couldn't have gone another inch. I suddenly realized that I was not in playing condition and required plenty of work prior to the upcoming Jamboree.

1948 Lowell High Football Squad with Coaches and Trainers

Foreground: Bill Franks, John Craven, Taffy Tavaris, Freddy Harris. **1st row:** Coach Raymond Riddick, Norman Carver, Jim Fallon, Campbell Gibson, George Spaneas, Roger Sanborn, Jack Lardner, Louis Martino, Fred Pawlowski, Dick Sharp, Coach Bill Wilson. **2nd row:** Bob Lach, Bob Ready, Mike Kopacz, Donald St. George, Brian Reynolds, Ray Armstrong. Bob Lemire, Frank Linscott, Donald Conway. **3rd row:** Chris Drivas, Bob Picard, Menil Mavraides, Art Lemoine, Bernard Ratchin, Steve Genakos, John Meehan, Frank "Foozy" Coimbra, Titus Plomaritis. **4th row:** Bob Lovejoy, Don Jelly, Jack Reilly, Dave Felton, Bob Ayers, Earl McQuade, Charles Chiklis, Paul Bue. **5th row:** Roland Brousseau, Francis Toupin, Phil Riley, Bob Burgoyne, John Janas, Anthony Picanso, Charles Jones, Tony Britt. **6th row:** Allan Scott, Don Maloney, Jim Spanos, Frank Roberge, Dan Richards, Ernest Ruszczyk, Don Toupin, Paul Melanson, Joe Pinook. **7th row:** Philip Thomas, Peter Libby, Stanley James, Nathan Smith, top row: Coach Al Mangan & Coach Tony Archinski.

COMPLETE 1948 LHS SCORES

Lowell 6, Lynn English 0
Lowell 20, Peabody 0
Lowell 33, Nashua 0
Lowell 17, Manchester Central 0
Lowell 6, Salem 6
Lowell 41, Haverhill 7
Lowell 34, Keith 0
Lowell 19, Lynn Classical 0
Lowell 28, Quincy 9
Lowell 20, Lawrence 19

Won 9 Lost 0, Tied 1
Points for, 224, Against 41

MEMORIAL BOWL
(Jackson, Miss.)
Bogalusa 12, Lowell 7

THE 1948 LOWELL HIGH FOOTBALL HIGHLIGHTS

PLOMARITIS SPARKPLUG DURING UNDEFEATED SEASON

NOTE—Senior **TITUS PLOMARITIS** went on to become the Eastern Massachusetts Class A Schoolboy Football Scoring Champion, with a grand total of 81 points, covering nine touchdowns, 24 conversion kicks and one field goal.

The following are newspaper highlights of his career.

LOWELL 41, HAVERHILL 7

LOWELL—The Red and Gray really showed its power, rolling up its largest score of the season, scoring in every quarter against the Hillies.

Hard-hitting fullback, **BRIAN REYNOLDS**, led the way, scoring three touchdowns, while left halfback, **TITUS PLOMARITIS**, shared the spotlight by booting five conversions in six attempts and tallied once himself.

Early in the second quarter, Plomaritis was a "one man gang" on his touchdown drive. He tossed a 20-yard pass to end Menil Mavraides down to the visitors' 14, and then he waded through the entire Haverhill team before being dropped at the one-yard line. He crashed over for the TD on the next play, and then added the PAT to give Lowell a 14-0 lead at the time.

LOWELL 28, QUINCY 9

QUINCY—Bouncing back with a vengeance after trailing host, Quincy, 9-0 at halftime, **COACH RAY RIDDICK**'s club poured across 28 unanswered points in the final two quarters to remain undefeated, in a game played here in the rain before a capacity crowd of 12,000.

It was **TITUS PLOMARITIS**, a scatback who can really scat, who set off the spark which turned what, for a time, looked like an upset defeat into a complete rout. His hard running and accurate passing accounted for three LHS touchdowns.

Throughout the disastrous first half the slippery ball stymied the Kirk Streeters, causing fumbles. However, in the third quarter Lowell finally caught fire and scored, followed by a three touchdown spree in the final stanza to keep its unbeaten record intact.

Plomaritis set off the spark which turned the Red and Gray offensive machine into a roaring blaze which just couldn't be extinguished. The diminutive left halfback passed for one touchdown, set up another and scored a third, as well as kicked four conversions.

"We just went into the dressing room and got a few things straightened out," was the way Coach Riddick expressed the late change in his squad.

LOWELL PLAYERS GUESTS AT BC-HC GAME

BOSTON—Head Coach, Ray Riddick, Captain and center, Roger Sanborn, left halfback, Titus Plomaritis, and end, Arthur Lemoine, traveled to Boston as guests of Boston College at the BC-Holy Cross gridiron battle.

Prior to this annual traditional game the undefeated Red and Gray football representatives were also guests at a luncheon held at a downtown hotel.

LHS RALLIES TO DEADLOCK SALEM

SALEM—An inspired Salem High team rose to its greatest heights when it ruined three of Lowell High's seasonal records by holding the Red and Gray gridders to a 6-6 tie before 10,000 fans at Bertram Field.

Going into the contest, Lowell boasted of an undefeated, untied and unscored upon record.

Salem recovered a fumble at the Lowell 25 in the second quarter, and it converted this miscue into a touchdown. This was the only time that the Witch City club was able to cross midfield during the afternoon.

TITUS PLOMARITIS again came to Lowell's rescue, when just after the second half kickoff he spearheaded an 85-yard march, carrying the brunt of the attack, to tie the score and preserve the Riddick team's undefeated record. Bob Swan tallied the TD on a seven-yard end sweep.

Plomaritis attempted a field goal with five seconds left, but on one of his rare misses the boot went off to the left as the game ended.

PLOMARITIS-LED LOWELL MAKES LYNN CLASSICAL ITS SEVENTH VICTIM, 19-0

LOWELL—**TITUS PLOMARITIS** scored one touchdown, passed for the other two and added an extra point as Lowell High defeated Lynn Classical, 19-0, to retain second place in the Class A ratings before a crowd of 11,000.

The start of the game was held up for 35 minutes while city workers distributed several tons of sand over the field, which was a quagmire following heavy rains.

"It's like trying to run through the sand on Hampton Beach," one of the Lowell backs commented between the halves.

The Red and Gray took an early lead on a 15-yard Plomaritis to **BOB SWAN** touchdown pass, and Titus plunged over from the one in the second quarter, after fullback **BRIAN REYNOLDS** accounted for 16 of the last 17 yards on three successive rushes.

Swan scored the final TD in the fourth quarter, taking a 28-yard aerial from Plomaritis on the six and romping over.

Lowell was just as sturdy defensively as it was powerful offensively, holding Classical to a total of just 35 total yards.

The victory was the Riddick team's seventh of the season, against one tie with Salem, its most wins in a decade.

LHS FAVORED OVER KEITH FOR CITY CHAMPIONSHIP

LOWELL—October 31, 1948—Coach Ray Riddick's undefeated Lowell High Raiders are heavily favored over Keith Academy in their annual battle for the city schoolboy football crown. Kickoff takes place this afternoon at 2 P.M. at Memorial Stadium.

The Red and Gray carry a 5-0-1 record into the contest, and it has outscored its opponents 123-13 thus far.

Keith, coached by former Dracut and Lowell High mentor, Spencer Sullivan, stands at 3-2-0 for the season, and has been outscored 57-55.

The Thorndike Street team, a member of the Catholic Conference, is a costly foe for Lowell High as a win over the Class B division Comets only gives LHS eight points, while a triumph over the remainder of its Class A opponents nets 10 points apiece.

The two-point differential has annually cost LHS several Eastern Mass. Class A championships.

THE STARTING LINEUPS

LOWELL	KEITH
(89) Mavraides, LE	RE, Pollinger (29)
(77) Carver, LT	RT, Grenier (21)
(69) Lach, LG	RG, Hand (38)
(52) Sanborn, C	C , McGuire (39)
(64) Meehan, RG	LG, McCann (26)
(78) Ready, RT	LT, J. Miller (44)
(88) Lemoine, RE	LE, Stagnone (36)
(24) Fallon, QB	QB, Hansbury (46)
(42) Plomaritis, LHB	RHB, Toomey (49)
(32) Swan, RHB	LHB, Walsh (48)
(34) Reynolds, FB	FB, Sloan (37)

LOWELL HIGH TROUNCES KEITH, 34-0

PLOMARITIS RUNS WILD IN ONE-MAN SHOW

LOWELL—Titus Plomaritis, the jet-propelled Lowell High left halfback, staged a one-man scoring show as he sparked Coach Ray Riddick's undefeated Red and Gray gridiron gang to a one-sided 34-0 victory over city rival Keith Academy on the Memorial Stadium turf before an estimated crowd of 10,000.

It was Lowell's sixth win in seven starts (one tie) this season, and puts LHS in the thick of the battle for the Eastern Mass. Class A title, along with Malden.

PLOMARITIS, whose name seems to rhyme with touchdownitis, had his piston-like legs pumping in perfect precision. The 155-pound ex-paratrooper scored three of his team's five TD's, in addition to kicking four PAT's, for a total of 22 points for the day. He also hurled an eight-yard scoring pass to end, **ARTHUR LEMOINE**, while lineman, **JOE CONNORS** —who had transferred from Keith along with quarterback, **JIMMY FALLON,** and big tackle, **BOB READY**—collected the final touchdown when he ran back a pass interception some 40 yards.

WRAPPING UP THE ROUT

Plomaritis' scoring runs were two, eight and 15 yarders, and he set up the latter score with a 23-yard breakaway.

Lowell completely dominated the final statistics, out-gaining Keith in first downs, 13-3, yards rushing, 251-17, and total yards, 281-61.

Following the game, Keith Coach, **SPENCER SULLIVAN**, lauded the Lowell club by saying: "They've got a powerhouse. They had too much for us and there's no use saying they didn't. Those boys were really hot today and they took advantage of every break."

NOTE—Titus commented that he played the entire Keith Academy game with two cracked ribs. "Coach Riddick sent me to team physician, DR. **JOHN MALONEY**, because of discomfort in the rib area. Following x-rays and examination, Dr Maloney pointed out that I had two minor rib fractures and suggested I take a week off, but I insisted that he tape me up and clear me to play, which he did"—and the rest is history.

FINAL NOTE—Keith Academy turned out to be Coach Riddick's most one-sided opponent as his Red and Gray team rolled up an overall 19-1-1 winning record over the Comets in their 21 meetings, before the series was mercifully terminated in 1968. Keith dropped football completely the following year.

RIDDICK REASON FOR RISE OF LOWELL HIGH, LIFTS SCHOOL FROM BOTTOM OF CLASS A IN TWO YEARS

By Ralph Wheeler

LOWELL—November 20, 1948—Any story about Lowell High School football would have to start with its tremendously successful coach, **RAY RIDDICK**. The former Lowell High, Fordham University and Green Bay Packers' end has consummated an amazing renaissance in his two seasons as head coach of football in the Spindle City.

Football was at its lowest ebb at Lowell when Riddick made his coaching debut in 1947. The teams of the previous seasons had lost more games than any other school in the state, dropping eleven successive contests.

Riddick's first and most important job was to rid his squad of a defeatist complex. Just how well he succeeded is indicated by the '47 season's record of six victories against four losses, the best of any Lowell team since 1935. The Red and Gray also outscored the opposition 141-108, to finish sixth in the Class A schoolboy competition in Eastern Massachusetts.

BECOMING CHAMPIONSHIP CONTENDER

Last year's foundation was the ground work for this year's great team, which has won eight games and tied one, to become runner-up to pace-making Malden in the race for the Class A championship.

Lowell is favored to defeat traditional rival, Lawrence on Thanksgiving Day and Malden will be a top-heavy favorite to win over traditional rival, Medford. If both teams should complete their seasons undefeated, Malden would win the title by a mere few points.

(NOTE—THE MINUS TWO POINTS SUFFERED BY LOWELL DUE TO PLAYING KEITH ACADEMY PROVED COSTLY TO THE RED AND GRAY.)

Lowell's impressive record for this season is all the more amazing when it is realized that last year's one-two punch of **WALTER "TICKIE" KULIS** and **TARSEY KOUCHALAKOS** graduated in June. Kulis was a triple threat who reached his peak in the game with Lynn Classical last fall when he emerged with a much better passing percentage than Classical's fabulous **HARRY AGGANIS.**

PLOMARITIS, KEITH TRANSFERS ARRIVE

Lowell 48 Coaches Dream Cartoon

TITUS PLOMARITIS, an Army Paratrooper veteran who returned to Lowell High this fall after playing service football in Japan, has been a great asset in taking up the slack caused by the loss of Kulis and Kouchalakos. The 155-pound halfback is a sharpshooting passer, one of the hardest runners of the schoolboy season and a deadly placekicker.

Other important additions to this year's Lowell team were quarterback, **JIMMY FALLON,** tackle, **BOB READY** and lineman, **JOE CONNORS,** all transfers from city rival, Keith Academy.

These four newcomers, with the veteran nucleus of a pair of star ends in **MENIL MAVRAIDES** and **ARTHUR LEMOINE,** an outstanding center in captain, **ROGER SANBORN,** and a veteran utility player in **BOB SWAN,** have backboned the best Lowell team in more than two decades.

LOWELL-LAWRENCE 1948 FOOTBALL GAME

Program Cover

Lawrence High School

—— Starting Line-up ——

C
Walsgerber
23

LE	LT	LG	RG	RT	RE
Vitale — / Campagnone		Annaldo	Varitimos	Wooles (Capt.)	Gregorowlc:
40	47	21	18	24	50

QB	LHB	RHB	FB
D'Angelo	Callagy — |	Sarcione — |	Jasinski
15	42	17	48

—— Squad List ——

15	D'Angelo	QB	28	Curtis	G	40	Vitale	LE
16	Fitzgerald	LHB	29	Ursillo	E	41	Harrison	B
17	Sarcione	RHB	30	Rowe	E	42	Callagy	B
18	Varitimos	RG	31	Hey	B	43	Becotte	C
20	Donovan	E	32	Manning	E	44	Matthews	QB
21	Annaldo	LG	33	Burba	C	46	DeLuca	B
23	Walsgerber	C	34	Welner	T	47	Compagnone	T
24	Wooles	LT	35	Sullivan	G	48	Jasinski	FB
26	Sweeney	B	38	Nigohosian	G	50	Gregorowicz	RE
27	Laudani	G	39	Baggett	C			

SCORE	1	2	3	4	TOTAL
Lawrence	6	0	6	7	19
Lowell	0	13	0	7	20

Lowell High School

—— Starting Line-up ——

C
Sanborn
52

LE	LT	LG	RG	RT	RE
Lemoine	Carver	Meehan	Lach	Ready	Mavraides
88	77	64	69	78	89

QB	LHB	RHB	FB
Fallon	Swan	Plomeritus — 3.	Reynolds
24	32	42	34

—— Squad List ——

10	Gibson	HB	48	Lemire	FB	72	McQuaide	T
14	Godreau	HB	50	St. George	C	74	McNamee	G
24	Fallon	QB	52	Sanborn	C	76	Garland	T
26	Reilly	QB	54	Lovejoy	C	77	Carver	T
28	Armstrong	QB	56	Felton	C	78	Ready	T
32	Swan	HB	60	Ayer	T	80	Sharp	E
34	Reynolds	FB	61	Conroy	G	81	Pawlowski	E
36	Ruszczyk	G	62	Picard	G	82	Spaneas	E
40	Jelley	HB	64	Meehan	G	84	Drivas	E
42	Plomeritus	HB	66	Lardner	G	88	Lemoine	E
44	Martino	HB	68	Connors	T	89	Mavraides	E
46	Coimbra	G	69	Lach	G			

—— OFFICIALS ——

Umpire ----------------------------- Herman Gill
Referee ------------------------------- Dan Silva
Head Linesman ---------------- Tom McNamara
Field Judge ----------------- Frank Brennan

Starting Line-ups

Lowell High School Statistics

NO.	NAME	POS.	WEIGHT	HEIGHT	AGE
10	Campbell Gibson	H.B.	160	5' 9"	16
14	Roger Godreau	H.B.	165	5' 9"	16
24	James Fallon	Q.B.	160	5' 8"	17
26	John Reilly	Q.B.	150	5' 9"	15
28	Ray Armstrong	Q.B.	165	5' 6"	16
32	Robert Swan	H.B.	180	5'11"	18
34	Brian Reynolds	F.B.	168	5'11"	15
36	Ernest Ruszczyk	G.	153	5' 6"	17
40	Donald Jelley	H.B.	170	5'10"	17
42	Titus Plomeritus	H.B.	170	5' 8"	19
44	Louie Martino	H.B.	160	5' 9"	16
46	Frank Coimbra	G.	160	5' 8"	18
48	Robert Lemire	F.B.	165	5'10"	15
50	Donald St. George	C.	150	5' 7"	17
52	Roger Sanborn	C.	175	5'10"	17
54	Robert Lovejoy	C.	180	6' 1"	17
56	Dave Felton	C.	175	5'11"	18
60	Robert Ayer	T.	165	5'10"	16
61	Donald Conroy	G.	165	5' 7"	16
62	Robert Picard	G.	165	5' 9"	16
64	John Meehan	G.	160	5' 9"	18
66	John Lardner	G.	175	5' 9"	18
68	Joseph Connors	T.	178	6'	18
69	Robert Lach	G.	175	5' 8"	17
72	Earle McQuaide	T.	185	5'10"	17
74	John McNamee	G.	165	5'10"	17
76	John Garland	T.	230	6' 1"	18
77	Norman Carver	T.	185	5'10"	18
78	Robert Ready	T.	200	6' 2"	16
80	Richard Sharp	E.	155	5'11"	18
81	Robert Pawlowski	E.	160	5'11"	17
82	George Spaneas	E.	190	6'	15
84	Chris Drivas	E.	170	6'	18
88	Arthur Lemoine	E.	190	6' 2"	18
89	Menil Mavraides	E.	195	6'	17

CORRECTIONS NOTES FROM TITUS:----

"The program's roster misspelled my name and botched up my official weight and height!!

"Officially, I was not 170 pounds and stood 5'8". I was actually 155 pounds and 5'5 1/2" at the time of the Lawrence game."

Lawrence Scoring

	TD	PA	Ttl.
Gregorowicz	6	0	36
Callagy	5	4	34
Sarcione	4	1	25
Vitale	3	0	18
Matthews	2	0	12
Jackinski	1	4	10
Sweeney	1	0	6
Visillo	1	0	6
Total	23	9	147

Lowell Scoring

	TD	PA	FG	Ttl.
Plomeritus	6	21	1	60
Reynolds	8	0	0	48
Swan	7	0	0	42
Gibson	2	0	0	12
Connors	2	0	0	12
Lemoine	2	0	0	12
Mavraides	1	0	0	6
Sanborn	1	0	0	6
Linscott	1	0	0	6
Total	30	21	1	204

Lowell High Statistics

THE KICK THAT CHANGED HISTORY

(Editor's note)—Following are the lead paragraphs of a column written by Sam Weisberg that appeared in the sports section of The Lowell Sun newspaper on December 16, 2007:

"After many years of witnessing Lowell High football action, I believe the name that placed the Red and Gray on the gridiron map was **PLOMARITIS.**

Titus Plomaritis returned from the service in 1948 to lead LHS to its first undefeated season, climaxed by his memorable exploits in the Thanksgiving game at Lawrence. His clutch game-winning conversion kick ranks as one of the most famous plays in school history, sending Ray Riddick's club to its first bowl game.

After playing Bogalusa in the Memorial Bowl in Jackson, Miss., a country-western personality penned a hit song titled TITUS PLUMMERITIS.

Titus went on to become the placekicker for Harry Agganis' Boston University teams and then became a successful chiropractor.

Incidentally, his son Titus 'Buddy' Plomaritis, Jr., quarterbacked the last undefeated Lowell High team, in 1970." and was the placekicker for four years.

Note: Another item that appeared in The Lowell Sun, on Nov. 24, 2010, titled **"THE GREATEST THANKSGIVING GAMES OF ALL TIME"**, was as follows:

1948—LOWELL 20, LAWRENCE 19

Titus Plomaritis scores all 20 Lowell points, including the clutch winning conversion kick, clinching Lowell's first undefeated season and establishing Ray Riddick's program as a state and national powerhouse.—**SAM WEISBERG.**

PRELUDE TO "THE GAME"

NOTE: Following are excerpts of a column written by Ambrose Kilerjian, Lawrence Sunday Star sports editor. These words appeared in the official Lowell-Lawrence game program of November 25, 1948.

"This year's classic between Lawrence and Lowell at the Mill City Stadium, where an undefeated and once tied Red and Gray eleven from Lowell, coached by Ray Riddick, meets an almost equally strong Blue and White team from Lawrence, coached by James Jordan.

This year's contest between the two strongest teams in the entire Merrimack Valley will be their 51st annual encounter, in a series that started back in 1895. Since that first meeting, when Lowell was a 4-0 winner, Lowell has won just 13 games, while Lawrence has won a total of 27, with no less than 10 ties recorded.

These Turkey Day clashes are the type of a game in which anything can, and usually does happen. They're the type of a clash at which the average fan will stand and roar 'till his throat is raw, and applaud 'till his hands are red. **(HOW TRUE! THIS ACTUALLY TOOK PLACE IN THIS GAME).**

Lowell fans this morning will have their chance to roar for the likes of Titus Plomaritis, Brian Reynolds and Robert Swan, three of the best backs on any high school team in New England. Plomaritis will do most of the kicking for the visitors and what pitching the Red and Gray mentor calls for. He'll do some running, **(AGAIN, ANOTHER PREDICTION THAT CAME TRUE)** along with Reynolds, Swan, James Fallon and the other capable backs from the Spindle City.

The Lowell line, which will have a weight advantage over the home eleven has such capable performers as Captain Roger Sanborn, the team's leader, who holds down the pivot position, two fine ends, both on the offense and defense, in Art Lemoine and Menil Mavraides; a couple of husky tackles in Norman Carver and Robert Ready; and two equally strong performers at the guard spots in John Meehan and Robert Picard.

The Lawrence contingent has lost but three games all season. The Blue and White was a 12-7 loser to Dover early in the season, and in their last two outings the Lawrencians dropped two contests by the margin of a point. They were a 7-6 loser to Somerville and a 14-13 loser to Haverhill.

In the Lawrence line this morning Ernie Gregorowicz and Emil Vitale will hold down the end positions; Captain Al Wooles and A. Campagnone will be at the tackle slots; Frank Annaldo and Teddy Varitimos will be the guards, and Joe Waisgerber will be the center. These will be the lads who will tell the story of whether Lawrence will come out on top or not, for they will have the responsibility of stopping the fast Lowell backs, and giving the ace Blue and White aerial artist the protection he needs.

We refer, of course, to Jerry Callagy, the last of the six Callagy boys at Lawrence High, who has gained state-wide recognition.

With Callagy will be Robert Matthews and Louie Sarcione, who hold down the halfbacks slots, and Frank Jasinski, who does a measurable amount of work from his fullback slot, to the bark of the signals of Jerry Callagy.

That's the Lawrence-Lowell picture today. Lowell is the favorite, but strange things have happened in the past and probably will today.

May the better team win.

(AND IT TURNED OUT TO BE LOWELL, THANKS TO THE FOOT OF TITUS PLOMARITIS!!).

THE GREATEST FOOTBALL GAME IN LOWELL HIGH HISTORY
—NOVEMBER 25, 1948, LAWRENCE MEMORIAL STADIUM

(Game story excerpts reprinted from the Lowell Sun)

WHEW!!—BUT STILL UNBEATEN
LOWELL EDGES
LAWRENCE, 20-19
Plomeritus Scores All Local Points As
Kirk Streeters Cop Ninth Victory
By Joe McGarry

LAWRENCE—The mark of a true champion!!

The Lowell High School football team displayed that mark beyond a shadow of a doubt yesterday morning as it came from behind on two different occasions to gain a hard earned 20-19 victory over Lawrence High in the traditional game played between these clubs at Memorial Stadium in the downriver city before a crowd of 14,148 rabid fans.

Although much credit goes to the entire team, it was Titus Plomaritis, the diminutive, hard-running Red and Gray halfback who stole the show by scoring all 20 points garnered by the locals.

It was Plomaritis who for the most part set up these touchdowns and it was Plomaritis who carried Lowell through its first undefeated season in the history of the school.

GREAT COMEBACK

For those who were at the game, there is very little to explain the activities of the ball carrier, who reached his peak in the final inter-scholastic game of the regular season. When the chips were down, he and the entire club proved their worth by bouncing back to stay in the ball game.

The climax of the whole game came late in the fourth period with Lowell trailing, 19-13, with just seven minutes of playing time remaining. Taking a short punt on its own 44, which Menil Mavraides grounded, Lowell punched down the field to the four yard stripe, where with fourth down and as many yards to go, the lad who came in for all the plaudits swept his own right end behind beautiful blocking to cross the goal line standing up with the tying touchdown.

When he tallied this score, the fans in the end zone bleachers swarmed down from their seats and just about smothered Plomaritis. He tried to get away, but to no avail as fan after fan pounded him on the back and it took some time before the available police could restore order and clear the field so that Plomaritis could attempt the all-important conversion kick.

After order had once again been restored, the teams lined up for the kick, and here the game, which incidentally was one of the best contests seen in these parts in many, many years, reached its climax.

The team lined up. Jimmy Fallon, the quarterback, who had been handling the ball in all plays from the "T", was to hold the ball.

THAT BIG POINT

The ball was snapped by center and captain, Roger Sanborn. Fallon touched it down as 14,000 fans held their breaths. The Lawrence line tried to charge through to block the kick, but the stalwart Red and Gray forward wall, which time and again had proven its worth this fall, rose to its greatest heights and not a Blue and White jersey penetrated the Lowell backfield. Plomaritis came forward, swung the right foot which had produced so many extra points this year—**AND THE BALL SAILED TRUE TO ITS MARK.**

Referee, Dan Silva raised his arms above his head, signifying that the try was good, and there was no holding the Lowell contingent as it stormed over the playing surface expressing its feelings with every lad in a Red and Gray jersey who came along.

Three plays later the game ended.

SECTION TWO

CALLAGY GREAT

The downriver club got off to a flying start in the game. It was Gerry Callagy (whose performance was just overshadowed by Plomaritis), who set the spark to the Lawrence offense, which came within an ace of turning the trick. Callagy pitched two touchdown passes and romped 40 yards for another. Trailing 6-0, after the first period, this was the signal for Lowell to take the wraps off its offense and get down to serious business of getting back that touchdown.

As the second stanza got underway, Brian Reynolds, Bob Swan and Plomaritis alternated in carrying the ball until they reached the four yard stripe, where with fourth down and inches to go, Plomaritis went right up the middle and into the end zone for the score. Plomaritis then added the extra point and Lowell was in front, 7-6.

Shortly before the half ended, Lowell was to increase its lead. Taking over at its own 42, after a quick kick had been returned by Campbell Gibson, Plomaritis again came into the spotlight on the first play from scrimmage. The hero of the game took the ball and started on a wide sweep around his own right end. As Plomaritis hit the outside, he spotted a wide hole between the tackles, cut back and picking up a couple of downfield blockers, went 58 yards to score. He shook off a last ditch shoestring tackle and dove into the end zone, and Lowell was now in front, 13-6. The conversion was no good by the nearly-exhausted Plomaritis, and the teams went into the clubhouse for the intermission.

Neither team was able to do much during the third period, but the fireworks erupted in the final stanza.

Callagy dropped back to pass, but a gaping hole opened in the Lowell forward wall, and seeing this the Lawrence ace broke through, eluded a couple of tacklers, and raced 40 yards for the touchdown. The kick again failed and Lowell now held a slender 13-12 margin.

Lawrence recovered a Lowell fumble on the ensuing kickoff, setting up another Lancer touchdown which put the home team in front for the second time during the course of the morning. After seven plays, a Callagy to Louie Sarcione pass netted the score, and this time the Callagy boot was good and it was now Lawrence 19, Lowell 13.

Then came the dramatic Red and Gray drive which had even the hardiest Lawrence fan on his feet. Seven minutes were left to play.

THE PAYOFF DRIVE

Mavraides fell on the kickoff on the Lowell 44, and Plomaritis picked up a first down at the Lawrence 44. A Plomaritis to Arthur Lemoine pass clicked to the 35, and again it was Plomaritis who carried on two consecutive plays to move the ball to the 26. Gibson, Reynolds and Plomaritis each took a crack at the line to pick up a first down at the eight.

Then came the climax which had every fan in the stadium on his feet.

Gibson was dropped back at the nine, Plomaritis bulled through to the six and Reynolds was piled up at the four.

This left the situation with fourth down coming up and four yards to go. The team went back into a huddle. Sanborn called the signals. The club lined up and the ball was snapped to Plomaritis.

With the same blocking which had provided an earlier touchdown, the Lowell ball carrier started out around his own right end. This time he kept to the outside and his interference cleared the way. On the one it seemed certain that he would be dropped, but he managed to keep going and moved across the magic stripe to tie the score.

FANS GO WILD

This was when the fans went wild and commenced to pour out of the stands. The police on duty tried vainly to restore order, but it was impossible. The people in the end zone swarmed all over Plomaritis, and it took some time to clear the field so that the attempted conversion could be made.

The rest of the story is history. Every football fan in Greater-Lowell knows what happened as the fans on the far end of the stadium spilled over the field to watch the kick. It was a happy ending to a story authored by Coach Ray Riddick and a group of youngsters who just wouldn't be denied.

As the sound of the foot hitting the ball resounded across the stadium there was a hush, but it was just for the moment—and then the Lowell crowd really let loose.

Lowell had annexed its first undefeated season in history and it was set for a bowl trip to Mississippi.

But what happened on the playing field as the final whistle blew was calm to the scene in the Lowell clubhouse as the boys vented their feelings on the coaching staff and everyone else in view. Assistant coaches Bill Wilson and Tony Archinski came in for their full share of the glory, and well they might.

Plomaritis was undoubtedly one of the happiest guys around, but the fact that he personally had provided Lowell with 20 valuable points didn't phase him in the least. All the credit went to the other boys on the club, who had played their hearts out.

Captain Roger Sanborn, who calls all the offensive and defensive signals, came in for a major share of the praise, and ends Arthur Lemoine and Menil Mavraides couldn't be left out, as well as tackles Norman Carver and Bob Ready. Bob Lach and Jack Meehan displayed the type of stuff at their guard positions which goes to make up a championship team.

Jimmy Fallon, although he carried just once, handled the ball on about every play, and boys like Plomaritis, Swan, Reynolds and Gibson, who had done the bulk of ball carrying, couldn't say too much about the way that Fallon handed the ball off as they came through the line.

Fred Pawlowski, Dave Felton and Earl McQuade carried out their assignments to a T.

In fact, the entire club went overboard to present its coach, its school and its city with the very best—**AN UNDEFEATED SEASON!!**

Yes, the boys showed the mark of true champions.

4TH DOWN
4 YARDS FROM THE GOAL LINE
4 SECONDS ON THE CLOCK
—AND TITUS SCORES THE TYING TOUCHDOWN!!!!

(NOTE—following is the caption that appeared under the above photo, printed in the Lawrence newspaper the day following THE GAME)

"Fiction came to life Thanksgiving morning at Memorial Stadium, when in the annual Lowell-Lawrence football clash, with four minutes to go, the ball on the 40 yard line, a drizzle started to set in, and the score Lawrence 19 Lowell 13, a young gent by the name of Titus Plomaritis pulled a Frank

Merriwell. He personally conducted the **GRANDEST, FIGHTINEST** Lowell High team to the goal line and on fourth down skirted his right end for a touchdown to tie the score. He then booted the ball between the bars for the winning point. Here is Titus (No. 42) scoring the touchdown, with teammate Brian Reynolds being seen throwing the deciding block on a Lawrence player."

THE HISTORIC WINNING KICK

The game-winning PAT kick is shown headed towards the goalpost during the final seconds of play, which immediately set off a mad rush of Lowell High fans to swarm around kicker Titus Plomaritis. As a result, the game ball, as well as Titus' helmet, were taken. The enthusiastic crowd mobbed the field, and it took 20 minutes to clear the gridiron. The kick was good but it took another 20 minutes to restore order. The clock does not move on PAT's and the Red and Gray still had to kick off. Thus, **IT TOOK 40 MINUTES TO PLAY THE LAST FOUR SECONDS!!**

NOTE—Following is Leo Monahan's story of the Lowell-Lawrence game that appeared in a Boston newspaper on November 26, 1948.

Plomeritus, Lowell
Nip Lawrence, 20-19
By LEO MONAHAN

LAWRENCE—Titus Plomeritus of Lowell outshone Lawrence's Jerry Callagy yesterday at Lawrence Stadium as Lowell eked out a 20-19 win over underdog Lawrence. Lowell had to come from behind to win this one on Plomeritus' conversion.

Lawrence surprised right away as it tallied in the first period on a 22-yard aerial from Callagy to Emelio Vitale. His try for the point was wide. Lowell came right back in the second with Plomeritus scoring twice to put the visitors ahead 13-6. His first score climaxed a 64-yard march which began late in the first quarter and saw Titus rack up five first downs before smashing over from four yards out. His try was good. His second score was the thriller of the game as he scampered 56 yards around end after Lawrence had kicked out on the 42-yard line,

After a scoreless third period, Lawrence snapped back to register two touchdowns with Callagy featuring both scores. Jerry's best play of the day was a 44-yard dash around left end after he seemed to be trapped while trying to pass. He converted to tie it up at 13-all and then Captain Al Wooles of Lawrence recovered a free ball which had hit a Lowell man on a short kick. Two Callagy passes brought the ball from the 44 to the nine whence a Callagy to Lou Sarcione pass put Lawrence ahead 19-13.

Bowl-bound Lowell snapped right back with All-Scholastic Plomeritus carrying most of the way as Ray Riddick's charges went 56 yards in 16 plays with the omnipresent Plomeritus bucking over from four yards out and then converting.

(NOTE—Plomaritis name misspelled throughout story.)

HERE IS ANOTHER GAME STORY FROM A LAWRENCE PAPER

LOWELL 20
LAWRENCE 19

LAWRENCE—Titus Plomaritis, the man with the musical name from Lowell High School, was a one-man band against traditional rival Lawrence, the chunky 19-year-old halfback scoring all of his team's points as Lowell got back on its feet twice to edge Lawrence, 20-19, in the 51st encounter between the Merrimack Valley rivals before a frenzied overflow turnout of 17,000 here yesterday.

Plomaritis scored three touchdowns, one a sparkling 54-yard run, plowed over for the equalizing touchdown in the closing minute of play when Lowell was losing, 19-13, and then booted the extra point which gave his mates their narrow victory margin.

Lawrence took an early 6-0 lead, but Lowell marched 64 yards with the ensuing kickoff, smacking into the tackles with relentless fury. Plomaritis, Bob Swan and Brian Reynolds consumed yardage in huge gulps to move the ball to the Lawrence four, from where Plomaritis bulled across.

An exchange of boots gave Lowell possession on its own 42 late in the second period, and Plomaritis once more brought the already limp audience to its feet with a 54-yard touchdown jaunt on a wide end sweep around the right side.

Apparently, outclassed Lawrence stuttered through the scoreless third period, then came rushing back into contention in the opening minutes of the fourth. Gerry Callagy scampered 44 yards for a touchdown, but he missed the point-after, and Lawrence capitalized on a fumbled kickoff on the next play to build up a 19-13 advantage.

The fans were going wild. Lowell was distressed and time was running out. That's when the blocky Plomaritis sparked his mates to a 56-yard drive down the field. It was Plomaritis and Swan, then Plomaritis and Campbell Gibson, right down the field.

The Lawrence defense stiffened in the shadow of its own goal posts, and on fourth down Plomaritis took off around right end, bowling over two Lawrence players to score.

That tied it up, 19-19, and Plomaritis completed his Herculean day's work by coolly booting the winning point.

TITUS'S OWN VERSION OF HIS TYING TOUCHDOWN RUN

It is interesting how much credit one gets when he scores the tying touchdown or kicks a winning PAT.

My analysis is that it couldn't happen without team blockers on either occasion.

When the Coach sent a play in and the quarterback called it in the huddle, I listened intently, primarily to focus on my assignment. If it was my job to block a defensive end or a linebacker, I set my sights on that ballplayer and applied every ounce of energy in my body to protect my fellow teammate to carry out his assignment. I would expect likewise when the situation was reversed.

I remember exactly what was going through my mind over sixty years ago when the Coach called my number at such a critical time. We were trailing, 19-13. It was fourth down on the four yard line and showing only four seconds on the clock. I told Brian Reynolds, my lead blocker, as we broke the huddle, **"I'LL BE ON YOUR TAIL, TAKE ME IN!!"**

It was one of the most sensational moments of my athletic life. I honestly believe that this exciting moment would have never occurred without my supporting cast leading the way.

With nearly 20,000 fans filling the stadium, and standing six deep around the track, they were unmanageable, running onto the field. Someone took my helmet and another fan took the football. It took twenty minutes to clear the field before we attempted the point after touchdown (PAT) kick.

Roger Sanborn, our center and captain, said, **"GUYS, THIS IS IT, GIVE TITUS A CHANCE!!"**

As we broke the huddle, I said to Jimmy Fallon, my holder, "Jimmy, get it down and I'll get it over."

THE REST IS HISTORY!!

THE LOWELL SUN

Lowell Sun Publishing Company, Publishers.
15 Kearney Square, Lowell, Mass.   Published Daily Except Sunday

FOUNDED 1878 BY THE LATE
JOHN H. HARRINGTON

LOWELL, MASS., FRIDAY, NOVEMBER 26, 1948

Whew!

Throw away the book! And include the dictionary and the encyclopedia! We've got to get new adjectives!

Whatta game! Whatta team! Whatta coach! The score of course was Lowell 20, Lawrence 19.

But that doesn't tell the half of it. It was without a doubt the most thrilling, the most exciting, the most chilling Lowell-Lawrence football game played in over a generation, if not in all history.

It was more than just a football game. The dampened atmosphere breathed saturation with a resurgence of Lowell men's pride in things Lowell.

Our good friends in Lawrence were great in defeat. They were up, up, up, 'way up for that game yesterday, just as they were expected to be. Those down-river boys gave it everything they had.

But when the clouds were darkest, when all seemed lost, our Lowell boys headed by Titus Plomeritus, reached to the skies and dragged forth that silver lining. What gave Lowell people their big kick was not that Lowell won, because that was expected, even though maybe not by as slim a margin as one point, but that the boys came from behind to win in the last fleeting seconds of the game.

Yes, Lowell won by only one point. But in one sense it isn't so much whether they won or lost; it's how they played the game. They played, as they have all year, to win, and they won it. A very good football team in any man's league, Lawrence had everything to win, and nothing to lose. Our boys had everything to lose, and almost nothing to win. But they won the ball game. So now it's:
Roll, Lowell, Roll,
Roll, Lowell, Roll,
Right Down and Thru
That Mississippi Bowl.

The Lowell Sun Editorial

CELEBRATING ONE OF HIS BIGGEST VICTORIES

...was Coach Riddick, after Lowell nipped Lawrence, 20-19, in 1948, giving the Red and Gray its first undefeated season ever. Titus Plomaritis (R), who scored all 20 of Lowell's points, and Gerry Callagy (L), who was responsible for all of the Lancers's scoring, flank Ray in lockerroom after Turkey Day classic.

Celebration Continues

Titus Plomaritis #42, with a happy bunch of his teammates, in the locker room, immediately following the most exciting Lowell-Lawrence football game of its historic rivalry, dating back to 1888. Scanning photo from the left, Donald St. George, Bob Lemire, Campbell Gibson, Ernie Ruszczyk, Jack Lardner (later became U.S. Secret Service Agent assigned to Jacqueline Kennedy), Bob Ayers, Roger Godreau, Tom Conway, Jimmy Fallon, Billy Franks, Louie Martino, Jack Riley, Dan Maloney, Fred Pawlowski and Titus's proud brother, George Plomaritis, far right in street clothes.

Celebrating with the Three Lowell High School Coaches
Tony Archinski, Line Coach
Ray Riddick, Head Coach
Bill Wilson, Backfield Coach
Scanning from left: Campbell Gibson, Roger Godreau, Bob Swan, Coach Archinski,
Titus Plomaritis, Coach Riddick, Joe Connors, Art Lemoine,Norm Carver, Coach
Wilson, Dave Felton, Jim Fallon, Lou Martino & Captain Roger Sanborn, directly in
front of Coach Riddick.

Lowell-Lawrence Statistics
By FRANK BREEN

	LOWELL	LAWRENCE
Score	20	19
First Downs	10	9
Yards Gained Rushing	212	87
Forward Passes Attempted	5	21
Forward Passes Completed	2	9
Forward Passes Intercepted By	2	0
Yards Gained Passing	13	13
Number of Punts	4	4
Average Yardage of Punts	29	40
Punt Returns (ave. yds.)	7	15
Fumbles	2	1
Fumbles Recovered By	0	3
Penalties Against	4	3
Yards Lost By Penalties	50	25
Kick-Offs	4	4
Average Yardage Kick-Offs	51¾	20¼
Kick-Off Returns (ave. yds.)	0	18

Lowell Lawrence Statistics

The 1948 Lowell High School Athletic Staff

Shown above are the head coaches and chief officials of the 1948 Lowell High School sports staff. Left to right are: Ray Riddick, football; Al Mangan, trainer and former Olympics walking competitor; Donald McIntyre, athletic director; Tony Archinski, basketball; Mike Haggerty, track; and Stan Stoklosa, baseball. Notice that only four major sports for boys were represented at LHS during that era, compared to today's multitude of events, for both boys and girls. On the page to follow are the complete listings of today's athletic events, officials and coaches at Lowell High.

LOWELL PUBLIC SCHOOLS ADMINISTRATION

Superintendent	Jean Franco
Assistant Superintendent	Claire Abrams
Deputy Superintendent	Jay Lang
Assistant Superintendent	Ann Murphy
High School Headmaster	Edward Rozmiarek
Athletic Director	Jim DeProfio

LOWELL HIGH SCHOOL ATHLETIC DEPARTMENT

BOYS SPORTS	COACH
BASEBALL	DAN GRAHAM
BASKETBALL	SCOTT BOYLE
CREW	JESSICA MURRAY
CROSS COUNTRY	PHIL MAIA
FOOTBALL	JOHN FLORENCE
GOLF	DICK O'LOUGHLIN
GYMNASTICS	SAMNANG HOR
HOCKEY	BILL DONAHUE
INDOOR TRACK	PHIL MAIA
LACROSSE	BRUCE WALKER
OUTDOOR TRACK	DAVE CASEY
SKIING	CHRIS ZACHERER
SOCCER	BILL BETTENCOURT
SWIMMING	RICK BATTISTINE
TENNIS	TBA
VOLLEYBALL	PAUL MCCARTHY
WRESTLING	GEORGE BOSSI

GIRLS SPORTS	COACH
BASKETBALL	JIM CARDACI
CHEERLEADING	JOHN BEATON
CREW	JESSICA MURRAY
CROSS COUNTRY	MARYBETH MCKENNEY
FIELD HOCKEY	LISA KATTAR
GYMNASTICS	SHANNON MARTINS
INDOOR TRACK	TIM PATTERSON
LACROSSE	DANIELLE CLERMONT
OUTDOOR TRACK	TIM PATTERSON
SKIING	CHRIS ZACHERER
SOCCER	KATE RYAN
SOFTBALL	RICK O'BRIEN
SWIMMING	CHRISTIN MONAGHAN
TENNIS	JENNIFER CAREY
VOLLEYBALL	RAKSMEY DERIVAL

**2011 Lowell Puplic Schools Administration and
Lowell High School Athletic Department**

A Football Giant—at 5'5" ... A True Triple Threat

TITUS PLOMARITIS UNANIMOUS STATE ALL-STAR

Lowell High's senior left halfback, **TITUS PLOMARITIS,** following his spectacular return from the U.S. Army Paratroopers, completed a sweep of 1948 Massachusetts schoolboy football honors when he was named to All-Star teams by every Greater-Boston major newspapers.

Following are several of these All-Scholastic presentations:

THE BOSTON POST—"In permanent recognition of his outstanding brilliance on the playing field, his sportsmanship, his worth to his team and his exemplification of the high ideals for which the game stands, **TITUS PLOMARITIS** of Lowell is hereby designated **"BACK"** of the **BOSTON POST** All-Scholastic Football Team of 1948. Approved this 6th day of December A.D. 1948.

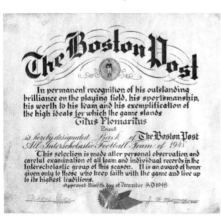

Other well-known gridders voted to The Post's All-Star squad included ends, **Arthur Lemoine** and **Menil Mavraides** of Lowell, back, **Gerry Callagy,** and end, **Ernie**

113

Gregorowicz, of Lawrence, fullback, **Sam Pino,** of Somerville (future powerful running mate of Plomaritis at B.U.) and back, **Armand Colombo,** of Brockton (eventual famous longtime coach at Brockton High).

BOSTON TRAVELER—"Halfback **TITUS PLOMARITIS,** Lowell—When graduations sapped the Lowell backfield last year, many fans wondered what would happen. They got their answer in Titus, who blossomed overnight into one of the best backs in the state. He's 5 feet 5 inches and weighs 155."

Also among the Travelers' All-Star selections were such famed gridders, **Lou Tsiropoulos,** of Lynn English (later to be a Boston Celtic), **Jim Buonopane** of Malden (to become All-New England linebacker at Holy Cross) and **Joe Andrews** of Durfee (named captain of this team).

BOSTON AMERICAN—"A star-studded 'Cream of the Crop' of Massachusetts schoolboy gridders, including backs **Don Mackey** of Malden, **Richie Doyle** of B.C. High, the above-mentioned **Colombo** and **Andrews**, and of course **PLOMARITIS**, in addition to ends Charlie **Pulsford** of Melrose and **Tsiropoulos**, tackles **Henry O'Brien** of Arlington and **Mike Doohan** of Malden Catholic, guards **Ray LeClerc** of Beverly and **Buonapane**, and center **Jack Granville** of Quincy.

Official All-Scholastic Team

BOSTON GLOBE— "**TITUS PLOMARITIS,** halfback, Lowell—the 'Pine Tree', as **Coach Ray Riddick** calls him. He came to Lowell last year as an unknown and has risen to the top of the pile on his ability to pass, run and kick with a high degree of success.

Every opponent is more than ready to admit that Plomaritis is the hardest man to stop because his little legs are always on the move as he drives for that extra yard. Along with a couple of other Lowell players, Titus has paved the way for another successful season and a post-season bowl game in Jackson, Mississippi."

ADDITIONAL 1948 HONORS BEFALL TITUS

TITUS PLOMARITIS was named to the Radio Station WESX All-Scholastic unit, whose certificate stated, "This certifies that Titus Plomaritis has been chosen by his opponents, because of outstanding achievement in High School Football, for the position of All-Scholastic Halfback".

Radio Station WESX was owned by North Shore Broadcasting Company.

PLOMARITIS was selected to play in the annual North Shore All-Stars vs. Boston Suburban All-Stars game, which took place at Lynn's Manning Bowl on December 5, 1948.

Also members of the North Shore All-Stars squad were Lowell High teammates, **Menil Mavraides, Arthur Lemoine, Bob Swan** and **Jack Meehan,** while **Ray Riddick** served as one of the coaches.

The Boston Suburban team won the game, 27-7, but the Lowell players came into prominence on more than one occasion. Mavraides set up the North Shore's lone touchdown by blocking a kick, and Plomaritis followed with the point-after kick to give his team an early 7-0 lead. However, the Boston Stars made it no contest during the second half.

Lemoine saw more action than did any other member of the squad, playing a good part of the game, and Meehan also played a good part of the time in the line on offense.

PLOMARITIS SCORES IN CAMBRIDGE JAMBOREE

CAMBRIDGE—September 11, 1948—The second annual Joseph Q. Sullivan Football Jamboree took place before 10,000 spectators at Russell Field in North Cambridge, with Lowell, Dedham, Brookline and Waltham scoring victories.

The four pre-season contests offered many thrills, but Lowell High unveiled a super-dreadnaught ground attack that all but drove Watertown out of the stadium in two 16-minute periods, with a 13-6 triumph.

Titus Tallying Touchdown

Lowell High star left halfback Titus Plomaritis (42), who led his team to a 13-6 win over Watertown in the Cambridge Jamboree, is seen going over for the first touchdown of the game on a five-yard run. Photo by Jimmy Jones, Boston Post.

In other games, Dedham downed St.Mary's of Brookline, Brookline High beat Cambridge Latin, and Waltham topped Rindge Tech—all by 6-0 scores.

LOWELL HIGH, which looms as a powerhouse this coming season, sent the fans home talking about left halfback **TIM LOMERITUS** (yes, that's the way the Boston newspaper spelled it, instead of **TITUS PLOMARITIS**) who ran and passed Watertown dizzy.

The former U.S. Army Paratrooper ripped through tackle and circled the ends on four consecutive plays, before scoring the game's first touchdown from the five-yard line, and he followed it up by kicking the extra point. Later in the game, No. 42 broke loose for a 40-yard gallop.

Fullback **BRIAN REYNOLDS** tallied the other Lowell six-pointer.

THE BOGALUSA BOWL GAME

Lowell High School Starting Lineup
Front, left to right: Art Lemoine, Norm Carver, Jack Meehan, Captain Roger Sanborn, Bob Latch, Bob Ready, Minnie Mavraides, Rear: Campbell Gibson, Jim Fallon, Bob Swan, Titus Plomaritis. Missing from photo is Brian Reynolds, who alternates at fullback. Lowell Sun photo.

LOWELL EDGED OUT, 12-7; LOSE BY ONE-YARD MARGIN

By Frank Sargent
Lowell Sun Sports Editor

JACKSON, MISS., Dec. 11—Don't throw away that welcome mat, folks, because your kids are still heroes. They emerged on the short end of the 12-7 count in their game with Bogalusa High here last night, but they're still among the gamest youngsters we've ever had represent us on any athletic field.

They didn't win last night, but they didn't lose a single thing. They played one of the best ball games they've ever been in and you can't take a single thing away from them. Jackson thinks they're wonderful and we know you do, too, so keep that welcome mat out, the kids will be looking for it when they get back—and they justly deserve it.

GLORY IN DEFEAT

"Come back and play for us any time you want, kids, you were great!" Jackson fans shouted into the bus bearing the heart-broken Lowell High gridders.

"Keep your chins up, fellows, you were wonderful!" fans kept shouting into the bus, but the boys couldn't hear them. Tears were streaming down their cheeks, and that setback was beating like a trip hammer on their weary heads. They had lost. They were "down"—and that's the sign of a champion—they hate to lose.

It was the first time all season that a Lowell High grid club had emerged on the short end of a decision, but this Ray Riddick coached outfit couldn't have lost to a better club. The Bogalusians were wonderful in victory and they would have been just as grand in defeat—because it was the type of ball game which was heartbreaking for either club to lose.

RAVE ABOUT GAME

Long after the cheers and groans of Tiger Stadium had become history, downtown Jackson was still talking about the ball game. It was one of the finest games ever played in Jackson, and long after the Lowell boys returned to their hotel the 12,000 fans who sat in on last night's grid proceedings here were still raving about the game.

"Those teams were wonderful," and "What a ball game" were heard all over the city. Everybody here who didn't attend the game took it in over the radio. There wasn't a soul in Jackson last night who didn't know all about the game and there wasn't a solitary person in the city who wasn't ready to shake the hands of the Lowell youngsters and tell them how grand they were out there at Tiger Stadium.

There's no getting away from it, this game here last night made history. Even officials who handled the contest were amazed at the high caliber of play on the part of both clubs.

Bogalusa's quarterback, **CLIFF SPRINGFIELD**, handled the ball like Mandrake. He was superb, and so were all of his teammates. That is, all

120

except Von Thomas, the fellow the officials caught trying to stamp out a cigarette butt on **TITUS PLOMARITIS**'s face. The boys from Louisiana taught us a lesson in forward passing, and Plomaritis ran like the rabbit the Bogalusians are always shooting at, but always missing.

AIR POWER

The game, as expected, found Bogalusa displaying its greatest strength through the air and Lowell using its sheer power to wear down the Southerners. Both types of play paid off. Bogalusa used passes to gain its second touchdown. Lowell capitalized on its running attack to register its only touchdown and then went via the same route, to the lip of the goal line for what promised to be the game's winning touchdown, only to catch those fingers in the door, and the thing slammed shut on a fumble which meant the difference between victory and defeat.

BIG PRE-GAME HIT

One thing which made a big hit with the fans, especially those from Lowell, was the way each and every starting player was introduced. About ten minutes before starting time the teams lined up at opposite ends of the field. All lights were extinguished and the public address announcer named the players, one by one, and the boys dashed toward midfield in the maze of a spotlight glare. This was something new to Lowell fans.

Both squads dressed at their hotels and then made the trip to the stadium via bus. In this way, the coaches were able to keep their boys right in their midst until an hour before game time.

RIDDICK PRAISES BOGALUSA

By Joe McGarry
Lowell Sun

JACKSON, MISS.-Dec.11—Even in defeat they were great.

Time and time again during the past season, the Lowell High School football team had come from behind to pull important victories out of the fire. Last night at Tiger Stadium the same situation prevailed, but this time the gods of fate stepped in and robbed the team of a victory and instead placed it on the short end of a 12-7 score in a contest against Bogalusa High, the Louisiana state champion.

RIDDICK GETS EYEFUL

But despite the defeat the boys showed themselves to be real champions. They dropped a game to a club which was described by Coach Ray Riddick as, "The best high school club I ever have seen." This is high praise coming from a coach who was so used to meeting the best in the business.

There is no doubt in the mind of this writer that the better club on the field lost the ball game, and some 10,000 of the 12,000 fans who jammed Tiger Stadium for this intersectional clash, are ready to back this statement.

As has been the case in the past, the Lowell aggregation had that ability to come from behind.

Bogalusa scored first, and then the Red and Gray gridders put on the pressure to hold the Louisiana boys until the fourth period, when they came from behind to knot the score on **BOB SWAN**'s touchdown, and then go into the lead as the educated toe of **TITUS PLOMARITIS** bisected the uprights with the all-important point.

THE COSTLY FUMBLE

In the long run, however, it was a combination of the aforementioned gods of faith, and the passing ability of **CLIFF SPRINGFIELD** which spelled the difference. It was the fumble on the one-yard line with just about a minute of playing time remaining which robbed the undefeated Massachusetts co-champions of a sure victory. At this time the score was 12-7 Springfield's passing ate up most of the yardage on a six-play drive of 80 yards, which led to the second Bogalusa TD.

No one has any regrets about the outcome, for the Lowell boys did themselves proud all the way. True, the Lowell fans, and the entire official party, would have been very much pleased with a victory, but the important thing about the entire situation was the way the boys conducted themselves on the field. In fact, this is emphatically brought out in the statistics, which show that Lowell failed to draw a single major penalty.

MORE LOWELL FUMBLES

During the first period, Lowell had the better of the deal, and held the ball a good two-thirds of the time. However, as was to be the case later in the game, fumbles proved very costly during this session.

With Plomaritis, **BRIAN REYNOLDS** and Swan alternating in the ball-carrying department, Lowell moved down to the Lumberjacks' 35, where the attack was stalled by a fumble, which Bogalusa recovered.

Lowell bounced right back and started another drive, which was terminated by the second costly fumble of the night.

In this series of downs, the only "dirty" action of the game was forthcoming, and as a result Bogalusa lost its best lineman for the remainder of the game.

After moving the ball to the Lowell 21, quarterback, **JIMMY FALLON**, handed the pigskin to Plomaritis, who advanced to the 27. After he had been tackled and was definitely downed, **VEN THOMAS** moved into the pileup and proceeded to plant a cleated foot in the Lowell halfback's face. For this action, the officials, who were on the ball all night long, tagged Bogalusa with a 15-yard penalty and gave Thomas a sideline seat for the remainder of the game.

Things were rolling along fine until it moved into "fumbleitis" territory on the 38, and another miscue in the Lowell backfield handed the ball to Bogalusa. **BILL GRAHAM** then tight-roped down the sideline to the Lowell 14, and three plays later **DON LEE** raced into the end zone from six yards out. Springfield's kick was wide.

THE RED AND GRAY MOVES IN FRONT

Lowell gained the lead, 7-6, in the fourth period. After an exchange of punts, The Riddick club started a successful scoring drive. Taking the ball on its own 39, Lowell started to march. Reynolds went up the middle to the 44, and Swan and Plomaritis alternated in doing most of the lugging right down to the lip of the goal, from where Fallon moved into the end zone. However, a back in motion penalty moved the ball back to the five, but on the next play Swan went around left end for the tying score, and "**THE TOE**"— Plomaritis—converted for the go-ahead point.

With time running out, Bogalusa immediately took to the air, and in six plays regained the lead which it had relinquished momentarily.

Springfield was the big gun in this attack, pitching three passes, including the touchdown heave to Graham.

THE HEARTBREAK OF THE SEASON

Then came the heartbreak of the ball game—and of the season—as far as the Lowell fans were concerned.

In the stands there wasn't the least doubt in the minds of any of the Lowell fans on hand for the contest, that Coach Riddick's warriors couldn't come back and pull the decision out of the fire.

The boys promptly proceeded to show these fans that they could do it. After taking the kickoff on to the 35 (Swan had returned it from the 12), Plomaritis and Reynolds shared the spotlight in the early stages of this drive. However, it took Swan's fourth down gamble which brought the crowd to its feet.

This came after Lowell had apparently bogged down on the Bogalusa 45. With fourth down and 11 yards to go for a first down, the ball was handed to the fleet-footed halfback and he took it around his own right end and moved to the 30 for the first down.

This kept the attack rolling and it advanced down to the three-yard stripe—where fate stepped in.

By this time the clock was running out and had Lowell been able to tally, it would have been at least a 13-12 lead and it didn't look as though Bogalusa would have time to score.

But, as things turned out, it just wasn't in the cards, and after recovering the costly fumble, Bogalusa just stuck around killing the clock— and killing Lowell's hopes.

BOGALUSA HAD SPEED—AND BREAKS TO WIN; PLOMARITIS AND SPRINGFIELD STAND OUT IN THRILLER

By Wayne Jackson
Jackson, Miss., Clarion-Ledger

In an environment fit for kings, and they were kings last night, Lowell and Bogalusa met on the turf of Tiger Stadium before over 12,000 fans in the third annual Memorial Bowl football game, which was sponsored by the Jackson Touchdown Club.

Winding up the week-long celebration was plenty of dancing by both the Massachusetts visitors and the Louisiana Lumberjacks in the Robert E. Lee Hotel, but immediately following the final whistle the shouting was all by Bogalusa, which won 12 to 7.

Using speed, a flashy aerial attack, and a set of brains not always found in a quarterback, the Lumberjacks grabbed a 6 to 0 lead in the second quarter from the heavier Yankees, lost it in the fourth period because of the talented toe of Titus Plomaritis, and then fought back in the same quarter to get the winning marker on a 16-yard touchdown pass from Cliff Springfield.

Now it was Lowell's turn to march, and the Yanks marched from their own 12 down to the Bogalusa one-yard stripe, only to lose it on a fumble and time soon ran out.

PLOMARITIS KICKED IN FACE

The officiating was tops, unquestionably fair and impartial to both sides. One illustration of this came when Plomaritis was deliberately kicked in the face and knocked out for a few minutes.

Even before most of the fans were able to see that Plomaritis was down, the officials had called a 15-yard penalty against Bogalusa and had ejected the Bogalusa player responsible for the dirty work from the game. It was, of course, an attempt to eliminate Plomaritis from the action, an attempt that failed, since Plomaritis went on to play a great ball game.

THE BOGALUSA SLANT

By Bob Landry
Sports Editor
Bogalusa Daily News

JACKSON, MISS., Dec. 10—Lowell and Bogalusa gave 12,000 shivering fans a ding-dong football game here tonight in Jackson's third annual Mississippi Memorial Bowl game, and only the slender thread of fate swung the balance to the Lumberjacks from Louisiana, who recovered a Lowell fumble on their own two-yard line with a minute left to play and hung doggedly to a 12-7 margin.

It was a great game to win—a tough one to lose. But none who saw the classic could deny the battling underdogs from Bogalusa fought a good fight from the opening whistle.

The kids from up East ripped the Lumberjacks' center, they breezed around the ends, and they tossed a fair share of successful passes to roll up 18 first downs—certainly enough to win most ball games. But, when the chips were down in the waning minutes of the game, the same **LADY LUCK** who frowned upon Bogalusa three weeks ago and lost them their only contest this year, felt a little bad about the deal, smiled, tapped **BHS** quarterback, **CLIFF SPRINGFIELD**, on the shoulder and showed him a loose ball, fumbled by the Lowell quarterback.

Springfield, without so much as a thank you to The Lady, fell on the pigskin and the Lumberjacks froze the game out in four plays.

TITUS NEARLY PULLS IT OUT

Bogalusa went out in front early in the second quarter on an end sweep by **DON LEE**.

It was the fourth quarter before Lowell roared back into the ball game, knotting the count at 6-6 on a five-yard sweep by **BOB SWAN**, and when **"TERRIFIC" TITUS PLOMARITIS** threaded the uprights for the 7-6 lead, it looked pretty good for the New Englanders

However, Bogalusa took the ensuing kickoff and in six plays regained the lead, on a 16-yard Springfield to **BILL GRAHAM** pass. The extra point failed and it remained 12-7, Bogalusa.

Lowell quickly turned on the heat with eight minutes to go, but used up a great heap of time in getting down to the Lumberjacks' two, taking five consecutive first downs to get that close to pay dirt. Yet, when they got that close, the cupboard was bare. Bogalusa took the ball on a fumble, and held on until the curtain came down.

A guy on his way home didn't put it into fancy words, but he summarized the concentrated opinion of the 12,000 fans when he said, **"BEST BALL GAME I'VE SEEN THIS YEAR."**

RIDDICK HAS NO REGRETS

NOTES FROM JACKSON

By Frank Sargent

JACKSON, MISS.—"You can quote me as saying that Bogalusa is the classiest high school club I've ever seen in action," said LHS Coach Ray Riddick as he dressed after last night's 12-7 loss to the Lumberjacks.

"The Bogalusa passing was superb and the backs handled the ball well at all times," added Riddick. "But I haven't too many regrets. I know exactly what mistakes we made, but we all got a taste of high school football as it is played down here and we're not even thinking about any alibis."

Captain Roger Sandborn holds placement as Santa gives place kicking specialist, Titus Plomaritis, 42, a few pointers? Lowell Sun photo.

The Lowell Coach also thought the officials did an exceptionally fine job.

One of the officials on top of the crucial fumble play that lost the ball game for Lowell was quoted as saying that the Red and Gray's heart-breaking fumble was a very clean one with the ball simply popping out of

his arms from the force of the impact when the boy hit the line. "It just popped out from the force of the pressure," the official commented, "and with it popped the Lowell victory."

GOOD SPORTS FROM LOWELL

Although they felt badly about losing the close ball game, the Lowell High gridders proved themselves good sports last night when they shook off the jitters which set in after a loss and attended the Bogalusa-Lowell dance at the Robert E. Lee Hotel here. The locals congratulated the Lumberjacks on their victory and received a loud burst of applause when introduced at the dance.

Lowell's gridders are nursing several bumps and bruises today.

PLOMARITIS is wearing more facial adhesive tape than a kid giving himself his first shave with his old man's straight razor.

There are also several bits of evidence that our boys absorbed a few knocks around the line—but, of course, those Bogalusa boys will not feel like chopping wood today, either.

MESSAGES FROM HOME

Coach Riddick was bombarded with phone and wire messages all day yesterday. Among those offering best wishes were Football Coach Denny Myers and John Curley of Boston College, Peabody High coaches and players, Lucy O'Heir, Virginia McCarron, Doris Sullivan, Virginia Doulmes, Rose Guwiazda, Mary Leahy, Alice Currie, **MRS. MARGE RIDDICK**, Rev.Bro. Firmin, CFX of Keith Academy, Jack Donahue, president of the Mass. State Coaches Assn., Lowell Chamber of Commerce, Kenny, Dick, Lowell Harvard Club, Jim Butler, Boston newspaperman Jerry Nason, Bella's Market, Keith Academy Athletic Assn., Harvard Coach, Art Valpey, "Whoops" S. Ivley, Paul "Bucky" Sullivan, Central Office Forces N.E. Tel. & Tel. and a host of others.

There was also a tremendous turnout of Lowell fans at the game. Some of those spotted in the stands included Arthur Keenan, Sy Solomont, Mendel Shapiro, Ed McMahon, George Mavraides, Billy Mavraides, Ned Brox, Paul Brunelle, Phil McGowan, Mr. and Mrs. Norman Carver, Phil Scannell, Art Lemoine, Lowell Police Captain Owen Conway, Bill Cohen, John Maguire, Eddie Conway, Mr. & Mr. Al Caswell, etc.

STILL A GREAT TEAM

By George McGuane
Lowell Sun

LOWELL—December 11, 1948—Take it from this corner, Lowell High has nothing to be ashamed of in that 12-7 setback down in Dixie last night.

Ray Riddick's boys played a great game and a good brand of football. For our dough, the Red and Gray appeared like the better club. It certainly played a smart brand of ball. The same goes for Bogalusa.

The Southerners displayed heady stuff when they hung on to the pigskin and ran the clock out in those valuable final seconds of play. They did just what the book calls for in such a case. They held the ball until the fourth down by snuggling up through the middle of the line to avoid the possibility of a fumble and a chance to kill the clock and win the game.

As far as we could see, the old chips were scattered on that Lowell fumble down near the "Gate to Heaven", that old touchdown stripe. It meant the difference between victory and defeat.

But, a fumble is one of those bug-a-boos of football and something that you can't blame on a team, a coach or a player. Fumbles happen to the best ballplayers in the business.

We had a great ball-club going to Mississippi, and as far as we're concerned we have a great ball-club coming home. They fought their hearts out for us.

Lowell High still has the heartstrings of this community— even in defeat.

Titus Plomaritis embracing his cousin, Electra Varkas, of Jamaica Plain, at South Station as Lowell High School football team returned home from its trip to the Memorial Bowl game with Bogalusa High of Louisiana in Jackson, Mississippi. Boston paper photo.

LOWELL TEAM RETURNS HOME
December 19, 1948

LOWELL—The gallant Lowell High football squad arrived at Boston's South Station tonight, coming home from its trip to the Memorial Bowl game with Bogalusa High of Louisiana in Jackson Mississippi.

Among those being enthusiastically greeted were Head Coach Ray Riddick, met by his wife Marjorie and their two daughters, Marjorie Rae and Betty, and star left halfback, Titus Plomaritis, who was embraced by his cousin, Electra Varkas, of Boston.

The Red and Gray players, coaches and officials were taken by surprise as snow failed to keep thousands from watching a gala parade held in downtown Lowell as they arrived home.

LOWELL ROARS "WELCOME HOME"

Ten thousand men, women and children lined downtown streets in a blinding snowstorm tonight to roar a "Welcome Home" to the returning Lowell High football team, coming from a fortnight's trip through the South and a heartbreaking Bowl game loss to Bogalusa High in Jackson, Mississippi, on December 10.

The entire squad and coaches were paraded through the streets on fire apparatus and then taken to the Lowell High School auditorium where 2000 others gave them the accolade usually reserved for victors.

Many friends and relatives of the players jumped the gun by going to Boston to meet the train from New York at the South Station at 5:45 P.M.

The last lap of the 4000 mile journey, that included stopovers in New Orleans, Washington and New York, was made in buses, with a transfer to fire trucks at the Chelmsford line. Police cruising cars formed an escort for the three mile ride to the school.

THE CITY POURS ON HONORS

Greetings of the city were extended by Mayor George Ayotte and City Manager John J. Flannery, followed by thankful remarks made by Head Coach Ray Riddick. It was one of the most spontaneous expressions of appreciation ever witnessed here.

Lowell lost to Bogalusa, 12-7, losing the ball via a fumble on the one-foot line with only about 40 seconds remaining in the game. But, tonight a visitor well might have thought that the cheers were for a team that had won an inter-sectional championship.

NOTES BY TITUS: I found it interesting when reviewing the newspaper clippings that the ticket prices for the good seats were $2.40 in the concrete stands. End-zone seats, where temporary bleachers were erected, were $1.00 and would only be available when the gates opened.

The list of ticket locations, printed in the Jackson newspapers, had one name in particular that really stood out, "**LUCKETT SEED AND FEED**". (See related Mississippi State stories).

Yep! That's the same **JAZZ LUCKETT. (See Miss. State Story)**

MISSISSIPPI STATE JOURNEY

NOTE: The following will clarify how, when and what events transpired that prompted country comedian Jerry Clower to feature the **"TITUS PLUMMERITIS"** episode on the side-one cut one portion on his album **"AMBASSADOR OF GOOD WILL"** when he was honored with a "Jerry Clower Day" at Mississippi State in 1970.

It all started at the conclusion of Lowell High's first football bowl game, December 10, 1948, in Jackson, Mississippi, against Bogalusa High School, the Louisiana State champions.

Following the game, a gentleman approached me and introduced himself as **JAZZ LUCKETT**, a member of the Mississippi State University's Alumni Club. He asked me to join him with his wife and daughter, a nice looking Southern Bell standing by his side, for a post game snack, to discuss a possible visit to the campus of Mississippi State in the spring of 1949.

When I asked Coach Riddick for permission, he replied in the affirmative and informed me that he had been contacted by several coaches from Southern colleges that were interested in me and suggested that I enjoy the occasion, **BUT NOT TO MAKE ANY COMMITMENTS.**

Jazz, as I found out, was a successful businessman, the owner of "Luckett Seed and Feed". His physical stature was close to mine, and now add that his beautiful daughter, with her Southern accent and charming smile, was by his side, a perfect combination to entice a candidate!!

Mr. Luckett next contacted me through the Lowell High Athletic Office, and we coordinated my visit to take place during Lowell's February vacation. Mr. Luckett said that he would make all the travel arrangements and he would be at the airport to pick me up.

Advice from Coach Riddick before departing was to take advantage of the free trip to visit Mississippi State University, however, "**DO NOT MAKE A COMMITMENT!!**"

PRACTICING AT MISSISSIPPI STATE

As promised, Jazz Luckett picked me up at the airport in Jackson, Mississippi, drove me to the Mississippi State campus and introduced me to the head football coach, **"SLICK" MORTON".**

I practiced with the team all week, with close to 100 players including returning veterans and a large contingent of recruits. The coaches were mostly impressed with my placekicking skills, especially my field goal quick delivery and accuracy at 45 yards, which would be equivalent to 60 yarders today.

Several times during the week, either Jazz or someone else with authority would pick me up after practice and take me to a lavish billiard parlor. They had apparently gotten wind of my discussion with Coach Riddick and Mr. Saunders, a good friend of Riddick's and the owner of **SAUNDER'S MARKET** on Gorham Street in Lowell.

When I told Coach Riddick that I preferred ownership of a billiard parlor to college, he pulled another gem out of the hat, and again he was looking out for my best interest. Believe me, it was all pre-arranged, when Mr. Saunders stated, "Titus, anybody can own a billiards parlor. However, if you go to college you'll have all the tools necessary to own the best billiards parlor in the country!!".

Later, I visited Harvard University with Bill Wilson, my backfield coach at Lowell High, and a Harvard alumnus. He assured me of a full scholarship, but that walk through the corridors of Harvard frightened the crap out of me.

Saturday was the conclusion of spring practice, which included their annual game scrimmage in front of over 40,000 fans and alumni. Coach "Slick" Morton, with his assistants, posted the sixty-six players chosen to participate in the game on the locker room bulletin board. They divided the team into two squads, thirty-three on each of the Red and Blue units. The Red squad had the first, third and fifth elevens, while the Blue squad had the second, fourth and sixth elevens. They had me on the Blue squad, as the sixth left halfback, and informed me that I would be doing all the kicking for my unit.

FOLLOW CLOSELY, IT'S HARD TO BELIEVE WHAT HAPPENED

On the opening kickoff, the left halfback on the Blue squad was injured, and halfway into the first quarter the second left halfback also got hurt.

Coach Morton came over to me and asked, "Wanna play some ball, boy?" I remember getting so excited that I said, "Yes", and started running out on the field without a helmet, when the coach called me back and said, "Get yourself a helmet, boy."

Not expecting to play, other than kicking, I did not have a helmet of my own. The trainer quickly pulled one out of his bag of surplus equipment, stuffed it with paper and put it on my head. Out I went into the huddle with the helmet resting on the bridge of my nose.

I played the entire remaining fifty minutes of the game and had another memorable exciting experience similar to the Lowell-Lawrence game on Thanksgiving. I scored three touchdowns, kicked five extra points and nobody penetrated my zone as safety-man on defense.

This leads to **THE LAST PLAY OF THE GAME.**

NOTE: Remember, in that era there was no such thing as offensive and defensive teams. You had to play **BOTH WAYS.**

The quarterback for the Red team was a big boy, standing over six feet and weighing over 200 pounds. As the play developed, my instinct told me not to bite for the bait, so I just kept my eyes on the QB, who was drifting by himself to his right while the whole line and other backs were running to the left. Sure as Hell it was a bootleg in the making.

You have to envision what was developing. The QB was not fast, but he was gaining momentum all by himself, with me being his only obstacle to the end zone. Instead of waiting for him to get to me, I decided to attack, so I focused on his legs, just below the knees like a Fighter Jet setting his laser on an enemy plane. Putting my jets on full speed, I hit him exactly where I had him beamed in.

The collision was heard across the entire stadium, but I felt an immediate shock-like pain down my right arm. However, I jumped to my feet quickly as I always did so not to show the enemy any weaknesses.

Can't say the same for the QB, as he landed on his head and required several minutes of attention as the game ended.

When inside the locker room after the game, I couldn't raise my right arm over my head to remove my jersey, so I had the trainer cut the jersey off so I could take a shower. When in the shower the trainer returned and told me the coaches wanted me in the coaches' room immediately. After wrapping a towel around my waist, the trainer escorted me into the coaches' room.

THE SCENE TO REMEMBER

There they were, five coaches in a dimly lit room, all smoking cigars, sitting on stools, stark naked with their balls hanging to the floor.

The first comment made by Head Coach "Slick" Morton was: "Tartus, my boy, we want you here at Mississippi State."

The dialogue continued for several minutes, from one coach to the next. "We're gonna make you an All-American…we'll make you a super star… you'll have your own billiards parlor…" and they went on and on with more promises.

It all sounded great. However, all I could think of was Coach Riddick's departing comment, **"DO NOT MAKE A COMMITMENT."**

With all the flattery and promises, it was very difficult to say no, so I quickly concocted a fairy tale, saying that I promised my father, a Greek immigrant who didn't speak English, that I wouldn't make a decision without his approval.

I left the nakedness of the coaches' room wearing my towel like a Grecian robe, but also with the increased throbbing pain in my right shoulder, like a Greek warrior.

Jazz Luckett was beaming like a light bulb and as happy as a peacock when he greeted me while I was exiting the stadium locker room. There were accolades aplenty from him and his Alumni friends, but not letting on that I was hurting, I kept my right arm close to my body, which seemed to minimize the pain.

Jazz and I had pre-arranged plans for me to take all my belongings when leaving the University facilities after the game, and to spend the last evening at Mr. Luckett's home. He was to drive me to the airport the next day for a noon departure.

It was about 2 A.M. when the pain became unbearable and my moaning awakened the Luckett's one after the other. Jazz sensed that something was wrong and he rushed me to the hospital.

YEP! YOU GUESSED IT!!!

This is the other **COLLAR BONE FRACTURE** that I related to earlier when I was roller skating on the Saunder's Market side of Summer Street about ten years prior and went head first into the open manhole.

Within an hour, head coach, "Slick" Morton, and the athletic director were at the hospital. They remained throughout the X-Ray findings and figure eight splinting, and when all the dust settled, we had a discrepancy of when I was returning to Lowell.

MASSACHUSETTS ACE TO ATTEND STATE

JACKSON (MISS.) DAILY NEWS FEB 28-1949

I wanted to leave on my scheduled flight at twelve noon, as my concern was that our Massachusetts school break ended that day and classes would resume on Monday morning. The Coach insisted that I remain locally until the doctor cleared me for travel. He, in fact, called Headmaster Sullivan on Monday morning, explaining my heroics and game-ending tackle that resulted in a fractured collar bone.

I also spoke to Mr. Sullivan, as I was concerned about getting behind in my school work, and he assured me that he would personally inform my teachers of the incident and not to worry as I would be able to make it up when I returned.

I was a house guest at the Luckett's for the next four days before returning home.

The Jackson (Miss.) Daily News and all the locals were congratulating me and as much as if I had made a commitment. They kept saying that I was attending Mississippi State in the fall.

Titus Plomaritis, 19-year-old backfield star of the Lowell, Mass., High school eleven that met the Bogalusa, La., team in Jackson's Memorial Bowl game last December, will be listed among the freshman footballers at Mississippi State next fall. Following a week's visit to Mississippi State, during which he worked out with the Maroons in spring training, Plomaritis was offered and accepted an athletic scholarship. Plomaritis weighs 168 pounds and is a fast and shifty ball carrier. He also plays well on defense and is an expert place-kicker. He was chosen on the official All-Scholastic eleven of Massachusetts last season.

PUNCH LINE TO THIS STORY

JERRY CLOWER was one of Mississippi State's outstanding tackles, playing on the Red team that took a beating from our Blue team.

Twenty years later, he was honored by Mississippi State University with a **JERRY CLOWER DAY**. He accepted with an impression of **"TITUS PLUMMERITIS"** (misspelled, but what else is new?) and honored me with the first title of his comedy album, **"AMBASSADOR of GOOD WILL"**.

My personalized autographed copy in 1977.

SIDE NOTE: Interesting how I first heard about this recording. It seems that Richard (Dick) K. Donahue, one of our (Claire's and my) dear friends, who also was one of President Jack Kennedy's "Irish Mafia", had just returned from a Nike business meeting in Hawaii.

He called our house and spoke to Claire, relating, "While returning from Hawaii today, up about 30,000 feet, I was listening to the comedy channel and just about dozing off, when I heard this comedian relating a funny story about Titus. I suddenly opened my eyes and turned to look in all directions, because I thought he was on the plane playing some kind of game with me."

NO JOKE!!

It wasn't long before it played nationwide, as I received phone calls from relatives and friends in California, Florida and Michigan, as well as the entire Greater-Boston area.

DON'T GO AWAY—IT'S NOT OVER YET

It was 1995 when we received a call from our son, Titus, Jr., an orthopedic surgeon living and practicing in Eden, North Carolina. We were in Florida at our winter hide-a-way, Willoughby Golf and Country Club, in the town of Stewart.

Titus, Jr., said it was important for us to get a flight to North Carolina because he was successful in contacting and convincing **JERRY CLOWER** to perform at the annual Chamber of Commerce Benefit that was sold out.

Our son spoke to Jerry just before the show, told him that I was there, sitting in the front row, and asked if he could do the skit about me. He said, "I don't know if I can remember that far back, but I"ll do something".

Well, he didn't lose a beat as he embellished the original recording for fifteen minutes, and had the standing-room-only audience cheering and applauding continuously, finishing up with something like:

"Y'all thought that Titus Plummeritis was a **FICK-TISH-SHUS** name— well it's not. Heees here in the front row—**STAND UP, TARTUS!!**"

When I stood up, at 5'5", he repeated, **"I SAID STAND UP!!"**

So, I jumped up and stood on my seat, **GAVE A PARATROOPER SALUTE TO JERRY,** and that closed his performance, with a thunderous ovation by, as Jerry would say, "A hootin' and hollarin'" audience.

The Following article and photo by Patty Bournival, appeared in the Salem Observer July 28, 1978, Salem, New hampshire.

Name's hard to forget

by Patty Bournival

PELHAM - Titus Plomaritis is a name that's becoming familiar to residents all over the country.

It seems that the chiropractor with the euphonious name is the subject of a comedy routine being broadcast by country and western radio stations throughout the country.

The album by Jerry Clower is also available to passengers on at least one major airline.

The question, of course, is why Titus Plomaritis.

Well, it all goes back to 1949 when the Lowell High School football star was invited down to Mississippi State University to view the campus as a possible college selection.

While he was there, he joined in with the university's football team at practices. On the last scrimmage of that spring, 50,000 alumnus gathered in the stands to see what prospects looked for the fall season.

For Titus who played in the scrimmage, it was one of those days when nothing could go wrong.

He had an outstanding day with three touchdowns, a field goal and four points after. Clower, who was playing opposite Titus, apparently never forgot the tremendous show that Titus put on that day.

When Clower visited his alma mater in 1976, he told the students of the day when he met his match in Titus Plomaritis.

In the recording that was made from that appearance, Clower says *"One day a fellow walked up. His name was Titus Plummeritis, and he was from up in New England, and he was the runningest man I've ever seen. He would reverse the field sometimes just to show us how he could run through us."*

He continues that just when he had Titus tight around the waist *"he wiggled and went straight up in the air and came down on my back and stomped me and was off. I was lying on the ground,*

beating my fists and hollering, and my teammates said Jerry, chase him? I said, 'Lie still. He'll be back by here in a minute."

Titus, who does not remember Clower, began getting telephone calls and letters shortly after the record was released from old friends and acquaintances who had heard the recording.

He has received letters from over 30 states from colleagues and old football rivals who do a lot of traveling.

Titus guesses that Clower still remembers him because of his play and his unusual name. He admits that he is shocked to think that he is still remembered for that day 29 years after it happened.

"I'm extremely flattered," Titus said.

The Plomaritis family now has four copies of The Ambassador of Goodwill by Jerry Clower. All of the copies were given to them by friends who had heard the album. One copy was a gift from Clower that is autographed with a "God Bless You."

Clower, who spells Titus's name on that album Plummeritis, and Titus have not yet spoken. Both have called the other one twice, but have been unable to make a connection.

Titus, who does not receive any royalties from the album, is anxious to talk with Clower.

He is hoping to get Clower to appear for a Raymond E. Riddick Memorial Scholarship Fund fund raiser.

Titus finds the whole incident unusual, and his family, Rep. Claire, Titus Jr., a medical student at Guadalajara, Mexico, Lyn, a learning disability specialist working on a Navajo reservation in Arizona, Steve, a student at Kirksville (Miss.) College of Osteopathic Medicine, and Diane, a student at Boston College, find the album about their husband and father amusing.

TITUS PLOMARITIS holds his autographed copy of Jerry Clower's album featuring a comedy routine "Titus Plummeritis".

Names hard to forget

When Jerry Clower visited his alma mater on March 15, 1976, he told the students, of the day when he met his match in Titus Plomaritis.

In the live recording made at that appearance, Clower says, "Good gracious alive, that's some kind of sumptin' another—I love un every one of ya. I don't know of any place that I'd rather be, than right here and for me to do a show at Mississippi State University is like throwing a rabbit in a briar patch. I have been here before—I have—I played football at Mississippi State University. Back in—yeah, I remember, back in the spring of '49. We

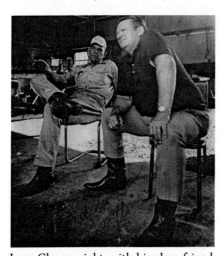

had 13 weeks of spring training an there was a lot of walk-ons and every Saturday there was a big scrimmage. We did the best we could—to hold our-po-sish-ons because there was so many walkin-ons goin out for football— I was afraid they may break my plate and give it to one of them. So I was putting out all I could and one day a fellow walks up. His name was Titus Plummeritis, and he was from up in New England, and that was the runningest thing I have ever seen in all my life. He would reverse the field sometimes just to show us how he could run through us. Jus' getting' it. They pitched the ball to him one time on a quick

Jerry Clower, right, with his close friend, Cary S. Chief Hill as it appears on the back side of his album "The Ambassador of Good Will" recorded live at Humphrey coliseum, Mississippi State University on March 15, 1976

pitch an I wuz playin left defensive tackle—an I busted through an got him around the waist, and commenced to squeezin' him and was gonna take him down to the ground. An about that time he wiggled and went straight up in the air—come down on my back and stomped me and bellied back around to the other side and I'z lying there beating the ground with my fist and hollering, and my teammates— dog go-in said—Jerry, get up an chase him. I said, 'lay still. He'll be back here in a minute.'"

PRESIDENTIAL CAMPAIGN— HIGH SCHOOL that is!

Now, back to Lowell High School, following the Bogalusa Bowl game and just after the Christmas break,1949. That's when Buttsie Correa and a handful of our classmates convinced me to run for president of the senior class.

Buttsie took the lead and was my campaign manager. Remember, that was the pre-television era, so the campaign didn't cost 100 million; actually about five bucks did the trick.

Once elected, it was evident that the senior class officers and my campaign chairman wanted to break from the norm of having the Senior Prom at the Lowell Memorial Auditorium in downtown Lowell. Mr. Brown, our senior class advisor, tried to convince us that it was more prudent and easier to supervise our large senior class of over 600 students at the Auditorium. I guess he didn't realize that's just what we were trying to avoid, more supervision.

As it was, we won out and had the Prom at the Tyngsboro Country Club, just four miles from the high school. Again we broke from the norm and controlled the ticket sale money rather than giving it to Mr. Brown to pay the costs.

We had a great group of classmate volunteers to help with the signs, decorations, band selection, refreshments and everything else needed for a great farewell. They were sure that we spent every dime collected.

HERE COMES THE STATEMENT OF THE CENTURY

I had sights on a petite member of the junior class for my Senior Prom date, Claire "Smokey" Hebert. Although her initial response was **NO**, she was convinced by some of her girlfriends and eventually said she would have to ask her father.

She related the following, "When I asked my dad if I could go to the Senior Prom, he said, 'What's that?'".

She explained that it was a dance that high school seniors had just before graduation, and that she would be with all her friends, would have supervision and would be home right after its conclusion.

He then asked, "Who will you be going with?"

She replied, "Titus Plomaritis."

He asked, "What kind of a name is that?"

She replied, "He's a Greek boy."
He asked, "Aren't there any French boys?"
NOW, Here's what you've been waiting for,

"DAD, I'M ONLY GOING TO THE PROM WITH HIM, NOT MARRYING HIM!!"

Claire Hebert & Titus Plomaritis at Lowell High School Senior Prom May, 1949

The future proved her wrong! December 1, 1951.

CLAIRE A. HEBERT

"Smokey"

89 Aiken Avenue Entered from St. Louis. Activities: National Honor Society. Future: Stenographer. Hobbies: Dancing, bowling, football, swimming, sewing.

OH, OH, I ALMOST FORGOT!!!

My prize photo of Lowell High School's 1949 Year Book, is of our Senior Class Officers with Claire's inscription, who has been and still is my "sweetheart and private secretary" for sixty-three years and counting.

For those of you that cannot read the inscriptions from Claire "Smokey" Hebert to me, please be my guest as I type in bold text.

Top: **With loads of LOVE to my favorite football player, "Titus"**
Below: **"Smokey"**
Bottom: **Claire "Smokey" Hebert Private Secretary to Titus Plomaritis**

From Claire's 1950 Lowell High School Year Book Photo with my evaluations:

Claire "Smokey" Hebert's

Future:

Stenographer—Excellent

Hobbies:

Dancing—my best partner

Bowling—terrible

Football—my best fan

Swimming—total failure

Sewing—outstanding

LOWELL SUN CHARITIES

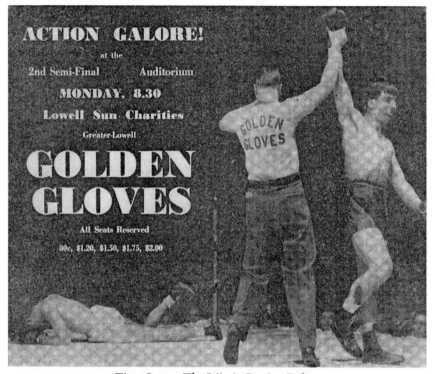

Titus Scores Tko Win in Boxing Debut
Titus Plomaritis, star of the recent undefeated Lowell High School football team, is having his right hand raised by Referee Jimmy McCarron after he floored Eugene Mazza for the fifth time to score a third round TKO victory in his amateur boxing debut during the Golden Gloves 147-pound division at Lowell Memorial Auditorium.

PLOMARITIS ENTERS GOLDEN GLOVES

LOWELL—"The Man of the Hour" in Lowell High's many football conquests in an unbeaten 1948 season is in "the lineup" again, this time in the second of the 1949 Golden Gloves amateur boxing classics under the Lowell Sun Charities auspices.

Titus Plomaritis, whose trusty toe booted many telling points, particularly the unforgettable "point after" that broke a 19-19 tie with rival Lawrence, and gave Lowell an unbeaten season...whose plunge for the tying touchdown and extra point from placement that Thanksgiving morning put Lowell into the Jackson, Mississippi, bowl game against Bogalusa of Louisiana...is entered in the Golden Gloves.

TITUS PLOMARITIS. Sun Staff Photo.

WELTERWEIGHT NOVICE

Plomaritis has been drawn from a record-breaking list of 184 entries to compete in the 147-pound welterweight class in the Novice Division.

How Plomaritis will fare as a noble-hearted novice boxer is in the lap of the gods. But, they have been saying up around the Lowell YMCA, where he does most of his physical training, that he is as handy with the gloves as the next novice—and consequently, he gets the same start in fair competition with other inexperienced novices that all these willing and ambitious youngsters deserve.

Titus makes no claims about himself. He merely sent in an entry blank without accompanying comment. He was, however, taken quite aback when the Sun photographer posed him for an action picture for Sun readers at this stage of the pre-fight period.

His comment then indicated a fine modesty that is characteristic of a true star who doesn't need anything but his own ability to recommend him. Said Titus: "Why my picture in The Sun as a boxer?

You've been publishing pictures of really good boxers all along!" Told that The Sun thought it appropriate that his pre-fight photo be published to give a lot of prospective fans a preview. Titus only added: "That's very nice of everybody. Thank you." And that was all.

The Lowell High star on Coach Ray Riddick's unbeaten, but once-tied, team has been picking up pointers from Roy Andrews and Jimmy Cook, a couple of professional boxers of fine reputation who do a lot of training at the YMCA.

ROOTING FOR TITUS IN GOLDEN GLOVES

By Frank Sargent
Lowell Sun Charities

LOWELL—If you're a real Golden Gloves fan and know all about the all-star array of talent due to sport its wares in the upcoming bouts at Memorial Auditorium, you need read no further. In fact, if you've already got your tickets for Monday's first show we'd prefer you'd quit reading this stuff now.

However, if you don't know the fistic feats which are in store for Golden Gloves fans, continue along, brother, and you'll realize you're in for more than a view of the picturesque architecture which goes with a visit to the Auditorium.

PLOMARITIS TO PUT ON GLOVES

Certainly you all remember **TITUS PLOMARITIS**, the Lowell High gridder with so much dynamite that he personally piled up all 20 points against 19 for Lawrence High on Thanksgiving day.

Well, Titus is going to don the padded mitts and see if he packs any fistic talent to go with his gridiron class.

All Lowell folks will be out to root the little fellow to victory, while

Lawrence rooters will be on hand to see if it is possible to stop the chunky left halfback.

Yeah!, there's a lot of fancy band music, there'll be many well-known celebrities on hand—and once again the usual "refreshments" will be available.

PLOMARITIS IN TKO WIN

By Joe McGarry
Lowell Sun Charities

LOWELL—With 3990 rabid fans looking on, new stars appeared on the fistic horizon last night as 44 boys swept into action in the 22 bout card of The Lowell Sun Charities second preliminary show in the 1949 Golden Gloves tournament at the Memorial Auditorium.

There were many new faces and several old faces in the ring last night as the 1949 amateur boxing classic of New England took up right where it left off last week, and it continued until midnight with the fans tearing down the house as they vented their feelings one way or another on the outcome of fight after fight where a particular favorite was involved.

Just eight of the 22 bouts went the limit and of these three were split decisions.

TITUS COMES THROUGH

Titus Plomaritis, who helped the Lowell High School football team to its undefeated season during the past year, shed the shoulder and hip pads for the padded mittens and stepped into the ring for the first time.

It didn't take long for Titus to get the feel of boxing, for his opponent—Eugene Mazza of Pittsfield—was far from being a soft touch, and for a time he had the former Lowell High halfback in plenty of trouble. But, as was the case, when he tried an off-tackle plunge, he refused to go down and rallied to eventually pull out a TKO win in the third round.

LOCAL BOY GETS BOOED

Plomaritis knocked Mazza down in the first round and again in the second, but he brought a chorus of boos down on his neck in the latter canto when he apparently hit Mazza after the latter's knee touched the canvas, but to veteran fight officials at ringside, this was chalked up to inexperience and over-anxiety, and the entire matter, as far as the officials —and the boys themselves—were concerned, was soon dropped.

In the final round, Plomaritis really got to his opponent, and after dropping Mazza three times, Referee Jimmy McCarron stepped in and halted the proceedings, bringing Plomaritis his first ring victory.

TITUS IN STELLAR PERFORMANCE

By Tom Gallagher
Lowell Sun Charities

LOWELL—A packed house jammed Memorial Auditorium last night for the second preliminary of the 1949 Golden Gloves, sponsored by Lowell Sun Charities.

It was a turn away crowd. As early as 8 p.m., hundreds were lined outside the ticket window, and a detail of police, under the efficient direction of Captain Francis M. O'Loughlin, estimated that more than 1000 were unable to obtain tickets.

When the first pair of fighters entered the ring at 8:30 p.m. there wasn't an unoccupied seat in the house.

The show was easily one of the most scintillating and spectacular since the inception of Golden Gloves' competition here.

THE MOST OUTSTANDING BOUT

Without question, the outstanding bout of the evening was the 147-pound novice between Titus Plomaritis, the All-Scholastic left halfback on Lowell High School's brilliant football team, and Eugene Mazza of Pittsfield.

Titus, making his debut as an amateur boxer, proved that he not only can play football, but can fight as well.

In the third and final round, he flattened his opponent for the fifth time and was awarded the fight on a technical knockout.

However, the bout was anything but one-sided. Titus absorbed a terrific amount of punishment in both the second and third rounds, but his effective counter-punching with a good right hand spelled the difference.

That, and a fighting, competitive heart which he exhibited on many occasions during Lowell High school's 1948 gridiron's season.

TITUS IN KNOCKDOWNS GALORE

Mazza displayed an effective left jab and tagged Titus repeatedly. But Titus kept that right flailing, scoring a knockdown in each of the first two rounds, and three knockdowns in the final round.

No other bout during the evening evoked as much audience reaction.

RETIRES AS UNDEFEATED BOXER

NOTE—This was the one and only bout of Titus Plomaritis' boxing career, as he quickly announced his retirement from the ring to concentrate on his future collegiate and successful football career.

ALSO, he closely followed LHS football coach Ray Riddick's "fatherly" advice to "Get out of boxing before you get killed—and **STICK TO FOOTBALL!!!**"

FIRST ALL-STAR FOOTBALL GAME, 1949

LOWELL—Sharpened by nearly three weeks of intensive training while in residence at Lowell Textile Institute and Phillips-Andover Academy, Greater-Lowell and Greater-Lawrence teams will clash tonight at Lowell Memorial Stadium in the first annual Inter-City All-Star football game.

This championship contest, under the Lowell Sun Charities' auspices, may carve new and ultra-glamorous football history in this part of New England. The program gets underway at 8 P.M., with the kickoff taking place promptly at 8:45.

THE STARTING LINEUPS

GREATER-LOWELL
Pollinger, Keith, LE
Bartis, Nashua, LT
Meehan, Lowell, LG
Sanborn, Lowell, C
Hand, Keith, RG
Carver, Lowell, RT
Lemoine, Lowell, RE
Fallon Lowell, QB
Plomaritis, Lowell, LHB
Finan, Concord, RHB
Swan Lowell, FB

GREATER-LAWRENCE
LE, Gregorawicz, Lawrence
LT, Gaudet, Punchard
LG, Varitimos, Lawrence
C, Tamagnine, Johnson
RG, Langlois, Haverhill
RT, Broderick haverhill
RE, Chetson Punchard
QB, Valhoulle, Haverhill
LHB, Foley, Newburyport
RHB, Mercier, Haverhill
FB, Tyler, Pinkeron

GREATER-LOWELL COACHING STAFF
Ray Riddick—Head Coach—Lowell
Bernie Megin—Assistant Coach—Concord
Ed Murphy—Assistant Coach—Dracut

Al Mangan—Trainer—Lowell
Stan Stoklosa—Manager—Lowell

COMPLETE GREATER-LOWELL ROSTER
LOWELL HIGH—Captain Roger Sanborn, John Meehan, Titus Plomaritis, Bob Swan, Fred Pawlowski, Norm Carver, Jim Fallon, Arthur Lemoine, John Garland, Joe Connors.
KEITH ACADEMY—Ed Hansbury, Paul Hand, George Pollinger, Gus McGuire, John Walsh.
DRACUT—Jim Phillips, Milt Monoxoles, Jim Dadoly, Gerry Pednault.
CHELMSFORD—Ed Bishop, Warren McHugh.
CONCORD—John Wetherbee, Richard Finan, Joe Callahan, Jim Alexander.
NASHUA—Bob Bartis.
WILMINGTON—Art Spear, Bill Chisholm.
TEWKSBURY—Dick Patten.
BILLERICA (HOWE HIGH)—Frank Luciano, George Gracie.
AYER—Phil Dynice.
BURLINGTON—Dick Garibotto.

PICOGRAPHIES

Titus Plomaritis
Lowell High School

LEFT HALFBACK

Reams could be written about "Titko", one of the most colorful and

accomplished players to come out of Lowell High in some time. Last year he was named to every Boston newspaper's All-Star teams, the North Shore All-Star team, and the All-Star teams of radio's Bump Hadley and Bob Lester.

President of his senior class, yearbook representative, honor roll student, veteran of 15 months service in the U.S. Army Paratroopers and ex-Golden Gloves boxer with a knockout victory.

His list of football feats is long. Last fall he scored all 20 points against Lawrence, kicked a point-after in the North Shore All-Star game, kicked a 38-yard point-after following three penalties that had forced Lowell back, and booted a 70-yard kickoff against Haverhill.

Son of Demosthenis Plomaritis, 29 Johnson Street, Lowell, he will enter Boston University in the fall.

He plans to get married after graduation, wants to be a physical education teacher, and his hobbies are repairing cars and swimming.

LOWELL SQUAD TRIUMPHS IN FIRST ALL-STAR GAME, GREATER-LAWRENCE BOWS, 6-0

PLOMARITIS SCORES TOUCHDOWN IN FINAL QUARTER

Friday, August 26, 1949

LOWELL—A hard-charging Greater-Lowell All-Star team edged out a 6-0 victory over a fighting Greater-Lawrence All-Star squad in the inaugural football extravaganza, sponsored by The Lowell Sun Charities, witnessed by a crowd of over 13,000 under the lights here at the Stadium last night.

PLOMARITIS STARS

From start to finish it was anybody's ball game, and if a little guy named Titus Plomaritis hadn't been around the star-studded attraction could have easily ended in a 0-0 stalemate.

It was Plomaritis, the former Lowell High All-Scholastic star who wears a set of jet-propelled legs, who accounted for the 6-0 edge that Greater-Lowell needed to provide the victory.

The big six points were collected just after the start of the fourth quarter when Plomaritis scooted off his right end and pounded his way into the end zone from nine yards away.

Fact of the matter is, that just about everyone on the Greater-Lawrence eleven knew that the Greek-American boy would be the ball-carrier when the chips were down, but yet they were helpless as he went circling around his right end to pay-dirt.

The downriver boys did try to rally and they came close to either gaining a tie, or a possible win, keeping the crowd on its toes and howling, before time ran out.

PLOMARITIS VOTED OUTSTANDING PLAYER

As the result of a poll of members of the press in attendance at last night's All-Star game at the Lowell Stadium, Greater-Lowell's Titus Plomaritis was chosen as the Outstanding Player of the contest.

As a result, the former Lowell High standout was the recipient of the first annual Lowell Sun Charities' Outstanding Player trophy.

There were 13 members of the press who voted, and 10 cast their ballots for Plomaritis, two voted for his teammate and end Arthur Lemoine and one ballot went to Greater-Lawrence tackle Dan Broderick.

KING AND QUEEN OF ALL-STAR GAME

Shown at left are the top performers and trophy winners in their respective fields of the first annual Lowell Sun Charities All-Star football game played at Lowell Memorial Stadium. The little lady is Carol Ann Thompson, Nashua, Queen of the All-Starettes, and with her is Titus Plomaritis, Lowell, who easily snared the award for the game's most valuable player.

PLOMARITIS, TELEPHONITIS BIG FACTOR IN ALL-STAR FOOTBALL VICTORY

By Frank Sargent
Lowell Sun Sports Editor

LOWELL—Plomaritis and telephonics were major factors in the Stadium's Lowell Sun Charities All-Star grid carnival last night.

The former was the little fellow with "42" on his back, who ran like the seat of his pants was on fire. The latter was what the rival assistant coaches were suffering from as a result of a handy phone connection between benches and press box.

Plomaritis kicked...Plomaritis passed...Plomaritis ran...Plomaritis blocked...and Plomaritis even tried to convert the point-after.

The powerful voice of Arthur Flynn, floating out over the waves of the public address system seemed strange if it didn't have Plomaritis mentioned once or twice in each sentence. At one time it seemed to say **"PLOMARITIS HANDS OFF TO PLOMARITIS, TACKLED BY PLOMARITIS!!"**

Of course, these weren't the words, but the little guy sure starred!!

BOSTON UNIVERSITY FOOTBALL

In the Mud at Philly
From left: Titus Plomaritis, Arnold Berg, Harry Agganis and Anthony Rando. B.U. lost to Villanova, 51-6 at Shibe Park, Philadelphia, PA., Nov. 22, 1952. Photo from Boston University 1953 Yearbook

PLOMARITIS BUOYS B.U's HOPES

September 13, 1949—Three members of the Boston University football coaching staff were chatting before a recent practice period at Nickerson Field in Weston.

"Now that Titus Plomaritis is here, your freshmen hadn't ought to lose a game." said one mentor to Silvia Cella, the new yearling coach.

Cella, a former B.U. star, smiled and said: "Could be."

Could be, indeed. Plomaritis, the Lowell lad with the rhyming name, is an asset to any outfit, for he was one of the greatest schoolboy halfbacks ever seen in this section.

He's diminutive, but dynamic. His teammates kid him because he has to sit on a pillow while eating in order to reach the table, but the little lad is a big gun in action.

WAS A PARATROOPER

"Yes, I weigh 165." he told us, which seems surprising, unless you observe the broad shoulders and well-developed muscles. "I'm 20, and standing five-feet-five."

Titus was selected as left halfback on the Hearst All-Scholastic football team last year. As a senior at Lowell High, he made 23 conversions, and also kicked two field goals. In addition to these feats, he carried the ball well enough to score a total of 80 points during the season.

In 1947, this athlete served as a Paratrooper in Japan, where he played on a headquarters team, making 26 conversions and three field goals.

Such a placekicking specialist is welcome to any coach these days, when the art seems to be somewhat neglected among colleges.

Plomaritis passes and runs with agility, too. He likes the single wing, which is employed by Coach Buff Donelli.

For hobbies, Titus repairs old autos and swims. His favorite food is lamb, prepared "Greek style".

"I'm taking a physical education course," he stated. "I hope to get a coaching job after graduation."

THE MAN WITH THE MUSICAL NAME

BOSTON—The most popular and publicized of the freshman football prospects at Boston University is left halfback Titus Plomaritis—"the man with the musical name"—from Lowell.

Standing only 5 foot 5 inches, Titus is an extremely deceptive and tricky broken field runner.

Pairing with him at halfback is George Schultz of Worcester, who is both big and fast. At fullback is "Slamming" Sammy Pino, the Somerville battering ram.

PLOMARITIS STARS IN B.U. FROSH WIN

BOSTON—November 5, 1949—Titus Plomaritis, former Lowell High star, connected for two perfect placements yesterday as the Boston University freshman team defeated Marianapolis Academy, 14-6, at Nickerson Field. In winning the game, the B.U. frosh overcame a 6-0 lead that Marianapolis held going into the second half.

The home team came back to score a touchdown in the third quarter, and then Titus kicked the point-after to put B.U. in front to stay.

WAITING FOR TITUS WITH OPEN ARMS

By Joe McGarry
December 1, 1949

TITUS PLOMARITIS seems destined to make the big time at B.U. in a big way, according to the report given first hand by four Terrier regulars at the Boston University Club meeting last night.

The quartet—Bob Whalen, Charlie Kent, Red Czarnota and Dick Fecteau—were unanimous in their praise of the diminutive scatback who brought many a fan to his feet while wearing the Red and Gray uniform at Lowell High School.

Czarnota was very emphatic in predicting that Titus would go a long way. "Although he's small, he can really move in the field," said Czarnota."Why, in fact the first time he scrimmaged against the varsity, he broke away for 80 yards on the first play."

"What did Buff (Head Coach Donelli) say to that?" he was asked.

"Oh, he just turned around and smiled at me" was the reply.

But, that generally is the feeling of the players themselves in regards to the prospects of the local hero, who just a year ago was sparking Coach Riddick's club to its first undefeated season.

TERRIERS RELYING HEAVILY ON SOPHOMORE GRIDDERS

BOSTON—Sophomores have been delegated to play a major part in the gridiron fortunes of Boston University this year, as the Terriers get set to launch their 1950 season against Duquesne at Pitt Stadium on Saturday.

Three sophomores will be in the B.U. starting lineup—right guard Len D'Errico, left guard Gerry Keane and right end Bob Capuano.

A trio of sophomores on a starting club is more than the usual quota. But Buff Donelli, beginning his fourth year as B.U. head coach, believes in starting them in right away, as long as they possess ability.

Not among the starters are sophomores Sam Pino, George Schultz, Nils Strom, Bob Gagnon, Bob Doblas, John Hurstak and Titus Plomaritis.

However, Plomaritis has been assigned the job as kicking extra points and field goals. Besides that, the former Golden Glover from Lowell is **THE SHIFTIEST BACK ON THE TEAM.**

MOVING UP AS A SOPHOMORE

1950—This was my sophomore year at B.U. and I had made great progress moving up to the second LHB spot on the varsity behind Bobby Whalen, our senior all conference Left Half Back.

Harry was my biggest booster, primarily because when he threw a pass in my direction I'd go after it like going after my Shirley Temple Oatmeal Dish. I almost always caught up to his errant passes. (South Common discipline all over again)

You must understand that in that era, freshmen were not eligible to play varsity football. Our freshman team ran the upcoming opponent's plays against the varsity and I was usually assigned the jersey of their running back. Whenever I made a good play against the varsity, Harry would tap the coach on the shoulder with a grin on his face.

As for our freshman team, I was the leading scorer, and had 21 consecutive PAT's.

DONELLI ASSIGNS PLOMARITIS AS TERRIERS' PLACE KICKER

BOSTON— September 18, 1950—Titus Plomaritis, the former Lowell High footballer and Golden Glover, has been assigned the kicking duties at Boston University by coach Buff Donelli.

The 5'5" sophomore halfback did all the extra-point kicking for the successful freshman team last fall, as well as in high school.

It was nothing for the elusive Greek boy to score a touchdown, then drop back and boot the ball between the uprights.

"He has been working very hard at it," said Donelli, "and I hope he gets many opportunities once the season starts. After all, the more chances he gets, means the more touchdowns we score."

Plomaritis has a real job ahead of him trying to win a regular berth in the Terriers' starting backfield. He is a left halfback, and all he has to do is beat out Bobby Whalen, a unanimous All-New England choice last year, and Charlie Hanson, one of the top prospects ever to show up at Nickerson Field.

But even with that, Titus is expected to see a lot of service and is sure to win the hearts of the fans who flock to Fenway Park during the fall.

TITUS RETURNS TO LOWELL STADIUM

Circa November, 1950

LOWELL—It seemed like old times to see **TITUS PLOMARITIS** whipping around the Stadium greensway during yesterday's Lowell High workout.

Titus, present placekicking specialist at Boston University, took a day off from his Hub chores to visit the Lowell camp and give some of Ray Riddick's lads a few pointers in the art of putting the ball between the uprights.

There isn't a man better qualified for the job, for the diminutive lad who wrote football history here a couple of years ago is certainly a perfectionist in this capacity.

Right now, the main aim of the Red and Gray gridders is to get in shape for the crucial test with Lawrence on Thanksgiving Day, and realizing that this extra point business may mean a lot. Titus took some time in instructing the boys in this art.

As he waltzed around the Stadium surface, it looked like a long lost son returning to the fold.

"This certainly feels great," said the B.U. star as he placed a boot cleanly between the uprights, "and running around here makes me feel right at home again."

Not many fans who were in the stands at Lawrence two years ago will forget the performance turned in by this lad, who personally accounted for all the points as he paced Lowell to that memorable 20-19 victory which climaxed the first undefeated season—and a bowl game appearance—in the history of the school.

PERFECT IN VARSITY DEBUT AT PITTSBURGH

PITTSBURGH, PA. October 8, 1950—Quarterback Bill Pavlikowski proved an apt successor to All-American Harry Agganis, hitting 12 of 20 passes and a touchdown toss, while **TITUS PLOMARITIS** added three clutch points as they led Boston University to a 21-7 victory over Duquesne before 12,000 fans here at Pitt Stadium yesterday.

Plomaritis, a sophomore from Lowell, made his varsity debut for Coach Buff Donelli's Terriers by being perfect as the placekicker, connecting on all three of his point-after attempts.

TITUS KICKS THREE MORE

BOSTON—A desperation 30-yard pass with 30 seconds remaining in the game gave St. Bonaventure a 25-21 uphill victory over favored, but unlucky Boston University at Fenway Park last night.

The pass, from Ted Marchibroda to Stan Zajdei, left 12,135 fans frustrated and erased the great ball carrying of Chuck Hanson, who scored all the Terriers' touchdowns on runs of 80, 28 and 60 yards.

Lowell native **TITUS PLOMARITIS** connected with all three point-after kicks for B.U. to maintain his perfect average and now has six conversions in as many attempts.

TITUS' FIELD GOAL SCALPS INDIANS, 16-14

BOSTON- November, 5, 1950—A fourth period field goal by **TITUS PLOMARITIS,** Boston University's sophomore kicking specialist, gave the Terriers a 16-14 win yesterday over a rugged William and Mary eleven on the soggy turf of Fenway Park.

Rain before game-time cut the attendance to a slim 3606—the smallest crowd to see a major college football game here this season.

Most of the fireworks came in the fourth quarter, which opened with B.U. trailing the Indians, 7-6. On the first play of the quarter, the Terriers' stocky fullback, Sam Pino, broke through for a 75-yard touchdown sprint, followed by a Plomaritis PAT kick.

The Terriers increased their margin with five minutes left to play, when their kicker with the rhyming name set one between the uprights from the 8-yard line—which eventually proved to be the margin of victory—to make the score 16-7.

The visiting William and Mary team put on a sparkling passing game in the waning moments to make it close, pushing over a touchdown, but time ran out before the Indians could get the ball again

TITUS NOW BITIS

BOSTON—There are all kinds of personal fouls, but the most unusual of the year occurred at Fenway Park yesterday when the foul turned out to be a bite just before the first half ended.

Between halves, Coach Buff Donelli of Boston University said to Titus Plomaritis: "What the devil did you do to get a 15-yard penalty?"

"I couldn't help it, coach," answered Titus. "Some guy tackled me and kept rubbing his hand over my mouth—I just couldn't resist the temptation, **SO I BIT HIM."**

NICKNAMES FOR THE TWO B.U. HEROES

After the Terriers' two-point win over William and Mary at rain-drenched Fenway Park, someone suggested that the lyrics of the new Terrier fight song include "Slam, bam, give it to Sam (Pino),"—with perhaps the melodious monicker of **"TITUS PLOMARITIS REFRAIN IN THE RAIN."**

The two sophomore buddies gave the soggy fans a fourth quarter demonstration of fighting spirit which will long be remembered.

Slamming' Sam Pino, the 190-pound fullback, rumbled 75 yards for a go-ahead touchdown, while Plomaritis—a 165-pound kicking specialist—clinched the contest with an 18-yard field goal. The chunky Lowell youngster's successful kick, which came with 4:56 left in the game, transformed him from "goat" to hero, as he earlier missed several placekicks in the rain, which ruined his season's record. Up to yesterday, he had eight straight conversions to his credit. But, he came through in the clutch when it counted to sew up the B.U. win.

MORE PRAISE HEAPED ON TITUS

LOWELL—We've got to doff the old fedora to **TITUS PLOMARITIS,** the hydrant-sized star of the 1948 Lowell High football club, who place-kicked the Boston University team to a 16-14 win over William and Mary at Fenway Park yesterday.

The fellow is just a little guy, but he's got it when the chips are down. Titus is always best under pressure—as those of us who took in the Lowell-Lawrence game of 1948 will recall. That was the game where he scored all the points (20-19 win) and was the leading light in keeping the LHS club unbeaten.

He's just a sophomore at B.U. and is considered a top asset by Coach Buff Donelli.

B.U. SCUTTLES MARINES, 16-0

BOSTON—November 8, 1950—Powered by fullback Johnny Kastan's two touchdowns and 105 yards running, Boston University out-battled Camp Lejeune's dogged Marines for a 16-0 victory before a slim crowd of 5000 here at Fenway Park yesterday

The Marines dismayed their few supporters by fumbling three times, each near the B.U. goal line.

Given a second try because Camp Lejeune was offside, **TITUS PLOMARITIS** booted a 19-yard field goal, after missing from the 24, in the third period.

PLOMARITIS READY AGAIN

BOSTON—With the cast on his fractured left wrist removed earlier this week, **TITUS PLOMARITIS** of Lowell, clever running back and placekicking expert, took part in his first regular practice with the Boston University grid squad yesterday at Nickerson Field as the Terriers prepared for a clash with N.Y.U. tomorrow.

A former Lowell High star and All-Scholastic, Plomaritis has been keeping up with his placekicking and has entered games to kick extra points since the William and Mary tilt, when the fracture was sustained.

PLOMARITIS TO BEAR WATCHING

November 10, 1950—For the first time this year, Boston University will be taking to the gridiron a prohibitive favorite, to the expense of New York University.

The game is expected to give B.U. coach Buff Donelli a chance to employ some of his promising sophomores whom he hadn't been able to use earlier.

The boy who will bear watching is Titus Plomaritis, the ex-Lowell High Golden Glover, whose field goal snapped a three-game losing streak for B.U. against William and Mary last week.

The 5'5" dynamo is the shiftiest back on the team, and he is looked upon as a future star at B.U., and tomorrow he should get his first varsity chance.

BOSTON UNIV. ROUTS NYU, 41-13; PLOMARITIS KICKS FIVE POINTS-AFTER

BOSTON—November 11, 1950—Despite three costly fumbles, Boston University's Terriers overpowered a weaker, though well-drilled, New York University football team, 41-13, today as a small audience of 3724 shivered at Fenway Park.

Former Lowell High standout Titus Plomaritis was one of B.U.'s stars of the day as he was successful on five conversion kicks during the rout.

DAD MADE B.U. GRIDDER PAY
WAY AT LOWELL HIGH

By Tom Monahan
(Circa 1949-50)

The ordinary high school star who advances to college football often is awed by the hard work ahead, but not **TITUS PLOMARITIS** of Lowell.

Instead, Boston University's fireplug freshman halfback with the euphonious name currently is congratulating himself on catching the gravy train. For the ordinary high school star may play football while working his way through college, but Titus had to work his way through high school so that he could play football.

Not only that, but he first had to deceive his parents and then join the Army so that he might play a game he learned to love, and at the same time assure himself an education.

DAD FELT FOOTBALL WAS WASTE OF TIME

According to Titus, it all goes back to a **"KIND OF AN OLD-FASHIONED FATHER."**—For Pa Plomaritis, born in Greece and brought up in Old Country tradition, felt not only that football was unimportant, but a waste of time.

"I disagreed though," relates Titus. "So in my freshman year (at Lowell High) I decided I was going to play football anyway."

Just what things Titus doesn't reveal. But one of them was the item that Lowell had lost 19 games in a row and there was a big fuss about the coaching situation. At that time, older brother George, who now is a teammate at B.U., came up with an idea.

"I played the first five games of my sophomore year," recalls Titus, "then George talked me into joining the Army. George has the brains in the family, I guess, but he figured we could join the Army and get in on the G.I. Bill of Rights and get to college, so I went with him. We wound up in the Paratroops and spent some time in Japan. Then, in 1948, we were back home again."

RETURNING TO HIGH SCHOOL

It turns out that while he was in the Army he had gone to school and studied, giving him the credit of one year of high school that he had missed. He figured that he needed the fourth year of high school, though. And, besides, he was still **UNDER THE AGE LIMIT FOR HIGH SCHOOL FOOTBALL!!**

George, on the other hand, also had a year of high school left, but he was just over the Bay State age limit. So, George took himself to Maine and Biddeford High, where he finished his high school credits and won All-State rating as a halfback.

"My father was still against playing football," continues Titus. "He used to say: 'Football, football. You can't eat a football!' So, the only way I could play was to get a job and pay for my room and board. I wanted to play football, so I got a job."

THE JOB ACTUALLY was two jobs. Every day, after football practice, he worked in a shoe shine parlor, polishing shoes of his Lowell fans, and on Saturdays he worked as a soda jerk in a local restaurant.

EVERY THING TURNS OUT SWELL

"My father still didn't like football," reminisces Titus, "but he couldn't say much. I was paying for my room and board, and George was, of course, up in Biddeford doing the same thing."

Wasn't it kind of tough to be tripling up on scholastic work his football and his jobs?

"YOU CAN SAY THAT AGAIN," murmurs Titus.

Of course, at Boston University, Titus doesn't have to work after school. The G.I. Bill takes care of his education and gives him a monthly allotment. So, it's just playing football and studying with duties showing movies to the Nursing School via the Visual Aid Department.

And, how about Pa Plomaritis? How does he feel about things now?

"OH, HE THINKS IT'S SWELL NOW," grins Titus, "although he never went to a football game. Everything is okay now, Why not? This is the best University in the world, and this is the best football team in the country!!"

WEDDING BELLS AT B.U.

Marco Landon, an outstanding end, was the Best Man at my wedding to **CLAIRE HEBERT**, on December 1,1951, and all the other ushers in our wedding party were also members of my Boston University football team.

I received a lot of flack from the coaches during the following spring practice, as Head Coach Buff Donelli was of the premise that by getting married, I would lose a step in my quickness, which meant that I had to work twice as hard to prove myself going into my senior year.

SIDE NOTE: I remember my bride coming up to Peterborough, N.H., our pre-season football training site, one evening with her cousin, our designated look-out guard, while we made whoopee in the back seat of the car. If Coach Buff ever caught me I probably would have lost my scholarship. **AH!! SHE'S WORTH IT!!**

TITUS—FORGOTTEN MAN OF B.U.FOOTBALL

September, 1952—The forgotten man on the Boston University football team may wind up as a starter this fall when the Terriers tackle their toughest slate in history.

TITUS PLOMARITIS, the 5'5" dynamo from Lowell, has laid claim to the No. 1 left halfback berth by his outstanding play in spring drills.

The former paratrooper was one of the best football players ever produced at Lowell High.

As a freshman, he was a starter. But when he moved up to the varsity as a sophomore, he had to play behind Bob Whalen. Last year, he had to buck another great player, Lindy Hanson.

In the pre-season scrimmages, Titus was terrific. It was assured he would see a lot of service even though he would be an understudy to Hanson. But he broke his wrist and fell way behind.

He is determined to make this his big season.

He is the shiftiest runner at Nickerson Field, being extremely difficult to pin down in the open field. He has all the poise of a seasoned veteran, and despite his size, does a good job on defense.

PLOMARITIS will have keen competition from Archie Cataldo, Billy Taylor, Don DeFeudis and Joe Terrasi.

PERFECT NIGHT AT SYRACUSE

SYRACUSE, N.Y.— September 27, 1952—Titus Plomaritis, former Lowell High All-Scholastic grid star, place kicked all three extra points for Boston University here last night.

However, the visiting Terriers were whipped by the favorite Syracuse University team, 34-21.

Plomaritis had one good kick nullified because of a penalty, but the next went over perfectly for three straight.

FIRST VARSITY START AT LEFT HALFBACK

November 15, 1952—**TITUS PLOMARITIS**, one-time Lowell All-Scholastic standout and present Boston University senior, will make his first varsity start for the Terriers in their farewell Fenway Park appearance of the football season against New York University this afternoon.

Nov. 15, 1952 Boston University Vs. NYU. Titus was appointed Game Captain By Head Coach Aldo "Buff" Donelli and presented with the game ball as he scored a touchdown and kicked two PAT's resulting in a 14-7 victory.

Titus, whose previous efforts mainly have been confined to placekicking specialties, was named yesterday by Coach Buff Donelli to the left halfback assignment left open earlier in the week when Don DeFeudis was shifted to the troublesome fullback berth.

TITUS' DAY — Plomaritus circles NYU end and recovers
fumble

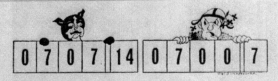

| 0 | 7 | 0 | 7 | 14 | 0 | 7 | 0 | 0 | 7 |

Saturday, November 15　　　　　**At Fenway Park**

Terrier Strategy Near Tragedy

With Agganis still watching from the sidelines, the
Terriers had to rally for a last-period touchdown to edge
spirited New York University. Coach Donelli's fourth-
quarter strategy almost cost the Scarlet and White the
win over the once-shrinking Violets.

Game captain Plomaritus kicked a 14-yard field goal
with only three minutes remaining, but an offside penalty against the Violets gave the Terriers the choice of a
first down at the one. Accepting the penalty, the Terriers
were immediately penalized 15 yards for an illegal play.

Lavery's circus catch of an O'Connell pass brought
the ball back to the one, from where Moriello bulled
over. Early in the second quarter the Terriers marched
82 yards for a TD, Plomaritus scoring from the 15.
NYU's touchdown was the result of a 55-yard aerial
from quarterback Ray Cadieux to end George Beschner.

PLOMARITIS SPARKLES IN 14-7 B.U. WIN

BOSTON—TITUS PLOMARITIS, a senior kicking specialist making his first start of the season at left halfback, accounted for eight points in Boston University's 14-7 victory over New York University here at Fenway Park last night. In the second quarter, B.U. climaxed a 15-play, 83-yard drive with Plomaritis sweeping 15 yards for a touchdown, and then he followed it up by booting the conversion.

The Terriers, playing without their triple threat quarterback, Harry Agganis, found themselves tied, 7-7, with the visiting N.Y.U. Violets late in the fourth quarter, when B.U. pushed across the winning touchdown on a one-yard line buck by Mario Moriello. A 15-yard Phil O'Connell to end Tom Lavery pass play set up the score.

Plomaritis followed by kicking his 13th conversion in 17 tries this season.

100-YARD GAME IN THE PENNSYLVANIA MUD

The setting for the worst football game in the Harry Agganis era at Boston University was a 51-6 drubbing by Villanova at rainy Shibe Park in Philadelphia, on November 22, 1952.

We had heavy rain for two days prior to the game and a steady rain fell throughout the game. Harry was nursing a bad cold and a shoulder injury, so Coach Donelli decided to install a special offense specifically for this game. He wanted to protect our star quarterback who only saw limited action from any further injury.

This new offense was a form of a single wing, with the ball coming directly to me from the center, only about three yards deep. We used this formation for about seven out of ten plays. I would make a complete pivot with the ball in hand and either pitch it with my back to the defense or complete the pivot and keep it following my big tackle, Don Fraser from Somerville, Mass., for a short gain in the mud.

It turned out to be **THE ONE AND ONLY 100-YARD GAME OF MY VARSITY CAREER.**

Villanova was a heavy favorite as it was. However, with my four-yard touchdown run in the first quarter we had the score tied at 6-6 going into the half. But, they were too strong and kind of gave us a real good licking in the second half, outscoring us 45-0 over the way.

NAME SPELLING FINALLY CORRECTED

A Boston sportswriter had a very interesting visit from a young B.U. athlete yesterday.

Ever since his schoolboy days at Lowell High, the writers had trouble with the spelling of his name. Once and for all, on the authority of the young man himself, his name is **TITUS PLOMARITIS.**

THE UNFORGETTABLE
HARRY AGGANIS

The late Harry Agganis was the most outstanding athlete I ever had the privilege of knowing, and to have him as a friend and teammate is beyond belief.

Harry's accomplishments in football and baseball at Boston University are in the history books, which made him a **"HALL of FAME"** phenom, and I will attempt to relate a few incidents that occurred behind the scenes that will further exemplify his kind and unselfish demeanor.

Look closely under Harry's right knee, to find me, yep, misspelled again, often referred to as the "Silver Greek" because Harry was always called the "Golden Greek".

BECOMING A TENNIS WHIZ

This setting was our pre-season football camp at Peterborough, N.H. At the end of each day we had a cool-down period of about one hour when we were allowed to swim, play horseshoes or just lie down and rest our exhausted legs from double sessions.

JOHN TONER, who was our team captain the previous season, was one of the assistant coaches and also served as B.U.'s tennis and golf coach. Coach Toner brought a bag of tennis balls and a few tennis racquets to camp and he commenced to give us just a few basics of service and volleying.

Harry never held a tennis racquet in his hands before this camp, and I watched in amazement as within two weeks time he was giving Coach Toner a head-to-head tennis match just like you would watch at Wimbledon.

HARRY TEACHES THE COACHES

Our mode of transportation at that time was with Mohawk Airlines. We would travel in two prop planes with a fairly even split division of players and coaches—remember, that was the pre-jet era.

On many occasions as we were airborne, traveling to Miami, California or to one of our distant opponents, it was a common sight to watch Head Coach **BUFF DONELLI** and Backfield Coach **ED DONNELLY** sitting with Harry and **GEORGE SALIMA**—our All-American end—designing special audible plays for that particular upcoming game. They used sugar lumps on a small table as a means of positioning the defensive players, and what options Harry and George would have on certain downs. Well, nine out of ten times it was Coach Buff agreeing with Harry's views.

Titus and Team-mates: left to right—George Salima, Titus and Gerald Keane.

Harry was way ahead of his time, as he was actually calling automatics (changing the plays at the line of scrimmage) long before it became popular in the Big Leagues for players like Tom Brady and Peyton Manning, as an example.

Left to Right: Harry Agganis, Mario Moriello, Titus Plomaritis and Lenny D'Errico.

BEGGING OFF THE LIMO

Another reflection of Harry's humbleness is when we landed on foreign soil, like the Miami or Los Angeles airports.

There would usually be a limousine waiting there, with one of Boston University's **"GREEK HIGH ROLLERS"** to whisk him off independently.

I was standing directly next to him one time when he politely begged off, with a believable excuse like, "I'm sorry to disappoint you, but we have an important team meeting tonight and then an early curfew."

THE GREEK CONNECTION

Another memory of **HARRY AGGANIS** is from the summer of 1949, after the Lowell Sun Charity All-Star game.

Harry congratulated me and stated that I played well and deserved the MVP award. He was with **ED DONNELLY**, one of the Boston University assistant coaches, and he related that he heard I was still considering Mississippi State University, but he came to assure me that B.U. would be a better fit.

Harry also mentioned two things that always stuck in my memory bank. First, how he decided to go to B.U. which would also apply to me, by playing close to home, where I would eventually settle down and start a business, which would be beneficial with my name recognition.

Second, Boston University had embellished its football schedule and would become a national contender.

Thus, we definably went down in history as the "**GREEK CONNECTION**".

MY FIRST NEWS OF HARRY'S DEATH

Whenever I hear the name "Harry", it reminds me of **HARRY AGGANIS,** my teammate and friend at Boston University.

The memory of Harry's death will always remain with me. Claire, Titus Jr. and I were returning to Lowell, from Burbank, California in late June, 1955, when the news come over the radio.

We were so devastated that we had to pull over to the side of the road. Literally in shock, we found ourselves crying in disbelief. It must have been a good thirty minutes before we were able to continue on our journey home, for the birth of our second child, Lyn, on August 26, 1955.

THE BIOGRAPHY OF A LEGEND

By George Sullivan
Boston Herald Traveler

HARRY AGGANIS was born on April 20, 1929, at his lifetime home in West Lynn, Mass., the seventh and last child of Greek immigrants.

He became a high school legend when he led **LYNN CLASSICAL HIGH** to an overall 30-4-1 record in three seasons, completing 326 of 502 passes for 4149 yards and 48 touchdowns, scoring 24 more TD's himself, in addition to kicking 39 extra points.

Over 20,000 fans would be overflowing Lynn's famous Manning Bowl week after week to watch him—so popular that some games even were carried on the budding new means, television.

Remarkably, while still a schoolboy, he was playing football in Miami's Orange Bowl, and baseball in New York's Polo Grounds, Chicago's Wrigley Field and Boston's Braves Field and Fenway Park.

After leading Classical during his junior season to an 11-0-1 record (29 TD passes) and the national championship, Tennessee University Coach **GEN. BOB NEYLAND** said "He could step into any college backfield right now." Then, as a senior and captain of the All-American schoolboy team, famed Notre Dame Coach, **FRANK LEAHY**, labeled him "the finest prospect I've ever seen."

At least 67 colleges sought him and scouts camped on his doorstep, as he had to sneak in the back door for supper.

THE BIG DECISION—BOSTON UNIVERSITY

Why he decided to attend Boston University? The reasons were: because he didn't want to leave his widowed mother, because he wanted to play for nobody else but **COACH BUFF DONELLI**—and because he just plain liked the institution.

In Harry's sophomore year he led the Terriers to six straight wins, before losing to powerhouse Maryland, 7-6, during the Terrapins' bowl season. He set three B.U. team records that season: touchdown passes in a game (4), TD passes in a season (15) and punting average (46.5 yards).

He was reluctant to put his name in the NCAA record books, as he was within eight TD passes of the mark with four games to go. Coach Donelli told him "You can beat the record," but Harry replied: "Who wants records? Let's win games." And Donelli mused: "Sometimes I wonder who's the coach and who's the player."

A TRUE ALL-AMERICAN

Harry Agganis, a remarkable quadruple threat, was a 50 minutes player, calling both offensive and defensive signals—quarterback on offense, safetyman on defense, punter and placekicker (before **TITUS PLOMARITIS** arrived), for both kickoffs and **PAT's**.

He was an old-fashioned legitimate All-American, becoming the cover boy of national magazines and was the subject of three full-length features in the prestigious **SPORT MAGAZINE**.

Harry was activated in the U.S. Marine Corps Reserve during the Korean War buildup just before the 1950 season, and he served a year.

FORSAKING THE NFL AND TURNING TO BASEBALL

Harry was the Cleveland Browns' No. 1 draft choice as a junior, when the famed Browns' coach and founder, **PAUL BROWN**, called him "the man who will succeed Hall of Fame Q.B. Otto Graham."

Nicknamed **"THE GOLDEN GREEK"**, Harry eventually turned down a $50,000 offer from the Browns, and almost sure stardom in the sport he loved, instead turning to baseball and signing for less money ($40,000) with the Boston Red Sox. He batted an even .300 in two seasons at B.U.

Harry left B.U. holding eight university football records, and he concluded his gridiron career with a great performance in the 1953 Senior Bowl Game at Mobile, Alabama. Both his high school and college retired his **NUMBER 33 JERSEY**—long before he died.

Although his education was twice interrupted by the service, he returned during the baseball off-season to study, and he won his degree in June, 1954, rushing up Commonwealth Avenue to the commencement after a Sunday game at Fenway Park.

Harry was able to play two seasons with the Red Sox, with a career batting average of .261 and a slugging mark of .404, as the starting first baseman for the Sox. In 1954 he collected 109 hits, belted 11 homers and had 57 RBI over 132 games.

He managed to play in 25 games during the fatal 1955 season and was batting a hefty .313—**WHEN TRAGEDY STRUCK**.

THE WORLD IN MOURNING

The great athlete was stricken by virus pneumonia in May, 1955, and then again less than a month later while on a road trip. He appeared to be recovering, only to die suddenly and almost unbelievably of a massive pulmonary embolism on June 27 at Sancta Marie Hospital in Cambridge.

Flags were flown at half-mast, newspapers printed editorials and congressmen issued tributes from the Capitol floor. Nearly 30,000 people, including governors, consuls, educators and the biggest names in sports, filed past the alter at St. George Greek Orthodox Church in Lynn, as his body lay in state. Over 20,000 lined the mile-and-half cortege route to Pine Grove, a cemetery on a hillside overlooking the Manning Bowl.

Over 400 churches in North and South America held memorial

services—an honor customarily reserved for Greek royalty and statesmen. A Lynn square, a concrete athlete stadium at Camp Lejeune, N.C., a portrait in Baseball's Hall of Fame at Cooperstown, N.Y., and a Memorial Scholarship Foundation—all carry the name of Harry Agganis, who was a special legend.

SECTION THREE

RAY RIDDICK

MY COACH

MY PATIENT

MY FRIEND

March of 1948 was the time in my life when I returned to Lowell High to complete my high school education and try out for the football team under Coach Raymond E. Riddick.

Lowell Sunday Sun feature article—Nov.23,1970. Then—1948 Joy with the Coach, in the locker room, following Thanksgiving day victory over Lawrence. Now—1970 giving Coach Riddick a Chiropractic Adjustment in the locker room.

As it was, he would be my third head coach at LHS. I had Coach Henry McCormick in 1944, my freshman year, and the following two years were "physical fitness training" under Coach Herb Cochran, with **ONLY ONE WIN.** As a sophomore I received my first varsity lettered "L-45" sweater.

An earlier chapter (Paratrooper Story) explains the details of my early departure from high school in 1947.

For those of you, especially from the Lawrence area, who had my age as old as 24, my date of birth was and still is **SEPTEMBER 6, 1929!!** My "legal playing age" was being disputed by many of our opposing teams, but any math course on the planet always comes up with the same results, **EIGHTEEN YEARS OLD** at the beginning of the 1948 school year.

Coach Riddick was more than my football coach. He, like Stan Stoklosa, was like a big brother who was quick to compliment me when correct and scold me when wrong, however, always with a helpful and comforting explanation so as not to discourage me from achieving.

When reviewing game films, which was quite often, at least two nights a week for the entire 1948 season, he would relate some of his Navy experiences to compare with my military stint, as similarities, and as a means of getting into my head. **WELL, IT WORKED.** You see some people call it brainwashing, however, the Coach was so genuine that he totally won my trust, knowing that it was in my best interest, because he always finished with something like, **"GOING TO COLLEGE WILL BE JUST AS EXCITING FOR YOU AS IT WAS FOR ME."**

HANGING ON TO THE BALL!!

If I had to pick one incident that was paramount in completing our first undefeated season, it would be in our locker room of the game at Quincy.

The Quincy game took place just one week before our annual Thanksgiving rival game with Lawrence High School. We were trailing, **NINE TO ZIP** at the half and I had fumbled twice in the first half.

When Coach Riddick finished his halftime pep talk and we all jumped up ready to run out yelling as we would normally do, the Coach had one of his paws pressing down on my shoulder, which prevented me from getting up with the rest of the team. Before he let me up from the bench, he leaned over and said, **"HANG ON TO THE F...G BALL!!"**

AND DID I EVER!!

I had an outstanding second half, catching two punts on the dead run, daredevil style that gave us great field position, scored a touchdown, threw a TD pass, kicked four PAT's and made several open field tackles on defense as we went on to win, 28-9. We remained undefeated going into our Thanksgiving morning rivalry with Lawrence.

GREAT ATHLETE, GREAT COACH, GREAT RECORD

Raymond E. Riddick was born in Lowell, Mass., on October 17, 1917, during the midst of World War I.

He attended Collinsville Grammar School in Dracut and entered Lowell High School in 1931. Then the legend began.

During his four years at Lowell High he became one of the greatest all-around athletes in the school's history, starring in football, baseball and track, in addition to playing hockey, basketball and swimming.

Football was **HIS SPORT**, though. He was the starting right end during his final three years, going on to captain the 1934 Red and Gray eleven. For his brilliant all-around play in his senior year, Ray was named to the All-State team as an end and was selected to the Lowell Sun's All-Merrimack Valley squad.

The Boston American newspaper gave the following thumbnail description of Ray when he was named All-State; "At 196 pounds, 6 foot 1 and a half inches and 17 years of age, Riddick is a smashing end, seldom waiting or fading. He is a fine blocker. Fast, rugged and an ace pass receiver, with reach giving him an advantage. On defense he never let a play get outside, often wrecking the interference and making the tackle. An intelligent, good student taking college course classes, with hopes of going to Columbia."

Following his graduation from LHS in 1935, Ray starred in the strong Lowell Twilight Baseball League as a catcher and cleanup batter for the South End's team. He led the League in batting in 1937, with a .457 average for twenty games.

In track, Ray became the greatest shot putter in the city's history, and his 53 feet, 4 and a half inches for the 12-pound shot at the indoor Paige Street Annex still stands as a record.

Ray attended Archmere Academy Prep School in Claymont, Delaware, in 1935 and 36, where he played football, baseball and captained the track team. He led the football squad to its best record ever, and in his track debut he broke a meet record at the University of Delaware for the 12-pound shot put, with a throw of 47 feet, 9 inches.

Then, instead of attending his first hope, Columbia, Ray wound up at football powerhouse Fordham University in New York City, where he received his Bachelor of Science degree in 1940. At 6'2" and 215 pounds Ray developed into one of the top defensive ends in the country for his final three seasons, under the tutelage of famed coaches Hugh Devore, "Sleepy" Jim Crowley and the legendary Frank Leahy.

After being named as an All-Metropolitan end by the New York Telegram, Ray was selected to play in The Fresh Air Fund College All-Star Game in 1940. Then 225-pound Riddick was immense in leading the All-Stars to an upset 16-7 win over the NFL Eastern Division champion New York Giants before 43,000 fans at the Polo Grounds.

Ray then played three seasons in the National Football League with the famed Green Bay Packers, coached by Hall of Famer "Curley" Lambeau. He was the starting right end for the Packers, playing on the opposite wing of the great Don Hutson. He played both ways, offense and defense, and in a game against the Cleveland Rams he became the first 60-minute man in Green Bay's modern history. After the 1941 season, Riddick was named to the second team All-Pro eleven following the Packers' closing at 10-2.

Ray married Marjorie Haynes on July 1, 1941 and the couple eventually became the parents of Raymond, Jr., and daughters, Elizabeth and Marjorie. They were later blessed with grandchildren Barry, Brian and Christopher Dick, and Matthew and Jonathan Miller.

"THE COACH"—ONE OF A KIND

Ray Riddick No. 5 Green Bay Packers Vs. Chicago Bears, November 3, 1940.

Ray played three years for the strong St. Mary's Pre-Flight School service team at Moraga, California. The paymaster of the team was none other than Gerry Ford, later to become the president of the United States. Riddick eventually left the Navy with the rank of full lieutenant.

The coaching bug finally hit Ray Riddick, and he accepted an offer to coach the ends at Dartmouth College in Hanover, N.H., under head man, Tuss McLaughry, in 1942.

However, he had one final fling in pro football as he returned to the Packers late in the 1942 season, rejoining the team in time to face the Giants. Having just time for a half hour workout prior to the start of the game, Ray still went out and caught a clutch pass from QB Cecil Isbell to set up the touchdown that enabled Green Bay to pull out a 21-21 tie.

Having decided that coaching was to be his life now, Ray went back to Dartmouth College in 1946 and was again The Big Green's end coach. The Lowell High job opened up the following year, and a legend began.

THE RED AND GRAY SAVIOR

Riddick actually had applied for the head football coaching job at LHS as far back as 1940, but he received no encouragement from the Lowell School Committee at that time, and Spencer Sullivan was voted to the position. Sullivan had been the coach at Dracut High and eventually wound up as mentor at city rival, Keith Academy.

Ray again nearly lost out for the Lowell High position in 1947, when Buzz Harvey appeared to have the berth all locked up. But at the last minute, Harvey decided to remain as the Nashua, N.H. coach.

It is not really known, but a letter printed in The Lowell Sun, penned by longtime LHS grid fan Archie Kaufman, who was residing in Waltham at this time, urged that Riddick be appointed Red and Gray coach. This time the Lowell officials agreed and **THE LEGEND BEGAN** on Kirk Street.

Ray entered the picture here in 1947, and it was a dark scene at that time as Lowell High football had reached rock-bottom. The Red and Gray teams, under besieged Coach Herb Cochran, were doormats to all their opponents in the mid-1940's, and even intra-city rival, Keith Academy, was beating Lowell.

However, the picture soon changed under the Riddick command and football was reborn at Lowell High as a twenty-nine year dynasty was underway.

Ray's first team posted a winning 6-4 record, and the following year the Red and Gray rolled to the school's first undefeated season in the school's history, and went on to play in a bowl game in Mississippi.

AN AMAZING RECORD UNVEILED

Ray Riddick's LHS teams rolled up 180 victories over a twenty-nine year span, and this included ninety-one shutouts. Amazing schoolboy records notched by Ray's squads over nearly three decades included:

Ten undefeated seasons,
Six Eastern Mass. Class A championships,
Four bowl appearances,
A 36-game undefeated streak,
Additional winning streaks of 18, 14, and 13 games, and
Winning 52 out of 54 games from 1951 through 1957, including 32 shutouts.

BESTOWED BY HONORS

Among the many prestigious honors that fell on Riddick's shoulders were as follows:

    Eastern Mass. Coach of the Year (twice),
    New England Football Officials Memorial Award, and
    Inducted into the Mass. Schoolboy Coaches Hall of Fame.

ADDITIONAL CAREER HIGHLIGHTS

Riddick was also one of the few schoolboy football coaches in the nation to have second generation players, such as Titus, and "Buddy" Plomaritis, the

Titus Sr., Titus Jr. & Coach Riddick

Bobby Lekites, and Jimmy and Tim Fallon. Titus Plomaritis received the game ball following the Manchester Central game in 1948, and Titus, Jr., "Buddy", was awarded the ball against the same Central team in 1970. Titus and "Buddy" were the spark-plugs of the first and last undefeated Lowell High teams in history, twenty-two years apart.

One final highlight of Ray Riddick's coaching career is his powerhouse 1967 LHS eleven. In his own words, "Overall, this was the best Lowell High team I've ever coached".

Coach and his pupils
"Coach Ray Riddick is shown pointing out instructions on the locker room backboard to three of his star players in 1961. L-R: Paul Lenardson, Walter Nelson and Tom Machardo". (Lowell Sun Photo)

Boston sportswriters also labeled the '67 Red and Gray machine as **ONE OF THE BEST SCHOOLBOY ELEVENS IN STATE HISTORY.**

That illustrious team rolled to a perfect 9-0 record, including seven shutouts and outscoring its opposition 299-12.

Riddick also was head coach in The Lowell Sun Charities' annual All-Star Football Game for 26 years.

SCOUTING FOR RAY

After graduation from high school, I attended Boston University on a football scholarship and attended Lowell High football games whenever it didn't conflict with my B.U. game schedule.

Coach Ray Riddick always had me come into the LHS locker room, introduced me with kind words and accolades and I would say a few words of encouragement prior to the opening kickoff.

Several years later, while completing my chiropractic education at the Chiropractic Institute of New York, Coach Riddick called to inform me of a nationally ranked football team, St. Michael's High. Lowell was scheduled to play St. Michael's in New Jersey, and the coach asked if I would do him a favor, only if it didn't interfere with my studies, to scout the team for him. YES, was my reply, without hesitation, as at that time I think I still had the coaching bug in my blood. It was also a great break from my chiropractic studies.

NOTE—One of our requirements for playing football for Coach Aldo "Buff" Donelli at Boston University was to submit a completed playbook at the end of each season.

I took the assignment very seriously and won the award in my senior year. My playbook contained diagrams with explanations of every single play, offensively and defensively. The last chapter explained in detail: **"HOW TO SCOUT AN OPPONENT"**.

Coach Riddick asked me to do another scouting assignment of a future LHS opponent from the New York area, and again I gladly performed this duty. That, my friend, is why I was so excited to do scouting reports for a coach that gave so much and asked so little. Summing up on this topic of scouting reports, I appreciated how humble the Coach was with his remarks in passing credit on to my reports, rather than with his own coaching preparations. **OH, YES**—Lowell did come out victorious on both those road games!!

Mass. Wednesday November 16 1955

The Lookout

By FRANK SARGENT
An Excellent Scouting Job
Helped Lowell Last Sunday
Riddick Praises Plomaritis
Didn't Miss Boat On Lancers

ALTHOUGH MOST LOWELL HIGH FOLLOWERS WERE pleased with the club's win over Snyder high here Sunday, some were a bit disappointed that it wasn't a closer ball game. However, it could well be that a former Lowell high star did such a good job of scouting the New Jersey gridders that the Red Raiders were that much better prepared for what the visitors had to offer.

Plomaritis Did Good Job

Remember Titus Plomaritis, the hydrant-sized back who scored all the Lowell points in that rugged Lowell-Lawrence game of 1948? The same Titus who starred in the Memorial Bowl at Jackson, Mississipi the same year despite the fact that he had his face stepped on early in the game. Well, Titus is now attending a chiropractic school in the New York area and took the trouble to watch Snyder high in a couple of their games.

Plomaritis

"He gave me such a detailed report of what to expect from these fellows," says Ray Riddick, "that I thought he must have been a member of their backfield. He furnished diagrams, punting and passing data that was of great value. Then, he came to the Sunday game here and worked the roof phones for me. He did a wonderful job."

Didn't Do Anything Strange

As he continued to describe Titus' fine job, Riddick said, "The Snyder lads didn't do a thing that Titus hadn't mentioned somewhere in his report. Naturally I'm not going to give away any secrets but I will say that he didn't miss a trick in watching the club. It's nice to have a fellow like this ready to help you. The minute Titus heard we were going to play the Jersey club he offered to watch them in action. He's quite a football analyst. He also helped me in another game this season and again in this one his report was tops."

ESTABLISHING THE SCHOLARSHIP FUND

Wonder why I loved the guy so much and worked around the clock with a group of his former football players to establish the **"RAYMOND E. RIDDICK SCHOLARSHIP FUND?"**

The answer to that question was because he did so much for me and influenced my life and the same for just about everybody he coached.

HOW IT ALL STARTED

Shortly after the Coach passed away, on July 14, 1976, at the age of 59, I received a call from George Spaneas, relating that he and several of Coach Riddick's former football players were having a meeting at his Windsor Restaurant and asked if I could attend. That was the beginning of the plan to form the memorial Scholarship Fund. The first meeting was more or less open discussions of different ideas. What, when and how could we do something to honor the Coach?

We met weekly for several weeks and then came up with the idea of establishing a scholarship in his name. A five to ten thousand dollar figure seemed like a reasonable goal. However, after a couple of beers and the more we talked, the higher the stakes grew.

I remember sitting with Al Lenzi, Paul Keefe and Spaneas, when I commented, "With proper public relations and support from the Lowell Sun and radio station, WLLH, we could reach a goal of $25,000!!"

At first they thought I was kidding. However, it didn't take long to convince them that I was serious.

UNANIMOUS!!!—GOAL SET AT $25,000.

FORMING THE COMMITTEE

L to R—George Spaneas, Paul Keefe, Dr. John Janas, Stan Stoklosa, Al Lenzi, Sam Weisberg, Atty. George Eliades, Tom Clayton, Dr. Titus Plomaritis and Mayor Leo Farley, signing Proclamation of April 17, 1977 as Ray Riddick Day.

Along with a handful of Coach Riddick's former football players we formed a committee to make plans to honor the late gridiron mentor. This committee included skilled and professional people who all had the same respect and admiration for the Coach as we did.

Once we agreed on the date to hold a mammoth "Coach Ray Riddick Scholarship Fund" affair, in conjunction with a major fund drive, we contacted Lowell Mayor Leo Farley. He was receptive to proclaiming April 17, 1977, as "Ray Riddick Day" in the city. This date fell on the day of our planned big affair at The Windsor Restaurant.

COMPLETING THE COMMITTEE

We contacted Tom Clayton, the **"RADIO VOICE OF THE MERRIMACK VALLEY"** on station **WLLH**, and he was overwhelmed with our intentions and graciously accepted the task of Toastmaster. Stan Stoklosa, who taught most of us the art of accounting and who had been handling all the Lowell High School Athletic Department finances, was a perfect selection to handle the receipts from ticket sales, plaques and related business. Attorney George Eliades agreed to take care of the by-laws and legal issues, while Sam Weisberg of The Lowell Sun newspaper handled all the necessary research in preparing a memorial booklet of the Coach's accomplishments. George Spaneas was appointed the General Chairman of the committee and handled the refreshments and arrangements at his own Windsor Restaurant in Dracut on the big night, April 17.

Rounding out the committee, Paul Keefe was to be Spaneas' Vice Chairman and completed the task of contacting all the captains of Coach Riddick's 29 LHS football teams in order to get them involved in ticket sales to their respective teammates. Dr. John Janas Jr., agreed to handle, through his office, other secretarial duties, including communications to dignitaries and invited guests. Al Lenzi took on the difficult task of Ticket Chairman, and I (Dr. Titus Plomaritis) happily agreed to **CARRY THE BALL** and serve as Coordinator.

RIDDICK COMMITTEE WEEKLY MEETINGS SET

Now that we had our full committee in place, we held our first official meeting, with all in attendance, at George Spaneas's Windsor Restaurant in Dracut, Massachusetts, on Wednesday, January 19, 1977. As a group we were in agreement that if we were to accomplish our goal of $25,000 we all had to assume some of the responsibilities and to meet on a weekly basis to share and coordinate happenings for that week. Wednesdays seemed to be convenient for all so we agreed to meet every Wednesday at 7 p.m.

GEORGE SPANEAS was ever so gracious in offering his conference room for the weekly meetings, relating that Wednesdays were not busy during evenings and he would be close by to attend the meetings. **TOM CLAYTON**, although unable to attend weekly meetings, was able to keep his radio listening audience abreast of our progress to reach our goal and remind the public daily of the date, location and cost of only $10 to attend.

Attorney **GEORGE ELIADES** related that he wouldn't be able to attend weekly meetings. However, he would keep his telephone line open to handle any legal problems and would begin working on the establishment of the bylaws for "**THE RAYMOND E. RIDDICK SCHOLARSHIP FUND**". **DR. JOHN JANAS**, also unable to attend every Wednesday, used his office staff to draft and send correspondences to the invited guests, including everyone that touched any aspect of Coach Riddick's athletic career throughout the United States and beyond.

The remaining committee members met weekly with progress reports and Stan's updates of monies in the bank. I disseminated this information to five newspapers and seven radio stations on a weekly basis. **PAUL KEEFE**, who was in charge of contacting the captains of Coach Riddick's 29 teams, did a superb job, reporting from week to week on how many more he was able to locate even though many had moved out of the area. **AL LENZI**, with his business charm, smoothly handled the ticket sales, and better yet was able to have them printed gratis and saw to it that absolutely no one was to be admitted without a $10 ticket.

STANLEY STOKLOSA opened a checking account and kept us abreast from week to week, of how well we were doing. He sometimes would pull out the whip and state, "We had a bad week, so let's all make a few more phone calls to our friends and relatives." **SAM WEISBERG**, a dead ringer for Dominic DiMaggio or Woody Allen, methodically researched and authenticated every aspect of Ray Riddick's athletic career and single-handedly created a sixteen-page souvenir booklet that was to be handed out to each and every $10 ticket holder as he or she entered the Ray Riddick Tribute on April 17, 1977.

WEEKLY LOG OF TICKET SALES AND INCOMING FUNDS

JANUARY 26—$900. Although we did not as yet have tickets, each committee member purchased ten tickets in advance to open the checking account.

FEBRUARY 2—$2200 all from ticket sales. It was at this time that we realized we needed another source of income to reach our goal.

BILL ROBERTSON, better known as **"BROB"**, a retired well-known cartoonist formally with the Boston Herald newspapers, volunteered to create a cartoon depicting Coach Riddick's entire athletic career that we would be able to use as another incentive in soliciting donations. Drawing on my Boston University audio visual aids education, and by adding my door-to-door Watkin's Products salesmanship experience, I was able to transform the cartoon into a certificate. I had Janet Lambert Moore artistically inscribe the donors' names at the top of the **"CARTOONED CERTIFICATES"**, and then had the certificates permanently mounted on walnut wooden plaques, so they could be presented as donations.

Certificate of Appreciation
to

for your Generous Donation to the

"Raymond E. Riddick Memorial Scholarship Fund"

We then promoted them as tax deductible donations, and with the help of the twelve news media mentioned earlier, they were given as outstanding mementos of Coach Riddick's eulogy for a donation of $100, or more.

MARCH 2—Stan reported that we had just reached the **$7000** mark. It was a little discouraging and it looked like I had made an overzealous judgment with my goal of $25,000. However, always having had the positive attitude to succeed, I packed my briefcase with Riddick memorabilia, headed out for the next three days and bombarded every radio station and the five newspapers from Nashua, Manchester, Lawrence and Salem. I personally saw editor, **CLEM COSTELLO**, at The Lowell Sun.

The following weeks showed the results as Stan's accounting of monies in the bank as follows:

MARCH 9—FUND REACHES $10,000.

THERE'S NOTHING HE WOULDN'T DO

By Paddy Bournival
Salem Observer, Salem, NH—
March 9, 1977

Next month at the Windsor Restaurant in Dracut, Massachusetts, friends, relatives, and the athletes who played for him, will come together to pay tribute.

Just recently inducted into the Massachusetts Coaches Hall of Fame, the dinner will be in the honor of the late Raymond Riddick, a man who has done a lot for the youth around this area.

HISTORIC SMILES — Titus Plomaritis (left) and Coach Ray Riddick had something to grin about back in 1948. This photo was taken moments after Lowell defeated Lawrence 20-19 to go undefeated for the first time since 1894. Plomaritis is co-ordinator for a tribute dinner in honor of Coach Riddick in April.

In last week's **OBSERVER**, we mentioned most of Coach Riddick's statistical accomplishments. One which we left out; Riddick was head coach of the **LOWELL SUN CHARITIES ALL STAR GAME** for 26 years and was responsible for sending dozens of football players on to college.

But to have a scholarship named after you, statistics isn't the only aspect of a person you look at.

Co-ordinator for this dinner, with all the proceeds going to the Raymond E. Riddick Memorial Scholarship Fund, Titus Plomaritis shares with us Ray Riddick, "He was like a third parent to all the kids who played for him," recalls Plomaritis, a running-back for Riddick back in 1948. "All the players idolized him, looked up to him and listened to him."

At 6' 3 1/2", Riddick was a very soft spoken, kind hearted man mentioned Plomaritis.

"On the football field as well as off the gridiron, Riddick always had time to take you aside when you asked or needed advice or just to talk to you," stated Plomaritis. "He was a warm gentle man."

Plomaritis went on to say that Riddick "was a grass roots developer".

"When you get kids in life at the age of 15-16, they are easily influenced," explained the Pelham Chiropractor. Riddick had a way of pointing the kids in the right direction."

Riddick, who died of cancer on July 14, 1976, always put the welfare of his kids before anything else.

"Ray had college, professional, and all kinds of offers with much higher pay, but refused them all," remarked Plomaritis. "He really wasn't concerned about making lots of money. He'd rather spend time with his players."

Riddick coached a total of 1,485 athletes in his 29 years at Lowell and the figure is not known how many of them went on to college.

Some coaches would try to get their players into the best college. Not so with Riddick. "Coach Riddick wanted the best for his players, so much so he wouldn't send you to a big college if he felt it was academically too tough," said Plomaritis. "Too many good players are hurt that way and Riddick knew this because he had gone through it himself."

There wasn't anything Ray Riddick wouldn't do. He spoke to all kinds of service groups accepting no money in return.

He never took credit for the countless numbers of wins his team recorded. It was always, "the kids and coaching staff deserve all the credit."

Riddick was a once in a lifetime type of fellow.

On January 29, 1977, the day Riddick was inducted into the Coaches Hall of Fame, compliments a Massachusetts High School football program, dedication and loyalty to the city, and constant exemplification of sportsmanship and self respect for his fellow man were echoed by people who knew him.

This is why there is a Raymond E. Riddick Memorial Scholarship Fund and you can be part of it by purchasing a ticket to this dinner.

Tickets are $10 each and are available from surrounding radio stations and newspapers including the **OBSERVER.**

A tax deductible $100 contribution will get you a plaque with Coach Riddick's eulogy on it.

MARCH-16—Fund reaches **$14,000.**

D2 THE SUNDAY SUN, LOWELL, MASS., MARCH 20, 1977

Riddick Fund gets $500 check

The Lowell High Alumni Association made a $500 donation to the Ray Riddick Memorial Scholarship Fund this past week, boosting the drive's total to over $14,000.

Shown above at the presentation of the check at the high school are members of the Scholarship Fund Committee and the LHS Alumni Club. L-r: Dr. Titus Plomaritis, fund coordinator; Dr. John J. Janas,

fund secretary; Brendan C. Sullivan, club president; Peter Stamas, high school headmaster; Paul Mann, club treasurer, and John Lang, club vice-president.

MARCH-23—Fund goes over $15,000.

THE DOCTOR, RAY RIDDICK AND A LABOR OF LOVE

By Rick Stewart
Lawrence Eagle-Tribune
Thursday, March 24, 1977

Dr.Titus Plomaritis walked into the Eagle-Tribune office last night with an armful of releases, letters and facts and figures—a foot-high stack of paperwork overflowing from a tired-looking briefcase.

Dr. Titus Plomaritis will talk your ear off about Ray Riddick and the Ray Riddick Memorial Scholarship Fund that he and several others are in the midst of creating. He spends—on the average—about 30 hours a week doing just that. Thirty hours a week above and beyond his normal work week.

Why, the question was asked? What are you killing yourself for?

"You're the second one today to ask me that," said Plomaritis. "I'll tell you..."

THE NAMES PLOMARITIS AND RIDDICK go a long way back.

Back to 1947 when Titus Plomaritis was playing service ball in Japan and Ray Riddick was coaching his very first Lowell High football team.

Plomaritis had played football for Lowell in 1945 and '46 but had opted for the paratroopers instead of his junior year in 1947. And so at age 17 he found himself in Japan, paratrooping and playing service football against talent straight out of college and the pros. It was better than tending the chickens and milking the cows every morning on his father's farm and, as Plomaritis himself admits, "I was a bit of a problem kid." And so on to the service.

But Riddick had this thing about eligible football players—good eligible football players who looked like they might not bother to graduate from high school. And so Riddick and Plomaritis wrote back and forth, at least once a month, and by the spring of 1948 Plomaritis was back in Lowell, ready for spring practice. By the fall of 1948 he was ready for his senior year.

AND WITH PLOMARITIS running Lowell's single wing attack from the tailback slot, the Red and Gray went undefeated at 9-0-1. Lowell capped the year with a 20-19 win over Lawrence as Plomaritis scored all 20 points on three touchdowns and two PAT kicks.

"But I was almost never on time for our games," confessed Plomaritis. "They were on Sundays and I used to have to hop out the window and bicycle seven miles to the stadium. My father was from the Old Country and he believed that when you turned 14 you should quit school and start working on the farm."

But Ray Riddick was from the New Country, the country of the American dream, and he believed that Titus Plomaritis should finish school and even go to college.

"I didn't want to finish high school," said Plomaritis, "but Ray would say, 'Stay in school. I'll get you a scholarship. You can go to college.'

"And he did. I went four years to Boston University and I never paid a penny."

AND AFTER FOUR YEARS of undergraduate work, Plomaritis started in on becoming Dr. Titus Plomaritis. Dr. Plomaritis, as in chiropractor. As in—now —successful chiropractor. Thanks to Ray Riddick, the kid from the chicken farm had it made.

Well, almost.

"When I graduated I still didn't have an office. It was being built," said Plomaritis. "So he hired me as a freshman coach—out of his own pocket—he hired me as a freshman coach so I'd be drawing a salary and then when the office was finished he bought me the furniture for it because I didn't have the money."

Which brings us to the whole point of this exercise.

THE POINT THAT LOVE has a way of doubling and tripling and quadrupling itself.

Ray Riddick, you see, died of cancer last July. But guys like Titus Plomaritis, George Spaneas, Paul Keefe, John Janas, Stan Stoklosa, Al Lenzi, Sam Weisberg, George Eliades, Tom Clayton and all the others who were touched by Ray Riddick in his 29 years of coaching, won't let him die. They won't let him stop touching the lives of others.

And so they have set up the Raymond E. Riddick Memorial Scholarship Fund so that Ray Riddick can keep sending kids to college, so that Ray Riddick can keep on doing what he did best.

Right now the Fund has gone over the $15,000 mark. The goal is $25,000 to create a perpetuating fund and everybody is allowed to contribute.

On Friday, April 1, a group of NFL players will participate in a charity basketball game at the Scondras Memorial Gym in Lowell with all the proceeds going to the Scholarship Fund. Admission will be just $1.00. The players will be donating their time. All profits will go to the Fund.

THEN ON SUNDAY, APRIL 17, the Windsor Restaurant in Dracut will host a "Tribute to Coach Ray Riddick Night" with guest speakers from throughout Riddick's 44 year football career. Admission will be $10.00 and will include a souvenir booklet. The restaurant is being donated, gratis, and the booklets are being printed for the same non-existent fee. All profits will go to the Fund.

Ex-Boston Herald cartoonist Bill Robertson has also drawn a detailed cartoon depicting Riddick's football career. All contributions of $100.00 or more receive a special wood-framed reproduction of the cartoon, inscribed specifically to the donor. The cartoon and all reproductions were donated, gratis to the Fund.

And so the love doubles and triples and quadruples. And guys like Dr. Titus Plomaritis work 30-hour weeks after business hours to see that it does.

"...**AND YOU ASK ME WHY** I do all this?" said Titus Plomaritis. And at that point there was no need to ask.

MARCH 27—Fund goes over 20,000.

NOTE:—On March 27, Bob Hilliard of the statewide New Hampshire Sunday News ran a full page, eight column article that included a photo of Coach Riddick and myself, and also included a picture of Brob's cartoon.

Although he masterly covered, in outstanding fashion, every aspect of the committee's intent of establishing a perpetual scholarship in Coach Riddick's name, I did not want to lose you with repetitive pages of similar commentary. Some of the highlights from his article that have not appeared elsewhere are as follows—

RAY RIDDICK SCHOLARSHIP FUND TRIBUTE SET

By BOB HILLIARD
New Hampshire Sunday News—March 27, 1977

MANCHESTER, N.H.—If only about an eighth of his friends show up to pay homage to the late Ray Riddick, Lowell High's famous football coach, it should be enough to fill the Boston Garden.

The tribute to Coach Riddick will be held April 17—a Sunday—at the Windsor Restaurant in Dracut, Mass., with festivities starting at 7 p.m.

Proceeds from the tribute will be channeled into a scholarship fund, with an announced goal of $25,000. More than $20,000 has already poured in, testifying to the great respect and admiration in which Riddick was held.

RIDDICK DIED last July at the age of 59, following 29 glorious seasons with the Red and Gray of Lowell High.

On January 29 of this year Ray Riddick was inducted into the Massachusetts Coaches Hall of Fame, a fitting tribute for a man who had spent the greater part of his lifetime coaching, and counseling, the young men of Lowell.

Until Riddick came along at Lowell High, Manchester Central teams held the upper hand. Those were the incredible **HUBIE McDONOUGH** coaching years, and not many Massachusetts teams were beating The Little Green then. Riddick arrived as coach at Lowell, the year after Hubie retired. And things began to hum. Against Central, Riddick went 16-4-2, including 12 straight wins in one span.

But Central wins during the Riddick era were sparse, so frequent, in fact, as to be an occasion to remember.

NASHUA AND LOWELL also had a thing going, too. A real rivalry. That is, until Riddick's appearance. Nashua led in a series that started in 1919, 13-11-4. Close. Then, Riddick came, and it went 21-7-1 over Nashua, the Panthers finally beating Ray for the first time in 1959. Against Riddick, Coach **BUZZ HARVEY** of Nashua was on the losing side, 16-5-1. Many of those games were close, and might have gone either way. But, it was no disgrace to lose to Riddick. He was a master craftsman on the gridiron.

In 1963, Lowell held Nashua's Greg Landry to four completions in 14 passes, and won, 27-6. Landry later was the star quarterback of the NFL Detroit Lions.

Ironically, the two figures spearheading the Raymond E. Riddick Memorial Scholarship Fund tribute have New Hampshire connections. **TOM CLAYTON,** a prominent radio personality in Lowell, is the Toastmaster, and he played for Manchester Central. **DR. TITUS PLOMARITIS,** now a resident of Pelham, N.H., was an outstanding halfback for Riddick, once scoring all of Lowell's points in a cliff-hanger 20-19 victory over Lawrence.

Clayton, a hefty tackle, played against Riddick on the field, not against Riddick the coach, and he scored the only touchdown of his career against Lowell on a blocked punt in the end zone.

DR. PLOMARITIS, a chiropractor, played on the first undefeated football team in Lowell history, also the first bowl team. At Boston University, Plomaritis was in the same backfield with the legendary Harry Agganis, who later starred at first base for the Boston Red Sox before his death at the young age of 25.

Manchester Mayor **CHARLES "DICK" STANTON,** who played a bit of halfback himself in Lowell, at Keith Academy, remembers Riddick well.

"I knew him as an excellent coach," Stanton said, "and as a fine gentleman. He knew how to handle 'em, too. No baloney from the players. And they admired and respected him. It was a mutual respect on both sides."

The Mayor played under Coach **SPENCER SULLIVAN** at Keith. Sullivan was a former coach at Dracut and Lowell High.

ED McMAHON, of Johnny Carson's "Tonight" T.V. show, will be one of the prominent figures invited to the Riddick tribute. McMahon came out of Lowell and was an outstanding athlete there. His cousin, same name, Ed McMahon, played on the LHS team with Riddick at Lowell in 1934. He is now a prominent architect in the city.

PLOMARITIS, a small but lightning-fast running back, was also Riddick's passer in 1948, and he pulled off many a completed aerial, although, as he explains: "I never saw one of them after the ball left my hand. I was usually flat on my back. I went by the roar of the crowd. If I heard the crowd let loose, I knew that the pass had found its mark."

Many of Ray's players over the long period will be in attendance, giving fans and players alike a chance to reminisce over old times.

A nice affair in the making, and a good chance to help some deserving boy or girl to a scholarship in the name of a legendary coach, a coach who turned things around at Lowell High.

APRIL 6—Fund at $23,500

RIDDICK FUND NEARS GOAL

Salem Observer, April 6, 1977

There are only eleven days left to purchase your tickets to the **COACH RAY RIDDICK TRIBUTE** get together, Sunday, April 17, at the Windsor Restaurant in Dracut, Mass.

Currently, according to coordinator Dr. Titus Plomaritis, the Scholarship Fund stands at $23,500, just $1500 short of the committee's goal.

This figure was reached over the weekend as a result of an all out benefit basketball game between the National Football League All-Stars and the Lowell All-Stars.

Relaxing After Charity Hoop Game
L to R: Mike Esposito, Don Macek, Jim McKay, Fred Steinford, Titus Plomaritis, Mike Kruczek, and Al Lenzi

It was an overflow crowd that witnessed the game and saw a last second jump shot by Billy Quirk that gave the Lowell Stars an 84-82 win. But more importantly, of course, $833 was raised for the Ray Riddick Memorial Scholarship Fund.

Wilmington's Mike Esposito of the Atlanta Falcons, Pittsburgh Steelers quarterback Mike Kruczek, Oakland Raiders kicker Fred Steinford and San Diego Chargers Don Macek were among the 20 professionals on hand for the game.

"It was a glorious affair, enjoyed by all," exclaimed Dr. Titus Plomaritis. "The professionals were very gracious to the kids by posing for pictures with them and signing autographs."

PLOMARITIS WENT ON to say that tickets are still available for this affair, which will bring together some great names under the roof of the Windsor Restaurant. Tickets are $10 each and available from surrounding radio stations and newspaper offices.

Pat Sullivan will represent Bill Sullivan, president of the New England Patriots, at the Hors D'oeuvres affair. He will be joined by several Patriots players.

Plaques are still available with a tax deductible $100 contribution. For your donation, you will receive a beautiful, personally inscribed plaque with Ray Riddick's eulogy on it. These you may purchase from Dr. Titus Plomaritis.

Speaking of these plaques, some of the students in Lowell have been going to teachers and students raising the $100 to have a plaque hung in their school.

APRIL13—FUND TOPS $25,000.

RIDDICK SCHOLARSHIP PASSES GOAL

Salem Observer, April 13, 1977

The Ray Riddick Memorial Scholarship Fund has topped its projected goal of $25,000!!

With receipts for tickets, plaques and donations still pouring in. the current total is approaching $30,000, with **"THE BIG NIGHT"** still one week away.

Next Sunday night at the Windsor Restaurant in Dracut, the **"SALUTE to COACH RAY RIDDICK NIGHT"** will be held, with hundreds—perhaps thousands—of players, friends and fans of the late Lowell High football coach being on hand to pay tribute to Ray.

The sale of $100 plaques is nearing the 200 mark now, with each donor of that sum receiving a large laminated wooden plaque, depicting the career of Ray Riddick, plus the inscription of the donor's name.

These plaques will be available for one more week, and for further information contact Dr. Titus Plomaritis.

The souvenir pictorial booklet, containing a full biography of Riddick's life, plus many old photos and a complete year-by-year record of his 29 Lowell High teams has been completed and each person who purchases a $10 ticket for next Sunday's affair at the Windsor will receive a copy.

ONE OF THE LATEST donors for the plaque was the New York Islanders. Last week, coordinator for this event, Dr. Titus Plomaritis, received a letter from Ed Westfall of the Islanders with all the team's signatures—and a $100 check.

George Spaneas is the chairman of the affair, and Tom Clayton, "The Voice of the Merrimack Valley," will be the Master of Ceremonies.

The featured speakers will include a host of famous national and local politicians, sports celebrities, newspaper men and friends and relatives of the late football legend.

PUSHING DONATIONS FROM "THE BIG ONES"

This is a good time and place to relate my several visits to Telemachus "Mike" Demoulas, Bob Notini and Clem Costello during my weekly escapades searching for new sources of donations to reach our goal of $25,000.

When I'd go to Notini with my hand extended, he'd ask "How much did Mike cough up?" My reply would be the same every couple of weeks. I would say "Mike told me to come back after Notini's donation."

Clem Costello at "The Sun" insisted on being the last donor, which put me in a delicate situation. So, I played the "shell game" and gave each a fictitious number and promised never to reveal their donations, so they all felt they were the ones that put us over the eventual $50,000 final figure. To this day, only The Committee knows.

RAY RIDDICK TRIBUTE, APRIL 17, 1977

RIDDICK FUND REACHES $50,000

A TRIBUTE TO RAYMOND E. RIDDICK

SUNDAY, APRIL 17, 1977

One of the most successful fundraising events ever conducted in the Greater-Lowell area took place at the Windsor Restaurant in Dracut on the night of April 17, 1977, when the **"SALUTE TO COACH RAYMOND E. RIDDICK"** was held.

The event drew an overflow crowd of 2500 friends, fans and former players of the beloved late Lowell High School football coach, which also included many dignitaries from the sports, political and print worlds.

To make the evening's festivities more significant, the Raymond E. Riddick Scholarship Fund Committee, which conducted the gala affair, announced that the initial target of raising $25,000 was easily reached.

"Our original goal of $25,000 has been exceeded by $25,000!!" exulted George Spaneas, the event's chairman, as he opened the evening's program.

"In other words", he shouted over the roar and applause of the crowd, **"WE HAVE REACHED A GRAND TOTAL OF $50,000!!"**

The amazing part of the Riddick Scholarship Fund's success was the fact that the $50,000 was collected in less than three months time.

Those attending the gala, like those who had contributed, came from the length and breadth of the United States, Canada and even Mexico.

CLAYTON AT THE MICROPHONE

It seemed only fitting that Tom Clayton, the play-by-play radio announcer on local Radio Station WLLH, for Riddick-coached games over nearly three decades should be at the microphone again for the fundraiser.

But not even the amiable thunder of Clayton could quiet the exuberant huge crowd, who arrived an hour early and stayed late—standing all the while—and enjoying themselves to the fullest. They had good reason.

They represented men who had played with Riddick, for him and against him, including 29 Lowell High football squads he had coached, and two generations of men and women who sat in the bleachers and cheered.

Now they cheered again, as the evening's toastmaster introduced Riddick's daughters—Betty and husband Ed Dick, and Marjorie and husband Frank Miller—Ray's grandchildren, Barry and Brian Dick (twins, age 10), son Ray Riddick, Jr., …and, of course, the power behind the throne, Mrs. Ray Riddick.

MEMORABILIA ON DISPLAY

Each ticket holder in attendance received a 16 page Ray Riddick Memorial souvenir pictorial booklet, that was written and edited by Sam Weisberg of The Lowell Sun, which included a complete biography of the late coach, plus a host of photos and all his records.

Hot hors d'oeuvres were served and Ray's memorabilia was on display, including his Green Bay Packers uniform. All 29 of his LHS teams had separate displays, which included team photos and records. Paul Keefe represented these squads.

Special laminated plaques, which featured an illustration of Ray's career, were available for purchase for each donation of $100 or more. The donors' names would be inscribed on the plaques, and thus far 250 had been sold.

INTRODUCTIONS AND FEATURED SPEAKERS

Rev. David M. Jones, pastor of Matthews Memorial Church, characterized Riddick as "a coach with a conscience—he applied the Golden Rule in a day when such rules were outmoded and outdated."

DR. TITUS PLOMARITIS, coordinator of The Fund drive—and the first Riddick-coached athlete to himself receive a scholarship through the Coach's help—said "two words—**THANK YOU**," a good many times... to the news media; to artists Bill Clark of The Sun, creator of a portrait of Riddick to be presented to Mrs. Riddick; Bill Robertson, who drew the figures on the memorial plaque, and Janet Moore; to George Poirier of Lowell, restorer of sundry old photographs of Ray's teams; to Sam Weisberg of The Sun, for research; to The Demoulas Foundation, Lowell Sun Charities and Notini Brothers for donations comprising the drive's final $10,000, moving it over the $50,000 mark.

Dr. Plomaritis then emotionally recalled Coach Riddick's 180 wins, 10 undefeated seasons and six State Championship teams.

"His spirit drove us...that's why we got there...thank you, Ray Riddick!!" concluded Dr. Plomaritis, close to tears.

"An outstanding job," applauded Lowell Mayor Leo Farley, as he stepped to the podium to announce that the Lowell City Council had proclaimed that date, April 17, as "Ray Riddick Day."

THE MAIN FEATURED SPEAKERS

Clement C. Costello, editor of The Sun and founder of Lowell Sun Charities, stepped to the podium to recall that the newspaper played a part in persuading Riddick, who had been playing for Fordham University and then The Green Bay Packers, to return to Lowell—"one of the most fruitful actions we ever undertook."

He lauded the Memorial Scholarship. "Ray gave too much to the city for his name to soon disappear," Costello added.

U.S. Senator Edward Brooke, among surprise visitors at the event, said he had not had the privilege of knowing Ray Riddick, but that Riddick had "left an impact on this earth, and had been truly a great giant."

U.S. Rep. Paul Tsongas, a Lowell native, told the gathering that a proclamation honoring Ray Riddick was already part of The Congressional Record and copies of which could be had by writing to him.

A telegram from **PRESIDENT JIMMY CARTER** was also read by Rep. Tsongas, lauding the establishment of a scholarship honoring The Coach.

State Senator B. Joseph Tully then told of a resolution passed by the Massachusetts Senate detailing Riddick's accomplishments, copies of which had been mailed to Lowell High School.

State Rep. Philip Shea lent a light note, recalling attending all the games in 1956-57 for free—as the team's water boy. Rep. Shea also recalled a resolution passed by the Massachusetts House in honor of Riddick.

Arthur Kelts, executive vice president of The Greater-Lowell Chamber of Commerce, rose to laud the tribute to Riddick and the great response to the Scholarship drive.

Ralph Wolfendale, representing Lawrence High, lauded Riddick as "one of the top coaches in the United States, and the greatest guy I've ever known."

Joe Nolan, Riddick's first football coach at Lowell High back in 1932, recalled how he was astounded at the effort Riddick put in. "The reason Ray Riddick was such a good coach was his own practical experience—he had to labor to develop to the extent he did," said Nolan.

RAY'S OLD TEAMMATES SPEAK

Harry Jacunski of the Yale coaching staff, a former teammate of Riddick at Fordham University and The Packers, commented: "It was a happy day for thousands when Ray went into coaching. As a coach, he was also a teacher, and a teacher effects eternity. No one can tell where the influence stops."

Jacunski also lauded Ray Riddick, Jr., adding: "He endeared himself during four outstanding years on the Yale campus, and he had been among the top ten at Yale."

John Balian, a teammate of Coach Riddick when he played at Lowell High, told the gathering of an incident when Ray was a junior at Fordham. "The game with rival Pittsburgh was tied. Riddick, an end, was put in as a tackle, and he did the job as a tackle. He was hurt, but went back into the game, and the coach later said that even an injured Ray Riddick was better than most at tackle, even though he was an end."

Buzz Harvey, football coach at Nashua High, who was one of Coach Riddick's arch-rivals—on the gridiron—recovering from eye surgery last week, commented: "throughout our rivalry over the years, Ray Riddick was a true gentleman and one of the most respected coaches in the United States."

Scheduled speaker Walter "Bill" Wilson, Jr., Riddick's first selected assistant coach at Lowell High, had the misfortune to be hospitalized on this night, but wired his congratulations regarding the Scholarship Fund.

"He gave so much of himself," Wilson said of Riddick.

MANY MORE HIGHLIGHTS

There were appearances by Leon Gray and Ray "Sugar Bear" Hamilton, representing the New England Patriots and The National Football League, both telling the welcoming crowd that it was a "great honor" for them to be part of the occasion.

Numerous telegrams were received, among them one from Ed McMahon, co-host of Johnny Carson's TV Tonight Show, and a Lowell native. "It was an honor to have known Ray," McMahon said, adding that "his dedication, loyalty and success spoke for themselves."

Special recognition was also made to other well-known people in attendance, including Wilmington's Mike Esposito of the NFL's Atlanta Falcons and former Boston College star running back, plus longtime Lowell High backfield coach Joe Polak, and many others.

Scholarship Fund committee members Stan Stoklosa, Al Lenzi, Dr. John J. Janas and Atty. George Eliades made several special presentations, and Ray Riddick, Jr., spoke in behalf of the Coach's family.

YES, RAY RIDDICK was honored, as a man who will never be forgotten by the sports fans of the Greater-Lowell area, and a man who made Lowell High School football nationally recognized.

Now, some fortunate Scholarship winners will benefit over the years from the Memorial Fund that carries Raymond E. Riddick's name. —That's the way Ray would have wanted it!!

BACK PAGE OF SOUVENIR BOOKLET

The Scholarship Fund Committee is extremely grateful to the following for their outstanding PUBLIC SERVICE during our drive in establishing the Perpetual "Raymond E. Riddick Memorial Scholarship Fund."

LOWELL SUN AND LOWELL SUNDAY SUN
Sam Weisberg
NASHUA TELEGRAPH
Ted Bryant
LAWRENCE EAGLE TRIBUNE
Ralph Vigoda and Rick Stewart
SALEM OBSERVER
Andy Hartery
MANCHESTER UNION LEADER-SUNDAY NEWS
Joe Barnes and Bob Hilliard

WLLH - Lowell, Mass.
Jack Peterson
WCAP - Lowell, Mass.
Joe Shimko
WOTW - Nashua, N.H.
John Spence
WCCM - Lawrence, Mass.
Bill Callagy
WVNH - Salem, N.H.
Ken O'Quinn
WJUL - Univ. of Lowell
Bob McCann
WSMN - Nashua, N.H.
Ed Lecius, Jr.

CENTRAL MIDDLESEX, Lawrence St., Lowell, Mass.
BUCKLAND PRINTING, Willie St., Lowell, Mass.
BILL CLARK, *Cartoonist*, Lowell Sun
BILL ROBERTSON, *Cartoonist*, No. Andover, Mass.
JANET LAMBERT MOORE, *Artist*, Lowell, Mass.
JEANNE SLOTTA & SONS, David & Christopher, Chelmsford, Mass.
LAMINATING UNLIMITED, 1492 Park Ave., Cranston, R.I.
PAUL TAFT - BOWLERS WORLD & TROPHY SHOP, No. Chelmsford, Mass.
GEORGE OF LOWELL, *Photographer*, University Ave., Lowell, Mass.
SHAWPRINT, Chelmsford St., Lowell, Mass.

This souvenir booklet and program was printed and donated by:
SULLIVAN BROS., PRINTERS, 95 Bridge St., Lowell, Mass.

COMMITTEE:
GEORGE SPANEAS, *Chairman*
PAUL KEEFE, *Vice-Chairman*
DR. JOHN JANAS, *Secretary*
STAN STOKLOSA, *Treasurer*
AL LENZI, *Ticket Chairman*
SAM WEISBERG, *Research Chairman*
ATTY. GEORGE ELIADES, *By-Laws*
TOM CLAYTON, *Toastmaster*
DR. TITUS PLOMARITIS, *Co-Ordinator*

Back Page of Souvenir Booklet

20"x24" Walnut Plaques depicting a collage of photos and the won-loss record with scores of each game for every one of Coach Riddick's 29 teams.

A collage of each of Coach Riddick's 29 football teams was depicted on 20"x24" decorative Walnut Plaques and disseminated throughout the banquet hall.

It provided the early gathering a great source of information and memories of the legacy that the Coach left behind.

The Plaques were available for a donation of $50.00 toward the Riddick Scholarship Fund.

Riddick Memorial Fund Officers

Here is the first slate of officers of the Raymond Riddick Memorial Scholarship Fund Committee. Shown at the organizational meeting, which officially elected the officers, are, left to right: Dr. John Janas, secretary; George Spaneas, first vice-president; Dr. Titus Plomaritis, President; Al Lenzi, second vice-president, and Stan Stoklosa, treasurer. Sun staff photo.

RIDDICK FUND INCORPORATED

LOWELL—December 11, 1977—The Raymond Riddick Memorial Scholarship Fund was officially incorporated this past week, and the Scholastic Fund Committee has elected its first slate of officers and conducted its initial organizational meeting.

Dr. Titus Plomaritis is the Committee's president, with George Spaneas the first vice-president, Al Lenzi the second vice-president, Dr. John Janas the secretary and Stan Stoklosa the treasurer.

Others on the Committee include Paul Keefe, Atty. George Eliades, George Basbanes, Sam Weisberg, Ernest Dixon, Walter Nelson, Eric Thomson and Ray Riddick, Jr.

THE SCHOLARSHIP FUND, honoring the memory of the late, great Lowell High football coach, has already topped the $50,000 mark.

A scholarship, or scholarships, will be awarded to Lowell High students or graduates annually, and the amount spent will not exceed the earnings of the fund's interest. Thus, a perpetual fund will be available.

At the organizational meeting, held at the Windsor Restaurant, the by-laws of the Scholarship Fund were approved and a discussion was held on the number and amounts of the scholarships.

Four separate committees were formed, consisting of Ways and Means, Selections, Financial Needs and Investments.

First Riddick Scholarship Winners, 1978
L-R: Dr. Titus Plomaritis, President of Lowell High"s Riddick Memorial Scholarship Fund, Ann McNamara, Peter Martin and Maureen Raymond. Sun staff photo.

Second Riddick Scholarship Winners, 1979
L-R: Lowell High's Susan Petullo, Karen Gillis, Daniel J. McCafferty, Mrs. Raymond Riddick, Daniel F. McNamara, Todd Beati, Candice Bedrosian, Ann C. McCormack. Sun staff photo.

BENEFIT BOOSTS RIDDICK FUND

Attending Saturday's theatre night benefiting the Raymond E. Riddick Memorial Scholarship Fund were, from left, George Spaneas of the scholarship fund committee; Paul A. Keefe, ticket chairman; Mrs. Raymond E. Riddick; Dr. Titus Plomaritis, Committee President; and Al Lenzi co-chairman. Sun Staff photo by Mike Maher.

LOWELL—April 14, 1980—More than 400 people made the first annual Raymond E. Riddick Memorial Scholarship Fund "Theater Night" at the Merrimack Regional Theatre a major success.

Patrons of the Scholarship Fund viewed the MRT's production of "Vanities", while at the same time were helping to increase the amount of the Fund, named after the late Lowell High School football coach.

Each year, the Scholarship Fund committee awards scholarships to deserving Lowell High seniors. In the past two years the committee has granted 10 scholarships, totaling $5,000.

Among those seated in the front row at the Theatre were members of the Riddick family, including Mrs. Raymond E. Riddick, Sr., Mr. and Mrs. Raymond E. Riddick, Jr., Mr. and Mrs. Edward Dick and Mrs. Frank Miller.

Many different people worked towards making the evening a success.

'**IT WAS A JOINT EFFORT,** and a highly successful one," noted **DR. TITUS PLOMARITIS,** president of the Scholarship Fund Committee. "This just shows that the people of Greater-Lowell haven't forgotten the legend that was Ray Riddick."

Others on the committee include co-chairman, Al Lenzi, George Spaneas, Dr. John Janas, Jr., Stan Stoklosa, Atty. George Eliades, Atty. George Basbanes, Sam Weisberg of The Lowell Sun, Ernest Dixon, Jr., Walter Nelson, Jr., D. Eric Thomson and Raymond E. Riddick, Jr.

Artist Janet Moore was in charge of ticket arrangements, and Spaneas donated refreshments.

Six members of the Lowell High School Girls Officers donated their services as ushers. They were Nancy Callahan, Sheila McCarthy, Lisa Picard, Salette Maia, Mary Crowley and Norma Poisson.

RAYMOND A. SULLIVAN

Mr. Raymond A. Sullivan, Headmaster at Lowell High School, still remains in my memory—going back to my high school days—because it seems that at every turn in my life I felt his hand on my shoulder turning me in the right direction.

MR. SULLIVAN INTRODUCTION

My first contact with Headmaster Raymond A. Sullivan occurred shortly after entering Lowell High School, in my freshman year in the old building on Kirk Street. That building housed all the ninth graders entering from schools that only had eight grades.

We were having an introduction presentation by the freshman floor-master in the assembly hall, when I was singled out and sent to the main office for discipline.

In a fatherly manner, Mr. Sullivan explained that when I placed my feet on the back of the chair in front of me it was showing disrespect for Mr. Brown during his address to the freshman class. He told me that the punishment was a one hour detention after school, and he also related that his door would always be open for me and that he did not expect to see me again unless it was under more pleasant circumstances.

This brings to my mind the barber shop incident when he was extremely instrumental in getting my father to reverse his position so I could remain in school. Then again, he gave me fatherly advice to take advantage of the post war G.I. Bill that would provide me with a free college education.

Mr. Sullivan also took me aside to explain the importance of keeping up with my studies while away in the Army. He provided me with the necessary study information and courses that I would need to be eligible to return as a senior to complete my high school education and qualify for college.

When I was leaving his office he gave me a relatively tight hand shake with his arthritic right hand and gave me a paper with his left hand. The paper contained two phone numbers—one was the high school number and the other was his home number. Then he stated that if I had any questions with the study courses or needed his help that **I WAS TO CALL HIM COLLECT.**

RETURNING TO HIGH SCHOOL

When I returned to Lowell High School fifteen months later as a veteran of the U.S. Army Paratroopers, Mr. Sullivan had me come to his office and again using his Headmaster and Fatherly skills, reminded me of our first encounter when I was a freshman. He frankly stated that, "now as a veteran and being older than most students, you will be in a position to influence some of the younger students, **SO SET A GOOD EXAMPLE!!"**

Mr. Sullivan also reviewed my high school credits and selected the classes and teachers necessary for my college preparation. I remember him taking me into the classroom of Mr. Reardon, who had the reputation of being the toughest English teacher at LHS, and briefly discussing my family history and the need of his assistance.

Well, Mr. Reardon not only gave me extra attention, he drove me twice as hard as any football coach I've ever had. It seemed like I was having English for breakfast, lunch and dinner, with extra homework and tutoring during recesses.

NUMBER ONE FOOTBALL FAN

As I reflect back in time, I can now envision that Mr. Raymond A. Sullivan had to be the greatest football supporter in the history of Lowell High School. Not only did he attend every game, he also had the four oldest of his six children—Brendan (age ten), Raymond (nine), Neil (eight) and Brian (seven)—with him, either standing in back of the players' bench or sitting nearby.

This is a great photo of our Lowell High School, Hall of Fame, Coach Ray Riddick with me by his side with my helmet in hand. Our expressions tell the story of an anxious moment as the coach grinds his teeth. Directly in back of him is our trainer, Taffy Tavaris and to the right is Assistant Coach Al Mangan. Notice in the background, another sell out standing only crowd. Lowell Sun photo

He always was the first to congratulate me on a good play and was ever so forgiving when I fumbled or the likes.

His other two children—Ellen (age four) and Quentin (three)— at the time remained at home with their mother, Marguerite, listening to Tom Clayton broadcasting the games live on their radio.

NOTE—that was the non-television era!!

COMING TO THE RESCUE

A few years later, I transferred from the Los Angeles College of Chiropractic (LACC) in California to the Chiropractic Institute of New York (CINY) in New York City.

The main reason for transferring was that we were expecting our second child, Lyn. Claire had such a tough delivery with Titus, Jr. she preferred having the same obstetrician, Dr. Herb Abrams, MD., in Lowell, Mass.

Sullivan Tappan Inn—I shared the room with Paddy on the top level, left corner window facing Oak Tree Road—Currently called Oak Tree Inn

Mr. Sullivan again came to the rescue when he heard that Claire was to remain in Lowell with her parents—Francois and Laurea (Doyon) Hebert— while I was searching for living accommodations and attending school in New York.

He called his brother Leonard, who owned and operated the Sullivan Tappan Inn in Tappan, N.Y., which was situated only thirteen miles from the George Washington Bridge and twenty-five miles from West Point Academy. Headmaster Sullivan explained my dilemma to his brother and asked if he could provide me temporary living quarters.

Without hesitation, Leonard replied in the affirmative. After all, he only had eleven children of his own.

BEING A SULLIVAN FOR SIX MONTHS

Leonard (Lenny or Sully) and wife Mary Edna treated me like one of their own, but trying to keep track of their children and remember their names was more difficult than most of my classroom work.

For the next six months I had the pleasure of being a Sullivan, as they all treated me like I was just another member of the family. I never met a bunch that was so kind, compassionate and caring for one another.

I am listing the whole clan, even the three oldest who were not living at home at the time. I did eventually meet them and was able to witness that they were all from the same mold.

The Sullivan clan is as follows:

Cornelius (Connie), 21 years old, married and serving in the Army,
Anne Marie, 20, and attending college and later entered the Sisters of Saint Dominic in Caldwell, N.J.
Hugh (Hughie), 19, and in college,
Mary Agnes (Aggie), 18, working in the restaurant and later entered the Sisters of Saint Dominic,
Patrick (Paddy), 17, my buddy, roommate and personal guide of the Sullivan establishment,
Edna (Goggy), 15,
Leonard (Lenny), 13,
Michael (Mickey), 10,
Thomas (Tommy), 8,
Brendan, 6, and
Eileen, 4.

BUSY IN THE RESTAURANT

For the next six months I used my Dutch Tea Room skills in the restaurant. Having always been an early riser, it was not difficult for me to get into the kitchen, wash the dishes and pots and pans from the previous evening's business as a means of showing my appreciation for the temporary room and board accommodations.

Many times I was reprimanded by the Sullivan clan for my actions. However, my insistence prevailed, and on weekends when it was exceptionally busy I helped at the bar and even waited on tables when they were shorthanded. **IT WAS ONE OF THE MOST PLEASANT EXPERIENCES OF MY LIFE!!**

Oh, I almost forgot to mention that Claire came up for a weekend visit after Lyn was born and Steven was presented nine months later!! MUST HAVE BEEN THAT SULLIVAN SYNDROME!!

SULLIVAN HISTORY LESSON

My six months stay at the Tappan Inn was somewhat of a history lesson relative to Headmaster Sullivan's six siblings and the closeness of the families. By seniority they were: Veronica, Raymond, Father Walter (a Dominican priest), Fred, Leonard, Marion and Earnest, an attorney and funeral director from Lowell.

When Leonard passed away in 1961, his son, Patrick, took over the leadership role of running the Sullivan Tappan Inn at the age of twenty-two.

A year later, Patrick married Kathleen and they, like all the Sullivan's, punched out four quick ones, all boys, in 1963, 1964, 1965 and 1967.

Sullivan family reunions started shortly thereafter, hosted by Edna (Leonard's widow) and Patrick & Kathleen at the Sullivan Tappan Inn. A news clipping from 1970, titled **"IT'S A FAMILY AFFAIR"** included a photo and a short paragraph which said it all : "130 Sullivan's shown at their third reunion that started 10 years ago, coming from all over the United States, including the entire Sullivan clan from Lowell".

Please notice the smiling faces of Raymond and his sister Veronica in the photo. That, to me, shows **LOVE AND KINDNESS** that cannot be found in text books.

IT'S A FAMILY AFFAIR WITH
PADDY AT THE GRILL

Pat Sullivan dishes out the goodies for Sister Anne Sullivan and his mother Edna

X-MAS EVE RITUAL

For many years it was a ritual on X-Mas Eve to visit with Mr. Sullivan, tip a glass of spirits and reminisce about my early days at Lowell High School. This continued on until the early 1970's.

Titus, Jr. graduated from LHS in the spring of '71 and, as luck would have it, with Mr. Sullivan still at the helm, he informed me when "my attention" was needed.

Several years later when Titus Jr. graduated from Boston University School of Medicine, Mr. Sullivan put him in touch with his son Raymond, who was an orthopedic surgeon practicing in the Boston area. Dr. Raymond Sullivan, just as warm and helpful as his dad, was quick to offer assistance to Titus, Jr. and recommended the best procedures to follow in locating an available orthopedic residency.

TEACHING AT LOWELL HIGH

Let me set the stage for one of my Lowell High School teaching experiences.

Mr. Sullivan once again came to my aid, this time by providing me with a substitute teaching job, filling in for a biology teacher on maternity leave. I was in the process of setting up my private chiropractic practice in the Lowell area and by then we had three children—Titus, Jr. (six years old), Lyn (four) and Steven (three), with Diane due on April 17, 1959.

One of my biology classes seemed to have all the kids that were waiting to come of age to bail out of school. Noisy and disruptive would be an understatement, and you will have to envision the setting to appreciate this story.

The room was on the third floor of the attached old building on Kirk Street, with creaky hard wood floors and old hanging ceiling lights.

Now, it was this particular day that I was determined to get the attention of the rowdies in the back row. I remember instructing the class to turn to a particular page in our class biology book that showed the muscle structure of the butt and lower extremities. However, I didn't get their attention until I jumped up and stood on top of the desk.

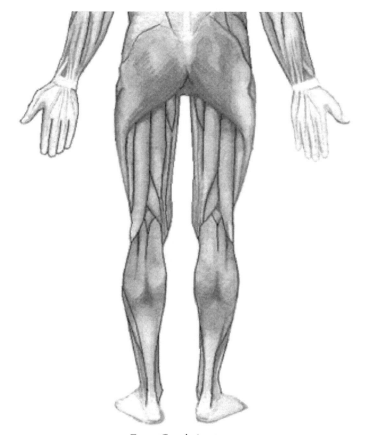

From Grey's Anatomy

I then stated in a considerably louder tone that I was going to demonstrate how I, as a former U.S. Army Paratrooper, used these same muscles to protect my legs and body from breakage when jumping out of an airplane in Japan. You could hear a pin drop, which was not the norm for this particular class.

I proceeded to verbalize as I demonstrated the exact posture when debarking from the plane to landing on the ground:

Standing in the plane's open doorway, looking out into space to remove the fear component,

Knees close together and slightly flexed,

Chin tucked into chest to prevent whiplash,

Elbows tucked close to the sides of my body with my hands in front, wrapped around the reserve parachute in case the main chute didn't open.

NOTE—By this time the back row group had moved to the empty seats up front.

I continued as if making an actual live jump, explaining that when leaving the plane, as instructed in paratrooper training, one had to count aloud **SLOWLY**:

ONE THOUSAND
TWO THOUSAND
THREE THOUSAND

If the main chute didn't open at the three thousand count, then pull the emergency chute. I explained that if in haste, like a lot of beginners do, one counted real fast one-two-three and pulled the emergency chute prematurely, two parachutes might open and clash with each other, causing them both to collapse. **DRASTIC RESULTS!!**

Now, back to the classroom and on top of the desk, in perfect deplaning posture **I JUMPED OFF THE DESK**, landing on the balls of my feet, and in a high vocal tone related to the class as I was performing the paratrooper landing maneuver:

"GASTROCNEMIUS AND ONTO THE GLUTEUS MAXIMUS"—as shown on page—

Because of the loud noise and the paint dust that fell from the ceiling below and the lights shaking as if preparing to collapse, two teachers rushed into my classroom with the intention of rescuing me from uncontrollable students, only to find me in complete control and the kids in their seats and waiting for the next episode!!

What made me do it? **Boston University Flashback!** One of my Phys. Ed. Professor's famous quotes was, " **A GOOD TEACHER CAN REACH EVEN THE UNDISCIPLINED BY FINDING HIS INTEREST**".

In this case, the interest was a practice jump from the platform tower to the ground or from desktop to the floor, **SAME PRINCIPLE.**

For the next twenty years, at all our class reunions and school functions, Mr. Sullivan related that story and we had a good laugh as he would say , "Those kids will never forget the **GASTROCNEMIUS AND GLUTEUS MAXIMUS** muscles."

CLOSURE—Mr. Sullivan's assistance continued on, then to our son, Titus, Jr's guidance through high school and on going until his peaceful departure to a better world in May of 1988.

STANLEY J. STOKLOSA

Having Stan as my math/accounting teacher in my freshman year at Lowell High School was like winning the lottery. Not only did he treat me like his kid brother, he became my **PEN PAL** when, at 17 years old, I went into the United States Army Paratroopers and served time in Japan (see paratrooper story).

"MISTER BASEBALL"

Stan served forty-four years as a teacher/administrator at LHS and was one of the most successful baseball coaches in the state of Massachusetts, compiling an overall record of 286-171-3 (a .626 winning percentage) during a twenty-four-year span, before retiring following the 1968 season.

He was inducted into the Massachusetts State Baseball Coaches Hall of Fame in 1974 and Lowell High School's Athletic Hall of Fame in 1986, the first class of inductees.

Additional honors came in 1992 when the dedication of "The Stanley J. Stoklosa Athletic Foyer" took place, and then in 1999 the Lowell High baseball field was officially renamed "**The Stoklosa/Alumni Field**". This was also the site of the Lowell Spinners' first home, and midget auto racing took place here just before World War II.

Stan's best fan during his baseball career was his beloved wife, Kay, who passed away in 1998. She was a fixture seated in the stands during most LHS games when her husband was in the dugout. The Stoklosa Middle School on Broadway Street, Lowell, was named in her honor as she served many years on the city's school committee.

STAN AND KAY FOREVER

Stan's field   Katherine Philbin Stoklosa Middle School

What better tribute to two very special people in my life than placing Stan and Kay side by side for Eternity; as Stan would say, **"A PERFECT DOUBLE PLAY."**

STARRING ON THE MOUND

Stan was an outstanding pitcher for Lowell High in 1934 and '35, with the latter team advancing as far as the State Tourney finals, eventually losing to Somerville. In 1934, he pitched for the Lowell American Legion squad that went to the championship game with Springfield.

Continuing his mound exploits, Stan hurled for Boston University for four seasons, followed by two years of action with a semi-pro team in New Hampshire.

Stanley J. Stoklosa and Katherine (Philbin) Stoklosa would get my vote for the most dedicated couple of the century after 49 years of marriage.

TAKING COMMAND IN THE DUGOUT

Stan began his coaching career at Lowell High in 1945, and he stayed in command of the Red and Gray nines up through 1968.

"Stok's" teams competed in the tough Greater-Boston League for nineteen years, finishing in second place no fewer than nine times and apparently winning one championship with a 14-2 record, only to lose the title on a replay of a protested game. His teams never finished lower than fourth in the talent-loaded GBL, which included such powerhouses as Somerville, Everett, Malden, Medford, Quincy, Revere, and Chelsea.

Lowell then joined the Essex County League in 1964, facing rivals Lawrence, Lynn Classical, Lynn English, Salem, Saugus, Beverly, Haverhill and Peabody. Stan's Red and Gray squads were major contenders in this circuit, capturing two Essex League championships and winding up second twice during his final five seasons at the helm, posting an overall record of 80-31-1 during that span, 56-23 in League play.

THAT CHAMPIONSHIP FEELING—1964

The 1964 season emerged as a memorable one for Stok, as his LHS nine wound up with a 19-5 record for the complete season, winning the Essex League crown in its inaugural campaign and nearly capturing the Eastern Mass. Class A championship, being edged out by Waltham, 2-1, in the semi-finals at the M.I.T. diamond. The strong pitching of fireballer Larry Connell and the change of pace mound work of Pete Bouchard carried Stan's club nearly all the way to the State crown. Connell posted a 12-1 record, with a 0.79 earned run average, along with 159 strikeouts in 98 innings.

The most memorable victory that season took place here at Alumni Field when Lowell shocked No. 1 seed Catholic Memorial, 6-4, in an earlier tourney game. Frank Kasilowski's home run over the centerfield fence was the winning blow, off star pitcher Skip Lockwood, who signed a $100,000 contract with the California Angels the next week.

Stan's final season as LHS mentor, 1968, had him emerging with an Essex League championship and a 15-6-1 record. Brian Martin and Tommy Whalen were the big guns of this club, with Martin pitching the only perfect game in Lowell High history—a 2-0 victory over Peabody on May 28. Stan's finale as LHS coach took place at the Shedd Park diamond as the Red and Gray lost to city rival Keith Academy, 3-2.

The Hall of Fame coach was a master at developing outstanding pitchers, and sixteen of his overall players eventually signed professional contracts. Among these were such standouts as Leo Parent, Bill Ecklund, Nick Macaronis, Jimmy Fallon, Sam Goodsoozian, Bud Slattery, Ray Michel, Tommy Whalen and Larry Connell.

BASEBALL CAREER ROLLED ON

Stan became a "Bird Dog" scout for the Brooklyn Dodgers, Philadelphia A's and the Baltimore Orioles, scanning the New England area for young diamond talent. He also managed the Nashua, N.H., team to the Twin State League championship for the Dodgers.

Stok was also a major contributor to the youth baseball scene in Lowell. He became an organizer and leader for a host of city programs, being a founder of the Prep League and Connie Mack League and serving as president of the Lowell Babe Ruth League, in addition to coaching Lowell to the State Prep League championship.

ENTERING THE "HALL"

Stanley J. Stoklosa finally received his highest honor when he was nominated to the Massachusetts State Baseball Coaches Association's Hall of Fame by close friend, Mike Skaff, who succeeded him as Lowell High coach. He was formally inducted at the Clinic and Hall of Fame ceremony held at Brandeis University on February 2, 1974.

Stan was previously honored by the Greater-Lowell Baseball Umpires Association at a testimonial affair upon his retirement as **LHS** coach.

BEST DRESSED TEACHER

Stan was voted the best dressed teacher at Lowell High, year after year. I later found out his secret. "You see, his dad was the best tailor in town," pointed out Mickey Finn, who was a second baseman on Stok's first **LHS** team, "and being the proud father that he was, wanted to be sure that his son attended school with a classy wardrobe".

Another little secret was that Kay, as a student at that time, was mesmerized by Stan's charm and good looks as well as his wardrobe. The rest is history!!

A WEDDING PHOTOGRAPHER

OH!! There is one little addition to this story. Stan hired me to take their wedding pictures. As I reflect back in time (1950), I can now appreciate even more that Stan was just trying to help me financially as I had just opened **TITUS' PHOTO STUDIO** on Gorham Street and had very little experience in candid weddings.

My fiancée, Claire Hebert, helped with the phone and over-the-counter transactions while I was matriculating at Boston University during the week in the offseason.

At times, Stan acted as my business manager, without a contract or compensation, and he solicited my services for his sister in law's (Dorothea "Dotty" Philbin) wedding to Dr. Paul Burke, also in 1950.

REMINISCING WITH STAN

I make it a point to either call or visit with Stan several times a year, as he is currently ninety-four years old and has been failing in health, including blindness.

My most recent visit with the coach was in March of 2012. We sat in his living room reminiscing about our sixty-five-year relationship, going back to my freshman year in high school when he was my accounting teacher.

I always have fun in relating to Stan's accounting class and how his technique in teaching made it easy for me to make a simple mathematical decision, like the following:

When I first tried out for the football team as a freshman and the coach said, "All the linemen to the left and all the backfield candidates to the right," I noticed that fourteen kids moved over with the line coach and about fifty moved over with the backfield group. **STAN'S ODDS** dictated that I had a much better chance of making the team as a lineman than in the backfield. He was right again as I did make the team as a guard and the backup place kicker, perhaps the smallest in our conference.

For those of you that are not football oriented, it takes **SEVEN LINEMEN and FOUR BACKS** to make up a full team.

SIMILARITIES

Stan quite often would use baseball lingo when comparing our likenesses. At our most recent get-together, he told me where to sit in his living room, knowing that he could not see me but by doing so we'd be facing each other and he'd talk in my direction.

"Titus, in all my years of baseball the **TRIPLE PLAY** was the most difficult to accomplish", he said. Then he went on to give me a brief history lesson, "We have commonality in that we were both **LHS** senior class presidents, me in 1935 and you in 1949. We both went to Boston University on athletic scholarships, me in baseball, 1935-38, and you in football,1949-1953, and we have both been inducted into **LHS** Athletic Hall of Fame, me in 1986 and you in 1996. Now, that's a triple play that odds makers in Vegas would have trouble making book on."

He continued as if still in the classroom, giving me a math lesson: "Add the fact that my father was born in Poland and your father was born in Greece—that's what is called a **GRAND SLAM!!**"

PAY BACK TIME

Stan reminded me of one of his greatest memories, that he refers to as **TITUS'S PAYBACK TIME**, when back in the early 60's I had accepted the role of Lowell High School Boosters Club president, in what he described as "a time consuming, thankless job." He reminded me that the leadership produced a ten-fold increase in membership, and promotional events that raised funds, which in turn provided a sundry of benefits to the school's athletic programs, including the much-needed **AUTOMATIC PITCHING MACHINE FOR THE BASEBALL TEAM!!**

16 THE LOWELL SUN, TUESDAY, APRIL 9, 1963

Pitching Machine at Lowell High

Lowell high baseball Coach Stan Stoklosa and Booster club president, Dr. Titus Plomaritis, left, look over the school's new pitching machine along with front line hurler Larry Connell. The machine, donated by the Boosters club, got its first workout at yesterday's practice session. Batting is the Red and Gray's catcher Mike O'Brien.

STAN IN RETIREMENT

Stan watches his beloved Lowell high team in action at Alumni Field in 1969 during his retirement years.

THE END OF A LEGEND

Stanley J. Stoklosa, "MISTER BASEBALL" for the city of Lowell for over seven decades, celebrated his final birthday on November

Stan in Retirement
Stan watches his beloved Lowell high team in action at Alumni Field in 1969 during his retirement years.

13, 2011, passed away on Friday, June 8, 2012, at the age of 94 at a local Healthcare Center.

Stan had been in failing health for the past few years, and had been aided and comforted by his devoted friend Martin "Mickey" Finn.

At Stan's services, I finally met Elizabeth Parker of Loomis, California, whom I've been communicating with by phone and e-mail over the past 18 months. She introduced me to her brother John Stoklosa, from St. Croix, Minnesota and her sister Jean Ballard from San Francisco.

She sent me the following letter when she returned home, "it was such a joy to meet you in person as we wished Godspeed to dear uncle Stan, I look forward to reading 'Titus' as I have heard so much about your amazing life story, and it would be delightful to read it in your own words. Stanley must have felt very honored to be part of the book."

LOWELL HIGH BOOSTERS CLUB

REVIVAL OF THE BOOSTERS CLUB

LOWELL—Circa 1962—The Lowell High School Boosters Club, once faced with extinction, has been rescued and revived with a bang, thanks to the election of Dr. Titus Plomaritis as its new president.

The man who led the Lowell High football team to its first undefeated season and its first bowl game 14 years ago, has been elected to head the Club for the 1962 season, and hopefully beyond.

Others voted to join the former LHS star left halfback as Club officers include Sam Hovnanian, first vice-president; Dave Stecchi, Sr., second vice-president, and Paul Donovan, treasurer.

Also, the new board of Directors is now composed of Ray Archambault, William Burke, John Machado, Walter Nelson, Sr., Josephine LeBourdais, Dennis McLaughlin, Richard Campbell, Joseph McCarthy, Ray Wojcik, Ray Beland, Edward Moore, Joseph Moore, Jack Noonan, Cliff Folkins, Mendel Banks and Manuel Avila.

SEEKING TO PUSH MEMBERSHIP OVER 1,000

Bolstered by an official proclamation, signed by Lowell Mayor Joseph Downes, which officially declared the next seven days as "Lowell High Boosters Club Week", the Boosters are staging a mammoth drive to push their membership over the 1,000 mark.

Club President **DR. TITUS PLOMARITIS** announced that the co-chairmen for the big week are two past presidents of the Club—**RAY ARCHAMBAULT** and **DAVE STECCHI, SR.** —plus another hard-working member, **MENDEL BANKS.**

The Boosters will take over the downtown area on Thursday night, as members of the Lowell High band, cheerleaders and girl officers will assist

241

Club members in their efforts to enroll new members among the horde of shoppers.

President Plomaritis points out that anyone is eligible to become a member, whether he or she attended Lowell High as a student.

NOTE—The drive was a success, as the official members totaled 1,245, and it became a nationwide drive.

GOVERNOR OF HAWAII ENROLLED

Dr. Plomaritis, former Lowell High and Boston University scatback and place-kicking specialist, credits **RAY ARCHAMBAULT**, a past president, for the nation-wide membership distinction.

"Ray dreamed up the plan to extend the membership all over the country, and saw it through," says Dr. Plomaritis, "putting in many hours."

Dr. Titus Plomaritis LHS Boosters Club President, left and Ray Archambault, past President hold the bulletin board display of memberships covering every state in the USA and a few foreign countries. Lowell Sun photo

Dr. Plomaritis went on: "Ray wrote to Lowell natives, servicemen, and in general just about everybody ever connected with Lowell, and the plan materialized. Even the Governor of Hawaii holds membership!!"

THE CLUB'S HISTORY AND NEW PLANS

The LHS Boosters Club first came into being back in the "historic" 1948 season, with the late Pete Lamson as president.

The Club spent $1,400 that year for a banquet and awards for the undefeated football team, and in succeeding years a total of $4,915 has been spent toward similar awards and banquets for Lowell High teams in all sports.

Other presidents of the Club over the years included Courtland Burkinshaw, Robert Turcotte, Dick Silver, Robert McGee, Dave Stecchi,

Sr., Paul Donovan, Richard Campbell, Joseph Moore, Slifford Folkins and Raymond Archambault.

The Club now meets every Wednesday night during the football season at the Lowell High cafeteria, where films of the previous LHS football games are shown, with **COACH RAY RIDDICK** on hand to outline the action. Meetings are open to the public.

HONORING THE RED AND GRAY ATHLETES

The Boosters Club went on to hold many successful affairs to honor the Lowell High athletes.

The Club presented its first annual Appreciation Dance at Lowell Memorial Auditorium, at which LHS athletes, cheerleaders, band members and baton twirlers were hailed for their efforts on behalf of their high school and its athletic program.

Special awards were presented to athletes on the basketball, track, baseball and golf teams. The football awards were presented early the previous winter at a special gridiron banquet staged by the Boosters Club.

RIDDICK HONORED—Another affair sponsored by the Club took place at a North Chelmsford restaurant, to honor the LHS athletes and coaches of all the Red and Gray teams of the past year.

Over 100 athletes were feted, and a special honor was awarded to Coach **RAY RIDDICK**, in tribute to his 100th football victory at Lowell High.

Place Image 115 here at full page width, center aligned. Caption underneath, "600 IN TRIBUTE OF LHS ATHLETES"

600 in Tribute of LHS Athletes

May 13, 1962, Riddick Honored at LHS Boosters Banquet. Ray Riddick, center, Lowell high head football coach, was honored last night at the Boosters Club Appreciation dinner dance which was held for Lowell high athletes of the past year. The event was staged by the Boosters club at a Dracut restaurant and Riddick was singled out for recognition after he posted his 100th victory as the Lowell high grid iron mentor during the last campaign, With Riddick, from left to right, are toastmaster Frank Sargent, Sun sports editor; Dr. Titus Plomaritis, president of the Boosters club; Raymond Sullivan, LHS headmaster and Paul Sullivan, LHS athletic director. Lowell Sun photo

MORE HONORS FOR RIDDICK—More than 600 players, parents, old and young alumni, and just plain fans jammed a Dracut restaurant for a banquet to pay tribute to members of Lowell High's athletic teams.

The gala dinner-dance, sponsored by the LHS Boosters Club, was a smashing success.

One of the special awards made following the banquet, which was toastmastered by Lowell Sun Sports Editor **FRANK SARGENT**, was presented to Head Coach Ray Riddick, in honor of his 100th victory at the helm of LHS grid teams since 1947.

"I contribute about one percent in trying to teach these boys how to play the game," Riddick stated. "They do the rest."

A giant cake, donated by former Lowell High lineman **BENNY PRICE**, of Price's Bakery, highlighted the occasion. The cake, weighing more than

60 pounds, was decorated with scenes depicting all sports played at the high school.

Special guests of the evening, in addition to the members of the football, basketball, baseball, track and golf teams, were several Boston schoolboy sports editors, representatives of the local radio stations, City Manager **CORNELIUS DESMOND** and Mayor **ELLEN SAMPSON**.

FAMED SPORTSWRITERS LAUD THE CLUB

By Ralph Wheeler
Boston Herald

(A letter sent to Boosters Club President Dr. Titus Plomaritis, after being invited to the Appreciation Dinner.)

BOSTON—Dear Titus—Thank you sincerely for your kind invitation to the Boosters Club's Appreciation Dinner for the Lowell High School athletes and my great friend, Ray Riddick.

I would love to attend, but my problem is, as in past years at other similar dinners, I do not drive, so I would have to bring a friend, who would drive me back and forth. I would be glad to pay for his ticket, but I do not like to impose on you in this respect in case you do not have sufficient room at one of the tables.

NOTE—Boosters Club President Dr. Titus Plomaritis took care of that problem, sending the appropriate amount of tickets.

I was just telling a Greek youngster, Billy Kipouras (also a sportswriter), whom I was lucky enough to get into the Herald Sports Department, that I have more friends in Lowell than in any other city, particularly Greek boys like yourself—Ted Kemos, George Spaneas and Minnie Mavraides.

Thank you again, Titus, and I hope we can get together.

Sincerely,

RALPH WHEELER,

Boston Herald Schoolboy Sports Editor

By Bill Kipouras
Boston Herald

SALEM—Unique is the only description for the Lowell High Boosters Club, which according to **DR. TITUS PLOMARITIS**, the Club's president, "is the only Boosters Club in the United States that has at least one member in each of the 50 states, plus foreign countries."

Numbering 1,245 members—its largest enrollment since the formation of the organization in 1948—the Lowell Boosters provide scholarships, achievement awards, trophies, donations to Red Raiders' bowl trips, and climaxes each year with the annual Appreciation Banquet for all Lowell High athletic teams.

FORMER ATHLETES JOINING CLUB

The Lowell High Boosters Club is seeing more and more former LHS athletes taking prominent positions in the current edition of the Club.

Among the 15 new members of the Board of Directors are six well-known former lettermen in football, basketball and baseball—Bob Avila, John Sarantakis, Jimmy Fallon, Ed Correa, George Spaneas and Minnie Malliaros.

PLOMARITIS TO LEAD LHS BOOSTERS CLUB AGAIN

LOWELL—Nov. 29, 1962—Dr. Titus Plomaritis was unanimously re-elected to the office of President of the Lowell High Boosters Club last night, and in appreciation of his past efforts in rehabilitating the Club he was presented with a gavel.

The election was held at the Lowell High School cafeteria, where a crowd of over 500—the largest of the year—jammed into the cafeteria to watch movies of the Lowell-Lawrence Thanksgiving Day football game, and to elect new officers of the Boosters Club for the 1963 term.

Boosters Expect 5,000 Signatures

BOOSTERS PETITIONERS—DR. Titus Plomaritis, seated second from left, president of the Lowell Boosters Club, holds petitions distributed at recent club meeting held at the Lowell YMCA. The Boosters hope to impress the school committee with public support of their request to obtain the 1963 program concession for high school athletic events. Others in the group are, from left, Mrs. Barbara Drewniak, secretary; Ben Price, vice president; and Dennis McLaughlin. Standing: Sam Hovnanian, William Burke, Dave Stecchi Nat Matthews, Tay Archambault, Joseph Moore, Mendel Banks and Phil McDonnell. Lowell Sun photo

BENNIE PRICE was elected first vice-president, and other officers voted in unanimously were **MENDEL BANKS,** second vice-president; **PAUL DONAVAN**, treasurer, and **BARBARA DREWNIAK**, secretary.

Following the official business, Lowell High Coach **RAY RIDDICK** showed colored movies of the Thanksgiving Day football game, and interpreted several of the key plays.

Dave Banks, Captain Tom Machado and Larry Begley received applause for their fine performances shown in the movies. Banks scored twice; Machado turned in a stellar effort on both offense and defense, and the movies also showed Begley making numerous tackles.

It was also announced that the Boosters will present their annual awards dinner to honor the players, scheduled to be held at the Polish-American Club on December 13.

BOOSTERS HONOR ALL LHS ATHLETES

By Howard Iverson
Lowell Sun

LOWELL—May 17, 1963—The Lowell High Boosters Club honors members of all **LHS** athletic teams, coaches, cheerleaders, the band, baton twirlers and girl officers. No one is overlooked.

Under the very able leadership of **DR. TITUS PLOMARITIS**, the **LHS** Boosters Club has grown by leaps and bounds over the past two years. It is a thriving, active organization, working toward the betterment of the Lowell High athletic program.

"Our primary object," says Dr. Plomaritis, "is to stimulate as many boys and girls as possible to participate in sports. We feel that an annual Appreciation-Awards Night, which takes place tonight at the Auditorium, creates interest in the athletic opportunities available to high school students. We hope to encourage more and more youngsters to try out for the various teams."

In that direction, the Boosters Club president voices whole-hearted approval of the junior high expansion program initiated by new Athletic Director **AL MANGAN.** Fourteen basketball and baseball leagues in each junior high have been proposed by Mangan as a method of ultimately strengthening the high school hoop and diamond squads.

"Al Mangan has taken a step in the right direction," says Dr. Plomaritis. "Constructive programs such as this are needed if we are to effectively promote interest among the high school eligibles in all sports."

BOOSTERS HELP IN BIG TURNOUTS

The Boosters are also doing a great deal to create enthusiasm among potential athletes. Their vigorous efforts—awards nights, scholarships, the baseball pitching machine, etc.—are being rewarded on several fronts.

Over 120 boys turned out for baseball this spring, a near-record number of candidates for Coach **STAN STOKLOSA**.

While it would be presumptuous to give the Boosters full credit for this fine turnout, it is certain that their sports promotion campaign was responsible for much of this increased interest in baseball this season.

WINLESS BASKETBALL TEAM NOT FORGOTTEN

LOWELL—With the behind-the-scenes help of the Boosters Club, the 1963 Lowell High baseball team was rejuvenated when a near-record 120 boys tried out for the team.

However, on the downside, the Red and Gray basketball squad was in the midst of doldrums, just completing a winless season, losing over 20 straight games, including a pair of setbacks to city rival Keith Academy, 68-47, and 58-37 (loss No. 19).

LHS Boosters Basketball Banquet
From left, John Abraham, Assistant Coach, Dr. Titus Plomaritis, Boosters club president, Henry Lisien, Head Coach and Peter Trivers, Capt." Lowell Sun photo

During the early 1960's, basketball was at the bottom of the totem pole at LHS. Many of the school's leading athletes—such as Dennis Canney, Brent Nelson, Bruce Brown, etc.—decided to stick with their major sports and stay away from the bouncing ball activities.

"—And we did this despite the fact that **WE ALL COULD DUNK THE BALL!!**" commented Canney in a recent interview.

THE BOOSTER CLUB then decided to come to the aid of the LHS hoopsters, trying to soothe the memories of the recent disastrous season and raise their hopes for future campaigns.

The past season marked Henry Lisien's debut as head coach, with John Abraham the assistant mentor and Peter Trivers the team's captain. Lisien, also one of the top basketball referees in the area, was regarded as a brilliant mind in the sport, but LHS, unfortunately had to compete in the rugged Greater-Boston League at that time and had to face such powerhouses as Somerville, Everett, Malden, etc., and the locals just didn't have the manpower to stay with them.

LHS HOOPSTERS ON THE BOTTOM OF THE TOTEM POLE

With football and baseball dominating the interest in Lowell High sports during the early 1960's, the Red and Gray basketball team was always being overlooked—so the Boosters Club decided to step in to aid the maligned hoopsters.

Club President **DR. TITUS PLOMARITIS** made a phone call to **WALTER BROWN,** the founder (1946), president (1946-63) and general manager (1946-64) of the mighty Boston Celtics, who were in the midst of an eight-year streak as National Basketball Association champions.

Dr. Plomaritis pointed out to Brown the plight of the Lowell High five, and asked if the Celtics' mogul could help out.

HELP OUT BROWN DID!!

He invited the entire Lowell High squad, coaches and managers to attend a forthcoming Celtics' game.

WELCOMED TO THE GARDEN

The Lowell High basketball unit had tremendous seats, courtesy of Walter Brown and the Boston Celtics, right behind the Boston team's bench.

The members of the Red and Gray squad were given the lush opportunity to witness some of the all-time greats of Celtics' history in action, players such as Hall of Famers Bill Russell, Bob Cousy, Tommy Heinsohn, Bill Sharman, Frank Ramsey, Sam Jones, K.C. Jones, etc., and, of course, legendary **COACH ARNOLD "RED" AUERBACH.**

This Celtic team went on to post a 58-22 seasonal record, plus nabbing another NBA championship.

The Lowell youngsters thus were able to shake off memories of their dismal past season and look forward to their future exploits.

THE BOOSTERS CLUB was not done in coming to the aid of the 1962-63 Lowell High basketball team, also honoring the hoopsters with a testimonial banquet.

CLUB'S MEMBERSHIP BOOMING

Membership in the Boosters Club has increased many times its original number during the past two years, thanks to the untiring efforts of Dr. Plomaritis, Mendel Banks, Benny Price, Barbara Drewniak, Dave Stecchi, Sr., Ray Archambault and Bob Avila, to name only a few of its hard-working members.

Countless hours have been spent formulating plans for the ultimate benefit of all sports participants and athletes-to-be at Lowell High. The Boosters' plans for the immediate future are even more ambitious.

RALPH S. BATTLES

Ralph was my very first paying patient, who became one of my best friends and golfing partner at the Vesper Country Club (Tyngsboro, Mass.) right up to his early, unexpected demise at the age of 68, in 1983.

In 1958 it was quite common and economically prudent to live and practice in a home-office combination. We had located a suitable lot just five miles from downtown Lowell on Route 38 in Pelham, New Hampshire.

I should also mention that although we would have preferred setting up shop in Lowell, Massachusetts, it was not a licensed chiropractic state at that time. Chiropractors were being arrested for practicing medicine without a license. With three children and expecting our fourth, I could not take a chance of going to jail and leaving my family unattended.

We moved into our new three bedroom split level home-office in Pelham. However, the office component that occupied the entire lower level was not finished or equipped to handle patients.

THE SETTING here took place at Alumni Field, as Coach Ray Riddick had created an assistant football coaching position for me, not funded by the school department, but by him personally.

Now, with that said, following one of our practice sessions at Alumni Field, Ralph came to pick up his son Philip, who was the freshman quarterback. Ralph was limping as well as listing to one side, and Coach Riddick informed him that I was a licensed chiropractor in the process of opening an office in Pelham, and could help him.

When I told Ralph that my office wasn't ready to receive patients, he asked me if I made house calls. Without any hesitation I answered in the affirmative, got directions to his Tewksbury residence, rushed home to pick up my portable table and, quick as a rabbit, went off to treat my first paying patient.

Ralph presented with severe spasm and swelling to his lower back area, and that, in my judgment, could not withstand any type of manipulation.

253

I did the next best thing and reached into my little black bag for a bottle of analgesic ointment. I asked his wife, Martha, to bring me a basin of hot water and a couple of towels. I applied the moist towels and analgesic, followed with several minutes of soft tissue technique that seemed to give Ralph considerable relief.

I advised Ralph to remain home from work for a couple of days. He was a **CEO** for a company in Boston that made rivets for submarines. I made additional house calls on the following two days and was able to apply substantial manipulation to the low back area, with great success.

Ralph gave me a check for $250, along with a cock and bull story about always paying in advance for future treatments, when the truth was that in his conversation with Coach Riddick, he was aware that my mortgage was overdue.

Now, how much of an overpayment was that, considering that office visits were $3.00 at that time!!

DON'T GO AWAY, MY FRIEND, THIS IS NOT THE END OF THE STORY.

Ralph was also my first patient when the office officially opened shortly thereafter. He had a history of neck pain and stiffness that his medical doctor, Dr. Varnum with whom I had a good relationship, had very little success with.

Following a series of tests and X-rays, I proceeded to apply all my skills and training, including Manipulation, Corrective Therapeutic Exercises and Nutritional Supplementation. Ralph, considering his busy schedule, was conscientious in following his regime and never missed an appointment.

What was amazing to Ralph was that when his neck stiffness seemed to no longer be a problem, he related to me that he had experienced headaches for years when driving to and from work in Boston, and since getting his adjustments, the headaches had disappeared. From that day on he insisted on coming to the office for adjustments once monthly, like a religion, for the next twenty-five years.

WAIT!! THERE'S MORE.

VESPER AND GOLF

A few years later (1963), we entertained moving to Lowell, since chiropractic had become legalized and I had a Massachusetts license after passing the first Chiropractic Licensing Examination. But, after careful consideration, especially with the children developing neighborhood friendships and already being established in school, we opted to expand and stay in Pelham, New Hampshire.

About that time we entertained installing a swimming pool in the back yard of our two acre lot, when Ralph asked me if I would be interested in becoming a member of the Vesper Country Club (VCC).

Vesper Country Club, Tyngsboro, Massachusetts

Vesper is one of the oldest country clubs in the USA, founded in 1875, and having a barrel of history. It is an eighteen-hole, extremely well-groomed course with nine of the holes on an island surrounded by the famous Merrimack River. It is also equipped with an Olympic size swimming pool and tennis courts.

I remember Ralph saying, **"TITUS, YOUR FOOTBALL PLAYING DAYS ARE NOW HISTORY. HOWEVER, YOU CAN PLAY GOLF THE REST OF YOUR LIFE."**

Although we felt we couldn't afford it at that time, we realized it would enhance the social growth and development of our children, so we opted for Vesper instead of a pool in the back yard. As time would tell, we apparently made the right decision, seeing that all four of our children were on the VCC swim team and the three oldest later worked as life guards during summer vacations when going to college.

I was not aware of the VCC politics. You see, there was a five-year wait at that time. However, with Ralph on the Executive Committee and serving as president, he said he had a "chit" that would allow me preferential advance on the waiting list.

Dave Hackney, the country club golf pro for forty-four years, gave Buddy and Steven all the fundamentals of golf at the right age. Buddy played on the Lowell High School golf team for two years and lettered four years on the University of Vermont golf team, serving as captain his junior and senior years. To this day they both hold single-digit handicaps.

Now, for me, I never touched a golf club until in my 30's, and although I never became a single-digit handicap golfer, I have been and continue to be very competitive, applying my South Common discipline as well as my high school and college desire to achieve excellence. This makes up for my unconventional golf swing and small stature.

Dave Hackney could have retired much sooner if he ever charged me for all my lessons. He was so thoughtful and unselfish that if he saw me practicing incorrectly, either on the range or on the chipping area, which was often, he would nonchalantly drift over and correct my flaws. With his Scottish accent, he would say, "Now me lad, you can continue".

BEATING THE "BIG BOYS"

For this story I felt that it was necessary to review and record the number of times my name appears on the Championship Plaques that decorate the lounge walls in the Golf House at the Vesper Country Club.

Practice and determination, along with a desire to compete and never to be intimidated by the big guy or the long hitters as I did growing up on the playgrounds, high school and college, will substitute for the lack of a good golf swing.

I have gotten, and still get great satisfaction in competing in and winning matches against a six-footer over 200 pounds that outdrives me by fifty yards. Ralph always advised me not to chase the long hitter, just keep the ball in play and beat him on the green.

I especially find it stimulating when a match is to be decided on the last hole or sudden death, because it reminds me of kicking a **PAT or FIELD GOAL TO WIN THE GAME.**

REMINISCING WITH THE COLLINS FAMILY

Just recently, on a Sunday afternoon, I joined a threesome at Vesper, one of whom was Paul W. Collins, and the other two were Paul's grandson, Justin, a pre-med student at Worcester Poly Tech, and his son-in-law, George Stedman, M.D., husband of his daughter Justine, who was behind the wheel of Paul's cart and keeping score.

On many occasions Paul was one of our Sunday foursomes in the 1960's and 70's. Paul was like a recorder, non-stop relating story after story of executed shots and long putts that he made to win a $2.00 Nassau from Ralph. Now, AT NINETY-THREE YEARS OLD, Paul still has the physical and mental ability to compete with his grandson.

Example—Justin and George both hit their tee shots a mile (250 yard range), while Paul, hitting from the front tees, had consecutive fours on three of Vesper's toughest holes, winning two of the three—and crowing like a rooster!! **IS RALPH A PROPHET, OR WHAT??**

BRAIN POWER

Ralph is always on my mind, especially when I play the eighteenth hole at Vesper, a par five, double dogleg that goes up a hill and then down a hill towards the green. Every time I reach into my bag for a club on that hole following my tee-shot, I can still hear Ralph in the background saying **"PUT THAT WOOD BACK IN YOUR BAG AND HIT YOUR FIVE-IRON!!"**

RALPH: "OUR VESPER SURVIVORS"

Vesper, like many other golf clubs, has favorite golfing groups playing on certain days from week to week. I've been playing with this so-called **Andover Group** for about twenty years. Originally they had close to forty players, now depleted considerably due to deaths or movement to Florida or Arizona. Although we play on Tuesdays, Thursdays, Saturdays and Sundays, we have an agreement that if you're not present by a certain time, the pairings will be made without you. The 2011 season started with the following golfers: Dick Adams, Joey Bashara, Gerry Bousquet, Tony D'Amato, Tom Fardy, Harlan Kelly, Larry Martin, Joe Levis, Phil McKittrick, Bob McKittrick, Bob Nazarian, Nino Palci, Vinny Popolizio, George Sarkisian and Mike Welcome (my current four-ball partner).

—AND THE BIGGEST PRIZE OF ALL?? Winning the annual Member-Member tournament with Ralph Battles, in sudden death overtime, in 1974. Extra special was having Dave Hackney make the presentation of the first "Dave Hackney Cup".

DAVID D. HACKNEY CUP
DR. TITUS PLOMARITIS & RALPH S. BATTLES
WINNERS 1974

Hackney Cup winners

The Vesper Country Club's annual member-member 36-hole golf tourney has been officially named "The David D. Hackney Cup" event, in honor of the 43 years of dedicated service rendered to the club by retiring pro Dave Hackney. The first such award was presented to the winning team of Dr. Titus Plomaritis and Ralph S. Battles, who won the tourney recently on the first hole of sudden death, following a three-way tie with Atty. Richard Drury and Walter B. Reilly, and Atty. Frederick Hoer and Henry Larson. Hackney is shown in the photo at right, making the award to the championship team. Dr. Plomaritis (L) and Battles (C). There were 92 teams competing for the prestigious award this year.

WINNING CHAMPIONSHIPS

Following is a list of my memorable championships at the Vesper Country Club:

Four Four-Ball Championships—
1968, with Ralph Battles (deceased in 1983)
1972, with Harry Briggs (no longer at Vesper)
1995, with Dick Bournival (deceased in 2008)*
2005, with Michael Welcome
One Club Cup Championship—1969
Six Senior Cup Championships—1995, 2000, 2001, 2002, 2007, and 2008.
Eight President Cup Championships—1968, 1974, 1995, 1999, 2000, 2006, 2010 and 2011**

*The 1995 Four-ball Championship was played in heavy rain, on the very last day permitted, or forfeit. My partner and good friend, Dick Bournival was in the hospital recovering from major surgery. I opted to take them on, carrying a 3 wood, 7 iron, pitching wedge and my putter. With Ralph in my head, "keep the ball in play and beat them on the green", and Dick in the hospital, I just wanted to be competitive.

The match went back and forth for fourteen holes, all even going down to the fifteenth hole, the toughest par four at Vesper. Marty Gruber and I got a stroke; I won with a five that put us one up with three to play. Bogies tied the sixteenth hole, staying one up with two to play. The seventeenth was and still is a tough par three under normal conditions. It was extremely tough that day as the pouring rain never let up. It took all three of us two strokes to get on the green. I was away and putting first from about thirty feet. They were both inside the ten foot range. I concentrated on just getting it close as the putting conditions were horrendous and felt that a four had a good chance of tying the hole. Well, would you believe that my putt went in and they both missed, making us the winners, 2 and 1.

When I called the hospital to give Dick's family the good news, they said he was so excited they had to give him a sedative.

**The 2011 Presidents Cup Championship was against a real gentleman, Don Therrien. He displayed outstanding sportsmanship, driving the cart to my ball, helping me in and out of the cart for eighteen holes. I went for my hip replacement with another championship in my trophy case.

BILLIARDS

My billiards skills started way back when I was a little guy, about five or six years old.

Whenever we had inclement weather, we drifted over to the Lowell Boys Club on Dutton Street, which was a real long Lou Groza field goal from the YMCA on the corner of Merrimack and Dutton streets.

They had all kinds of games to play that required two or more participants, but it was the pool tables that caught my fancy. Whenever I had a chance to play with or without an opponent, I remember practicing with the same intensity of practicing my placekicking outdoors.

Going to the next level was Scott's Pool Room on Middlesex Street where I received free coaching from the owner and his poolroom manager during rainy day afternoons when it wasn't busy. In exchange, when they had busy spells, I always volunteered to "rack the balls" so they could attend the counter and phone customers.

For those that do not know what "racking the balls" means, it's removing the balls from the six pockets and placing them into a triangular rack, then setting the lead ball on a spot at the other end of the table and removing the rack.

My pocket billiards skills carried over into high school and the military. However, I never touched a pool cue again until I was in private practice and joined the Lowell Rotary Club in the early 1960's. Practically all of the Rotarians were Greater-Lowell businessmen and belonged to the Yorick Men's Club, which had a half dozen billiard tables of which four were pocketless. The Yorick Club also had a restaurant that was open only to members and their guests—very popular for businessmen's (Martini) lunches.

Pocketless pool, otherwise known as carom billiards, is a variation of pool played with three balls on a pool table that doesn't have pockets.

Three billiard balls

Pocketless billiard table 4 1/2 x 9 feet with three diamonds on each end and seven diamonds on each side

There are two white balls and one red ball, and the object is to strike one white ball so that it strikes the other two, in any order. There weren't five players in the whole club that wanted to take the time to learn the skills of three cushion billiards, so most members played straight carom billiards.

Straight carom billiards removes the three cushion requirement and is worth one point each time you hit the red ball and your opponent's ball. One of the white balls has a red spot on it, the other does not. They are referred to either "plain" or "spot".

SETTING UP THE TABLE

The first player selects either of the two white balls to be his cue ball. The other white ball is placed on a spot on the board called "the head spot". The red ball is then placed on a spot on the board called "the foot spot". The player may place his cue ball anywhere within six inches of the side of the white ball.

The first ball struck by the cue ball must be the red ball. In subsequent shots any ball may be the first one struck by the cue ball. A point is scored when a player successfully hits both of the other balls, and yields to the opponent as soon as the current player fails to score. The opponent then plays the balls as they are positioned on the table, using the opposite white ball as his opponent. Players then take turns until one player has accumulated fifty points. In the event that a player uses the wrong cue ball on his turn he receives a one point penalty and loses his turn.

Now back to the Yorick Men's Club in the mid sixties. I was sponsored by several of my member friends from the Lowell Rotary Club who had followed my athletic career in high school and Boston University. They were all businessmen in the Greater-Lowell community.

I found carom billiards entertaining and challenging so much so that I purchased an antique pocketless billiards table from one of my Rotarian friends for ten cents on the dollar that needed slate repairs and a new table cloth. It fit perfectly into our recreation room and provided several years of recreation for our four children and me.

Within two years I was in the semi-finals of the Yorick Club carom billiards club championships, only to lose to a true gentleman, Ralph Runnels, whose fame was that he played an exhibition match against fifteen-time world champion, Willie Mosconi. Ralph was in his 70's at the time and lost in the finals to Bob Achin, who had won the previous two years.

Ralph could see my interest in becoming a better billiards player and suggested we meet once weekly during the winter months, for competitive toughness. We met every Wednesday from six to nine P.M. to play a game of 100 points. All matches in tournament play were fifty points, except the finals, which were 100 points.

Ralph taught me several game skills, including defensive leaves (difficult ball location for the opponent). But more importantly, he taught me how to play psychologically against Robert Achin, who had a reputation of getting under the skin of his opponents. It was a given that Bob and I would meet in the finals.

With thirty-two players in the "A Division" we each advanced without difficulty to the finals over the next two months. Several large posters announcing the date and time of the finals were hanging up everywhere, like wallpaper, even in the lavatories, saying **WEDNESDAY EVENING AT 6 P.M.**

BILLIARDS—THE CHAMPIONSHIP

The big night finally arrived!!

I was there at 5 p.m., had a light dinner with Ralph Runnels and then went over to one of the unreserved tables and was just practicing my stroke and trying not to get too excited.

By six o'clock the gallery seats had fifteen to twenty members and just about then Bob Achin drifted in, said he hadn't eaten yet and asked if I would allow him a few minutes to have a quick snack. I said okay.

We didn't start until 6:30 and Bob accomplished his psychological warfare as he had me upset from the start and had a commanding lead of 50 to 32 at the ten-minute lavatory break. I couldn't seem to cut into his lead and at about 9:15, it appeared to be over with Bob leading, 99 to 79, and needing only one more point for his four peat championship.

Then, all of a sudden, it seemed like flash bulbs going off in my head!! I felt totally relaxed and could clearly envision my next shot on the table as if practicing at home or with Ralph on our Wednesday evening scrimmages. Up to that time in our title match I hadn't had a run of more than three points.

I remember that Richard K. Donahue's dad and Ralph were the only two remaining in the gallery. They would tap a cue stick on the floor, indicative of a good shot. As my run approached ten, they got louder and louder, one shot after the other, some of the three cushion variety.

I ran twenty straight points and had the score tied at 99 and I had to make a decision as I was stymied. Either I played defensive or pull off a three

Lowell, Massachusetts, Yorick Club's Presidents from 1882

cushioned shot using the diamonds that I had practiced for the past two years. I pretended to be relaxed, but was so excited that I felt like my feet were not touching the floor.

I chalked my cue, stared at the diamonds over and over, set my left hand on the table, positioned my cue and proceeded to make a good smooth stroke and watched my ball hit the first diamond, the second diamond and as it hit the third diamond I knew it had a chance.

With the ball running out of steam it gently approached the two balls, and gave each a kiss on the cheek. Not only was I declared the new club champion, but my run of twenty-one also set a new club record!!

I can now understand the phrase: **DIAMONDS ARE A GIRL'S BEST FRIEND**. But, for me, it will always be James Bond's "**DIAMONDS ARE FOREVER**".

Note: It was about that time that I became more interested in golf and gradually drifted away from billiards—with that **21 GUN SALUTE** always in my memory.

December 22, 1968 **PELHAM BANK AND TRUST** prepares to open. Seated, Louis Fineman, Chairman of the board. Left to right, The Directors and Officers are: Ralph Boutwell, Edward King, James Stadtmiller, Ted Russem, Albert Maki, Ralph Harmon, Leo Sevigny, Dr. Titus Plomaritis, Atty. William McNamara, Leon Litchfield, (in rear), Chester Milnes, Leo Kahn, Thomas Allison, George Harris, Tom Waterhouse, Jr., and Bradford Fox.

Note: Louis Fineman, an extremely hard working cattle farmer, converted his entrepreneurial skills into building a shopping mall, then putting a group of business men together to incorporate the first bank in Pelham.

I Remember him coming into my office when I first opened with his farmer clothing and cow manure all over his boots and severe back pain. Once we resolved the dress code we became good friends that carried over to social events and golfing at Vesper C C, where we became regular golfing partners on Saturdays and Sundays until his passing on in 1995.

Also notice the two Directors to my right, Ralph Harmon, and Leo Sevigny, my first and second contacts in Pelham in 1957.

MY MOTHER'S FIRST AUTOMOBILE

The setting for this story goes back to when we first met Dick Bournival and his lovely wife, Florence, at the Quail Ridge Country Club in Boynton Beach, Florida, in the late 1970's.

Dr. John Markey, one of my chiropractic colleagues from North Andover, Massachusetts, also a member of Vesper, invited us to his Quail Ridge winter residence for a vacation and to view the possibilities of a likewise purchase.

Claire and I were considering a winter hide-away that would possibly become a retirement home later on, and at that time seemed like a good idea to locate in a facility that already had several other Vesper members which made for immediate familiarity.

Dick Bournival, my Vesper four-ball golfing partner in 1995, was a "SUPER CAR **SALESMAN**", exemplified in the sale of a car to my mother, way back in 1955. Dick told me this story many times over the years, so I will attempt to relate it, as I did when the family invited me to participate in a **"ROAST"** in Dick's honor just a few years ago, prior to his demise.

She was on the sidewalk, looking into the big show window of Bissonnette Motors on Central Street, next to the old Rialto Theater. Dick quickly walked out onto the street, introduced himself and asked if she liked that automobile. She said, "Yes, it's beautiful, but I cannot drive and I'm just walking up to meet my husband at the barber shop"—only a couple of hundred yards (two football fields) away when continuing up onto Gorham Street.

NOW IF YOU WANT TO SUCCEED
IN SALES FOLLOW CLOSELY

With Dick's charming car dealer demeanor, he convinced my mother that he could teach her how to drive, get her a license and give her the bargain of the century. When she replied that, "My husband would have to make that decision", he walked her to the barber shop (remember my mother spoke English) and introduced himself to my father, as my mother was translating. When my father heard the words, "great deal & bargain of the century", his ears perked (remember Irving's fruit stand story) as he was a real sucker for a bargain.

By then my mother got into his head with a few gems like, "You will never have to take a bus again…Mr Bournival is going to teach me how to drive and get me a license" …plus a few more, and when Dick saw an opening he jumped into the conversation with, "I will guarantee to teach her how to drive personally and get her a license **all for free**".

Dick was such a great salesman that he already had the sales papers in his pocket, walked back to his show room with a deposit and my father never even saw the car.

IT GETS BETTER!!

I probably should explain that although Dick and Florence were also members at Vesper Country Club, in Tyngsboro, Massachusetts, we really didn't get to know each other very well until we began socializing at Quail Ridge Country Club in Florida, where we both had a winter residence.

Dick became one of my regular golfing partners twice weekly in Florida, and Claire and I would join them for dinner almost every Saturday that we were down in The Sunshine State. That's when and where we heard these stories over and over, and they always brought laughter.

DRIVING LESSONS

Now, let me continue. As per Dick's agreement, he met my mother daily, with a demo similar to the 1955 Plymouth Savoy, the car on which he had the deposit and sales agreement.

Dick's explanation of my mother's inability to coordinate the floor clutch with the gear box was hysterical, "It felt like she was grinding hundreds of pounds of hamburg with each lesson. Her coordination of the brake, clutch and accelerator was absolutely nil. At times it felt like a rocker- dodgem at the carnival, where my head was rocking forward and backward in rapid succession." (Today it would be called severe whip lash.)

He would relate that following my mother's unusually lengthy "driver training" preparation, he next had to schedule her Motor Vehicles Examination with the Massachusetts Motor Vehicle Division.

Dick always continued with the story. He contacted "Oscar", one of his close ties at the Massachusetts MVD, explained how important it was to get her a license as it would consummate the car sale. The test was scheduled for the very first morning appointment and Oscar took her to the South Common area where there was very little traffic. Shortly thereafter, Oscar drove the car back to the dealer where Dick was anxiously awaiting the results.

Oscar handed Dick the keys and related: "I'm giving Niki Plomaritis a license as a favor to you, Dick, now keep her off the f—g roads!!"

NOW AN EXPERIENCED DRIVER?

Two days later, now that she was an experienced driver, she drove all alone to our apartment on Shore Parkway in Brooklyn, New York. She knocked on the door and after a big hug and kiss, I asked how she got there.

Her explanation of the entire story above took only about five minutes, and to this day, I find it hard to believe. I told her I was just about to go up to the Jewish bakery for Sunday morning bagels. She said, "Wonderful. Let me show you how good I can drive, in my new car".

Well, it was one hell of an experience, going through three stop signs and two red lights in less than a half mile, before I suggested she pull over to the side of the road. I tried to be kind in relating to my mom that the streets in Brooklyn have stop signs that are difficult to see, and with the sunrise in your face you can hardly see the traffic lights. However, my heartbeat was at about 200 beats a minute when she pulled over.

I further explained to my mom that driving in New York was no cakewalk, as I attempted to demonstrate cautious driving on our way back to the apartment with a bag full of bagels.

HANG ON, we're getting close to the end of this great travelogue.

My mother showed me the map that Dick Bournival highlighted for her with specific directions to my apartment as well as the return directions. She departed the next day at 2 PM, for what was normally a four hour drive.

Dick told the following story, "I got a phone call from your mother at 2 AM, and she said, 'Mr Bournival, I followed your directions to return to

Lowell, and I still haven't got there yet'. After a few questions I realized that she was near Provincetown on Cape Cod, approximately five hours from Lowell."

Dick would get all excited as he continued to relate the end of the story.

"It was about one month later when your mother brought the car in for its first service, which was included with the sale price. She said, 'Mr. Bournival, would you please take care of the **COUPLE OF DINGS**, from some of those careless drivers in the shopping center parking lots?' "

Dick said in his forty years of car sales he never saw anything like the car she brought in, purchased only one month prior. It looked like it just came from the **DEMOLITION DERBY.**

Then he would say, "How can you not love that lady?"

SECTION FOUR

THE DEMOULAS STORY

MIKE DEMOULAS AT PALM BEACH

Telemachus "Mike" Demoulas

I would like to share with you another fascinating memory that keeps flashing into my cranial wall every time that I drive by, or go into, one of the **DEMOULAS (MARKET BASKET)** supermarkets, reminiscing about Mike Demoulas and his wife, Irene (Psoinos).

The setting was April 1975, Palm Beach, Florida. I was there taking the Florida Chiropractic Licensing Examination from the Florida State Board of Chiropractic Examiners. My wife, Claire, came along for company and support, plus it was also serving as a little mini vacation.

Following the third and final day of the examination, as we had prearranged, I met her on the beach with a cooler containing ice and martini ingredients. It was a rather cool, late afternoon, and not considered a good beach day. However, with the intense examinations out of the way, the weather was secondary.

When in the process of making two giant martinis, we noticed that there was only one other couple on the entire beach, sitting on a blanket about forty-five to fifty yards or "one good field goal" away. I walked over to ask them if they would like to join us in having a cocktail.

RECOGNIZING "MIKE"

When I got closer, I recognized that it was **TELEMACHUS "MIKE" DEMOULAS.** What a surprise!! With over one hundred million people in the USA (at that time), I was meeting the one person to whom I delivered my first shopping bags of chickens when I was a chicken farmer at twelve years of age.

After our ecstatic hellos, I told Mike and his daughter that I had just completed the Florida Chiropractic Licensing Examination and was just getting ready to have a relaxing martini with my wife. They accepted my invitation to join us.

Mike related his purpose of being in Palm Beach, saying that he had taken his family on a vacation earlier in the year and at that time his daughter was unable to join them because of her final exams.

"This was a little private get-away, just for the two of us," he said.

This is a family photo currently stored in the Demoulas archives, of the original Demoulas Market on Dummer Street, Lowell, Massachusetts. That's "Mike" standing inside wearing a white apron.

We had fun reminiscing about how I would get off the bus in front of City Hall on Merrimack Street, in Lowell, Massachusetts, and then walk about 150 yards to the one and only **"DEMOULAS MARKET"** in existence at that time on Dummer Street.

City Hall, Lowell, Massachusetts
Current photo, taken while standing on Dummer Street where the first Demoulas Market existed nearly a century ago. The bus from Varnum Avenue made a stop in front of the City Hall, where I got off and delivered the chickens to Mike Demoulas. While being only 12 at the time, the big building with the clock on top was my landmark to leave the bus. Photo by Titus Plomaritis.

Mike actually remembered how I struggled with two shopping bags full of chickens, and how he came out of the market to help me with the last fifteen yards or so. He then related, for the benefit of his daughter, how he mentioned to me, after a Lowell High School football game in 1948, "You carried that football today much faster than you carried those two bags of chickens".

DINING WITH THE DEMOULAS'

Well, following our social hour, Mike insisted we join him for dinner as his guest, stating he had already made reservations, but would call ahead to change the reservations to four.

As luck would have it, we were staying at the same hotel, directly on the beach. Mike suggested that we leave our cars at the hotel and he ordered limo service in one hour, to allow time for a quick shower and change of clothes. Can you imagine how Mike was way ahead of the curve, even in that era, thinking about a **DESIGNATED DRIVER?**

It was a fine French restaurant that Claire and I were not accustomed to dining in. Mike graciously ordered for the four of us, using his hands to describe how the chef was to prepare the meal, and, with a little French accent, ordered his favorite bottle of French wine.

Wow!! What a great memory that repeats itself almost daily.

ADDITIONAL MEMORIES OF "MIKE"

Telemachus "Mike" Demoulas is a name that has a ring to it like "Titus Plomaritis". Well, many of you from the Lowell area have read or heard about some of his philanthropic endeavors. However, for the benefit of those who have not, I will share a few memories of a great person with a fabulous memory who never forgot where he came from.

When I started this project some six years ago, sifting though large storage boxes full of negatives and photos in the thousands, I began to visualize stories that related to the photos. I was having fun recollecting some outstanding memories when family members suggested that I put together a short memoir for posterity.

In doing so, I noticed how many times "Mike" came into play, like delivering chickens on Dummer Street, his encouraging comments following my high school football games, attending the Boston University vs. N.Y.U. football game, when the Lowell Sun announced that I would be starting for B.U. at halfback, coming though big time when we were establishing the Ray Riddick Scholarship Fund and then running into him unexpectedly in Seabrook or at one of the markets, when he would give me one of his contagious smiles commenting, "How is Dr. Titus Plomaritis today?"

It kind of gave me the feeling of how proud he was of my professional status, like his **KID BROTHER SCORING ANOTHER TOUCHDOWN**. That's when I realized how many times he's touched my life like a big brother.

CONTACTING ARTHUR "T"

Having never met Mike's children, except for the beach incident, I felt impelled to notify them of my intention to incorporate memories of their dad into my book, **"TITUS"**. I called the only number listed in the phone book and asked to speak to Mr. Arthur "T" Demoulas. A woman politely thanked me for calling Market Basket and transferred my call to another pleasant, soft-spoken voice, this one named Joanne. She informed me that Mr. Demoulas was not presently in his office, took my two phone numbers and said that she would leave a message on his desk and that he would call me.

I waited two days and called again. Same routine. The call was transferred to Joanne, and with a slight giggle of friendliness she stated, "Yes, the message is still on his desk, but I will leave another and he will call you."

Giving it another couple of days, I called again. This time the transfer went to another soft-spoken, pleasant voice. Her name was Sue, she related that Joanne was on vacation, but she would leave another message on Mr. Demoulas's desk and stated, "He will call you".

By now, it was beyond the disappointment stage, so I said to myself, "fuck it", and thought to myself that Mike would never treat me that way, so I totally abandoned that avenue of authenticating those memories.

A couple of days later, while driving over to visit my good friend, Stan Stoklosa, my cell phone rang and this is what I heard, "Hello, Dr. Plomaritis, this is Arthur Demoulas. What can I do for you?" I was so shocked that I almost crashed as I pulled over to the side of the road.

My temperament went from a tinge of anger to humble pie in a flash! I briefly explained the purpose of wanting to meet with him. He was very receptive and apologized for not getting back to me sooner. After reviewing our schedules, we agreed to meet the following Tuesday at 9 AM in his office, located at 875 East Street, Tewksbury, Massachusetts. He also took the time to give me directions, and in closing said he is very anxious to meet me.

Well, not wanting to interfere with his busy schedule, I planned on arriving at 8 AM with reading material. I apparently wasn't the only one planning on an early arrival, as the mammoth parking lot was full. When entering the reception area there was standing room only. All were well-dressed men and women with their brief cases and wares in hand.

The receptionist asked my name and purpose. She then relayed a message to Joanne, who told her to inform me that Mr. Demoulas would be with me shortly.

About five minutes later, I was in deep concentration, going over some of my notes in the Demoulas chapter when Arthur walked out into the reception area, gave me a royal welcome just like it was "Mike" all over again, with a big smile, a strong hand shake and, "Dr. Plomaritis, please come in."

He walked me to his office, saw to it that I had a comfortable chair and started talking about my football days at Lowell High. I swear to god that if I had closed my eyes it would seem as though I was listening to Mike all over again. Even if I failed math in school, it wouldn't require too much intelligence to deduct that he wasn't even born when I played football. I couldn't get over the similarities of his dad in his voice, his expressions and his personality.

I informed him of my book project consisting of my autobiography and related stories from news articles. At the same time, I shared some of my memories that related to his dad and asked if he knew which of his three sisters was with his dad in Palm Beach, Florida, in the spring of 1975. I explained further that if I could meet her, it would be even better.

He was extremely accommodating, stating he would get in touch with his sister and give me a call to set up a meeting. He then asked me if I would like a tour of the warehouse. I accepted his offer and took out my note pad.

TOURING THE MASSIVE WAREHOUSE

Now, understand that the warehouse is attached to the executive offices. However, getting there from his office required a diagram.

Not only does Arthur look like his father, but he walks like him also, moving with the fast quick-step. Trying to keep up with him with two good hips would have been a task in itself, however with my newly replaced hip, I really couldn't. Having so much pride, I skipped along so he wouldn't notice.

As I was shown around the vast warehouse, the growth from a small market to this vast building was a thrill to me. I have never seen a warehouse that spacious. It was gigantic. Nor have I ever seen so much food in one location. Arthur had a golf cart at his disposal, to track from one end of the building to the other. I was taking notes while sitting in the passenger's seat as he drove slowly, so

Arthur T. Demoulas with Dr. Titus Plomaritis, pointing to an upper level storage bin, being restocked loaded by a forklift at the spacious warehouse.

as to identify the groceries from bin to bin. He also made several stops to introduce me to some of his associates who would relate that they worked at this same location for twenty, twenty-five, and thirty years.

Now that prompted me to ask how big the warehouse was. Arthur's reply with pride in his voice was, "585,000 square feet." He continued, "This warehouse only contains dry goods, and it has to be restocked daily. Otherwise, it would be completely empty in seven days."

Then I asked, "If these are all the dry goods, where are the perishables?" He replied, "At our other warehouse in Andover. That one has approximately 500,000 square feet."

That adds up to over **ONE MILLION SQUARE FEET** of storage space alone. If Brent Musburger were the announcer on this tour he would say, "Folks, that's some kind of ride!"

THE GROWTH CONTINUES

All of a sudden, it was like a quiz show.

Titus: "How many Market Baskets are there?"

Arthur: "Demoulas Market Basket, more commonly known as Market Basket, is a chain of sixty-four stores, with thirty-seven in Massachusetts and twenty-seven in New Hampshire. Our first store on the Cape will open soon, along with five others by year's end, making a total of seventy by the end of 2012."

Titus: "How many employees do you have?"

Arthur: "About 20,000 wonderful associates."

Titus: "What are your sales?"

Arthur: "Approaching $4.0 **BILLION** annually." (Verified by Consumer Reports).

ADDED HISTORY—The original Demoulas store opened on Dummer Street, Lowell, in 1917, and the second market on Bridge Street was launched in 1957. When Mike passed away in 2003, there were fifty-eight stores.

As we approached the finish line, with a complete tour of the warehouse, Arthur brought me into Jimmy Miamis' office. Now that's another story, but I promise to make it brief.

Jimmy was one of Mike's younger helpers on Dummer Street when I was delivering chickens. He even remembers the hanging scale that was used for weighing incoming and outgoing goods. Remember now, that's when they were working with a shoestring budget. Being a little younger than Mike was somewhat beneficial, as Mike would take him to my football games in 1948. We played all our games on Sundays, and at that time the markets were closed on Sundays.

NOTE—Our football stadium typically sold out every Sunday, in the vicinity of 20,000 to 22,000 people. It was formerly known as Lowell Memorial Stadium, now called Cawley Stadium.

Arthur brought me into Jimmy's office, and he was on the phone. When he saw me, he said to whomever he was speaking to: "I'll call you back." He hung up the phone, came around the desk and gave me such a big hug that my feet came off the floor. He then started talking all about the football games he attended with Mike, and repeated what I've heard a thousand times about the Lowell-Lawrence game on Thanksgiving. I must admit, I never get sick of hearing it.

Jimmy's office is next to Arthur's office and it comes with a title of **EXECUTIVE VICE PRESIDENT.**

WORKING THEIR WAY UP

It's interesting how Mike was notorious for rewarding conscientious, associates, of which he had many. The two with whom I've had a personal experience with include **JULIEN LACOURSE** and **JIMMY MIAMIS.** Jimmy has been associated with the Demoulas family over a span of a lifetime.

Julien was a key member of Lowell High School's powerhouse football teams during the early 1950's under **COACH RAYMOND E. RIDDICK.** Coach Riddick introduced Julien to Mike Demoulas as one of his dedicated players, who was seeking part-time work. He then began his fifty-five-year career within the business in 1952, working on weekends during the football off-seasons as a bagger, packing groceries at the checkout at the Demoulas store on Dummer Street in Lowell.

Part-time became full-time when Julien graduated from LHS in the spring of 1954. He was promoted to Store Manager when the newly-built #2 Demoulas Market on Bridge Street, at the Dracut line, was opened on September 12, 1957, and it was then onwards and upwards in the business, reaching the pinnacle as **EXECUTIVE VICE PRESIDENT.** Julien continued on as Arthur T. Demoulas' Executive Vice-President until the time of his demise in 2007.

Julien, who as one of sixteen children, married Anne Carter of Haverhill, having first met at Lowell's famous Commodore Ballroom, and the couple was blessed with four children, Catherine, James, Timothy and Stephen.

NOTE—Several interesting tidbits concerning the life of Julien Lacourse—His oldest sibling, **JOAN,** was born on **MARCH** 22nd. His youngest sibling, **CLAUDETTE**, was born on **MARCH** 22nd. **JULIEN** died unexpectedly on **MARCH** 22nd.

REMINISCING about Jimmy Miamis and Julien Lacourse— Now, where in this world are you going to find two kids in their teens, both starting from boyhood ,working for the same employer and becoming that employer's **EXECUTIVE VICE PRESIDENTS?**

Before leaving from my scheduled "fifteen-minute" appointment that lasted over two hours with the most congenial people you could ever meet,

Arthur intercepted me and related that his sister, **GLORIANNE**, was the sister in question back in 1975 at Palm Beach, Florida, and wondered if I could come back next week to meet her.

I replied, "Yes, with bells on."

REUNITED WITH GLORIANNE

The following week I arrived early once more. I was sitting when Glorianne walked into the reception room and as she was preparing to tell the receptionist of our appointment, she recognized me, came over and gave me a hug and a kiss on the cheek, something you'd only expect from one of your children.

She had me follow her into the conference room. Arthur joined us for a bit, and then excused himself. We sat and talked for over an hour, and of course the beach incident was the main topic. She said she remembered it as if it were yesterday. The longer we chatted, the more teary-eyed we became, requiring tissue breaks from the many emotional memories of her dad.

Glorianne then had an archive book brought in, which showcased the history of the Demoulas/Market Basket chain. We turned page after page, viewing the great ads, pictures and slogans that produced "oohs" and "ahs" for a solid half hour.

MORE FOR YOUR DOLLAR

The enclosed nonprofit survey fits well with the Demoulas motto, **"MORE FOR YOUR DOLLAR"**, established in 1955.

The nonprofit Center for the Study of Services, a Washington based consumer group, conducted a pricing survey of 151 items in supermarkets throughout the country. Robert Krughoff, president of the Washington D.C. based consumer group that conducted the survey in seven U.S. metro areas, stated that no other chain offered Market Basket's level of savings (Boston Herald April 24, 2011). The findings were reported in Boston Consumers' Checkbook Spring/Summer 2011 magazine. The survey concluded that a family spending $150.00 a week on groceries could save $1,600 a year shopping at Market Basket compared to the average food store.

A LITTLE WIKIPEDIA HISTORY

"In 1917, Greek immigrants Athanasios (Arthur) and Efrosini Demoulas opened a grocery store in Lowell, Massachusetts, specializing in fresh lamb. They eventually sold their store to two of their six children, Telemachus ("Mike") and George Demoulas. By1950 the business had grown into a supperette and into a modern, fifteen supermarket chain, by 1970."

LIKE FATHERS, LIKE SONS

As we were reflecting on the history of the Demoulas/Market Basket business, dating back to 1917, I commented to Arthur T. Demoulas that, "I can count three generations of your family," Then asked the question, "Do we have another generation prepared to continue this fascinating success story?"

Arthur, who is married to the former Maureen Lewis, moved forward in his chair, and with pride in his voice answered: "Yes, Dr. Plomaritis. I have four children, Madeline, Telemachus Arthur, Irene and Mary, while my sisters Frances and Glorianne both have three, and Caren four. You see, we are all involved, and having fourteen children among us hopefully provides for a great bullpen!!!"

THE PLAQUE AT WHISTLER PARK

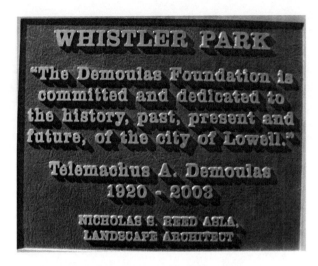

The Plaque at Whistler Park
Whistler Park is located at the site of the original Demoulas Market, that was founded by Athanasios ("Arthur ") and Efrosini Demoulas in 1917. The PARK is also located adjacent to the famous WHISTLER HOUSE.

In perpetuity, **WHISTLER PARK** is the exclamation point of the unforgettable memories of **TELEMACHUS "MIKE" DEMOULAS!!!**

LIKE FATHER, LIKE SONS (TITUS JR. & STEVEN TITUS)
By Sam Weisberg

The Plomaritis sons—Titus, Jr., and Steve—developed into **"CHIPS OFF THE OLD BLOCK".**

Before they both became highly successful in the medical profession, they were outstanding athletes in high school and college, following right along in their father's footsteps.

Papa Plomaritis enjoying a round of golf with his two sons. Left to right, Steven his youngest son, Titus Sr. and Titus Jr. with the shades.

ELDEST SON, Titus "Buddy", Jr., was the quarterback of the last undefeated Lowell High School football team in 1970. Twenty-two years earlier, his father was the star of the Red and Gray's first unbeaten eleven (1948).

As a sophomore in 1968, he successfully kicked six PATs in a row on Thanksgiving day during a 42-8 win against Lawrence. As a junior he scored a touchdown and booted thirteen conversions for the season, while as a senior he tallied two TDs and came through with twenty-two more points-after tries and a pair of field goals, good for a total of forty points over the unbeaten campaign.

"Buddy" was also a member of the Lowell baseball, track, wrestling, hockey and golf teams. Among his major exploits on the slopes took place when he won the gold medal for finishing first in a standard slalom ski race at Crotched Mountain, N.H., beating out the field of sixty of the top junior skiers in New England, while also posting the fastest time of the day, at fifty-two seconds flat. In addition, he captured several first places in Inter-Club ski races.

The multi-sport Pelham native attended the University of Vermont, where he played on the golf team for four years and captained the team his junior and senior years. He also skied on the UVM ski team his freshman and sophomore years, specializing in the slalom and giant slalom. UVM placed 2nd in the NCAA Division one championship his sophomore year.

STEVE turned in his major athletic endeavors in the sport of football, in New Hampshire and Maine.

The younger Plomaritis brother led Bishop Guertin High School in Nashua to the New Hampshire Division 2 state football championship during the 1973 season. He was the team's quarterback and placekicker, similar to his brother, connecting on all but three of his point-after attempts.

Steve was groomed by the best, as he was tutored by Benny Friedman, one of the greatest quarterbacks in gridiron history and the longtime head coach at Brandeis University. The Pelham gridder attended Friedman's Quarterback Camp, in New Jersey.

Steve went on to become a four-year letterman at Colby College, one member of "The Little Three" college circuit—which also consisted of Bates and Bowdoin—up in Maine. As he was in high school, Steve was the quarterback and placekicker for "The Mules" of Waterville, whose current enrollment is 1,838.

THE BROTHERS' RIVALRY

From family rivalry in sports to the arena of orthopedic surgeons—that highlights the story of **"BUDDY"** and **STEVE PLOMARITIS.**

Following were key moments of the brothers' medical careers.

TITUS, JR., partnered with Dr. Paul Burke, Jr., to heroically save a patient's life, after he had suffered a shotgun blast at close range in Lowell, Mass., in 1987.

STEVE, not to be denied, received nationally televised coverage for attending to Nancy Kerrigan's famous knee injury following a brutal attack with a heavy club in 1994.

Now the two Plomaritis brothers are stars in the world of medicine—
JUST LIKE THEIR FATHER WAS!!

PROUD PARENTS

We are the proud parents of four outstanding children who continue to grow on us. As I attempt to relate this story and describe their accomplishments, I find myself choking up as I turn the clock back some sixty-five years, to my high school days and wonder:
WHAT IF?

What if—I didn't stay in high school at age 14?
What if—I didn't go in the paratroopers?
What if—I didn't go back to high school?
What if—I never met Claire Hebert?
What if—I didn't go to Boston University?
What if—I didn't go to Chiropractic College?

None of the following could have ever happened unless all of the what if's were positive.

Plomaritis Children 1959:
Titus Jr., Lyn, Steven, Diane

Plomaritis Family 1979: Titus Sr., Titus Jr., Claire, Steven, Lyn, Diane

Plomaritis Family 7-20-2011 (Claire's 80th- B/D): front—l to r: Titus Jr., Titus Sr., Claire, Back—l to r: Diane, Steven, Lyn

Titus & Titus Jr.

Now let me attempt to briefly describe their accomplishments. Do you remember back in the early pages of this auto-biography when I mentioned my father's **"OLD COUNTRY"** educational mentality? Well, I believe Claire and I made up for it in spades.

We gave them the foundation, let them pick their colleges, and my chiropractic profession provided us the financial resources. The end results are that we have **"FOUR JEWELS"** to show for it.

TITUS, JR.— Graduated from the University of Vermont, in Burlington, and Boston University School of Medicine. He did his Orthopedic Residency at the Medical College of Ohio, in Toledo. He currently is a

Titus & Lyn

skilled Orthopedic Surgeon with a private practice in Eden, N.C., for the past twenty-five years.

LYN—Graduated from Keene State College with a Bachelors Degree in "Special Education". After working at an Hopi Indian Reservation in Arizona for one year, she decided to go back to school and get a Masters

Degree in "Talented and Gifted Education". She was recruited directly from the University of Northern Colorado by the State of Alaska.

After being honored for her twenty-year commitment, she went back to

Steven & Titus

school and now has a private practice as a Certified Massage Therapist, in both Delta Junction and Kennicott, Alaska as well as New Zealand.

STEVEN—Graduated from Colby College in Waterville, Maine, and from Kirksville Osteopathic College in Missouri. He then completed a four year Orthopedic Residency program in Canton, Ohio, and finally did a **FELLOWSHIP** at Henry Ford Hospital, in Detroit, in Shoulder and Knee reconstruction.

Steven became famous across the USA when he attended to Nancy Kerrigan's knee following a brutal attack with a heavy club at the World Figure Skating Championships, prior to the Olympics trials, in Detroit, Michigan, Jan. 6, 1994.

He now has a very successful Orthopedic Surgery private practice in Warren, Michigan.

Titus & Diane

DIANE—Graduated from Boston College with a Bachelor of Arts degree in English and Secondary Education.

She received a Master of Education from Framingham State College, Enhancing ELA Curriculum with technology. She received her PHD in Education at Northeastern University, Boston, MA. and currently is teaching English at Plymouth High School, in Plymouth, MA.

Now tell me, is that one hell of a foursome or what?

EXTRA-CURRICULAR ACTIVITIES
By Sam Weisberg

In addition to his stellar football exploits, first at Lowell High and then at Boston University, Titus participated in numerous athletic and civic volunteer projects throughout the Greater-Lowell area, during and after his gridiron playing days.

One of his pet projects was conducting football clinics with youngsters, teaching the future gridders the fine art of the sport. On many occasions the boys would come knocking at Titus' door, begging him to "Come out and give us some more tips."

A photo in **THE LOWELL SUN** depicted Titus holding a clinic at Hadley Field, located in the Highlands section of outer Lowell, as he was showing his younger brother, Anthony, and a group of boys how quarterbacks get set to take the snap from center.

The centers in the photo included Henry Fennell, Larry Cunningham, Richard Harrison and Fred Reslow. The quarterbacks were Phil Nyman, Richard Curran, Billy Stevens and David Godfrey.

NOTE—Titus' tips eventually paid off big, as Cunningham and Stevens later went on to star on the gridiron for **COACH RAY RIDDICK'S** Lowell High elevens. **CUNNINGHAM** became a flashy running back in 1955, and **STEVENS** kicked the winning PAT in a 7-6 verdict over White Plains High during a 1954 game played in New York, which enabled the Red and Gray to remain undefeated (9-0-0 final record).

ADDED NOTE—Stevens' exploit turned out to be Lowell's most famous successful kick since Plomaritis' game-winner against Lawrence some six years earlier.

Among Titus's other far-flung community projects were:—a volunteer physical education effort in Pelham, heading the highly-successful Ray Riddick Memorial Scholarship Fund drive, which netted over $50,000, and serving as president, plus completely reviving, the Lowell High School

Booster Club, which boasted having members from every state in the country, plus foreign nations.

PHYSICAL FITNESS AT ST. PATRICK'S SCHOOL

By Roy E. Hardy
Lowell Sunday Sun

PELHAM, N.H. —May 29, 1966— "The vigor of our country is no stronger than the vitality and well being of our countrymen. The level of physical, mental, moral and spiritual fitness of every American citizen must be our constant concern"—**JOHN F. KENNEDY.**

The above quotation, made by the late president during the time he occupied the White House, pointedly illustrates the importance of being prepared to keep America strong, but until civic-minded leaders in towns and cities throughout the nation make practical application of the learned advice, the full measure of preparedness may never be realized.

ONE MAN WHO paid particular attention to President Kennedy's Youth Fitness Program was **REV. GEORGE R. KILCOYNE**, pastor of Pelham's St. Patrick's parish, who decided to investigate the possibilities of instituting a regular physical training program as part of the parish school's curriculum, with a qualified instructor conducting the body building exercises.

Rev Kilcoyne quickly recognized that, in order to ensure a successful program, he must find a man with an extensive background in physical education, a man who would be willing to volunteer his time for what the pastor knew to be a worthwhile effort.

TITUS TO THE RESCUE

His search was short-lived. Contacting **DR. TITUS PLOMARITIS**, a Pelham chiropractor who played football for Lowell High School before going on to Boston University to win a degree in Physical Education, the pastor explained his idea to the local Chiropractor and asked if he would consider undertaking the task. Dr. Plomaritis agreed.

IN SEPTEMBER of 1964, armed with pamphlets and brochures obtained from Washington, St. Patrick's new physical director began classes with youngsters in the 4th, 5th, 6th and 7th grades, using the front lawn at the school for a "classroom" each Tuesday.

This pair of fifth graders demonstrated to the St. Patrick's Mens club how easy it was to do 10 pull ups and maintain a good smile. Left to right: Debbie Purcell and Lyn Plomaritis. Lowell Sun photo.

Since that time the physical training classes, or "PT" as the armed forces call them, have evolved into a polished, regulated program, complete with progress charts, grades and certificates of achievement. The results have been impressive.

'**WHEN I FIRST STARTED** the program it was obvious that many of the children had not been getting the proper exercise and, as a result, they were uncoordinated and not in prime physical condition," said Dr. Plomaritis. "I look at many of the students today who were in that first group and the improvement is remarkable. I'd be willing to match their fitness skills with any children in the country," he concluded.

Girls and boys at the school take their training in separate groups. Although the girls practice the same exercises as the boys, their standards are not quite so high and understandably so.

Each pupil is scored in performance of push-ups, sit-ups, pull-ups, squat-jumps, squat-thrusts, 50-yard dash, standing broad jump, 600-yard run and walk, softball throw and 120-foot shuttle run.

ONLY PUPILS in grades 4 through 7 undergo the extensive training. Youngsters in the first three grades participate in less intensive calisthenics, supervised by older pupils, but they are considered by Dr. Plomaritis to be a strong foundation in preparing the students for more extensive training in later months.

All the students are asked to do "homework" for a short period each day, and in some cases it has been reported that parents have joined their offspring.

"It should be a family program," the Doctor asserted. "Physical fitness is of primary concern to adults, but getting them started is a problem. Their children have provided motivation in many cases."

During the winter months, training continues indoors. The ground floor of the school, a spacious room with gymnastic equipment provided by the Men's Club at St. Patrick's becomes a "PT" hall.

FORMING A NATIONWIDE PROGRAM

THE AMERICAN CHIROPRACTIC Association recently adopted a special plan for physical fitness and has since set its sights on formulating a program for use in schools around the country.

Association funds were used to record an interview at the United Nations with children of diplomats from around the globe, to obtain a cross picture of various exercises used in other nations. Producing a recording, using much of the information received at the U.N., the ACA has sponsored a kit complete with colorful booklets and pamphlets on the body building for issuance to civic leaders. Dr. Plomaritis considers the kit an Invaluable tool.

The 10 balanced physical fitness activities are used to develop good posture, breathing habits, endurance, agility, flexibility, speed co-ordination and balance. As the ACA booklet denotes, "Physical Fitness Begins with Good Posture."

HAD PRESIDENT KENNEDY lived, he might have taken special pride in watching these students exercise their way to better health, because he, himself, was an advocate of such a program. He tried to interest others so that future generations would be physically prepared.

One of the keys to the success of a national program of this type is finding enough people willing to give their time and services to work with the youngsters on a regular basis.

St. Patrick's parish is fortunate in that it has just such a man—**DR. TITUS PLOMARITIS!!**

NEW PELHAM GROUP SPONSORS GIANT SPORTARAMA

By Gil Wood
Lowell Sun

PELHAM, N.H. —Circa 1962—There's a new deal for kids in Pelham, thanks to the birth of the Pelham Athletic Association.

Finishing Sportarama Plans

Dr. Titus Plomaritis, formerly of Lowell, looks over the program of events for this week-end's giant Sportarama which is being sponsored by the newly formed Pelham Athletic association. Events are listed for tomorrow and Sunday at the Sherburne school.

This organization, which has former Lowell High and Boston University football great, **DR. TITUS PLOMARITIS**, as one of its hustling spark-plugs, is awakening this community to the needs and benefits derived from an organized recreation program.

The biggest undertaking to date will take place this weekend in the form of a giant two-day **SPORTARAMA**.

According to Dr. Plomaritis, participants in the colossal event will hail from most of the cities and towns in the Greater-Lowell area, in addition to Pelham.

The **SPORTARAMA**, to be held at the Sherburne School, will come to a close Sunday night at 8 o'clock, when some 180 trophies will be awarded.

SATURDAY'S PROGRAM calls for 17 events, starting with 25-yard dashes for first and second grade boys and girls, at 9 a.m., and winding up with a teen-age record hop at 8 p.m. One of the highlights of the day will be a five-mile high school boys' cross-country run, listed for 11 a.m.

In addition to running races, there will be broad jump, baseball throw, bicycle slalom, basketball foul shooting, volleyball game, tug-o-war, softball game, and one of Sunday's features will be a Babe Ruth League tilt at 2:30.

Any organization of this type needs funds to operate. The organizers of the P.A.A. canvassed door-to-door for members and picked up a fine total of 500 subscribers at a dollar apiece. This kitty will be enhanced on Sunday noon by means of a roast beef dinner, which is open to the public at a nominal fee.

"The whole town's talking favorably about the Association and its aims," said Dr. Plomaritis, who is one of the committee members working on the

SPORTARAMA. "The boys and girls in Pelham need supervised recreation, just as kids anywhere else needs it. We feel that the Association's activities will enable the children of Pelham to participate with neighborhood communities in competitive athletic programs."

THE ASSOCIATION has set its sights on furnishing athletic equipment, proper supervision and recreation areas, all of which will assist in the social adjustment of Pelham's rapidly growing community.

The P.A.A. has organized and entered a team in the Inter-State Babe Ruth League and is well along the way to setting up a Little League program. A volleyball league for boys and girls of all ages is in the formative stage and the Association already has constructed and equipped two baseball diamonds.

Officers of the Association include Bruno Thibeault, president; Donald Burton, vice president; Ruth Richardson, secretary, and Jim Fenton treasurer. They comprise the **SPORTARAMA** committee, along with Dr. Plomaritis, Randy Richardson, Fred Manty, Jane Cardwell, Pat Vining and Harold Mansfield.

BOSTON UNIVERSITY MAJOR & MINOR BENEFITS

This section briefly tells how my BU Minor—of Audio Visual Aids has served me in one way or another throughout my entire life whereas my BU Major—of Teacher-Coach, was short lived but the outcome was astronomical. As you read through this book everything will unravel, all your questions will be answered and you will have had entertainment along the way.

FOOTBALL SCHOLARSHIP

I entered Boston University in the fall of 1949 on a football scholarship. Physical Education was my major with the intention of becoming a Teacher Coach. I selected Audio Visual Aids as my Minor to further enhance my photography skills as well as to learn more about the movie projection industry.

All of the scholarship students had to perform some school related service. Mine was showing educational movies to the nursing school students. In doing so I actually learned how to run and operate a projection business.

Each week, the nursing class instructor gave me the name of the following week's film. I, in turn, would reserve it along with a sixteen millimeter projector from our audio visual library.

After showing the movie I had the responsibility of inspecting, cleaning, rewinding and splicing if necessary in preparation for its next showing.

As it worked out, my minor courses provided immediate results financially. I learned from my professor, Dr. Krasker, the business aspect of renting movies from commercial venders for a weekly rate for $25.00, then showing it at least five times at $25.00 a pop to various town recreation groups as well as social clubs in the Lowell area. **SALESMANSHIP AT WORK.**

The 4x5 press camera was the most popular used by professionals in that era, for landscape, weddings, portraits, sports and all kinds of group pictures. I learned how to set up a dark room, develop my own 4x5 negatives, print proofs and enlargements, crop, create pamphlets and just about everything necessary to run a photography business.

Dr. Krasker issued me a Graflex Crown 4x5 press camera and gave me assignments taking pictures of tall buildings and designated landscaped areas. He also assigned action events, including sporting activities at Fenway Park at different times of the day and evening. I then had to develop my film, make proofs and enlargements.

As I was completing my first year, Dr. Krasker told me to take the camera home for the summer and continue to treat it kindly.

APPLYING BOSTON UNIVERSITY SKILLS

When returning to Lowell following my first year at BU, I opened a photo studio on Gorham Street, called "Titus' Photo Studio". I worked a few weddings with Ray Marchand and George Poirier, two well known professional photographers in Lowell, to learn the techniques and skills of taking candid weddings.

That's me, Titus Plomaritis with my fiancé, Claire Hebert, when I was attending Boston University in 1950, with the help of a football scholarship.

My only help came from Claire Hebert, my fiancé, a Lowell High School National Honor Student who was working as a private secretary for Edward and Florence Paris of Paris Shoe Corporation in Lowell, Massachusetts. She volunteered to help me get started and, to this day, **she continues to be my motivation and inspiration to succeed.**

NOTE: For those of you that require a brief definition of motivation, it's **"A DRIVING FORCE TO ACHIEVE YOUR GOALS".**

*****

My first candid wedding from Titus' Photo Studio on Gorham Street was that of Stanley & Kay (Philbin) Stoklosa (1950). It's interesting how many people over the years would approach me in a grocery store or some function and remove a wedding photo from their wallets or handbags to show me "Titus' Photo Studio" printed on the back side of the photo.

*****

By agreement, my tuition at the Los Angeles College of Chiropractic was offset by taking on the responsibility of School Photographer that consisted mostly of public relations and promotional brochures. The school provided me with adequate space and budget to set up a darkroom that could also be used for personal use. On weekends I took candid weddings for a studio in Burbank.

TITUS' PHOTO STUDIO

While attending Chiropractic College in New York, Mr. Sullivan granted me permission to set up a temporary studio for the Lowell High School Senior Prom. It was a source of much needed finances and we looked forward to that gravy train each year.

Payment was immediate with Claire collecting the money, taking students' names and issuing receipts. I, in turn, took the pictures and gave each photo a number that coincided with the receipt.

We had a smooth operation that got better each year. The initial orders were for a set fee of $5.00 that included two 5x7's with decorative cardboard frames.

With Mr. Sullivan's permission I sent the entire order to Lowell High School with the students' names and numbers on each envelope and they would pick them up in the main office. This saved me the cost of individual postage. I included my studio stamp "Titus' Photo Studio" and phone number on the back of each photo.

WORKING IN BROOKLYN

While attending Chiropractic School in New York I shot candid weddings on weekends for Marcy's Studio, Brooklyn, New York. I believe it was the largest studio in Brooklyn, with over twenty photographers specifically used for candid weddings.

It took me a whole year before I could work my way up to the top ten in seniority. They were so fussy that before they added me to their candid weddings list I had to shoot three weddings alongside one of their top ten photographers, duplicating his or her shots. The purpose was to examine the aperture settings and quality of the negatives. They loaded and unloaded my 4x5 cut film holders and did all the dark room processing and printing of proofs that they critiqued.

To survive their requirements and be added to the list of photographers was an accomplishment in itself. The top ten were always assigned to two or three weddings every weekend.

GOVERNOR'S PERSONAL PHOTOGRAPHER

As Governor Hugh Gallen's personal photographer I was granted special clearance by security to work side by side with President Carter's photographer when the Governor and President were in the same location or company. Eventually President Jimmy Carter and I were on a first name basis. I will explain in a story later on.

BU MAJOR—TEACHER COACH

I applied for several Teacher-Coach jobs and was interviewed for two of them. Neither were quality jobs but I would have taken either one if offered to me. They both opted to hire within, someone with experience.

I accepted an assistant football coaching job at Somerville High School, Somerville, Massachusetts as backfield coach. Football practice was from 4:00 to 6:30 PM, Monday through Friday with games on Saturdays. The job ended on Thanksgiving Day.

I enjoyed every minute of the coaching stint and felt that experience in my resumé would better qualify me for a quality Teacher-Head Coaching job the following year. I planned on keeping my eyes and ears open for any potential openings.

In the meantime I did use my basic science courses at BU to land me a job at the Bedford VA Hospital in Bedford, Mass. The position was Corrective Exercise Therapist, with Bachelor of Science as a prerequisite. It was quite an experience working with mentally unstable veterans. However, it was extremely rewarding every time I got a patient to come out of his shell and ask to play catch with a football, or baseball. The hospital job was from 7am to 3pm and worked into the coaching job just fine.

The following year I was the inside favorite for what was considered the best quality job available over the past several years, head football coach, Physical Education teacher and intramural director for an annual salary of $2,700.00 at one of the suburban schools.

I remember waiting outside in the foyer with several other candidates, for the School Committee to make the announcement. It was about 9:00 PM when we were informed that the position was no longer available because the coach who had given his resignation reconsidered. The consensus was that coach was holding out for a considerable raise.

As fate would have it, **THAT WAS THE LUCKIEST DAY OF MY LIFE!!** We immediately put our backup plan into operation.

I had already been accepted to the Los Angeles College of Chiropractic in Burbank, California. Within forty-five days, we sold our two-family house and used the money to purchase a new 1954 Custom Ford four-door sedan and a 38 ft house trailer from a dealer in New Hampshire.

CLOSE CALLS—FOURTH INCIDENT

The arrangements were for us to pick up the house trailer in Elkhart, Indiana, on the way to California. What we didn't know was that it was highly unusual for an automobile such as a Ford to pull a thirty-eight foot house trailer. The only experience I'd had pulling a trailer was when I was ten years old on the farm and pulled the cart with firewood for the furnace.

We prepared the back seat area of the car with a makeshift playpen for Titus, Jr., our one-year-old son, and off we went to Indiana to pick up our future home for the next four years.

The dealer was surprised to see that we were not driving a truck. However, he proceeded to install a hitch to our car and **BRIEFLY** explained the use of the electric brakes. Off we went, following our mapped route onto the famous Route 66.

After a couple of days I felt more comfortable driving on the right side of the road and watching the Volkswagen Bugs fly by me. We kept seeing billboard signs advertising some famous Caves that were listed as just off Route 66 which we thought would be a good stop for lunch as well as a scenic place for pictures.

We followed the signs that took us about one mile off the highway onto an unpaved road and down a steep one lane driveway that frightened the hell out of me as I wondered how we would ever get back onto the highway.

After practically choking on my quick lunch I started to make a u-turn and head out, when a farmer with a heavy Southern accent approached me and said he made a living of towing trailers such as mine up the steep graded driveway with his four wheel drive truck. Although five bucks at that time was a full tank of gas, I quickly agreed to his terms.

As he was connecting a heavy chain to the front of my car he instructed me to keep my hand on the electric brake switch and be prepared to activate it in the event we started rolling backward.

He started towing our car and trailer up the slope and it seemed like forever to get to the top while traveling about one mile per hour. When we got to the top and he was unhitching the chain he noticed a cable hanging under the car. He told me it was the cable to the electric brakes and must have been severed when I made the u-turn, and said if he had noticed it earlier he never would have towed me up the slope. Then he recommended a garage a couple of miles up the road where they could repair and reattached the cable.

It seemed like we were having one experience after another, starting with pulling into a gas station for gas and tearing down the canopy on the way out. However, **THE BIG SCARE** was yet to come as we approached the famous Needles Pass-Way—a great view with a gradual steep downhill run of over a mile.

As I started down, Claire was pointing out the great view to "Buddy" (Titus, Jr.) and my speed began to exceed forty mph. I started utilizing the electric brakes until they were no longer effective.

NOTE—I was never told that when the electric brakes were used too often they get hot and would no longer be effective.

My speed gradually increased to fifty, then sixty, and Claire, in her high screaming tone, shouted **"SLOW DOWN!!"** as I exceeded seventy mph. With my heart in my throat, I pretended to have the situation under control. With both hands tightly squeezing the steering wheel and the trailer behind me swerving and my peripheral vision noticing flipped-over trailers on both sides of the road it was then that I finally got to the bottom and gradually slowed down and pulled over to the side of the road. I then realized that somebody upstairs was once again looking after me.

PHYS. ED. CREDENTIALS AT WORK

I used my BU Phys. Ed. Credentials to acquire a part time job as Playground Supervisor, after my Chiropractic classes, from 3:00 to 6:00 PM, and Claire would plan her day to be at the playground at the same time. It was like having whipped cream on a chocolate sundae, playing with my son for three hours daily and getting paid for it.

When I transferred to the Chiropractic Institute of New York, I was able to use my experience as a Certified Corrective Exercise Therapist to acquire a full time job at the Brooklyn Veterans Hospital.

It was the best possible combination of schooling and practical training anyone could possibly ask for. I spent seven hours daily in school and eight hours a day in the hospital, applying everything I learned in school, especially the manipulation component of Chiropractic Training. I had two great advantages over my classmates relative to chiropractic adjustment training.

Let me first explain the setup. There were five Corrective Therapists including the chief. Every three months, my schedule was to rotate from medical, including amputees, to Neurological and then Psychiatric. The psychiatric patients were not classified as violent. Most were there for evaluations to justify their continued disability. Whenever the psychiatrists would show up in the clinic, these patients would go into their **BROADWAY SKITS**, like "goosing flies" or "repeating one's name over and over, until the doctor would leave the clinic".

My first advantage was that the Chief of the Corrective Therapy and the Physiatrist (a specialist in charge of Physical Medicine and Rehabilitation), were both aware that I was working toward a Doctor of Chiropractic Degree. For the next three years, we had a great working relationship. This included spinal manipulations on both of them when needed, especially Monday mornings following their golfing weekends, and Fridays, for relaxation, when they wanted an advantage over their golfing partners.

Secondly, my three month periods in the psychiatric clinic were barrels of fun. As I reflect back to those days, it's when and where my chiropractic manipulation skills excelled and moved me to the head of the class. Even the patients knew I was a chiropractic student and would line up in the clinic for adjustments, and relate, "I'm next, Doc".

To this day I still find it difficult in deciding whether my BU Minor or Major was the most beneficial throughout this long journey. Either way, it all became possible by way of an opportunity given to me through a **FOOTBALL SCHOLARSHIP!!!**

Thank you, **COACH RIDDICK.**

THE ROTARY CLUB

—Rotary is a world-wide organization of business and professional leaders that provide humanitarian service and encourages high ethical standards in all vocations.

The Rotary Foundation of Rotary International is a non-profit corporation that promotes world understanding through humanitarian service and educational and cultural exchanges.

LOWELL ROTARIANS HONOR RIDDICK

It was "Ray Riddick Day" at the Lowell Rotary Club as Rotarians honored the Lowell High School football coach for his 20 years as coach of the Red and Gray. Pictured making a plaque presentation to Riddick is former star Dr. Titus Plomaritis (third from left) who served as toastmaster. Also in photo are, left to right, Vice President James B. Williams, President Samuel S. Morse, Plomaritis, Coach Riddick, Mayor Edward Early and Superintendent of Schools Vincent McCartin. Sun photo by Alves.

LOWELL —(Circa, late 1966)—"Coach Ray Riddick is not only a great coach and a dedicated man, but one of the finest things that has ever happened to Lowell High School," said Athletic Director **AL MANGAN** as he addressed members of the Lowell Rotary Club, city officials, players of the 1966 LHS football club and former coaches and players, as the Red and Gray grid mentor was feted on the occasion of his completion of 20 years as Lowell High coach.

Introduced by **Dr. TITUS PLOMARITIS**, chairman of the Rotary Club committee and toastmaster, Mangan lauded Riddick and advised the audience that without the famed mentor, athletics as a whole would have suffered.

"He's just been a great man, on and off the field," added Mangan, a former U.S. Olympian in the walking event. "His devotion to duty is a year-round affair, and without him many boys would not have made it."

The occasion was marked by the presentation of a plaque honoring Riddick for his 20 years of service.

Dr. Plomaritis cited many of the Coach's records, most important of which was his mark of 135 wins, 36 losses and 14 ties, garnered during the two decades he has served as coach.

VINCENT M. McCARTIN, superintendent of schools, was the first of the speakers to laud Riddick. "He's been a great man and has straightened out many boys," said McCartin.

Mayor **EDWARD EARLY** also had words of praise of the Coach, as did Rep. **JOHN JANAS** and Headmaster **RAYMOND SULLIVAN,** all of whom expressed the hope that Riddick would be coaching here in Lowell for many years to come. (**HE WAS ABLE TO STAY FOR NINE MORE YEARS**).

NOTE—Ray Riddick received many offers to accept other football coaching berths, including colleges (Boston University was one of them) but he turned them all down to remain at Lowell High School, until his declining health forced him to retire after the 1975 season. His final 29-year record at LHS was 180-73-14, with 10 undefeated teams.

COACH RIDDICK accepted the plaque from the Rotarians, humbly, and thanked his family, coaches and the boys for making it possible for him to succeed.

"I never would have made it without help and patience from my family, devoted work by my coaches, and most of all by my players," said The Coach. "It's been a team effort all the way. I just hope it continues."

MEMBERS of Riddick's coaching staff who were present, and were introduced were: Joe Polak, Dave Stecchi, Art Andricopoulos, George Bossi, Frank Finnerty, and Team Trainer Tom Grady.

Guests included Riddick's family: wife Marjorie, son Raymond, Jr., and daughters Marjorie and Mrs. Edward Dick, and son-in-law Edward Dick.

MANY LOWELL HIGH PLAYERS of yesteryear were introduced, with GEORGE WOOD of the class of 1907 receiving a round of applause as the oldest player in the hall. **BAILEY TRULL** also laid claim to early fame as a Red and Gray player, but admitted that Wood preceded him.

TOASTMASTER Plomaritis, in addition to introducing guests and speakers, had much praise for The Coach for whom he played, and starred. "He exemplifies the Rotary Symbol—Spirit Above Self," said the Doctor.

Dr. Plomaritis was aided in honoring The Coach by Rotarians John P. O'Hearn, Dr. Costas Kokinos, Dr. George Gianis, Dan Mulhern, Wilfred Pearson, William Vrettas, Tom Balfrey, Courtland Burkinshaw, John J. Mahoney, Raymond Hardy, John H. Doherty, Edward O'Day, Joseph Hardman, Chapin Webb and Roy T. Johnson.

MEMBERS OF THE 1966 LHS football squad in attendance were: George Albert, Paul Broderick, Walter Brown, Chris Brustas, Tony Budge, Dennis Case, Dave Cavossa, Ken Cavanaugh, Charles Cormier, Chris Cox, Ron Crowe, Dave Currie, Jim Dowling, George Eklund, Frank Elliott, Arthur Farris, Robert Fawcett, Dick Gauthier, Tim Green, Ray Hanley, Chris Hantzis, Carl Holmes and Jim Hemphill.

Also, Jack Iby, Ed Janas, Bill Jozokos, Dennis Krysiak, Paul Lanoue, Tom McDowell, Dave Mills, Ron Ouellett, Al Pare, Steve Poznick, Rod "Rocket" Redman, Joe Roderiques, Jim Ryan, Tony Savaris, Tom Sheehy, Bob Tara, John Tighe, Al Varoski, Tommy Whalen, Alex Wilson, Walter Wilson, Tom Yates, Dennis Zannoni and Student Managers Craig Gallant and Paul Iverson.

FINAL NOTE—The above-mentioned 1966 Lowell High grid team wound up with a 7-1-1 record, with the only loss being a 14-8 setback to powerful Manchester Central. The tie was a scoreless deadlock with Salem.

HOWEVER, the following (1967) Red and Gray squad (9-0-0, 7 shutouts, 299-12 in points) was overall **"THE BEST LOWELL HIGH TEAM I'VE EVER COACHED,"** admitted Riddick immediately after the Thanksgiving Day, 22-0 victory over Lawrence at Cawley Stadium.

THE ROTARY CLUB AUCTION OF 1960'S

Standing left to right—Arthur Anton, Gerald A.Trepanier and Dr.Titus Plomaritis, sitting on the horse, Claire Plomaritis.

One of the Lowell Rotary Club'a fund raisers back in the sixties was an annual auction that was always the event of the year. The local merchants were most generous with their donations of merchandise and monetary contributions that made this a great success.

As you can see from the photos, the western attire provided some fun and games following the business part of the auction, headed by the famous Ken Harkins, "Auctioneer Supreme".

Rotary committee members: Sitting Left to Right—Connie Picard, Elaine Mongeau, Bob Mongeau, Claire Plomaritis, Titus Plomaritis, Frank McCaffrey, Marlene Johnston, Dan Mulhern, Mary Alice Mulhern. Standing left to right—Bob Picard, Charlie Johnston and unidentified couple.

ROTARIANS STRIVE FOR PERFECT ATTENDANCE, AND CURT GOWDY REMEMBERED TITUS

All our Boston University home football games were played at Fenway Park and the famed **CURT GOWDY**—who was the Boston Red Sox play-by-play announcer at that time—was also our B.U. football radio announcer.

He also was captivated with the name **"TITUS PLOMARITIS"**. I remember when I made my first varsity appearance, in 1950, all my buddies from Lowell told me how he electrified his listening audience by drawing out the name with a slow, low tone into a high pitch rhyme —"AN—HERE—COMES—TY—TUS—PLOM—A—RITE—US!!".

HOLD ON!! There is a connection to my story here.

GOWDY DIDN'T FORGET THE NAME

In the early 1960's I was a member of The Lowell Rotary Club that strived for perfect attendance. If a member of the Club was unable to attend its once a week luncheon meeting he was expected to make it up at one of the surrounding towns, so as to get credit for not missing that meeting.

One of the most popular locations for making up for a missed meeting was at **BISHOPS RESTAURANT** in Lawrence, Mass., where the Lawrence Rotarians met weekly.

Well, one day I was making up a missed meeting at Bishops and I noticed that Curt Gowdy, a Lawrence Rotarian who owned a local radio station, was in attendance. I walked over to his table and said: "Hello, Mr. Gowdy. I certainly remember you, but you probably don't remember me."

He stands up, gives me a big hug, and said: **"HOW THE FUCK COULD I FORGET TY-TUS PLOM-A-RITE-US!!"**

BACKGROUND TO OUR MEETING

Why was Gowdy a local Rotarian? Well, it seems that in 1963 he purchased radio stations WCCM and WCCM-FM in Lawrence, later changing the FM station's call letters to WCGY, to somewhat match his name.

These radio stations were a hotbed of area schoolboy sports during the Gowdy regime, but he sold his broadcast interests in 1994, and the stations became all-Latin.

He also owned stations in Laramie, Wyoming; West Palm Beach, Florida, and WBBX in New Hampshire.

THE SAGA OF CURT GOWDY

Curtis Edward "Curt" Gowdy was born in Green River, Wyoming, on July 31, 1919, and eventually became one of the nation's great radio and television sportscasters, being the longtime "voice" of the Boston Red Sox, before entering television, covering years of major national sports events, primarily for NBC Sports, and Olympic Games during the 1960's and 1970's.

Curt passed away on February 20, 2006, at the age of 87.

JOINING THE BOSTON RED SOX

In April, 1951, at the age of 31, Gowdy began his tenure as the lead announcer for the Red Sox, and for the next 15 years he called the games on WHDH radio and on three Boston TV stations—WBZ-TV, WHDH-TV and WNAC-TV.

He left the Red Sox after the 1965 season to join NBC Sports, where for the next ten years he called the national baseball telecasts of the Saturday afternoon "Game of the Week" and "Monday Night Baseball," plus the All-Star games in July and the post-season playoffs and The World Series in October.

A NATIONALLY FAMOUS VOICE

Over the course of his career, he was involved in the broadcasts of 13 World Series, 16 baseball All-Star games, nine Super Bowls, 14 Rose Bowls, eight Olympic Games and 24 NCAA Final Four basketball contests. He called all the Olympic Games televised by ABC, from 1964-84, and also hosted the long-running outdoors show "The American Sportsman" on ABC.

NOTABLE MOMENTS CALLED BY GOWDY

CURT GOWDY was present for some of America's most storied sports moments, including:—

TED WILLIAMS' home run in his final at bat, in 1960.
The AFL's infamous 'HEIDI GAME' of 1968.
SUPER BOWL number 1.
SUPER BOWL 3, in which Joe Namath and the underdog AFL New York Jets upset the NFL's Baltimore Colts, 16-7.
'THE IMMACULATE RECEPTION" catch by Franco Harris in 1972.
HANK AARON's record-breaking 715th home run in 1974.

GOLFING IN NEW ZEALAND
THE PINES GOLF CLUB,
PARUA BAY, NEW ZEALAND

Golfing in New Zealand
Left to right: Charlie O'Neil, Claire Plomaritis, Lyn Plomaritis and yours truly, Titus Plomaritis.

The above photo, taken by one of my golfing partners, shows the beautiful background from the first tee at **THE PINES GOLF CLUB,** in Parua Bay, Whangarei, New Zealand.

It's amazing how green the grass is, and that's with no irrigation system. They get plenty of rain, however, it never seems to interfere with play. The golfers seem to realize that rain is essential to keeping the grass green, so they all carry umbrellas.

With the exception of a handful of golfers, they all pull "trundlers", what we call pull carts. The yardage adjustment took me a while to get accustomed to, because the course is measured in meters, not yards.

They do have lawn mowers, although when I first got there they told me that the course didn't open until twelve noon, because the cows were having breakfast. It was their way of mowing the fairways. With nobody on the course that day and seeing a few cows grazing at a distance, I bit for it hook line and sinker.

The members at the Pines were extremely friendly and accepted me as if I was a life-long resident of the area. Some of the locals spoke with such a heavy accent and very little lip movement; I had difficulty understanding what was being said. Sometimes I would ask them to please repeat, and after two or three attempts I would just nod my head affirmatively, not knowing what the hell they were talking about.

I'll get back to golf in a bit, first let me relate to my meeting one of the regulars who befriended me, a gentleman named Jack Broome. He carries a strong 16 handicap, and is fun to play with. I would always try to be in his foursome because he was a fierce competitor and fun to have as a partner, although he had no mercy on me when I was on the opposing team. He also displayed a great sense of humor and was pretty good with the tainted stories. Jack was also instrumental in helping me become a seasonal member.

He sponsored me for a seasonal membership, which included unlimited golf, and explained that it qualified me to participate in the Tuesday and Friday "**HAGGLES.**" It would also be a great opportunity to meet the locals, who certainly proved to be a super bunch of friendly blokes.

A brief explanation of their "**HAGGLES**": Any member can just show up without reservations and type his name and membership number on a keyboard that's located on the porch, just outside the pro shop. Out pops a computer-ready score card with the handicap stroke holes already checked off. He then places it on a table and at 12:30 a gong sounds, indicating pairings are to be announced.

VERY SERIOUS GOLFERS

I quickly found out how seriously they take their golf, very seriously. As an example, on my first day in the 'Haggles" group, I was paired up with Shane, who wears a lower extremity prosthesis (artificial limb) as a result of a motorcycle accident. He has been given a nickname, "**SPLINTER,**" for obvious reasons. I found him to be a real easy-going, chain smoking, single handicap golfer with a great personality. However, the two guys we were paired with were of a different mindset.

The format was one best-ball of the foursome against the field, with a side match of two against two for the beers.

On the very first hole, being a little nervous and playing with a new group for the first time, I hit a ball out of bound, another into a creek and then three putted. Our opponents asked for scores. Knowing that my ball didn't matter, my partner had a par. I was somewhat embarrassed and quietly said, "Eight." Our opponent said, "You did like hell, you had a nine," and described each of my errant strokes almost like he had taken movies!

Once the round was finished, we all went into the clubhouse, and having lost to our two teammates, "Splinter" insisted on paying for the first round of beers. I planned on buying the next round, but it didn't happen. The blood match was only to see who bought the first round.

They certainly were a great group of guys to play with. I couldn't remember all their names so I contacted Jack Broome recently and informed him of my intention to include a short story relative to my memories at the Pines Golf Club and New Zealand. His comments were well received, which I will share with you.

JACK'S COMMENTS

"Your two visits to **THE PINES** have indelibly registered with we mug golfers how inadequate we are in our 60's versus you now in your prime.

Tony Workman, who recently had a prostate operation (he's fine now), has reflected on the occasion when you clambered down the bank on the right side of the fourth fairway. You showed us the wonderful balance and agility at eightyish, that we seem to have lost when we matured past teenage. You recovered the golf ball and climbed back to the fairway before Tony worked out the route for the ball recovery."

JACK'S IMPRESSION OF THE "HAGGLE" GROUP REGULARS

Bruce "Radar" Johnson is your "Radar" of Mash TV fame. We copied his appearance from our radar. Marcerllo Coffani, "The Mad Italian" was nicknamed "Prada," after the Americas Yachting Cup Italian entry. Keith Webb, who was club captain is an ex-London Bobby (cop). Shane Brando is a porter at Whangarei Hospital. He lost his leg in a motorcycle accident when he was a young tear away, and now is just an aging lout. We have nicknamed him "Splinter."

Graham Foggin, the very tall "Burglar," is on a handicap that does not represent his ability. Mahu Harris, is the Maori from Okaihau in upper Northland. He seems to have a continuing challenge with his lower denture. I've never seen him use that half of his dentures, but is a real neat guy.

Tom Brown, another Maori, is an insurance assessor. He usually sets the field on its way and does the presentation to winners of the "Haggles", entry fee $2.00 payable after the round.

Angus Lyell is a life member who organizes the annual golf trip to Australia, usually at Gold Coast or Sunshine Coast in Queensland. Phillipp Oxenius is the German with a great sense of humor. "Ve vill smash your fingers vith a hammer, ze German vay." He is an instructor of horse dressage and show jumping, and was at one time involved with the German Olympic team. Don "Spider" McKenzie is always with a yarn, encourages positive bar patronage, and is an ex-commercial avocado grower.

REMEMBERING JACK AND HIS WIFE

Now that you have a descriptive image of my golfing partners in New Zealand, let me relate a pleasant memory of Jack and his lovely wife, Jayne (pronounced Jaynee).

Following another grueling, competitive round of golf with Jack, I informed him of our planned departure the following day. He was quick to invite us over for a farewell cocktail and to meet his wife.

I thanked him for the invitation but explained that we wouldn't be able to accept because of a previous commitment. Further explaining that Claire, Lyn, Charlie and I had been invited to a farewell dinner party at Kay and Andy Mears', owners of a beautiful B&B. Kay has a reputation as a gourmet cook, so that we anticipated a seven course three hour affair.

Jack was persistent, saying no matter what time it was, just come over, relating that it's less than a mile away. He actually drew a map for me, because it's a curvy road with narrow driveways.

As anticipated, our evening started with wine and followed with delicious hors d'oeuvres, more wine, a scrumptious rack of lamb, outstanding gourmet dessert, and the clock struck midnight.

I felt it was much too late to go to Jack's. However, Lyn suggested that I should at least call him, just to be polite and thank him for the invitation. I called and before I could beg off, he said, "I've got the lights on, and will be expecting you in a few minutes."

With Charlie behind the wheel, we were there in about thirty seconds. The only problem was we had arrived at the neighbor's house. Fortunately, it was a friendly neighbor—without a shotgun—and with a long winding driveway, almost the same distance from Kay's and Andy's.

Well, as it turned out, we had a very enjoyable send-off, with Jack's "KINGS" Liquors. He is the owner of Kings Liquor LTD. We mixed various concoctions with fresh fruit juices, sitting on his deck with an outstanding view of the ocean under a full moon until 3 AM.

MEETING LYN'S AND CHARLIE'S FRIENDS

Titus removing a Spanakopita from the oven. Came out perfectly!

While in New Zealand, we stayed with our daughter, Lyn, and Charles O'Neil, our son-in-law.

Lyn is a retired school teacher who has retooled herself, and now has a private practice in massage therapy, with six months in Alaska and six months in New Zealand. They are very social with house parties practically weekly.

When it was Lyn's and Charlie's turn to cook, I offered to take part by preparing a Greek pita pie, **"SPANAKOPITA."** It took me four attempts before I could get accustomed to the spinach, feta and stove, so as to give it a "TEN" rating.

We met most of their friends, with whom they have a lot in common— **THEY LIKE TO PARTY!!"**

Following is a list of wonderful people who we ran into at various parties and gatherings during our stay in New Zealand:

Julie Tattley, who stands over six feet tall, is Lyn's closest friend. Even when she removes her shoes indoors I have to climb up on a chair to give her a hug.

Paddy Tattley is Julie's dad, who is a snooker champion. He has a professional-sized table in his huge attic, and we had a few good matches. However, I was not good enough to be a threat.

Cove at Low Tide
Titus and Claire Plomaritis, Ocean Beach, out in Whangarei Heads, New Zealand. Our favorite location for picnics and low tide walks. February, 2011.

Kay Tattley is Julie's mom. Daphne and Gary Peterken are Lyn's and Charlie's friends and landlords. We were there for Daphne's sixtieth birthday party, which was a beauty, and the buzz lasted for weeks.

Kay and Andy Mears are owners of a beautiful B&B, with an ocean view, where we stayed for two weeks during our first New Zealand visit.

Pene Richards is Charlie's co-worker at the Whangarei Hospital, where they work as X-Ray technicians.

Among the areas that we frequented were Onerahi, Waikaraka, Tamaterau, McLeod Bay, Taurikura, McKenzie Bay, Urquarts Bay, Parua Bay (location of The Pines Golf Club) and Ocean Beach, where we visited almost daily.

WOW! Another great memory!!

NEW LEFT HIP
DARTMOUTH HITCHCOCK MEDICAL CENTER

CATHOLIC MEDICAL CENTER

This chapter may better inform some of you, readers who are getting along in age and perhaps contemplating total hip replacement, and to others it may be very educational.

As for me, I'm having a ball reading my notes and relating my personal experiences from the beginning to their conclusions, especially sharing with you the involvement of my two orthopedic sons and their differences of opinions relative to what type of surgery would be best for dad.

IT ALL STARTED one day in March, 2011, when I made a sudden twisting motion while ascending from a chair. I felt an immediate sharp, stabbing pain in my left hip and groin area. Having experienced many of these episodes over the years I was not concerned, as they always dissipated within a few days to a week.

This time the pain lingered on for over two weeks and increased in intensity when weight bearing and walking, which prompted me to call both of my sons, who are orthopedic surgeons, for advice. Now, that created somewhat of a problem, because after giving them my symptoms, Titus Jr., who is located in North Carolina, and Steven, in Michigan, both insisted that I get to their offices immediately.

Having confidence in both of them, I decided to flip a coin to help me make a decision, and two days later Steven picked me up at the Detroit Airport. He drove me to his office, which was about thirty miles from the airport, in Warren, Michigan. Steven gave me the most thorough orthopedic examination that I could have ever imagined. He also called his specialist friends in the area who worked me into their busy schedules, for bone density, MRI and laboratory tests, to complete his diagnostic workup.

Dr. Steven shared all the test results and his personal findings with his older brother, Dr. Titus Jr. They both agreed that there was a hairline fracture on the neck of the femur and some osteoarthritic spurring throughout the hip joint.

Their advice and recommendations were similar, in that I was to try conservative treatment first; consisting of non weight bearing (use of crutches) for six to eight weeks, and calcium and Vitamin D supplements indefinitely, due to the loss of bone density.

.

I VISITED TITUS JR., during the period I was using the crutches. Then, following a steroid injection, I experienced a drastic improvement with practically no pain for the next two to three weeks. It seemed that surgery would not be required after all.

However, after playing a few rounds of golf and resuming full weight bearing, the pain returned with more intensity. They both agreed that a total hip (**ARTHROPLASTY**) joint replacement was the next step. However, Dr. Titus Jr., who has performed over 2,000 of these total hip replacements, suggested that I get another steroid injection and postpone surgery as long as possible. Whereas, Dr. Steven had a different opinion and felt that I should have the **ARTHROPLASTY** sooner, while still in good health.

I vacillated back and forth and finally made the decision to have my new hip as soon as **DR. SEAN FROST,** my orthopedist from Dartmouth Hitchcock Medical Center in Nashua, N.H., could put me into his surgical schedule.

Next came another difference of opinion from my two boys. Titus Jr. was a proponent of the lateral approach, while Steven was insisting that the anterior surgical approach, although relatively new, is less invasive and has a shorter recovery period. Titus Jr. explained that the lateral approach allows one to use a full sized curved (3 dimensional) collarless femoral component that completely fills the femoral canal. Titus Jr. also prefers to have his total hip patient, toe touch weight bearing for the first eight weeks, during which time the reattachment of the abductor muscles have plenty of time to heal to the bone, while the bone ingrowth into the femoral component occurs. He reminded me that the best measurement of success is how many decades the patient goes before he needs a revision rather than how many days post op before he can full weight bear.

OCT. 26, 2011—While having my pre-surgical consultation with Dr. Frost, at my request, he called Steven in my presence to address Steven's concerns on my behalf. Following his call with Steven, we went over the two options again, and at that time I decided to have Dr. Frost use the anterior approach.

Dr. Frost then stated he would refer me to one of his associates, **DR. GONZALES,** who only performs the anterior approach, and with great results. He also related that he was training for the anterior approach and within six months he would only be using the anterior approach, primarily due to the outstanding results being reported.

Within twenty-four hours I received a call from Dr. Gonzales' office, giving me the date of November third and directions to the Dartmouth Hitchcock Medical Center in Manchester, N.H. for a surgical consultation with Dr. Ricardo Gonzales.

MEETING DR. GONZALES

NOV. 3rd, 2011—Surgical consultation with Dr. Ricardo Gonzales at the Manchester Dartmouth Hitchcock Medical Center.

Dr. Gonzales greeted me with a friendly handshake and a big smile. After a few range of motion tests, he thoroughly explained the anterior approach with the use of a model prosthesis of the total hip.

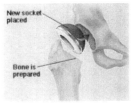

He stressed that this approach required less invasiveness, therefore allowing for a more aggressive rehabilitation program, which inevitably results in a more rapid recovery. **SOUNDED GOOD TO ME!**

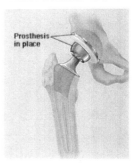

He then asked, "When would you like to have the surgery?"

I quickly replied, "Tomorrow."

He smiled as he looked me straight in the eyes and said he would have his booking secretary arrange the earliest possible date with his surgical coordinator and have his office contact me with additional instructions.

Nov. 4, 2011—Received a call from "Gillian", Dr. Gonzales' surgical coordinator, relating that, "We have your Total Left Hip Replacement surgery scheduled for Monday, November 28th." She also related that she had sent a list of pre-surgical appointments that must be completed prior to surgery.

Nov. 5, 2011—Pre-surgical exam by **DR. KALPESH PATEL,** including blood work and chest X-Rays.

Nov. 17th, 2011—11:30 A.M. appointment at CMC (Catholic Memorial Center) for pre-surgical paper work, surgical preparation and post-surgical home care or rehabilitation.

Nov. 22nd, 2011—8:30 A.M. appointment with **PATRICK McCARTHY,** Dr. Gonzales' P.A. at the Dartmouth Hitchcock Medical Center in Manchester, N.H., for final instructions and information relative to immediate pre-surgery and post-surgery activity.

McCARTHY, although lacking in Dr. Gonzales' personality and warmth was able to convey the following:

a—Discontinue all medications and food supplements, except for my blood pressure pill (25 mg atenolol).

b—Discontinue all food and beverages from midnight, Nov. 27th, except for the blood pressure pill with only a "thimble" of water on the morning of Nov. 28th.

c—Do not bring any personal belongings, jewelry, money, medications or even a toothbrush, to the hospital.

d—Dr. Gonzales and the Anesthesiologist will meet you just before surgery to insert an I.V. (intravenous) line, to provide fluids and medication during surgery.

e—Epidural anesthesia, as explained from Wikipedia, is a form of regional analgesia involving injection of drugs through a catheter placed into the epidural space.

The injection can cause both a loss of sensation (anesthesia) and a loss of pain (analgesia), by blocking the transmission of signals through nerves in or near the spinal cord.

f—When Dr. Gonzales' surgical team is ready, you will be taken to the operating room. There you will be given anesthesia. The anesthesia will help you sleep during surgery. Then an incision will be made, giving Dr. Gonzales access to your hip joint. The damaged ball will be removed and the socket prepared to hold the prosthesis.

g—Following surgery, you will be transported to the recovery room where your condition will be closely monitored. A catheter will be placed in your bladder for urine elimination and elastic stockings will be applied. You will also be outfitted with a Sequential Compression Device, an improved type of intermittent pneumatic compression system that includes inflatable compression sleeves to the lower extremities and a characteristic pressure modulation in order to reduce risk of clot formation, such as deep vein thrombosis.

h—Standing and walking may begin that same day, with the supervision of a physical therapist.

THE BIG DAY FINALLY ARRIVES

Now, with all the preliminaries done, it was the big day that I'd been waiting for, **NOV. 28th, 2011.**

7:30 A.M.—MICHAEL WELCOME, my best friend and four-ball golfing partner, picked me and my wife Claire up at our home and drove us to the Catholic Medical Center in Manchester, N.H.

8:30 A.M.—Check in. From the moment that I checked in at the registration desk my only experiences were pleasantries, smiling faces and gracious welcomes from department to department, very relaxing to the anxious patient, and that I was.

Following some brief paper work, we were then escorted to the surgical waiting room, where Dr. Gonzales gave us a warm greeting, explained briefly the approximate timetable of events, and also that Dr. Frost was able to re-arrange his schedule and would assist in the surgery.

9:15 A.M.—We were escorted to the pre-op surgical room where we met the pre-op nurses, **KELLY BRITTON, R.N.,** and **SANDY WATTS, R.N.** They were both extremely friendly, with bubbly personalities, like we were getting ready for a big party. Then, Dr. Gonzales introduced us to **DR. BOGURSKI,** the anesthesiologist, who also gave us a great big smile and a royal welcome. He very politely ushered his associate into our cubicle and introduced her as **JUDY ROY, R.N.,** his anesthesiologist nurse, and stated that she would be at my side throughout the surgery.

11:00 A.M.—It was here that Dr. Gonzales re-assured Claire and Michael that it was safe to leave and that he would contact Claire at the conclusion of the surgery.

WOW!!—With Claire and Michael heading home and me to the operating room, it was like having the bases loaded and our designated hitter, **DR. GONZALES,** coming to bat!!

THE RECOVERY

1:30 P.M.—This was the next time that I opened my eyes and the **THREE VISIONS** that appeared will remain in my mind forever:

1) Six clocks, all staring me in the face, all identical reading 1:30. Actually, there were only two clocks, side by side; I was having triple vision which accounted for the mathematical six.

2) The first sounds that I heard were in a very soft, soothing tone. "Hello, my name is Cheryl. You are now in the recovery room and in my custody." She had the most comforting smile to go with the voice, and was later identified as **CHERYL YIANAKOPOLOS**, recovery room R.N. What a great asset to the Catholic Memorial Center staff.

3) **"NURSING EXCELLENCE"**, an emblem that resembled a dart board from a distance. I was able to read this close-up during my rehab walking stints up and down the corridors over the next two days. Based on the professional personal services that I experienced, the sign was a great reflection, in spades, of the excellent nursing services provided at the Catholic Memorial Center.

OH, BY THE WAY, it was me, **THE PATIENT**, in the bull's eye slot.

4:00 P.M.—Cheryl wheeled my bed from the recovery room to my residence for the next three days, room E-121-2. Before departing, she introduced me to the floor nurse, **RENEE CHAPUT, R.N.** (3-11 P.M.). **KRISTIN MARCUM, R.N.**, would follow. Great peace of mind.

I WILL ATTEMPT to draw you a picture in words of what I looked like the first day:

1) Intravenous line, bag of fluids and meds attached to a stand on wheels, traveling by gravity down into the back of my left hand, for feeding fluids and medications into my body.

2) Another line with pain control medication from the same stand on wheels, into the epidural space of my spine via a very fine catheter.

3) A catheter from my bladder to a plastic bag attached to the bed frame, for urine elimination.

4) Elastic stockings on both lower extremities.

5) Inflatable compression sleeves to both lower extremities, for intermittent pneumatic pressure to reduce the risk of blood clots.

NOTE: Within twenty-four hours my occupational therapy and physical therapy were initiated and the catheters were removed, one at a time, as my progress showed steady improvement. I roamed the corridors with my walker every couple of hours and was encouraged with greetings of, **"HELLO, TITUS PLOMARITIS"**, from nurses, nurses' assistants, students and housekeeping.

OFFERING HEARTFELT THANKS

I would like to offer my gratitude to the following who all came into play during my C.M.C. hospitalization:

RN's, LNA's, PT's, OT's, students and environmental specialists Cheryl Yianakopolos, Kelly Britton, Kristin Marcum, Renee Chaput, Sandy Watts, Judy Roy, Jennifer Lynch, Sara Ashleigh, Sara Burkhardt, Columba Bisson, Stacy Richardson, Carol Dale, Catherine Exter, Jessica Turgeon, Joanna Dillon, Kristine Cherbonneau, Barbara Cormier, Ricky Donahue, Olga, Tara, and Carol Lapierre.

Last mentioned, **CAROL LAPIERRE,** doubles as a comic, or she should, as she was very entertaining to me and my roommate, **JOHN NORDLE,** creating much needed laughter.

Once she drifted into our room wearing an orange outfit, pushing a mop, happy as a lark, and commented aloud, "Wow! Look at you two birds, ninety and eighty-two, that's 172 years of brain power in the same room." Then she continued, "That's going to be my new lottery number, a definite winner!"

When I asked what her title was, she again brought laughter to both of us with the following, "It used to be House Cleaning, but now we are classified as Environmental Services, you know, like yesterday's Janitors are now Environmental Engineers."

MY ROOMMATE, JOHN

JOHN NORDLE became my roommate, checking in at midnight during my second day, with his oldest of three daughters, Marcia, by his bedside until 4 A.M. I remember because my first two nights there were hourly wake-ups, via a soft tap on the shoulder, with such lines as, "Time for your medication", "Time for your blood pressure and temperature," and "Time for your blood tests."

John's other two daughters, Pam and Nancy, as well as his granddaughters, Kayla and Christie, were all constant visitors, showing great love and affection for their father and grandfather.

John and I were each given an incentive spirometer, with instructions on its use, inhaling ten times each hour to free the lungs of fluids. The gages were set at moderate age differential goals. John must have been a hell of an athlete and competitor because I could hear him through the curtain, inhaling ten times every few minutes, wanting to exceed the goal given by his nurse.

"Hey, Titus, I just hit 1,000!" he commented. Then, about a half hour later, he piped in, "I just hit 1,200!"

He got me going and we must have sounded like two old Tribal Indian Chiefs, sucking on our peace-pipes. And yes, I did exceed my goal, reaching 2,500 and that's without getting down in a three-point stance!

THE BEST AND THE WORST

Every story has to have a best and worst experience.

THE WORST: 4 A.M. each morning, awakened from a sound sleep by a person closely resembling **VINCE WILFORK**, the Patriots' nose tackle, who devours little running backs.

"Blood test time," he said as he licked his chops, with his tools of torture in hand. Sixty years ago I could have faked him out of his jock. But today? No contest.

THE BEST: A great big shopping bag full of great experiences. However, topping the list was being picked up by my bride of sixty years, and driven home with a **NEW LEFT HIP!**

Dec. 1, 2011 was our sixtieth anniversary date and the day I was discharged with a new hip from C.M.C. and picked up by Claire and Michael Welcome.

HOME CARE, REHAB BEGINS

Dec. 2, 2011—A team of nurses and therapists, from home, health and hospice care, came to my home at the direction of Dr. Gonzales' office, to continue the rehabilitation of my new hip joint. They first scanned the house to remove any possible hazards, like scatter rugs, ornaments or obstacles located on the main pathways.

Daily inspection of the incision followed with a fresh dressing, and they set up a firm flat surface for exercises to be performed three times daily, followed by giving me safety instructions on the use of the elevated toilet seat and rubberized shower stool.

They also left a note pad to record digital blood pressure, pulse and temperature, to be taken every four hours, and finally they left a simplified chart and timetable for keeping track of the prescribed medications.

The team included: Angela Ackerson Henry and Megan Dimambrd (PT's), Barbara Goyette and Melissa Tiney (Nurses) and Paula Stark (OT).

Dec. 13, 2011—Discharged from home, health and hospice care.

DAILY CALLS FROM TWO PRECIOUS SONS

This is a great time to mention the two calls daily from Dr. Titus Jr. at 7 A.M, and Dr. Steven, at 7 P.M., as dependable as **BIG BEN** and always the same questions: color of stools, degree of swelling and amount of pain.

I just love those kids and can just imagine how the doctors, nurses and therapists attending to my recovery must have felt with those two guys constantly looking over their shoulders.

DR. GONZALES' POST-OP EXAM

NOTE—The following segment may be a little easier to follow if I mention that my two orthopedic sons repeatedly, practically daily, ask me if I was sure that Dr. Gonzales told me that there were no restrictions on weight bearing.

Dec. 14, 2011—Here were Dr. Gonzales' post surgical exam findings and comments:

1) He removed the dressing, took a real close inspection of the incision, and related that with no oozing or inflammation it would not require any further dressings, and it would be okay to take open showers, wetting the incision area.

2) He explained that the numbness to the lateral thigh area would dissipate over the next few months.

3) He was pleased with the range of motion, and related it was better than expected, crediting the faithful home physical therapy.

4) He wrote a Physical Therapy prescription for "**BALANCE THERAPY**" for gait, balance and proprioception.

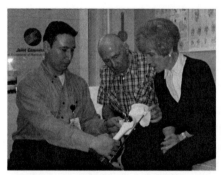

Dr. Ricardo Gonzales, explaining the "ANTERIOR APPROACH" to Titus and Claire Plomaritis

WHEN I QUESTIONED him again about my boys' concerns, relative to weight bearing at this early stage of post-op activities, he smiled, reached over to his desk for his replica of the total hip joint, and explained in detail to me and Claire the difference between the old conventional approach and the new "**ANTERIOR APPROACH**". He enthusiastically pointed to and manipulated the model in his hands. That had us both mesmerized, again relating immediate full weight bearing to the patient's tolerance level.

I asked Dr. Gonzales if he would mind placing a call to one of my boys and explaining his technique and rehabilitation expectations. Before departing, I gave him their office phone numbers, but realizing his busy schedule I figured that it would probably be a day or so before he would get time to call either of them.

AS BIG BEN STRUCK 7:00 that evening, Steven called and said he had a delightful twenty minute phone call from Dr. Gonzales.

Although Steven was convinced of Dr. Gonzales' success rate, relative to immediate full weight bearing, he still cautioned me to go fifty percent for the first four to six weeks, just to be sure the prosthesis had fused to the bone, stating that way I would be sure to be **BACK ON THE GOLF LINKS BY NEXT SPRING.**

PRESCRIPTION from Dr. Gonzales to the therapists: gait, balance and proprioception, and to wean from assistive devices post-op on weeks 4-6.

Dec. 15, 2011—Janet greeted me at the Balance Therapy reception desk, assisted me with all the necessary insurance forms, and introduced me to the physical therapists, Nancy, Chris and Peter, who would be working with me on an as-needed basis until my follow-up visit with Dr. Gonzales on Jan. 11, 2012.

DARTMOUTH HITCHCOCK MEDICAL CENTER-NASHUA

As you walk into the Dartmouth-Hitchcock Medical Center, Nashua lobby, the signs direct you to a holding area, where you are to wait for the next available Patient Accounts Customer Service personal.

JENNIFER FULTON of "Patient Accounts" is like an official greeter, and when I'm next in line she calls me up to her booth with the following in musical tone, **"GOOD MORNING, TITUS PLOMARITIS"**, as all the heads in the lobby turn in my direction.

She then proceeds to sign me in, handing me the necessary paper work for that day's appointments, with directions like: "laboratory, down one level, or Dr. Patel, third floor."

BIG AND GENTLE

After being discharged from CMC, my internist, Dr. Kal'pesh Patel from the Dartmouth Hitchcock Medical Center, Nashua, ordered additional follow-up blood tests.

With the memory of the Vince Wilfork look-alike at the CMC, I dreaded the thought of another torture session. However, I had toughened up a bit and prepared myself for the situation.

Well, this guy, **TERRY FRYE,** was about the same size as Vince, but so gentle. He must have been an offensive lineman, who was used to protecting little running backs because I never even felt so much as a pinprick.

POST-OP REHABILITATION

BALANCE REHABILITATION AND HEALTH SCIENCE is in the neighboring town of Windham, New Hampshire

For those of you who have read this book from the beginning, and have not skipped through chapters, you will understand that my extensive graduate and post graduate training, along with my forty years of private practice, qualify me to evaluate an excellent **PHYSICAL REHABILITATION** facility.

My personal total left hip rehabilitation at **BALANCE REHABILITATION** has been a pleasant experience and is rapidly coming to its conclusion. Having been an active participant and witnessing the multitude of techniques administered for similar conditions in a friendly environment, to the young and old (like me), is a testament of excellence.

PETER OLSON, PT, ATC, and **CHRIS PIERCE, PT, CSCS**, founded Balance in 2006 and opened the doors on February 14th of that year. The original seed for the idea that grew into Balance was planted during a whitewater kayaking run of the Contoocook River in Henniker, NH.

While working together at Merrimack Valley PT in Bedford, Chris and Pete discovered that they shared a love of the outdoors, and both had spent time running a variety of rivers on the East Coast and Western U.S.

On the Contoocook River, sometime around 2003, a conversation about opening a physical therapy practice occurred. At that time it was only a passing discussion without any action. Pete left to do a traveling PT gig in California, while Chris stayed in NH at the same practice. While Pete was gone, Chris started to look into some options for starting up a practice. After Pete returned the conversation was started again.

On a morning in which a boating trip was planned, instead of hitting the water, the two men sat down in a local Manchester café and began a plan to open what became Balance Physical Therapy and Human Performance, and later became Balance Rehabilitation and Health Science, LLC. **THE REST IS HISTORY!**

JASON MASSA joined the practice in a business management position, having recently graduated at the top of his class from SNHU Business School. This job evolved into practice manager.

Captains and Crew—Great Team

Left to right: Top row—Peter Olsen, Chris Pierce. Middle row— Jason Massa, Amy Spencer, Lindsey Bokuniewicz. Bottom row—Jess Erwin, Judy Antonucci, Nancy Manchester. Not pictured (missing in action)—Cathy Freeman, Janet Crudden, Beth Comerford. Cathy Freeman, PT, Nancy Manchester, PT, Lindsey Bokuniewicz, DPT; And the smiling faces at the front desk are Jessica Erwin, Judy Antonucci, Janet Crudden and Beth Comerford.

BISHOP'S FAMOUS RESTAURANT

Christmas Dinner at Bishop's Restaurant-1968
L to R: Joey Bashara, Titus Jr., Claire, Titus Sr., Lyn, Steven and Diane in front. It was
about this time that Joey was adopted, as part of our family.

I first met **JOE BASHARA** in the early sixties, better known as "Joey", one of
four family member owners of Bishop's Restaurant. His older brother, Abe,
was the other Bashara I got to know very well as the years rolled on.

Bishop's was located in downtown Lawrence, Massachusetts, and
famous for its Lebanese specialties and two-pound stuffed lobsters.

It seemed that a lot of my friends from Vesper Country Club, the Rotary
Club and the Yorik Club frequented Bishop's, and whenever we had dinner
engagements, be it with the Riddick's, Battles, Stoklosa's or other friends,
their choice was always Bishop's.

Now that the restaurant is closed and Joey and Abe are retired, let me let
you in on a little secret. Thursdays, Fridays and Saturdays were their busiest
nights, and their policy was not to take reservations. If you arrived at the

restaurant between six and seven in the evening, you would have at least an hour wait, sometimes two hours. The secret was to call the restaurant before leaving the house, and usually Vicki, Joey and Abe's sister would answer. Recognizing who we were, she would put our names on the list as if we just arrived at the restaurant. That way, our wait time would be somewhere between fifteen minutes to perhaps a half hour.

Joey could be recognized at the restaurant by his short, quick steps carrying menus under his arm like a paper boy selling the Daily News. As soon as my name was called on the loud speaker, Joey would greet me with a great big smile and "**HELLO DOCTOR**", at the archway, and I would feel privileged as he'd guide us to our booth or table.

The problem was, on Saturdays when about half the customers were regulars, they were all playing the same game. Joey would sometimes hide in the kitchen to avoid some of his friends because he couldn't accommodate everyone. So he would make up for it by sitting down at our table for a couple of minutes and insist on buying a round of after- dinner drinks.

JOEY BECAME FAMILY

As the years rolled on, it seemed that Joey was getting attached to our four children because when Claire and I went to Bishops without them, he would always say, "Where's the kids?" He would call them all by name when they were with us, which is quite a feat, because even to this day I address Titus as Steve, and Diane as Lyn, and vice versa. The kids get quite a kick out of it, because they claim they'd all be millionaires if they got a quarter for every time I called them by their wrong name.

When Titus Jr., "Buddy" as Joey called him, was playing football at Lowell High School, he would go to the ball games with me, and get as excited as I would every time Buddy would complete a pass or make a short gain on a keeper.

1971 Lowell Sun Charities All Star Game. Joey Bashara on the side lines with Titus Plomaritis Jr., QB for the Greater Lowell All Stars And Coach Riddick.

Coach Riddick, one of Bishops' best customers, always allowed Joey and me to stand around the bench when seats were scarce. I remember when Buddy was a senior, he was probably the smallest quarterback in the country at 5'5" and 140 pounds and led Lowell High School to its last undefeated team in the history of LHS Football.

Well, following that 1970 football season, Titus Jr., was also the starting QB of the Lowell Sun All-Star Game in the Summer of 1971. Joey and I were on the sidelines for the entire game, with Coach Riddick's permission, like two proud parents.

Joey has had a lady friend for the past 43 years, with her nickname being "MADDY".

Claire and I dine with the pair quite often at the Vesper Country Club, and recently I inquired why the couple never got married.

Maddy replied that "Anytime marriage is mentioned, Joey has **A PANIC ATTACK."**

She also adds that they have had a very good longtime relationship.

THE MATINEES

This is a great time to inject this short story that partially includes Bishops Restaurant.

On several occasions Claire and I would reminisce about our children growing up, and she would tell me of Lyn inquiring why she never heard us making love sounds in the bedroom, which brought laughter to both of us.

Remember now, I had a home/office combination private practice. For several years during those growing up days of the children, I would schedule my patients on Tuesdays and Fridays, 8 A.M. to twelve noon, and 3 P.M. to 8 P.M.

I always was aware of the morning time on those days, to be sure all the patients were attended to and no procrastination. Claire would have the car all revved up at twelve sharp, in the driveway, ready for a fast get-away for a fifteen minute ride on the back roads to Bishop's Restaurant.

Lunches at Bishops were very popular, always crowded at noon, but Joey always sat us immediately, with the understanding that I had to get back to the office by 2 P.M. To this day I get tingles down my spine and other sensitive parts of my body just reflecting on those **MATINEES.**

THE SAGA OF BISHOP'S RESTAURANT

Bishops Restaurant of Lawrence, Mass., came into existence in 1949, when the owner of a small sandwich shop at White and Oak Street decided to sell.

ABE BASHARA and his brother, **CHARLES**, scraped together what they had managed to save while in the service. Their mother, sister, **VICKI**, and brother, **JOSEPH**, also chipped in with what money they had. They added that to a $1,000 loan, and the family became the proud owners of Bishops. The name of the newly-acquired restaurant was an Anglicization of the nickname, Bishy.

The original restaurant, founded in 1949 with a seating capacity of fewer than 100, was located on the first floor of a three-decker tenement. The restaurant quickly became famous for its massive orders of fresh-cut French fries and huge salads.

In 1953 the building was acquired. The next year it was torn down and replaced with a new structure, consisting of a 30'x90', and 2,700 square foot new restaurant at the same location.

THE NEW BISHOP'S OPENS

Bishops eventually left the White Street location, in 1968, under Urban Reconstruction, and the Bashara family then built and opened the spacious and eventually famous 450-seat restaurant on Hampshire Street.

The business quickly boomed, and the rich and famous came, a Saudi Arabian prince, three-time Academy Award winning actress, Meryl Streep, television star, Danny Thomas, his daughter, Marlo (later to head St. Jude Children's Research Hospital), comedian George Carlin, Boston Bruins big-wig Harry Sinden, Red Sox and World Series champion, Oakland Athletics Manager, Dick Williams, famed T.V. announcer, Curt Gowdy, all of whom shared holiday cards with the Bashara family. Even Jacqueline Kennedy Onassis was a frequent customer, when her son, John F. Kennedy Jr., attended nearby Phillips Andover Academy.

However, most of the regular Bishop's customers came from the Merrimack Valley, as it always attracted Middle Eastern-Americans seeking Lebanese cuisine.

The totally Mediterranean restaurant, which finally seated 850, served 30,000 legs of lamb per year, plus 500,000 pounds of rice, 25,000 heads of lettuce and 10,000 loaves of Arabian bread—just some of the ingredients which comprised the 400,000 meals annually.

HONORS GAINED BY BISHOP'S

Many honors befell Bishop's, especially in 1977, with the State of Massachusetts Small Business Award, followed by the Bashara family being invited to the White House to meet President Jimmy Carter.

The U.S. Small Business Association honored the Bashara family, brothers Charles, Abe and Joseph, and sister, Victoria, at a luncheon at the Pleasant Valley Country Club in Sutton. The annual award goes to the "The Outstanding Small Business Person of the Year", but with Bishop's Restaurant being such a family operation, the award had to be all-inclusive.

Following the public tribute paid to them at Pleasant Valley, yet another came from the Greater-Lawrence Chamber of Commerce.

THE GREATER-LAWRENCE BOAT PROGRAM SPEARHEADED BY ABE BASHARA

When Bishop's Restaurant closed its doors, I grew to know brothers Joey and Abe considerably better. They had always been supportive of whatever charitable program I was promoting, without ever expecting anything in return.

I have learned their pet charity for the past ten or so years, and I, along with our regular Vesper golfers, have supported Abe's annual fundraiser by attending the annual banquet for **THE GREATER-LAWRENCE BOAT PROGRAM,** his major fund raiser. When and if you ever get an opportunity to visit the **ABE BASHARA BOATHOUSE,** you will get goose bumps watching the underprivileged kids learning to swim and all there is to know about boating.

How it started and how it has grown to serve the Greater-Lawrence community is a great history lesson that I would like to share with you.

LAWRENCE—The Greater-Lawrence Community Boating program, a private non-profit program committed to provide safe, affordable boating for all Merrimack Valley residents, was incorporated in 1979, and has since been expanded by leaps and bounds.

Spearheaded by **ABE BASHARA**, Mayor Larry LeFebre and prominent businessmen, Bob Nazarian, Gene O'Neil, Mike Morris and Dick Barney, the boating program began with six boats and a temporary trailer.

The new program taught about 100 kids how to sail that summer, from a picturesque spot along the Merrimack River, which was donated by State Representative Thomas Lane. Since then, the Boating Program has grown to become a cherished institution in the City of Lawrence.

THE ABE BASHARA COMMUNITY BOATHOUSE

In 1987, a combination of public and private entities joined forces to begin

construction of the 10,000 square foot **Abe Bashara Boathouse,** which was opened in 1990.

OVER THE YEARS, the G-L Community Boating Program staff has taught over 30,000 youths from the Merrimack Valley to sail and row, many of whom are from the underserved communities of Lawrence and surrounding towns, who could not otherwise have an opportunity to learn and excel in boating.

The Abe Bashara Boathouse is an ideal facility complete with showers, locker facilities, function space, ample parking, and picnic area for the whole family to enjoy.

Many of the participants have improved enough to continue rowing and sailing in college and beyond, and also return to Lawrence each summer as experienced instructors.

THE GENEROUS BASHARA BROTHERS

Many times if a family was deserving of joining the boating program, but found that $150 was over its budget, **ABE or JOE BASHARA** would pay for that family's membership.

If you ever met Abe or Joe you could understand why you would be intrigued with their kind, unforgiving generosity to the less fortunate. You couldn't discover two loving brothers who find greater satisfaction in giving.

The Greater-Lawrence Community Boating Program's Boathouse was built, and eventually named in honor of **ABE BASHARA**, deservingly so as he gives 100 percent of his time, energy and financial resources to the program.

Abe, who is the Chairman of the Program's Board of Directors, conducts fundraisers every year which raise thousands of dollars. These drives also include giving away dinners and hundreds of donated gifts, such as Super Bowl, Red Sox and Bruins tickets. After he gives something away, Abe says, "Thank you, for taking it."

OFFICERS AND BOARD OF DIRECTORS, 2012

Chairman, Abraham Bashara
Executive Director, Jed Koehler
President, Bruce Baril
Vice President, Shaun Hardy
Immediate Post President, Larry J. Yameen
Treasurer, Kenneth Daher
Clerk, Vincent C. Manzi, Esq.
Secretary, Ellen Wright

Board of Directors—Lance Adie, Joseph Bashara, Eileen Bernal, Esq., Robert Bernier, June Black, Peter Blanchette, Tom Connors, Bud Crowninshield, Irene Crane, Patricia Degan, Joseph Deagan, Gil Frechette, David King, Mary Kountz, Charles Lopiano, David lacroix, Philip Loverriere, Sr., Robert LeBlanc, Esq, April Lyskoowsky, Esq., Jeffrey Marcoux, Frank Moran, Gary Mucica, Nelson Ortiz, Judy Perkins, Michael Petrilli, George Peters, Jr, Fred Shaheen, Peter Shaheen, Esq., Robert Sheehan, Bryan Sweet, Francisco Urena, and Evan Williams.

SECTION FIVE

LOWELL HIGH SCHOOL CLASS OF 1949

Senior Prom

TITUS PLOMARITIS, SENIOR CLASS PRESIDENT, WITH HIS SENIOR PROM DATE, CLAIRE HEBERT, AND HEADMASTER, RAYMOND A. SULLIVAN GIVEN THE HONORS OF CUTTING THE CAKE.

**The Riddicks and Stoklosas Were Invited
Guests at Lowell High Class of 1949 Reunion**
Left to right: Marjorie Riddick, Coach Ray Riddick, Kay Stoklosa, Dr.Titus Plomaritis,
Claire Plomaritis, Coach Stan Stoklosa.

REUNION REVIVED MEMORIES

By Sam Weisberg
Lowell Sun

LOWELL—June , 1969—The Lowell High Class of 1949 held its 20th reunion at the Pelham Inn on Saturday night, and members of this class helped to establish athletic history for the Red and Gray.

TITUS PLOMARITIS was the class president. Who can forget his exploits in leading Lowell to a 20-19 victory over Lawrence on Thanksgiving Day in 1948. That was the first undefeated football team on record at LHS, and it became the first Red and Gray squad to play in a bowl game—meeting Bogalusa (Louisiana) High in the Memorial Bowl in Jackson, Mississippi. Lowell fans contributed $14,000 to send the team down South.

GOING OVER THE ROSTER

The seniors on that famous gridiron unit included Captain Roger Sanborn, Jack Garland, Arthur Lemoine, Bob Lach, Dave Felton, Jack Meehan, Joe Connors, Norm Carver, Bob Sharp, Earl McQuade, Bob Swan, Bob Lovejoy, Jimmy Fallon, Fred Pawlowski, Bob Ayer, John McNamee, Jack Lardner, and, of course Plomaritis. **LARDNER** is remembered as being the security guard for Jackie Kennedy following the assassination of the President.

These seniors also participated in the initial Lowell Sun Charities All-Star game, won by Lowell, 6-0, over Lawrence, with Plomaritis being named the most valuable player of the contest.

The managers of the 1948 LHS eleven were seniors Bill Franks, Fred Harris and John Tavares. The latter, son of famous boxer Al Mello, is now the head of Model Cities in Lowell.

CHECKING OTHER LHS SPORTS

The 1949 Lowell High baseball team was edged out by Everett for the Greater-Boston League title, and the local seniors on the squad included Captain Sam Goodsoozian, Bob Callery, Frank Major, Jack McHale, Al Scott, Joe Connors, Fallon and Swan.

Leading the track team were Captain Julian Mroz, Joe Mello, Swan and Pawlowski. **MROZ** was the Northeast Interscholastic 1000 champion that year. Pete Kalergeropoulos captained the 1948-49 LHS basketball five, which had seniors Ed Correa, Gene Lightbody, Goodsoozian and Fallon.

PROMINENT UNDERCLASSMEN NAMED

Historic Red and Gray Eleven
The 20th reunion of the Lowell High School class of 1949 brings back memories of the undefeated Red and Gray football team of the previous Fall. Shown above was the starting eleven. The passers in the backfield, L-R: Bob Swan (32), Jimmy Fallon (24), Brian Reynolds (34) and Titus Plomaritis (42). The linemen, L-R: Arthur Lemoine, Norm Carver, John Meehan, Captain Roger Sanborn, Bob Lach, Bob Ready and Minnie Mavraides. Sun staff photo.

Senior Class Officers

Left to Right: Front John Shaw, first vice president; Titus Plomaritis, president; Charles Erwin, second vice president. Standing—Lorraine Pearsall. secretary: Thomas Ralls. treasurer.

Several of the more prominent underclassmen, whose names loom as sure future All-Stars, who were on these squads were Brian Reynolds, Bob Ready, Menil Mavraides, Leo Avila, Ray Armstrong, Leo Parent, Jack Reilly, George Spaneas and Harry Drivas.

Ray Riddick (football), Stan Stoklosa (baseball), Mike Haggerty (track) and Tony Archinski (basketball) were the head coaches of the major sports at LHS at the time.

25th LHS Reunion

Left to right Standing front, Dr. Titus and Claire Plomaritis. Rear, Left to right—Albert Mangan, Athletic Director, Armand Lemay, Coach Tony Archinski, Coach Raymond Riddick, Jimmy Fallon.

Lowell High School 50th Class Reunion

By Claire Ignacio

The 50th. reunion of Lowell High School, held in 1999, was surely a memorable one. Well attended by a roomful of senior citizens, there were many smiles, lots of laughter and a few tears. We all wore lapel pins made with a gold "50" and our hall banner, welcoming us to the Radisson, was highlighted by gold lettering.

SITTING; Carolyn (O'Connell) Clancy, Claire (Smith) Mousley, Patricia (Quinn) Kohl, Anne (Chandler) Patterson, Monica (O'Neill) Liston, Lorraine (Pearsall) McLaughlin, Patricia (McSorely) O'Brien, Norma (Conlon) McAndrews
STANDING; Gunnar Reslow, Claire (Paquin) Ignacio, Kay (Rynne) Fallon, James Fallon, Titus Plomaritis, John Shaw, Barbara (Leavitt) Silva, Margaret Lenzi, William Moriarty.

After our scrumptious dinner, we assembled in the reception hall for a picture taking session and many of the people who came unattended by a

spouse posed with another classmate. These pictures were later assembled in a booklet that became a souvenir for those who purchased them later. As I write this accounting of that reunion, I am looking at these photos and it is a treasure to me to be able to recount that fabulous time we had that weekend.

The LHS class of 49' hoists it's flag to celebrate their 50th reunion. Who better than Monica (O'Neil) Liston, that has served as our reunion committee treasurer from day one (with no shortages) and Lorraine (Pearsall) McLaughlin, our class Secretary.

Being on the committee afforded me the privilege of greeting the many classmates who arrived and pinning them with the pin that I lovingly made for each one of them. I saw faces that wore wrinkles, people walking with the aid of a cane and some with walkers. A few had to use a wheelchair. But...one thing that stood out in my mind were the smiles and bright eyes that each one wore despite their handicaps. They were happy, yes indeed. They ate heartily and conversed with each other and danced to a band that played the "old" favorites of our time. Band members were classmates too.

LHS 50th Class reunion: L to R: Monica Liston, Sec-Treas.; Jim & Kay Fallon Co-Chairman; Class Pres. Titus Plomaritis, Co-Chairman.

I was fortunate to share a table with the Plomaritis's and noticed Claire poking Titus a few times but paid no attention to her eye riveting glances. After the meal, Titus stood up and went to the podium to make a short speech. (his speeches are never short) He called me up to the front of the room and I nearly died. I stood next to him and he presented me with a gift that was totally unexpected. Well I had to make a little speech now and I was tongue tied. Thinking of our troops fighting in Iraq I requested that the entire room stand up and salute these brave people by singing **"AMERICA"** in their honor **IT WAS FABULOUS!!** my heart filled with pride and my classmates never faltered. Despite their ages, they all had strong voices and tears in their eyes. Many of them were veterans from WWII themselves.

OH! The gift? It was a beautiful silver bracelet in appreciation for the many years that I made the pins that we wore at all of our reunions.

President "Titus" with four Claires. 1999—LHS 50th Class reunion: L to R: Claire Plomaritis. Claire Ignacio, Titus, Claire Bourgeault, Claire Mousley.

Lowell High School 60th Class Reunion

By Claire Ignacio

YES! It was 60 years ago, and like the Field of Dreams, the classmates came. Filling the function room at Long Meadow Golf Club, the graduates and their spouses, along with many guests, enjoyed reuniting with each other in a fun-filled afternoon.

So many hugs and a few tears, among many unrecognizable glances, took place as the "oldsters" piled into the room for the pinning of their name tags. It was so memorable. Laughter soon replaced the anticipation of meeting an older generation of school mates and soon we were all one again. It had been five years since we met in this fashion and although a few more wrinkles may have been added, the familiar faces soon fell into focus and the chatter began.

The brightly decorated room brought cheers from the class of '49 as they encountered a few hundred maroon/gray clusters of balloons throughout the room along with an archway of the same that surrounded the silver numbers, "60," where the band, "The Comeback Kids," played songs reminiscent of our era. Those who were able danced and it was like a scene from the Commodore Ballroom of years ago.

Speeches were held at a minimum since we had two talented singers who performed for us. **ARMAND LEMAY** and **GEORGE TSANDIKOS** gave us a rendition, each in his own style, of "Toor-a-lor-a-loora" and "Bluebird of Happiness." They were rewarded by a room full of applause. A tribute to our troops followed by the singing of "God Bless America," an unscheduled

353

little surprise was received by everyone standing, in gratitude to these men/ women who are fighting for our freedom. I'm sure that there were many veterans in our group, also. Our "Reunion Queen," Monica (O'Neill) Liston was also honored.

Our class president, **TITUS PLOMARITIS**, presided over this event along with our quarterback, Jim Fallon, who recognized Bob Lach (one of the band members) and Norman Carver as the ones who saved their backs during the greatest football season of that time. Not to be left out, Francis Hickey, also a classmate and a member of the band, who later became a music teacher at Dracut High School, greeted the guests with the microphone as he walked around to the tune of our class song. While everyone sang, a march took place and the clapping of hands brought us back to Lowell High School in the year 1949.

CLASS OF 1949 REUNION COMMITTEE MEMBERS

Titus, then continued to thank the following classmates who have served on the reunion committees, from time to time, over the past sixty years, especially Monica (O'Neill) Liston, who has been our Secretary and Treasurer since day one. Also a special thanks to Jim & Kay Fallon who have served as my co-chairs.

Margaret Lenzi, William Moriarty, Claire (Paquin) Ignacio, Lorraine (Pearsall) McLaughlin, Bill Moriarty, Carolyn (O'Connell) Clancy, Edward Clancy, Norma (Conlon) McAndrews, Jack Gervais, Dan Silva, Ed Correa, Claire (Smith) Mousley, Gloria (St. Hillaire) Douglas, Jack Tenczar, Jack McHale, Jack McNamee,, Jack Shaw, Barbara (Meagher) Eastham, Walter McKenna, Patricia (Quinn) Kohl, Anne (Chandler) Patterson, Patricia (McSorley) O'Brien, and Barbara(Leavitt) Silva.

Finishing with: **"THANKS FOR THE GREAT RIDE"**

LAST OFFICIAL MEETING

The committee met at the Stonehedge Inn, Pawtucket Boulevard in Tyngsboro, Massachusetts on September 15, 2011, for a **"HIGH NOON"** luncheon. We chose Stonehedge for two reasons. One was for its sentimental connection, being only a long field goal (real long, about a mile) to Tyngsboro Country Club, the location of our 1949 senior class prom.

The second reason we chose this location was Monica's insistence that we close the bank account that was opened during our very first class reunion.

The consensus was, that we would order off the menu, exhaust the funds in the account and, if insufficient, we would pitch in for the balance. Well, when the luncheon bill was given to Monica, she reviewed it, as we all waited for the good news. It never happened, as she removed her glasses and commented, "Our account just about covered the appetizers, start digging".

Anyway, as always, it was a fun time having lunch, with a great group of classmates.

We all agreed that the 60th was to be our last official class reunion. As we parted, there were hugs, kisses and tears of happiness, as we all sang our **LOWELL HIGH SCHOOL SONG,** together for the last time.

LOWELL HIGH SCHOOL SONG

Lowell High School, Lowell High School
May we ever stand
Honest, Faithful, and Courageous,
Loyal to our land.

Lowell High School, Lowell High School
We shall all be true
To the ideals you teach us,
Through and through.

OUR SWIMMING CHAMPION

Home Again

Charlie Erwin returned to
swim in the same open water
race that he had won 50 years
earlier.

By Betsy Durrant

"I started to meet some of my Lowell High School classmates from the Class of 1949. Soon, a group of them appeared with signs. That newspaper article generated enough interest to create a mini-class reunion and cheering section for me!"

In the photo above, with Charlie kneeling, are Committee members, from left to right: Bill Moriarty, Lorraine Pearsall (our class secretary), Titus Plomaritis (class president), Jimmy Fallon, Anne Patterson, Kay Fallon, Mary Keefe (Charlie's cousin) and sitting is Cara Powell (Charlie's Granddaughter).

Just another excuse to have a "reunion," or what we called a committee get-together, occurred when Charles Erwin, my Lowell High School second vice president, decided he was going to compete in the famous Mike Rynne Swim, in the also famous Merrimack River on the banks of Pawtucket Boulevard in Lowell, Mass.

We, his classmates, were there with placards to root him on, following him along the river banks with loud cheers for the last 100 yards.

"GO, CHARLIE, GO!!" we shouted.

Charlie had won the same race, which took place a half century ago, on July 28, 1952. He set three goals for himself when he decided to submit his application for this July 4, 2002 two-mile event.

1. To swim to the finish line.
2. Not to come in last.
3. To post a time under one hour.

Charlie was **OUTSTANDING** as he accomplished all three of his goals, with a finishing time of fifty-six minutes, coming in forty-third out of sixty participants.

RETURNING TO HISTORY

NOTE—Much of the interview below with Charlie Erwin was authored by Betsy Durrant, a member of the Virginia Masters Swim Team and editor of her club's newsletter.

Famous author, Thomas Wolfe, once stated, "You can't go home again," but master swimmer, Charlie Erwin, begs to differ.

It seems that 50 years ago, Charlie, a native of Lowell, Mass. won the first-ever Mike Rynne 3-mile Swim on the Merrimack River.

Now, a half century later, on the Fourth of July, 2002, the 70-year-old Charlie found himself back in Lowell from his current residence in Virginia Beach, Virginia, stroking away in those familiar Merrimack waters as he was cheered on by his old high school classmates.—**HOME AGAIN!!**

"My wife, Dottie, and I were vacationing in Cape Cod this past summer, and we headed to Lowell, Mass.," commented Charlie, "that's where the Mike Rynne Swim was scheduled for the Fourth of July.

"Lowell is my hometown, but I hadn't been there for at least 20 years. The Swim was very nostalgic to me. I knew Mike Rynne, an admired and beloved Lowell police officer.

"When I called Jack Hall, the race organizer, earlier this year, I indicated that I had won the race 50 years ago. Jack contacted a reporter (Chris Scott) at The Lowell Sun, who subsequently called and interviewed me, and two days before the event an article appeared in the newspaper.

"That newspaper article generated enough interest to create a mini-class reunion (Lowell High, class of 1949) and a cheering section for me.

"The race itself was well-run, with 60 participants, and the winner was New England Masters Ed Gendreau, who finished the two-mile distance in 35:51. I placed 43rd and achieved my goals of swimming under an hour (56 minutes) and not coming in last."

HONORED BY THE CITY OF LOWELL

After the race, Charlie was called up to the stage by the river bank and the mayor of Lowell presented him with a special award—a City of Lowell citation.

"I have never been so stunned and humbled by all the attention that I received," added Charlie. "My memento this time was not a medal, but a citation—framed and now hanging in my den—something I will cherish for the remainder of my life."

THE PAST HISTORY OF THE RACE

Back in 1952 the Mike Rynne race began at the Vesper Country Club in Tyngsboro and headed downstream before ending at the Municipal Bathhouse, covering a distance of about three miles.

The race events in 1952 were launched when Rynne, on his 72nd birthday, pulled his memorable stunt of swimming across the Merrimack River while towing a rowboat carrying several adults—**WITH HIS WRISTS AND ANKLES BOUND TOGETHER!!**—This remarkable feat landed him an entry in "Ripley's Believe It or Not".

Charlie Erwin won the race, covering the distance in one hour and 35 minutes, finishing ahead of the former champion by five minutes. Mike Rynne was on hand to present Erwin with the winner's trophy.

REMINISCING WITH CHARLIE

Christopher Scott, The Lowell Sun, July 2, 2002).

Charlie Erwin, a retired U.S. Navy officer who served on an aircraft carrier, destroyer and oiler, was born and raised on Royal Street in the Lower

Highlands. His father was a salesman for the former Lowell Electric Light Corp.

Charlie began swimming at an early age, on Dracut's Long Pond during family vacations, and then on Westford's Nabnasset Lake. He eventually moved to the choppy waters of the North Atlantic, doing the Australian crawl and breaststroke along Hampton Beach, N.H.

Following his 1949 graduation from Lowell High, he completed several years of seminarian study at St. John's Seminary in Brighton before enrolling in Officers' Candidate School. He retired from the naval service with the rank of lieutenant commander.

"I guess I've always held something special for the water," said Erwin. "I've always loved boats, and I've always loved swimming."

LOWELL HIGH SCHOOL ALUMNI GOLF TOURNAMENT, 2004

Lowell High School Alumni sponsors an annual golf tournament each year in honor of a distinguished LHS graduate, and the proceeds go into a

family scholarship fund for that year's honoree.

Well, as luck would have it, in 2004 the honoree was Ray Riddick. I put a team together, consisting of myself, Joey Bashara, Titus Jr., and Molly, Titus Jr.'s youngest, who was only eleven years old at the time and ranked internationally as one of the top three eleven-year-old golfers in the world. At age thirteen she made it to the final qualifier at the U.S. Ladies Open, playing 36 holes with touring pros.

Buddy lettered four years in golf at the University of Vermont up in Burlington, was Captain his Jr. And Sr. Years. This meant that Joey and I were the two riders of our "**TWO HORSES**"—an expression in golf as great players.

The course was Sky Meadow, in Nashua, N.H., not an easy track and with tough greens to read.

We used Molly's T-Shot on twelve holes and Titus Jr.'s on the other six. However, we used Joey's birdie putts on eight holes, and I also made several good approach shots. So combined we came in eighteen under par and were declared the winners.

Place Image 176 here aligned to the left at 50% page width with text wrapping to the right and below the image. Caption underneath, "From left: Joey Bashara, Titus Plomaritis Sr., Molly Plomaritis, Titus Jr. Plomaritis

Inscribed by Molly "DEAR PAPOO, I LOVE YOU & YOU PLAYED WELL. MOLLY PLOMARITIS"

The photo at left is one of my prize possessions within my 2,500 plus aperture photo library. It is an autographed copy, by my granddaughter, Molly, of the winners of the annual Lowell High School Alumni Golf Classic, with the 2004 honoree being the family of Raymond E. Riddick.

Side note: My friend Dick Bournival, with a cocktail in hand, was on his porch at the fifteenth hole, tipping his glass and complimenting Molly on a great t-shot.

TITUS RETURNS, THIS TIME AS COACH

By Joe McGarry
Lowell Sun

LOWELL, September 24,1958 —Just 10 years ago new trails were being blazed across the Lowell High football horizon as a new era in Red and Gray gridiron history was born.

That was the year in which the Raiders were destined to come up with their first undefeated season in many a moon and one which found the club, under the guidance of a comparative "newcomer"—**RAY RIDDICK**—about to represent the school in the first post-season game in history.

BECOMING A LEGEND

Spearheading the attack in those glorious days was a diminutive scatback, who later was to become a legend in Lowell High football annals.

It was **TITUS PLOMARITIS,** who time after time pulled the fat out of the fire with breakaway runs and deadeye placekicking on field goals and conversions.

He will long be remembered for his feats in the Thanksgiving game of 1948 when he tallied all the points as Lowell wound up the season with a come-from-behind 20-19 victory over Lawrence.

Now, he has returned to the scene of his earlier gridiron exploits, but this time in a coaching capacity. He is now a member of the official staff of the Lowell High coaching regime and is working with the freshman-sophomore group, under the direction of former Olympian, **AL MANGAN.**

Now a Coach   Wednesday, September 16, 1964   The Lowell Sun

Titus Plomeritus Returns to Scene of His Grid Triumphs

It's Like Old Times

Former Lowell High football star Titus Plomaritis is back in town, this time as a coach for the Red and Gray's freshman-sophomore team. Shown above, at right, is Titus handing the ball off to his younger brother, Tony, during a workout. At left is Coach Al Mangan watching guard Bob Martin.

IT WILL NOW BE "DOCTOR PLOMARITIS"

Since leaving the Lowell High scene—as a player—a lot of water has gone over the well-known dam for Titus. He moved on to Boston University, where he also made a name for himself on the football field and thence, following his graduation in 1953, to California.

After a year of study in Los Angeles he returned to the East, settling in New York, where he won a degree as a chiropractor following study at the New York Chiropractic Institute, an affiliate of the school in Los Angeles where he studied while on the West Coast.

Since that time he has been as busy as the proverbial bee, passing examinations and what-have-you in New Hampshire, where he is due to open an office in Pelham in the near future.

A FAMILY AFFAIR AT LHS

In coaching the Lowell High frosh squad Titus may be in on the ground floor of another era, for one of his pupils is **TONY PLOMARITIS**, his 15-year-old brother. Although Tony, in all probability, won't see too much varsity action this year, he did make an appearance in the Jamboree last Sunday, and it certainly brought back fond memories as Number 42 trotted onto the field once again.

Titus hasn't been away from football completely since his graduation, as while attending school in New York he took time out to do all the scouting of St. Michael's in Union City, New Jersey, a future LHS opponent, for Coach Riddick. He also assisted in scouting the White Plains team when Lowell was playing that New York club, and as Riddick put it: "His assistance was invaluable."

Yes, it was just 10 years ago that a new era was being born, and with the know-how and fortitude of a guy like Titus Plomaritis, there may be more history in the making.

THE PLOMARITIS FAMILY TRADITION CONTINUES

Anthony "Tony" Plomaritis, the middle member of the Lowell High School football playing family, is shown at the far left of this photo taken at a 1960 Red and Gray practice. Other gridders shown, left to right, are "Tiny" Sheehan, Walter Nelson and Tom O'Hare...Titus, Sr., was the original Plomaritis family member to play for Coach Ray Riddick, followed by younger brother "Tony" and finally son Titus, Jr....Walter Nelson later became Titus, Jr.'s, freshman coach and eventually served as the LHS head coach and the school's athletic director.

YEP!! That's the same Tony that George and I carried on our shoulders to the Lowell Day Nursery, fourteen years earlier, prior to our military enlistment.

MEMORIES

MEMORIES OF LOWELL DAY NURSERY

Lowell Day Nursery, July 2011

After taking the attached photo, I called the Lowell Day Nursery, as it ties into one of my earlier stories, of going into the military, while attending Lowell High school in 1946.

I found it very interesting and felt it was worth passing on that it was founded in 1885, (that's 127 years) and still in business.

Well it certainly has memories, going back to the days when George and I carried our younger brother, Tony, on our shoulders, from the bus stop on Merrimack Street, to the nursery and then hustled up Hall Street to Lowell High School, which was about four football fields or a 440 yard track.

THANKSGIVING, 1948

The missing Lowell Lawrence **TYING TD** football.

Presented to me at the post game dinner dance with a ribbon tied onto it.

Janet Lambert Moore did the artistry and it's in my trophy case willed to Lowell High School!!!

Titus Got the TD; Who Got the Ball?

LOWELL—When Titus Plomeritus made the final—and tieing touchdown in yesterday's game at Lawrence, the fans in the end zone bleachers rolled down onto the playing field and swarmed all over the diminutive Red and Gray halfback. During the course of the mele the game ball disappeared to the satisfaction of some fan, and it was necessary to put a new ball in play before the try for the deciding point.

LHS BOY OF THE WEEK

LOWELL—Circa 1948—Titus Plomaritis, son of Mr. and Mrs. Demosthenes Plomaritis of 29 Johnson Street, and one of Lowell High's sharpest and most versatile seniors, has been named the school's **BOY OF THE WEEK.**

He graduated from Pawtucket Junior High School and is currently enrolled in the college course. He intends to follow mechanical engineering as his career.

"Titko," as he is known to his friends, takes part in football, baseball, ping-pong and boxing.

He is well remembered among local football fans for that amazing kick for the point-after touchdown in Lowell's win over Peabody. The kick had to travel over 38 yards, due to the Red and Gray's being hit with two successive penalties on the play.

THE FIRST ALL-STAR GAME MVP

TITUS PLOMARITIS, who led Lowell High to its first undefeated season (1948) and to its first bowl game in history, was the star of the 1949 Lowell Sun Charities initial Inter-City All-Star Game.

"Plomaritis ran, kicked, passed and blocked like a demon," stated The Lowell Sun.

Titus scored the only touchdown early in the fourth quarter with a nine-yard run in Greater-Lowell's 6-0 victory over Greater-Lawrence. A Plomaritis to George Pollinger pass set up the score.

Plomaritis was selected as the winner of the game's most valuable player trophy, receiving 10 of the 13 votes cast by members of the press.

HANGING OUT AT FENWAY

SAM PINO, a Boston University football teammate and one of my close friends, would grab me and say, "Come on, Greek, let's go to the game at Fenway Park today."

Needless to say, we would take in many baseball games at Fenway Park, due to the fact that we received reduced ticket prices because B.U. played its football games at Fenway, which was located just down the street from the University. We normally got good seats, as the Red Sox drew small crowds at that time, usually just a few thousand fans for day games, compared to sellout crowds of 36,000 nowadays.

WITNESSING MANY OF THE STARS

Fortunately, we were able to watch plenty of the top Major League big names of that early 1950's era, such as "The Yankee Clipper", **JOE DiMAGGIO,** who competed against his brother, **DOMINIC,** of the Red Sox. Both were great centerfielders.

When the Yankees were in town, the rabid Sox fans in the centerfield bleachers would all stand up and shout in unison, **"WHO IS BETTER THAN HIS BROTHER JOE?? DOMINIC DiMAGGIO!!"**

When Joe retired after the 1951 season, and he visited different ballparks, he insisted that he be introduced as "the greatest living former player."

We were also fortunate to witness the exploits of the fabulous Boston slugger, **TED WILLIAMS.** We were on hand the day that Ted gave the famous **"FINGER"** to his longtime critics, the press, and to the fans, who didn't get to admire and cheer him on until he returned from military service for the second time. Shortly after **THE FINGER** incident the Red Sox management roped off the deep part of the leftfield stands in order to keep unruly fans from "getting on" Ted.

On another day we saw the lowly St. Louis Browns in town, and the great **LEROY "SATCHEL" PAIGE,** who was close to fifty at the time, strike out Williams on three pitches—two change ups and then a blazing fastball right past Ted, who went back to the dugout and broke his bat against the wall.

However, we also saw "The Splendid Splinter" belt many tape-measure home runs, before he was called back into the Marine Corps during the Korean War.

CHARLIE "KING KONG" KELLER

One day the Detroit Tigers were playing at Fenway, and Sam and I took in the game.

Meeting Keller at Fenway Park
Titus, 2nd from left, and B.U.football teammate Sam Pino, far right, are shown with Tigers' Left fielder Charlie Keller at Fenway Park in 1950.

The Tigers were hot at that time, battling the Yankees for the top spot in the A.L standings. One of their recent pickups for the stretch drive was former Yankee slugger, Charlie Keller, and we had the good fortune to interview him and take photos just before the start of the game.

Keller, nicknamed **"KING KONG"** because of his fierce looks and big, bushy eyebrows, was a member of one of the greatest outfield trios in Major League Baseball history, and only a serious back injury probably kept him out of Hall of Fame contention.

Keller was the left fielder of the famous New York Yankees outfield of the 1940's, which also consisted of **JOE DIMAGGIO** in center field and **TOMMY HENRICH** in right.

Keller played eleven seasons for the Yankees, from 1939 to 1949, and again in 1952, being a member of seven pennant winning and six World Championship Bronx Bomber teams. He also saw service with the Detroit Tigers for two years, 1950-51.

Other Red Sox stars I remember witnessing in action during that period of time include Bobby Doerr, Johnny Pesky, Junior Stephens, Mel Parnell, Jack Kramer, Ellis Kinder, and Maurie McDermott.

SUMMING UP—It was much better sitting out in the sun with Sam Pino at Fenway Park than being stuck in a stuffy classroom.

FRANKIE HEBERT, VALIANT RINGMAN

NOTE—Frankie Hebert was the father of **CLAIRE HEBERT**, who eventually became **MRS. TITUS PLOMARITIS. YEP,** he's the same dad who didn't pull his punches when talking to his four daughters.

FRANKIE HEBERT

LOWELL—During late November, 1955, the city of Lowell lost one of its most popular boxers of the 1920's when **FRANKIE HEBERT** was killed in a tragic auto accident.

Hebert, who held the New England flyweight championship, was one of a host of prominent Lowell professional fighters, including Olympian, Al Mello, Phinney Boyle, "Irish" Billy Murphy, Tommy Leonard, Bobby Brown, "Red" O'Brien, etc., during "The Roaring Twenties" era.

At that time pro boxing was king in the city, with fight cards taking place repeatedly at The Crescent Rink, located on Hurd Street. A fire eventually demolished the arena, and boxing and pro wrestling then moved over to The Rex Arena, which also was a victim of a mammoth blaze.

"SARGE" PENS FAREWELL SALUTE TO FRANKIE

Lowell Sun Sports editor **FRANK SARGENT** wrote the following tribute to Frankie Hebert in his weekly **"LOOKOUT"** column on November 27, 1955.

"Funeral services were conducted yesterday for Francis Hebert. Some 32 years ago this same lad, better known as Frankie Hebert, reigned as New England flyweight (112 pounds) champion.

The fellow had a colorful ring career and veteran fight fans will recall that at the outset "Punch" Mayo managed the lad from Little Canada and sent him against some of the topflight boxers of the day.

Hebert fought over 100 professional fights during his career and met such noted mitt-men as Eddie Polo, Lou Perfetti, Wee Willie Woods, Davey Abad and others.

Abad and Hebert fought a great fight at Holyoke some 30 years ago. Abad came out of Panama and was the first boxer to beat the great Tony Canzoneri. In fact, he was also the first to trip up three-time World Champion Henry Armstrong. He and Hebert went the distance, with Abad getting the decision.

Abad, in 1927, remarked that Hebert was one of the toughest men he'd ever met, and considering that he had been in there with Hall of Famers Canzoneri and Armstrong and other top-notchers, this was a real tribute to Frankie.

Hebert turned in many top performances in the old Crescent Rink, and many Lowellians will recall the great battle he put up before losing the N.E. flyweight title to Harry Goldstein in Boston in 1926.

Another of our better fighters has gone to his eternal reward. Frankie was always a friend to young mitt-men and was always willing to share his ring experience with lads starting out on the fistic trail. He'll be greatly missed by the boxing gentry."

HIGHLIGHTS OF FRANKIE'S CAREER

NASHUA, N.H., July 22, 1924—Frankie Hebert of Lowell won the New England flyweight championship with a 10-round decision over **EDDIE POLO** of Waterville, Maine, here last night.

Hebert fought an aggressive battle, leading all the way, and scoring a knockdown in the fourth round.

A large delegation of fans from Lowell attended the open air show.

BOSTON—Frankie Hebert gained a close decision victory over **YOUNG DENCIO**, a little Filipino, in the main event here.

It was an interesting and hard-fought battle, with the little fellows traveling at a whirlwind clip throughout.

WORCESTER—Frankie Hebert defeated **DARK CLOUD** of Holyoke, who is considered one of the best flyweights in the East.

The Lowell boy made a great hit and several promoters who were at ringside immediately opened negotiations with Hebert's manager for the Lowell boy's services.

BOSTON—In the semi-final bout of the card here, Frankie Hebert and **GENE ROCHON** fought a slashing battle for four rounds, but Rochon sustained a gash under his eye and the hostilities were called off, with Hebert being awarded a technical knockout win.

LOWELL—September 12, 1924—In the main event here at the Crescent Rink, **"WEE WILLIE" WOODS**, flyweight champion of Scotland, won a knockout victory over local boy Frankie Hebert in a hard fought battle. The end came in the eighth round.

Hebert was the superior boxer, but the Scotlander's body punches— many of which were low blows according to the referee—eventually took their toll.

LOWELL—June 5, 1924—An All-Star card for the benefit of The American Legion Relief Fund and sponsored by the local Moody Club took place here at the Crescent Rink, and in the final event Frankie Hebert pounded out a decision over **JOHNNY THOMAS** of New Bedford in a thriller.

Hebert took command in the fifth round with a heavy body attack and he remained in the lead the rest of the way.

The proceeds of the All-Star program went to the American Legion Relief Fund, for the benefit of needy veterans of World War One.

MANCHESTER, N.H. —A large delegation of Lowell fans journeyed here last night to cheer on Frankie Hebert in his bout with National Flyweight contender **BOBBY BURKE** of Reading, Pa.

Hebert wore his New England championship belt for the first time, but unfortunately he lost the 10-round decision to Burke, who was in line to battle World Champion Pancho Villa of the Philippines.

GEORGE KOULOHERAS

LOWELL—Highly controversial…outspoken…feisty…a real-life legend… but a backbone of Lowell education for many decades…that's the story of the late **GEORGE KOULOHERAS.**

A longtime resident of the Acre section of the city, Kouloheras dedicated his life to the school children of Lowell.

Born in Lowell on January 25, 1913, he passed away just three days prior to his 98th birthday, on January 22, 2011.

Kouloheras graduated from Lowell High School in 1930, and he went on to study engineering at Northeastern University.

His employment as a mechanical engineer took place for over 40 years at Thomson Labs, part of the General Electric plant in Lynn, before retiring in 1978.

He helped design, develop, build and finally test and operate generators, motors, high altitude chambers, electric circuits and sound level meters which were used in the production of the first jet engines used by the United States military during World War Two.

REMARKABLE CAREER IN EDUCATION

Kouloheras became heavily involved in public education during the 1940's, when he was instrumental in the rebuilding of the Bartlett School in the Acre, and then serving several terms as president of the Bartlett School PTO. This was just the start of his six decades of service in promoting local education.

He was first elected to the Lowell School Committee in 1963, a position he held for many years. He also became a longtime board member of the Greater-Lowell Technical High School, located in the neighboring town of Tyngsboro. Thus, being on the pair of school boards, he reached his goal "to ensure the best educational opportunity for all Lowell children."

Kouloheras was a driving force in Lowell's extensive school building program of the 1990's, which saw 14 new schools being constructed. He was also instrumental in the building of the Greater-Lowell Technical High School, being a strong advocate of vocational education.

He enjoyed a deep friendship with Stan and Kay Stoklosa, attending a host of Coach Stan's baseball games, and serving alongside Kay on the Lowell School Committee in the 1980's. Many times George and Kay teamed up and voted with each other on controversial issues.

GEORGE AND KAY TEAM UP AGAIN

Lowell Sun
December 29, 1986

LOWELL—Pushing to reduce cigarette smoking among the city's school children, school committee members **GEORGE KOULOHERAS** and **KAY STOKLOSA** will tonight jointly sponsor a motion to seek a **"SMOKE FREE"** school system by January, 1987.

The motion, which says the school committee is responsible for protecting the academic and physical well-being of students, would prohibit students from smoking in schools, on school grounds, outside of buildings and at school activities occurring off campus.

"The motion is aimed primarily at Lowell High students," said Kouloheras.

High school students are already prohibited from smoking in school, but are allowed to smoke outside the building in Lucy Larcom Parkway and in the area between the new school building and the Merrimack Canal.

This motion would restrict smoking in those areas.

While he considered seeking a total prohibition of smoking in school buildings, Kouloheras said that he would not push to ban teachers from smoking in lounges.

At the same time, Kouloheras said that he is "looking forward to wide community support of PTO's and The Friends of Lowell High School in pushing programs to reduce smoking."

Kouloheras added that he expects the motion to easily pass at the meeting.

"Opposing the motion would be like being against motherhood or apple pie and ice cream." he said.

NOTE—Today's parents of Lowell school children can thank George and Kay's concerns for the health and well-being of our current generation.

HELPING TITUS AND THE BOOSTERS

Kouloheras was also a great help to **DR. TITUS PLOMARITIS** and the Lowell High School Boosters Club over the years.

"George and I often worked together for the benefit of the kids," Titus commented. "He was a great influence in aiding all the Lowell sports teams for quite a long time," added the several terms president of the Boosters Club.

GEORGE KOULOHERAS
(Family photo)

"George was a tremendous admirer of Coach Ray Riddick and the LHS football teams, particularly because his sons were standouts for the Red and Gray elevens," pointed out Dr. Plomaritis.

"He performed many services for Riddick," summed up Titus. "I can still remember him being astonished that the football team didn't have a washing machine available to clean the players' uniforms after practices and games. Well, he made his presence felt— and a washing machine quickly was installed in the Stadium's locker room. That was George Kouloheras at work for the kids."

RECEIVING A HOST OF HONORS

The veteran educator was honored in 1997, with the dedication of the George Kouloheras Educational Wing and Library Media Center at Lowell High School, and in 2000 Greater-Lowell Technical High named its athletic field house in his honor, for his contribution to technical education. He was also awarded a lifetime membership in the Massachusetts Association of School Committees.

ALWAYS MAKING HEADLINES

Kouloheras was a regular newsmaker in The Lowell Sun. Several of his actions included:

Tackling a fellow member (Dan Kane) during a school committee meeting
Refusing to call member Mary Ann Sullivan by her maiden name
Brawling with Athletic Director Al Mangan outside of Cawley Stadium and being banned from the Lowell High football game
Being an outspoken champion of English as the official language of Lowell
Blasting the appearance of a Gay Rights flag in the high school

Perhaps his final front page story in The Sun took place in 2004, when he was labeled as a hero, despite being ninety-two years of age at the time. He was driving down East Merrimack Street when he saw a man getting ready to jump off the bridge into the Concord River. He stopped the car, got out and grabbed the forty-four-year-old homeless man from behind, saving his life.

"I got him down and sat on him," Kouloheras said, preventing the suicide attempt.

A HAPPY FAMILY LIFE

Kouloheras was married for seventy years to his soul mate, Stella (Athanas), who passed away on September 8, 2006. The couple had five children, sons James, William and Harry, and daughters Daphne and Elizabeth. They later added nine grandchildren.

Kouloheras was an ardent follower of all the Lowell High and Greater-Lowell Tech sports teams, especially the Red and Gray football squads, as his sons excelled on the gridiron.

TITUS AND HIS PROTECTOR

JACK LARDNER, a guard on Coach Riddick's 1948 Lowell High's undefeated football team, continued in the protection business the rest of his life as a CIA agent for the United States Government.

Jack was assigned by Coach Riddick to protect Titus from the enemy, in this case the charging linemen.

PRESIDENT LYNDON BAINES JOHNSON assigned Jack to protect **JACQUELINE KENNEDY** following the assassination of **PRESIDENT JOHN F. KENNEDY,** on November 22, 1963.

IMPLANTED MEMORIES OF MY FRIEND THE COACH

I maintained a close relationship with the Coach, with a brotherly-like friendship, and I also was his "Personal Chiropractor"—Ray never needed a scheduled appointment.

NOTE: The Coach was also Lowell High School's drivers' education instructor, and it was a routine experience to see him at my office once a month, with the students waiting in the Drivers' Ed auto as he supposedly came in the office for directions.

Photo L to R: Titus Plomaritis, Jack Lardner, relaxing, prior to LHS's 1st bowl game, in Jackson, Miss., Dec.1948

His routine was to get on the scale for a weigh-in (always 265 to 270), get a full spine adjustment and, as he was leaving, would say, for the benefit of patients in the waiting room, "Thanks for the directions, Doc."

Another of his favorite comments when getting on the scale was, "Doc, I'm working on my diet and eating whole wheat Hollywood health bread." Then, when I would relate this to his wife, Marge, she would say, "Yeah, but did he tell you he's eating the whole loaf?"

MY BIGGEST BOOSTER

He was my biggest booster, whether it was a football player, a parent or another coach, he would direct them to my office, knowing that if it was out of my scope of practice I would steer them in the right direction.

Ray was a stickler for the players grabbing two towels after taking a shower. He would say, "Doc, if they would swipe the water off their bodies when leaving the shower, they would need only one towel," as he would then demonstrate, and to this day I swipe the excess water off my body before using my towel, and I can still envision the Coach's nod of approval in the horizon.

THE COACH'S GOLFING TALES

Now, golfing was something else. Dating back to our Rotary Club outings, Long Meadow Calcutta's and many years at Vesper, his golf swing never changed. His backswing was like John Daley's and his follow-through was twice as fast.

Whether being my partner or my opponent, he would say, "Doc, keep your eye on this one!" Actually, we all had to keep both eyes on his ball, because when he finished his swing he was facing the group in back of us, almost as bad as Barkley. He had a vicious "hook" with high elevation, sometimes crossing two fairways.

However, regardless of his swing, he was a lot of fun to play with and was aces on "The Nineteenth Hole."

One of Ray's favorite tales following a round of golf, when we would sit and chat over a couple of his favorite bourbon and water beverages, was about how he loved his wife and that he would be devastated if she ever broke a leg. After getting your attention, he would relate the following verbatim, "I went over to Lull & Hartford's (a specialty sporting goods store in downtown Lowell) just the other day and asked Elmer Rynne for the most expensive pair of ladies sneakers in the store, for my wife's Christmas present."

Curiously, we always had someone in our group ask, "Why sneakers?"

The Coach would smoothly down his bourbon and reply, "I don't want her to slip, the next time she's shoveling snow off the roof."

ANOTHER MEMORY OF THE COACH

I can still remember Coach Riddick's comments to me concerning my oldest son, Titus, Jr.

"Titus, you have to do something about that kid of yours," Ray began.

"Now what happened, Coach?" was my reply.

"He doesn't listen," Riddick followed up. "Coach (Joe) Polak sends in a play and 'Buddy' ignores it and calls a different play."

R.R. then continued, "Worst part of it is, it always works. He's so **f...g** smart that I have to reprimand him—with tongue in cheek. He explains that he was setting up a play, and the play that Coach Polak sent in was contrary to the one that was successful!

He memorizes every single play for every lineman and if he sees a blank face on anyone, he tells him what his assignment is before breaking the huddle," R.R. summed up.

THE PERPETUAL SCHOLARSHIP

Having been at the front end of Coach Riddick's Scholarship train, I feel privileged to have been a member of the team that created a $50,000 perpetual Scholarship in the Coach's name. I get goose bumps each year when reading the news of the new year's recipients.

WARNING BELLS RING OUT

Claire and I are shown with our improvised **BELLS SYSTEM** during Christmas time at our Bridge Street home in Pelham.

NOTICE THE BELLS, hanging on the inside of the front door at the right. The bells, very sensitive and noisy, were a souvenir we obtained from an underground restaurant, called Pataka, during a Chiropractic conference up in Canada.

The bells became our **ALARM SYSTEM** of knowing what time the children arrived at home, as we had curfews and we would not go to bed until they all were home.

Claire and I would usually be sitting watching television, but quite often would fall asleep, so then we became alerted when the bells would ring as the children opened the front door.

However, the kids always found a way of bypassing our security system. The older children would prearrange to have Diane, the youngest, to keep her eyes on us, and as soon as we dozed off she would sneak by and remove the bells and the last one in would place them back on the door.

MEMORABLE PLOMARITIS FAMILY REUNION

This was the final family picture taken where all seven Plomaritis siblings were together with our parents. The occasion took place in July, 1974, at Indian Rock Beach, Tampa, Florida. Back row, left to right: my sister Priscilla Mitchell, my brother George, my father Demosthenis, my mother Niki, and my brothers Timothy, Anthony and Joseph. In front are myself (Titus) at left and my brother David. My parents were Florida residents for over 20 years, following their move from Lowell.

REMEMBERING JERRY CLOWER

Every time I watch a Mississippi State football or basketball game on

television I am reminded of Jerry Clower, and his recording of my name and football experience.

Humphrey Coliseum at Mississippi State University was the setting where Jerry's live recording of **"THE AMBASSADOR of GOOD WILL"** album took place, on March 15, 1976, when the famed country-style comedian was honored with a "Jerry Clower Day".

Humphrey Coliseum at Miss. State University

On side one, cut one of the recording, he tells his audience how honored he was to return to Mississippi State because he was there before, and he goes on for about three minutes of football comedy relating to **TITUS PLOMARITIS** in a skit recording of his welcome back to the Humphrey Coliseum, which was the University's largest on-campus arena.

The Ambassador Of Good Will
1976 - MCA782

Titus Plummeritis	Flying To The Opry
Writing In My Bible	A Nickels Worth Of Cheese
Warm Water Heater	Marcel's Brother Goes To
Tough Nut	Jail
Clovis And Beck	Runnin' The Coon
The Wise Men	Uncle Versie Sees The
Dig A Dug Well	Ocean
Marcel Goes Quail Huntin'	Mr. Jake Ledbetter
The Pet Squirrel	The Clumsy Mule
Wanna Buy A Possum?	It Coulda Been A Lot Worse
The Headless Man	The House I Live In

Among the episodes on Jerry's recording is a comedy bit entitled **"Titus Plummeritis"**.

COLISEUM HOSTED MANY CELEBRITIES

Home of the Mississippi State's men's and women's basketball teams, nicknamed "The Bulldogs", this 11,000 seat facility also provides a venue for concerts, commencement exercises, trade shows and many other activities.

The Coliseum serves the University's 16,000 students and a trade area population of 925,000.

Since opening in 1975, "The Hump" has hosted performances by Garth Brooks, Tina Turner, Bruce Springsteen, Billy Joel, George Strait, Bob Dylan, Reba McEntire, Vince Gill, Jimmy Buffett and James Taylor, in addition to over thirty years of exciting Southeastern Conference basketball.

TALKING TO MRS. CLOWER

On November 11, 2011, I spoke to **HOMERLINE CLOWER**, Jerry's widow, and thanked her for taking my call. Her voice was youthful and thinking that she was one of her children, I asked to speak to her mother.

Once we got over my goof, we had a very pleasant conversation, and then I explained that I was the character who Jerry depicted in his first live album, **"AMBASSADOR OF GOOD WILL"**, at the Humphrey Coliseum.

I further explained that I was writing my autobiography and was interested in adding a few comments relative to her family. She was very receptive.

They were married fifty-one years when Jerry passed on, August 24, 1998. They had four wonderful children, Ray, Amy, Sue and Katy. The person on the back cover of the album was Jerry's best friend, **CHIEF HILL.** It was only a short time later, when she informed me of her son Ray's passing on, November 28, 2011.

Handshake on White House Front Lawn

Here was a BONDING HANDSHAKE, with eye-to-eye contact, that took place on the front lawn of the White House in Washington, D.C., between Titus Plomaritis (left) and the President of the United States, Jimmy Carter, during 1978.

This happening eventually turned out to be "Just the beginning of a great rewarding relationship between the President and myself," commented Titus.

"The outcome benefitted over fifty million American Chiropractic patients," added Titus, "because President Carter, in 1980, removed a clause in the Medicare Bill that mandated prior approval by an M.D. before a patient becomes eligible for Medicare coverage."

The Greek Archbishop (center) shows approval of the connection, while a Secret Service agent (right) is focused on the occasion.

GOVERNOR GALLEN'S FIRST
ORDER OF BUSINESS

L to R: Governor Hugh Gallen, Representative Claire Plomaritis, Secretary of State Bill Gardner and myself Dr.Titus Plomaritis.

Photo taken in the New Hampshire State House's Governor and Executive Council Chambers in January, 1979, when Dr. Titus Plomaritis became Governor Hugh Gallen's very first appointment—to the N.H. Board of Chiropractic Examiners.

NOTE:—Statistics revealed that Democratic Governors in the State of New Hampshire were a rare breed. From 1857 to the year that Hugh Gallen took office as the state's chief executive (1979) there had been only four Democrats that occupied the corner office for a total of twelve years. During that span of 122 years there were 35 GOP governors that occupied the top office.

NH FIRST IN THE NATION PRIMARY

October 24, 2011—in the New Hampshire Secretary of State's office, left to right—Dr. Titus Plomaritis, Bill Gardner, Secretary of State, Takeshi Hikihara, Consul General of Japan, Boston, and Charles Doleac, Portsmouth, NH, President of the Japanese-American Society of New Hampshire.

Note: On this day Governor Mitt Romney filed his papers for the first in the Nation Primary. Takeshi wanted to see firsthand and really got an eye full as Mitt made a grand entrance with his followers three abreast from the Sec. of State's Office all the way out to Main Street in front of the State Capitol.

Thirty-two years earlier, Bill Gardner orchestrated Governor Gallen's first appointment (my appointment to the NHBCE) and now continues to orchestrate the first in the nation primary.

GREETING PRESIDENT CARTER
IN NEW HAMPSHIRE

Titus and N.H. Representative Claire Plomaritis are pictured welcoming President Jimmy Carter at the State House in Concord in 1978 during one of the President's few visits to New Hampshire. The First Lady of New Hampshire, Mrs. Irene Gallen, is standing to the left of the President.

HELICOPTER ALARMS POLICE CHIEF BOUTWELL

My Bank Director buddy, Chief Ralph Boutwell, Pelham Police Department, came rushing over in his police cruiser, when he received an emergency call of a helicopter crash in Dr. Plomaritis's back yard. He shook hands with the Governor, wished me a happy 50th and with a healthy slice of cake in hand, he departed saying to himself."what will those Plomaritis's do next"?

GOVERNOR HUGH GALLEN just dropping in to wish me a happy fiftieth birthday, prearranged by my sneaky but adorable wife, Claire.

SAME COACH, SAME RESULTS

Shown above at Lawrence Memorial Stadium following the annual Lowell-Lawrence football game on Thanksgiving morning, 1970, are Red and Gray Coach Ray Riddick, flanked by the two Titus Plomaritis's—Junior, left, and Senior, right. The father and son Plomaritis's both led Lowell High to victories over the Lawrence High Lancers—some 22 years apart—at the same field, with the pair of dramatic wins clinching undefeated seasons for Riddick teams.

Titus Jr. had just quarterbacked Lowell to a 33-6 triumph, as he scored a touchdown, passed for another T.D. and kicked three PAT's, good for a total of 15 points. However, his Dad outscored "Buddy" by five points, when he accounted for all the Red and Gray's points in a stirring 20-19 verdict on Turkey Day, 1948.

Incidentally, both the Plomaritis gridders wore Number 42 on their jerseys.

Titus, Jr. went on to be a highly-successful Orthopedic Surgeon, while Titus, Sr., became a World-Renowned Chiropractor. By Sam Weisberg

BEST MAN, NOT FORGOTTEN

December 1, 1951—Immediately following the football season of my junior year at Boston University, we were married. Surrounding Claire (Hebert) Plomaritis are five of my teammates. Sitting, from left to right: Lindy Hanson, Arnold Berg, Claire, Tom Gastall, **MARCO LANDON** (my best man), and Gerry Pednault. Standing next to me is Ralph Norman, the photographer who took our wedding pictures and presented them to us as a wedding gift. Ralph also was one on my mentors at Boston University. Ralph eventually became the official photographer for Brandeis University and was always available whenever I ran into trouble with my photographic equipment.

Tom Gastall was a twelve letterman at BU and was signed by the Baltimore Orioles in 1955 as a catcher. In 1956, he died in a plane crash, while on his final solo flight to obtain a pilot's license.

My best man, Marco, accomplished a rare feat when he was inducted into two Massachusetts High School Halls of Fame, Leominster High School as a player and Fitchburg High School as a coach.

At BU, Marco's NCAA record of recording two safeties in one contest against the Miami Hurricanes in the Orange Bowl still stands.

VICTORY SMILES AT WHITE HOUSE
WITH THE PRESIDENT

*With best wishes
to Titus Plomaritis*

Jimmy Carter

President Jimmy Carter is shown congratulating Titus Plomaritis at the White House for his help following the President's victory over U.S. Senator Ted Kennedy in the Democratic primary election of 1980.

"THANKS, TITUS, your hard work was greatly appreciated," was the President's initial comment at their meeting following the "first in the nation's" primary in New Hampshire.

"I, in turn, thanked him for his intervention in removing the restrictive clause in the Medicare Bill that would have mandated referral from a medical physician before a patient would be covered and treated by a Chiropractor," replied Titus.

NOTE;—President Carter officially autographed this photo.

Lowell High School

To Dr. Titus Plomaritis
The Best class president
LHS 1949

Thanks from the class —

Treasured Gift from My Class-mates

A gift to Dr. Titus Plomaritis, 1949 Class President, from classmates at our Lowell High School 35th Class reunion, in 1984, by Artist Janet Lambert, one of our own, Lowell High School graduates.

DOCTORS TITUS, JR., AND BURKE HELP SAVE A LIFE

Life or Death Emergency Team
A dozen members of the St. John's hospital staff were involved in the battle to save Saturnino Maldonado's life.(L-R) Shown here are Dr. Paul M. Burke Jr., Dr. Titus Plomaritis Jr., Joanne Gustin, R.N., Donna Doherty, R.N., Marge Anderson, R.N., Dr. H. Scott Breen, Janice Ledbetter, R.N., Cindy Guilbert, R.N., Linda Sorrenti, R.N.,Tricia McFadden, R.N., Linda Kilbride, med. Tech. and Kathy Walker, R.N. Sun photo by David Brow.

LOWELL, MASS.—Doctors Titus Plomaritis, Jr., and Paul M. Burke, Jr., not only had similar backgrounds but they also teamed up with a group of staff members at Lowell's St. John's Hospital to save a gunshot victim's life.

The two local doctors were both Lowell High School graduates, both Boston University Medical School graduates and are both Medical Specialists.

Dr. Plomaritis, an orthopedic and spine specialist, and Dr. Burke, a general surgeon especially trained to treat visceral and vascular trauma, were called into action on March 12, 1987, to work with a team of doctors and nurses to try to save a man who received a shotgun blast to the back and lower chest at close range.

The patient, **SATURNINO MALDONADO, JR.,** a native of Comerio, Puerto Rico, had a serious lower chest wound with severe damage to his lung, liver, kidney and spine.

He was at first given only a five percent chance of survival, but with the attention given by Dr. Plomaritis (bone work) and Dr. Burke (blood work) and the ten other staff members, he miraculously recovered after three hours of surgery.

The patient's parents, who didn't speak English, were so grateful that they took out an add in The Lowell Sun newspaper, thanking the doctors, nurses and staff members for saving their son's life. They also delivered carnations and chocolates as a show of gratitude.

"It's gratifying," Dr.Burke said. "It's not often that we have someone on death's doorstep and then make an effort to save his life. I guess when the family recognizes it, it's nice," he added, proudly wearing one of the carnations.

THE VIOLENT BACKGROUND, AND SURVIVAL

What started as a street clash on Back Central Street unfolded into a dramatic emergency scene that made medical history in Lowell, and drilled home the impact of violence in people's lives.

The 20-year-old Maldonado's bloody, limp body was unloaded, face down on a stretcher in St. John's Hospital's emergency room. His blood pressure was dropping quickly. He was near death.

Maldonado was quickly wheeled across the hall to the Critical Care Unit, and his blood pressure was low. Dr. Burke, the surgeon on call that night, was brought in.

"When I came in, the magnitude of the injury really surprised me, " Dr. Burke commented. "He had a gaping hole. You could have easily fit a grapefruit through there."

Turning to police, who had unsuccessfully tried to question the dazed shotgun victim, Dr. Burke advised them that Maldonado had less than a five percent chance of surviving.

Dr. Burke, with the assistance of the only other surgeon available— orthopedic surgeon **DR. TITUS PLOMARITIS, JR.,**—began the procedures that eventually saved the patient's life. Plomaritis stabilized the spine injuries while "Dr. Burke did a phenomenal job repairing the damage to the vital organs, especially to the lacerated liver", commented Plomaritis.

DR. RONALD RANDAZZO

I first met Dr. Ronald Randazzo, a well-known local dentist, about 1975. I had a severe toothache during a busy day in my chiropractic office, and at least three patients, who were also patients of Dr. Randazzo, told me of his painless techniques and that I should call him for an emergency treatment.

I did just that, and not only did he attend to my immediate problem, but also a friendship continued to evolve from that day on.

I treated his back and he attended to my teeth until I retired in 1995. Now it's a one-way street, in that I'm not able to reciprocate. However, Ron continues to extend professional courtesy to me.

I built the first professional building in Pelham, the **PLOMARITIS PROFESSIONAL CENTER,** in 1983, and Ron built the second professional building in town during 1987.

OUR GOLFING MEETINGS

Now, let me describe his physical stature, because it will come into play shortly. He stands about 5'9", weighs about 135, and has very slender chicken legs, with no beef. However, he literally hits the shit out of the ball, carries a single digit handicap and is an outstanding competitor.

We both love to play golf, and although we belong to different courses we manage to get together at least a couple of times a year, playing in member-guest tournaments.

The Haverhill Country Club's three-day member-guest tourney has been a yearly ritual, with plenty of golf and a Saturday evening of great camaraderie, sharing the evening with Ron and his longtime lady friend, Catherine Keith. We always enjoy the scrumptious appetizers during an open cocktail hour, followed with an outstanding gourmet dinner and dancing to a live band.

The past few years we have been paired with some really fun

guys, namely Joe Massys, Bill Corcoran, Bill McIver and Dr. Frank MacMillan.

I get a a great kick out of watching some of the **HUGE GUESTS** that we have played against, some of whom were 100 pounds heavier than Ron, all swinging from their assholes, using the John Daly backswing, only to find themselves developing stiff necks watching Ron launch T-shot after T-shot with his smooth as silk delivery. They're so hell bent on outdriving Ronny that I go unnoticed with my bunt T-shots, then a good approach shot and one putt, many times winning the hole.

It seems to always go down to the final match in deciding who gets the first place prize in our flight, plus a piece of the side action.

BRINGING BACK MEMORIES

It is interesting how certain incidents that occur today will flash back to a great memory of yesterday. A great example would be what happened back in February, 1998, when I invited Ron and his son Anthony to spend a few days with us at our winter home at Willoughby Country Club, in Stuart, Florida.

The second day we were playing skins with carryovers, and we were at one of the par-threes. Ron hit the pin and the ball rolled about a foot away for an easy bird, but not good enough though, as Anthony got a hole-in-one. Then, I hit the pin.

Ron and I each lost five bucks to Anthony on that one hole alone as we had a five hole carryover. Anthony had his name permanently engraved on a brass plate, which was screwed onto a beautiful recreational spectator bench at the back of the tee.

Now, what makes that incident special is that in my fifty years of playing golf, including with my two sons who both carry a single digit handicap, I never came close to duplicating that feat: walking off the green with a total score of **FIVE, TWO BIRDS AND AN ACE.!!**

From that day on I've told that story a thousand times, especially whenever someone in our foursome gets a birdie and displays ecstasy. It kind of deflates his balloon in a hurry.

Happy Family Faces
My wife Claire and I with my Mother Niki and Aunt Irene Varkas (my father's only sister), a trio of tender loving, caring women that never stopped giving, without expecting remuneration. The four young ones are my brother George's children.
Front row, left to right: Kevin, myself (Titus), Alexander, Aunt Irene.
Back row, left to right: Dara, my wife Claire, Niki and my mother Niki.

THE SPORT OF KINGS

By Titus Jr.

Titus Sr. with his female passage red tail hawk, "Niki", which he named after his mom, my YAYA.

Dr. Titus Plomaritis, my dad, became a licensed falconer at the age of 80, in 2009. At that time he was the oldest apprentice class falconer in the United States. Falconry, often referred to as the "Sport of Kings", is the hunting of wild quarry in their natural habitat using a trained bird of prey (falcon, hawk, eagle, owl). Falconry is a sport that has been practiced for six thousand years, with it's roots being traced to central Asia. In many countries falconry has been declared a living heritage. It was first introduced to North America in the 1900's. Today, it is the most highly regulated sport in the United States. Titus Sr. responded to my request to become a licensed falconer and practice falconry with me and my wife, Jan.

DR. KEVIN MORIARTY

Claire's 80th Birthday

Left to right: Dr. Kevin Moriarty, Claire Plomaritis, your's truly and Laurin Moriarty, Kevin's lovely wife.

DR. KEVIN MORIARTY was one of my Chiropractic associates whom I've grown to love like one of my children. I remember the first time we met when **DR. JIM LATOURNEAU**, one of my dedicated Chiropractic C-PAC members, called and asked if I had room for another associate. Jim related that Kevin had a one-year-old and was just starting his private practice in Nashua, New Hampshire. Jim was acting like a professional placement agent, telling me some of the things that he knew I would like to hear. "Dr. Moriarty was an outstanding wrestler in college and has great hands." My comment was, "Okay Jim, give me his number." That was the beginning of a great friendship that still exists.

If I had to pick one memory, out of the many that exist, from our Plomaritis Chiropractic Office association, it would have to be the following.

LET ME FIRST give you the setting.

When Dr. Moriarty first started at the PCO, he would work with me, side by side, on Mondays, Wednesdays and Fridays, just so he could get familiar with my patients, techniques and patient management.

Usually Monday was my busiest day anyway. Well this particular Monday, after being away the previous week on an NBCE assignment, my appointment book was full, three across. I felt invigorated, returning to my patients after being away, so I instructed my office manger to accept any patients today, new or otherwise.

I mentioned my plan to Dr. Moriarty, that he would take all the new patients into the consultation room, do all the examinations, take whatever necessary X-rays, and that I would treat all the patients. What a mistake that turned out to be.

The five treatment rooms and the consultation room were occupied from 7:00 AM to 7:00 PM, and we took a half hour lunch break. The count at day's end was ten new patients to whom Kevin attended in a very professional manner, following thorough history taking, examinations and X-rays. He then moved them to the next available empty treatment room, with the X-rays on the illuminated view boxes and patient's file ready for my review.

I physically treated 102 patients that day, and needless to say, my arms and hands were aching for the days that followed. However, it was a memory that neither of us will ever forget.

REMEMBERING KIRK GIBSON

This one is a great 1989 memory of when I was in Warren, Michigan, to have my rotator cuff repaired.

One day playing golf at Vesper with my friend Ralph Battles, I made one of my "bad swings" chasing my partner's tee shot, resulting in immediate pain in my left shoulder, prompting my call to my son, Steven, in Michigan. He advised me to come to Michigan and stay as his houseguest so he could do the necessary examination with **DR. ROBERT TEITGE** to make a proper diagnosis of my problem.

Steven, the younger of my two orthopedic surgeon sons, received a **"FELLOWSHIP"** in shoulder and knee reconstruction at the Henry Ford Hospital in Detroit, under the supervision of Dr. Teitge, after completing his orthopedic residency in Canton, Ohio.

Following a barrage of tests and X-Rays, it was determined that I had a rotator cuff tear, requiring surgery which was performed by Dr. Teitge, assisted by my son, Steven. Following surgery, I had two weeks of scheduled rehabilitation in the Physical Therapy Clinic adjacent to the Teitge-Plomaritis Orthopedic Clinic.

KIRK GIBSON was also at the PT Clinic, having his troublesome hip evaluated, and we had a lot of laughter exchanging stories during those sessions.

The one that still rings my bell as a **"TEN"** is as follows—

I was the president of the National Board of Chiropractic Examiners at that time, and during one of my daily phone calls to **DR. FRANK HIDEG,** vice-president of the National Board, Kirk Gibson's name came up, which prompted Frank's brain to immediately switch from **NBCE** business to baseball.

"Titus, do me a big favor and have Kirk Gibson autograph a baseball for my son, Mike," Frank requested.

When I replied in the affirmative, he went on to explain the importance of it being an authentic National League baseball. Not knowing where to purchase it, I asked Frank "Where do I get such a specialty baseball?" He then told me to, "Go to any jewelry store, and specify authentic National League baseball."

Well, after searching all over hell before I found a jewelry store that had the baseballs that Frank specified, I decided to buy two, with the thought of having one autographed for my grandson, Nicholas Plomaritis, Steve's son.

THE NEXT DAY, when I was in therapy and Kirk was performing a fast gait test, I asked him if he would be kind enough to autograph a couple of baseballs, he said in a rather nasty tone, "Don't bother me!!" I was rather disappointed because we had been exchanging stories for several days, and I thought we had struck up a friendship.

Well, about ten minutes later, he came over to the table where I was getting therapy, sat down at the edge of the table and said he didn't mean to be abrupt, however, he was counting his laps for a required test, and now was free to see how he could help me.

I then told him that I would appreciate it if he would autograph a baseball for the son of a famous baseball coach in Paducah, Kentucky. He asked me what was the coach's name, and when I said, "Frank Hideg", his immediate response was, **"WHO THE FUCK IS FRANK HIDEG??**

DOCTOR HIDEG is a member of the Kentucky State Baseball Coaches Hall of Fame, having led the Paducah, Ky., Post 31 American Legion team to an amazing record over twenty years.

His teams rolled up an overall 831-294 record, having competed in eleven State tournaments and winning six of them. He saw that every one

of his players received scholarship offers to colleges or junior colleges, and over his two decades of coaching, not one of his players ever quit his teams.

I sent the "Authentic autographed National League Baseball" to Frank with a note explaining in detail what Kirk Gibson said when I asked him to autograph the baseball for the son of a famous baseball coach in Paducah, Kentucky.

Well, his son Mike thought the note was hilarious so he mounted the autographed baseball on the mantle along with Gibson's baseball card and the **NOTE** sent to Frank by me.

THE HISTORIC HOME RUN

Kirk Gibson belted one of the most famous pinch hit home runs in World Series history.

It occurred during the 1988 Series when Gibson was a member of the Los Angeles Dodgers, and it was hit off of Hall of Fame relief pitcher Dennis Eckersley of the Oakland Athletics.

Gibson, being on the bench with a serious injury, was called on to pinch hit late in the game by Manager **TOMMY LASORDA,** with the Dodgers trailing.

He hobbled up to the plate in the bottom of the ninth inning, and blasted an Eckersley pitch into the right field stands, giving the Dodgers the opening game victory and propelling them on to the World Championship. It was his only hit and **his only at bat,** in the Series.

Gibson limped around the bases, giving triumphant gestures with his arms—and this image has been repeatedly shown on televised baseball highlights over the years.

Gibson spent his most productive Major League seasons as a slugging outfielder with the Detroit Tigers, before winding up with L.A., where he was the National League's Most Valuable Player in 1988.

In recent years he has been a highly-successful manager of the Arizona Diamondbacks, leading them to the National League's Western Division championship in 2011, being named as N.L Manager of the Year.

Last Photo with All My Siblings

May 18, 1990: Photo of me with my six siblings at our mother's wake in Tampa Florida. It was the last photo of all seven of us together. Left to right sitting: my brothers Anthony, David, Timothy (deceased 2011), George (deceased 1993); standing: left to right— Joseph (born Christmas Day 1930), my sister Priscilla Mitchell and myself, Titus.

OKINAWA WITH MIKE DEMAURO

Mike DeMauro was Lowell High School's star halfback in 1946. He definitely had all- star talent, but unfortunately Lowell was going through a dry spell at that time, just a year before the Ray Riddick era began.

Titus (left) and Mike DeMauro discussing their Lowell High School football exploits.

I remember one day while waiting for a haircut in Spinelli's Barber Shop in Lowell, where Mike and I would meet occasionally and reminisce about football from our South Common, sandlot and high school days. The barber shop was located in Gallagher Square, a rather small business area at the corner of Gorham and Central Streets. Mike mentioned he was leaving for a couple of years to go to Okinawa.

Well, several years later, Claire and I had an opportunity to take advantage of a Boston University Alumni charter flight to Japan. When mentioning this to Mike in one of our letters, he stated that it was only a short flight from Tokyo to Okinawa and he would like us to be his house guests. When I mentioned this to Claire she wasn't receptive at first. However, when Mike said that the best Jade values in the world are in Okinawa, she said, **"BOOK THE FLIGHT"**.

THE SEVERAL GREAT MEMORIES OF TRIP

Well, that trip had two great memories that I'd like to share with you.

THE FIRST MEMORY was an evening at the opera to watch the most boring "Geisha Show," that by the way was recommended by the hotel concierge. We sat in the balcony for three solid hours waiting for the exciting part which never occurred. However, after the show is when the fun began.

Let me first set the stage. Before leaving the hotel we were given instructions on how to get to the theater, by subway, just a short walk from the hotel. We were also given a handwritten note, in Japanese, to show to the conductor, so he would tell us when to get off. The theater was, again, just a short walk from the subway station.

Now, leaving the theater at approximately 11PM, we were walking to the subway station in total darkness except for a few dim street lights. We could hear sounds of laughter and the aroma of barbecue cooking coming from an alleyway. After an uneventful evening at the theater we decided to explore, walking casually up the alley to where we found an overhanging canopy, with six locals sitting on stools.

They were apparently telling jokes in Japanese because one was talking and everyone else laughing. As we approached what was a small sake and barbecue concession stand, two of the men quickly offered us their stools. They were extremely friendly and humble, insisted on buying us hot sake and whatever the cook was barbecuing. One of the gentlemen was fascinated with Claire's blue eyes and blond hair. He was standing only about a foot away from her face, as she was sitting on the corner stool, and he kept saying, **"I WOVE YOU BWOO EYES!!"**

Well, after a dull start, it turned out to be the first delightful adventure of our vacation.

NOTE— Nowadays, whenever Claire and I have a disagreement, or a slight quarrel, all I have to do to calm the atmosphere is to whisper to her, **"I WOVE YOU BWOO EYES."**

Don't go away; the second adventure is even better.

THE SECOND MEMORY— We had booked a shuttle flight from Tokyo to Okinawa with the intention of staying over for one night and then getting back to join our Boston University group.

On the first day, Mike gave us a cook's tour, taking us to several points of interest and stopping in several of his favorite gift shops. Every time Claire was ready to jump on a good buy, Mike would give her the **"NO"** head sign, meaning, **"NOT YET, CLAIRE"**. He was just getting her primed for the great values ahead.

Well, what we had originally planned as a one day trip actually ended up with us staying in Okinawa for the entire week. Every day was a new experience, and every evening we were at a different night club with dining, dancing and stimulating entertainment.

When Mike took us to his house, I remember him saying we could take a Jacuzzi bubble bath, but we would have to start filling the tub at such and such time, about two hours prior to its use.

We were having a delightful time sipping bubbly champagne and cruising around the huge Jacuzzi, which had about ten jets. We were diving under the bubbles, playing hide and seek, when all of a sudden, the flood lights came on. My first impression was that son of a bitch was taking movies of us. He still denies it, saying that, **"THEY WERE SECURITY LIGHTS"**.

Mike was a great host. He wouldn't let me spend a dime. And yes, Claire came home with the greatest collection of Jade pieces for a fraction of their original cost.

DR. ROBERT EYRE—
WHO? WHY? WHEN? WHERE?

DR. ROBERT EYRE, who specializes in urology in Boston, Massachusetts, has thirty-six years of experience as an M.D., with three hospital affiliations and was educated at the University of Virginia.

Dr. Robert C. Eyre

Throughout this book, especially in the earlier chapters, you have read several passages concerning my brother George. Well, Claire and I visited him just shortly before he passed on, in May of 1993. We kind of surprised him with our unexpected visit, but George, being George, was jovial and his greeting remarks continue to remain in my memory. **"HI, TITUS. HI, CLAIRE. I'M A GONER".**

He then explained that he never saw it coming until it was too late, referring to his prostate cancer. His advice was to take advantage of his condition as a warning, which I did.

As soon as we got home, I called Titus Jr., and asked if he could locate one of his B.U. Med. School graduates in the Boston area who was specializing in Urology. Within twenty-four hours, he called back and said one of his friends and classmates, Dr. John Levin, recommended **DR. ROBERT EYRE.**

My medical records indicate that my first visit with Dr. Eyre was in June of 1993, and I have been faithful with my follow-up examinations twice yearly ever since.

Dr. Eyre is an expert in performing the so-called "nerve sparing" radical prostatectomy, removal of the prostate while sparing the nerves that are necessary for men to get an erection. However, he noted that not every patient's nerves are able to be spared, depending on where the cancer is located. "I try to spare the nerves whenever I can," he said.

411

I've included the photo above of a smiling Dr. Eyre, which is easier to look at, than of the graphics of the **UROLOGY POSE** for the prostate inspection, of which I do get flash backs every time **JAY LENO** cracks a joke about the doctors with the rubber glove!!!

"TITUS PLOMARITIS"

by Claire Ignacio

There are many kinds of heroes,
Filling many types of roles,
Some for courage, others fame,
Being brave in wars so cold.

This book depicts the hero,
In the days when he was young,
Showing many skills and triumphs,
As he climbed each ladders rung.

When one views the many pages,
Pride, respect will top the list,
For the man who struggled and became,
The giant that he is.

From a classmate sharing glory,
Always cheering like the rest,
I developed inner friendship,
And regard him as the best.

Thumb through history, gaze in wonder,
Then remember what you saw,
And like many other people,
You'll shake your head in awe.

Dedicated to Titko.....1995

You gave me many memories,
That I've added to my life,
My love, respect and gratitude,
To you and your dear wife.

Claire R. Ignacio

Class Prophecy

It seems just yesterday that we walked through the corridors of Lowell High School for the last time; and yet, if we would stop to think, we would realize that it's been all of ten years. Our classmates have gone many different ways, but all of them have found success in their chosen work. If you doubt my word at all, you need only read on to find out for yourself.

TITUS PLOMERITUS and his assistant, NORMAN CARVER, have coached a series of winning football teams at Mississippi State.

TITUS PLOMARITIS
"Titko"
29 Johnson Street. Entered from Pawtucket Junior High. Activities: President of Senior Class, football and baseball teams. Hobbies: Boxing, traveling, automobiles. Future: Further education.

ONE OF MY PRIZE POSSESSIONS IS THIS 1995 GIFT FROM
CLAIRE IGNACIO, AUTHOR, POET & 1949 CLASSMATE.

LOWELL HIGH SCHOOL HALL OF FAME INDUCTED IN 1996

Lowell High School Athletic Hall Of Fame

TITUS PLOMARITIS
Class of 1949

Renowned for one of the greatest single game performances in the storied history of the traditional Lowell-Lawrence Football Series, Titus Plomaritis etched a permanent place for himself in the annals of the Red & Gray football program.

A three year varsity performer for Lowell, Titus's senior year saw the dawn of the Ray Riddick Era at Lowell High. Titus was one of the key performers. As the all-purpose standout, he led the Raiders and Eastern Mass Class A in scoring with 80 points. As well as being a standout halfback, Titus was a superior place kicker, totaling 23 P.A.T.'s and 1 Field Goal.

It was at the Lowell-Lawrence game of 1948 that the 'Plomaritis Legend' was born. With a series of dazzling runs and kicks, Titus led the underdog Red & Gray, scoring all 20 Lowell points, including the game-tying TD and winning P.A.T. with but 4 seconds remaining. The 20-19 victory concluded Lowell's first ever undefeated grid squad and insured its first ever bowl appearance in Jackson, Mississippi.

Titus was a Consensus All-Scholastic Selection during this outstanding season.

Titus attended Boston University on a football scholarship. During his tenure as a Terrier, he was a two-way starter and frequently played the entire game because of his versatility as a kicker and kick returner.

Boston Area Dermatologist
Jeffrey S. Dover, MD, FRCPC

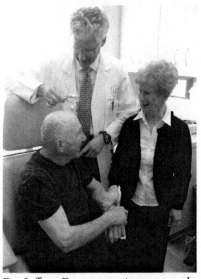

Dr. Jeffrey Dover examines my scalp twice yearly for a skin condition he calls rare, but controllable. My wife, Claire, by my side, with assurance that Dr. Dover will be gentle.

Dover's Smile really says it all. However, he has about three pages of credentials to go along with it, of which I will only go **SKIN DEEP.**

Dr. Dover graduated as the silver medalist, Magna Cum Laude with an M. D. degree from the University of Ottawa. His dermatology training was received at the University of Toronto followed by research fellowships at St. John's Hospital for Diseases of the Skin at the University of London in London, England, and a two-year photo medicine fellowship at the Beth Israel Hospital and the Massachusetts General Hospital of Harvard Medical School.

Dr. Dover is a former Associate Professor of Dermatology at Harvard Medical School, Chief of Dermatology at the New England Deaconess Hospital for over ten years and Associate Chairman of Dermatology at Beth Israel Deaconess Medical Center.

He is Associate Clinical Professor of Dermatology at Yale University School of Medicine, and Adjunct Professor of Medicine (Dermatology) at Dartmouth Medical School.

A Boston dermatologist, and director of SkinCare Physicians, Dr. Dover's research interests are lasers in medicine, cosmetic surgery and medical education.

PAUL SURPRENANT REVIVED TEACHING EXPERIENCE

Following is an interesting short story that will strike your funny bone, as it did mine.

PAUL SURPRENANT was a young Lowell High School student who lived in Pelham, N.H., back in the 1950's. He came from a large family that was not in a position to help him financially with his desire to attend college.

He is quick to give credit to his business and history teacher, Mr. Wyman Trull, for encouraging him to pursue a college education. Paul told me on many occasions how Mr. Trull got him his first job at one of Lowell's banks, just a short walk from the school.

Paul is now another success story, having attended night school for six years to get his business degree, then through dedication and hard work advanced from a teller to Senior Vice President and Chief Financial Officer at the Bank of New England, which has branches in Massachusetts and New Hampshire.

Paul is also a single digit handicap golfer, who has been my savior on many occasions when I needed an emergency fourth for a social round or for a tournament. He's one of those heavyweights I had mentioned earlier. However, this guy also has a soft touch around the greens, with a good putting stroke.

Well, would you believe it, recently we were on rain delay, playing at Scottish Highlands in the Pelham Police Association Annual Charity Golf Tournament, sitting at a table of eight, sipping on a cold brew. Out of nowhere, Paul starts telling a story about a biology class he was in some fifty years ago at Lowell High School, relating how the class was noisy with a bunch of unmanageable kids in the back of the room.

He continued, "The teacher jumped up on the desk, and he certainly got the group's attention as well as mine," relating that the teacher was a paratrooper and used these muscles every time he jumped out of a plane. Paul said, "Then he pointed to the page in the text book that described the muscle assignment for that day."

Continuing, but come to think of it, Paul was on his second beer, "The teacher jumped off the desk and was yelling, '**GASTROCNEMIUS GLUTEUS MAXIMUS**' as he rolled on the floor." Paul then told the group, "That teacher was **DR. TITUS PLOMARITIS.**" I congratulated Paul for remembering his muscle assignment, as we tipped our glasses and had a good laugh.

PELHAM POLICE RELIEF ASSOCIATION

Pelham Police Relief Golf Tournament, June, 2009—From left to right: Tom Fardy, Bob McKittrick, Mike Welcome and yours truly sitting, Titus Plomaritis.

I've been participating in the Dennis Lyons Memorial Golf Tournament, hosted by the Pelham Police Retirement Association since its inception, both as a sponsor and as a player. Usually played on the first Monday of June at Campbell's Scottish Highlands Golf Course, Salem, New Hampshire.

It has been so inspirational to observe Chief Joseph Roark with his team of assistants and volunteers cooking, serving meals, marshaling, raffling tickets, dispensing prizes, plus a sundry of other details, especially with their happy faces and **"THANK YOU'S GALORE".** These inspire me to be part of this annual charitable affair.

Then Chief Roarke opens the post dinner awards portion of the affair with pride in his voice, stating that: "ONE HUNDRED PERCENT OF THE PROCEEDS FROM THIS GOLF TOURNAMENT STAYS IN PELHAM, DISTRIBUTED TO THE VARIOUS CHARITABLE ORGANIZATIONS".

Dennis Lyons Memorial Golf Tournament, June 4, 2012—From left to right: Lt. Gary Fisher, Chief Joe Roarke, Michael Welcome, Titus, and Jim Moriarty.

He then graciously gives special thanks to his immediate assistants, Lieutenant Gary Fisher, Officer Allison Capringo and records coordinator Brenda Rizzo.

The catered lunch, food and refreshments on the course are provided by Jimmy Nagle from Chunky's Cinema Pub, Pelham, NH.

The charity golf tournament also raises revenue from a raffle, featuring exciting prizes, donated by local merchants.

Some of my golfing buddies who have played with me in this tournament over the years are: Robert McKittrick, Tom Fardy, Michael Welcome, Tony D'amato, Dr. John Bakke, Dr. Ron Randazzo, Paul Couillard, Joey Bashara, Paul Surprenant and Jim Moriarty.

CLASSMATE REVIVES GOLFING MEMORIES AT VESPER

Another great memory, this time, was rekindled at our LHS sixtieth class reunion that was held at The Long Meadow Country Club, in Lowell, Massachusetts, in 2009.

I was greeting some of my classmates as they entered, when Christine (Economopoulos) Demetriou came though the entryway. We simultaneously said, **"GARY"**, because we had both been on alert by Gary to be sure and recognize each other. He is her son and was also my golfing partner at

Vesper's Northern Twi League, of which Gary Demetriou is one of Vesper's current captains.

A little history of the **NORTHERN TWI LEAGUE** reveals that it is the oldest active Twi golf league in the United States. It was founded and incorporated in 1934, with three eighteen-hole courses (Tedesco, Salem and United Shoe) and three nine-hole courses (Bellevue, Bear Hill and Meadowbrook) as the founding charter members. Vesper Country Club was admitted in 1953 under the guidance of Bill Bradley and Ollie Stevens.

I am probably the oldest Vesper member, of the Northern Twi League participants, with a history of playing under the leadership of at least twenty captains. I was first invited to play for the Vesper team, by captains Robert McKittrick, George McQuade and Bill Brady back in the 1967 or 1968.

This memory is the best ever in the forty-five years or so, of playing in the Northern Twi League, I don't remember the exact year, but it was in the 1990's sometime. Vesper was to play at Oakley Country Club. Our Captains at that time were Phil Scannell, Jim Burns and Roy Johnson. The format was and continues to be ten players from each team with the captains putting together the pairing of two against two, better ball with one point front nine, one point back nine and one point for total (later the format changed to one point for each hole).

Well, one of Vesper's scheduled player's had an emergency, leaving our team a man short, and with not enough time for a replacement, Phil and Jimmy approached me and said, "Titus, we're sorry but under the circumstances we are going to sacrifice you, by sending you off in the last group against Oakley's fifth pairing".

Oakley always had a very strong team, including the two guys I was playing against. They didn't take me seriously and were horsing around taking impossible shots, figuring they would be certain winners.

Well, coming up the eighteenth fairway, the match was all even, I made another one of those great putts from the twenty foot range to win the hole and the match. When going into the clubhouse to join my teammates, I looked at the score board and all I saw were goose eggs on the Vesper side of the board, I was congratulated, by my teammates, for preventing a shutout, as I got the only Vesper point.

One of my good friends, Charlie DiGiovanni, who is a member of Oakley brings this incident up every time we get together, which is at least twice yearly. Only recently Charlie and I were on the phone, reviewing our summer calendars, to make golfing plans, for our annual home and home golfing outings. Sure as hell, the subject came up again. I mentioned to

Charlie that I was writing a book, and planed on mentioning the incident, but without mentioning the names, because I did not want to embarrass anyone. Charlie insisted I use the names, relating "everyone at Oakley remembers **TITUS PLOMARITIS** beating **RICHARD BRUHMULLER** (The **BROOM**) and **JACK MURPHY**", continuing, "You can't embarrass those jokers and I'm sure they would love to see their names in print".

2012 Vesper Captains: Gary Demetriou, Ken McPartland, Jim O'Donnell, Angelo Sakelarios, and Ed Stone

Vesper-Country Club

"Vesper-Country Club sits on Tyngs Island in the midst of the Merrimack River and was established in 1875 as Vesper Boat Club. In 1894 it merged with Lowell Country Club (founded in 1892) to create Vesper-Country Club.

Vesper has hosted numerous major golf events, including four Massachusetts Open championships, several Massachusetts

Vesper Country Club, Aerial View

Amateur Championships, and the New England PGA (held in 1977 and won by the Vesper host pro at the time, Tom McGuirk). The professional course record of sixty-five was set by Jeff Lewis during the 1990 Massachusetts Open.

Today, Vesper's golf course is considered one of the finest in New England. In 2008, the membership voted to completely rebuild all eighteen greens to USGA specifications and to restore the bunkers on the course. This rebuilding project was completed at the end of 2009 and overseen by architect Brian Silva, who attempted to be faithful to the original design and plans of Donald Ross.

With beautiful views of the Merrimack River, Vesper-Country Club has continued to be the preeminent social venue for the Greater Lowell area since 1875. They specialize in weddings, golf outings, bridal and baby showers, anniversary parties, holiday parties, class reunions, retirement celebrations, graduations, bar and bat mitzvahs, and bereavements."

CURRENT 2012—MANAGEMENT TEAM

David Mazur, Club Manager; Jeanne Morrison, Controller; Christina Coll, Member Services Administrator; Irene Collette, Special Events Manager; Lorelei Judge, Food and Beverage Manager; Sue Rondeau, Head Hostess/ Accounting; Paul Bellino, Executive Chef.

Pro Shop: Paul Boland, PGA Professional; Assistant Golf Professionals, Jill Leach, Keith Rogers, Andrew Chun.

Caddy Masters: Anthony Georgopoulos, Rob Satryb, Eric Karpinski, Dan Lampariello, Dan Murphy, Justin Chiklis, Pat Nelson, John DeVito, Payne Bourgeois.

FROM DISASTER TO GOOD FORTUNE

We, meaning my five closest neighbors, have had the misfortune of suffering drastic losses from power failures over the past five to six years. We all suffered losses of food from our refrigerators and freezers, and some of us had frozen water pipes, resulting in heavy financial repairs, plus the inconvenience of not being able to live and sleep in our own homes.

Well, following three consecutive winters of inconveniences and losses resulting from power outages, some for as long as a week, I contacted **WAYNE SOUZA,** a Master Electrician, who was the electrician who serviced my "Plomaritis Professional Center", for advice relative to buying and installing a generator that would service our needs.

Not only did he give me good advice on purchasing a "**KOHLER**" on line for a substantial savings, but he also assisted me with all the requirements and supplies necessary to build a platform in advance for the generator. My close friend, **MICHAEL WELCOME**, did most of the digging and cement mixing. He said my job was to, "**HOLD THE TAPE MEASURE!!**"

Thanks to Wayne's **UNSELFISH ATTITUDE** as a tradesman, just after the generator was installed we had two rapid fire power outages, one for two days and the other for five days, and with the generator automatically switched on within seconds. It resulted in absolutely no discomfort or losses. As a result, two of our neighbors observed our good fortune and they contacted Wayne for his professional services.

Now, there are three of us at the very end of the cul-de-sac who no longer fear disastrous power outages and they consider Wayne as our good fortune savior. **OH! BY THE WAY**— Wayne Souza just happens to be my wife, Claire's, nephew!!!I

Returning to Vesper CC Member Guest

May 17, 2012:—This photo was taken at Vesper Country Club with three very special people. That's me on the left just getting back to golfing following my new left hip replacement. Next to me is my dentist, Dr. Ron Randazzo, the one with the chicken legs who hits the shit out of the ball. To his left is my banker, Paul Surprenant, who also was one of my former biology students at Lowell High—and he still talks about my jumping off the desk, when I was teaching the class about the "**GASTROCNEMIUS AND GLUTEUS MAXIMUS**" muscles. On the far right is my dear friend, Charlie DiGiovanni, from Oakley CC (Belmont, MA) and Quail Ridge CC (Boynton Beach, FL). This foursome has had several years of golfing and socializing together, locally, in North Carolina and Florida.

SECTION SIX

CHIROPRACTIC

CHIROPRACTIC START TO FINISH

I guarantee you that this chapter, relative to the Chiropractic Profession, whether you are a doctor, patient, professor or a non believer, will go into the history books as one of the most interesting and exciting developments of **"WHATS NEXT"** in the culmination of a climactic conclusion.

I started in New Hampshire in 1958 with an ancient Chiropractic RSA (Law) that had not been significantly upgraded since 1921. Therefore, N.H. was regarded as one of the least desirable states to set up a Chiropractic practice, even if you had graduated from one of the accredited chiropractic colleges. But, it was a haven for those from the so called "Chiropractic Factories."

I, for one, had my B.S. degree from Boston University, my Certification in Corrective Exercise Therapy and my Doctor of Chiropractic Degree from the Chiropractic Institute of New York, which was one of the few Accredited Chiropractic Schools at that time.

FINALLY SELECTING NEW HAMPSHIRE

I will briefly repeat how I ended up in New Hampshire, just as I related in an earlier chapter.

My original plan was to set up my private practice in Lowell, Massachusetts, where I had excelled in athletics and had good name recognition. These were considered to be pre-requisites for a successful business or private practice, as stressed by motivational guest speakers throughout my years of higher education.

At that time (1958) we had three children, Titus Jr. (Buddy), five years old, Lyn, three, Steven, two, and soon expecting Diane, our fourth child.

Chiropractic was not legalized in Mass. until June 28, 1966. In 1958 chiropractors in that state were getting arrested for practicing medicine without a license.

We felt that with that state of affairs in Massachusetts, it would not be prudent to set up my private practice in Lowell, as planned, but to go across the state line into Pelham, New Hampshire, which was only five miles from downtown Lowell, to set up shop. Pelham was a town of only 900 people at that time. Our ultimate goal was to eventually move back to Lowell once Massachusetts became a licensed state.

LOCATION-LOCATION-LOCATION

How many times have you heard the saying, "location, location, location"? Well, I remembered it when I attended my first motivational lecture, when I was in my first year of Chiropractic at the Los Angeles College of Chiropractic, in Glendale, California.

The lecture was for the senior graduation class. However, I was the school photographer, taking photos for the school's promotional brochures and school photo library, which gave me an opportunity to observe at the senior level.

Two items that would actually apply to just about every occupation remained in my head, just as if it was yesterday.

"Firstly, when you are looking to build your combination home-office, which is now quite popular," the lecturer continued, "there are three very important factors to consider—**LOCATION-LOCATION-LOCATION!!**"

Secondly, he emphasized that, "your goal should be to go out and become the best Chiropractor in the whole world, not to see how much money you can earn. If you are a successful Chiropractor, you will have opportunities to invest some of your earnings—and that my friends, is the only way you will establish wealth!!"

SELECTING HOME-OFFICE LOCATION

This is my recollection of how and when I started my private practice. It was about one year prior to graduation from the Chiropractic Institute of New York, when we started looking for the first stage of the motivational speaker's implant.

It was a given that setting up a private practice in Lowell was not going to work, because the Massachusetts Chiropractors were getting arrested for practicing medicine without a license.

Our first option was to scout Pelham, New Hampshire, which was the closest bordering community to Lowell, only five miles from downtown Kearney Square. It was also a straight shot from the Bridge Street Bridge, facing directly into Pelham, resulting in both Bridge Streets by name, and is also Route 38.

We went directly to the only real estate office in Pelham and introduced ourselves to the Town Clerk, Mr. Ralph Harmon, who also operated Harmon Real Estate. He was extremely helpful in showing us available properties and building lots throughout the town. We kept in touch with him by phone whenever we returned to Lowell for a quick visit.

There was one great corner lot, consisting of two acres and also two building lots owned by a custom builder who had constructed all twenty-five houses in that development. Ralph introduced us to Leo and Phil, skilled carpenters, who were completing construction on the house directly next to the lot we were interested in. The sign in front of the building said "**SEV-A-TEL BUILDERS**", whose contractors we got to know very well. There are not too many of those folks around anymore. To this day we communicate with them via **X-MAS** greetings.

It didn't take us long to recognize where the name "**SEV-A-TEL**" came from after meeting the captains and crew Leo & Doris Sevigny and Phil & Loretta Tellier. Leo and Loretta were brother and sister, making it a family corporation.

With Doris and Loretta doing the painting and wallpaper hanging, and Leo and Phil doing the carpentry, it made for a real family business. The guys loved and appreciated their wives, naming the two streets adjacent to the lots that we eventually purchased, Loretta & Doris Avenues.

FINALLY BUILDING A HOME-OFFICE

Now, this is how we got started without a dime to our name.

Claire convinced her mom to loan us one thousand dollars, the bank's requirement at that time to procure a four percent mortgage, from a Lowell bank, whose President was Dr. Frank Hulslander's father-in law. Remember, Frank Hulslander was the Chiropractor instrumental in my pursuit of a Chiropractic career.

NOTE: Claire's dad died in an auto accident two years prior, which explains that the money came from the insurance settlement, into Mrs. Hebert's bank account.

SEV-A-TEL builders agreed to construct us a three bedroom ranch on one of the two lots, as well as finish the lower level into a four room office with a half bathroom. The agreement also included a hot-topped finished parking lot with direct access to the office—all for $21,000.

They were so accommodating, they even gave me a twelve month option to buy the adjacent lot for $500. And yes, we repaid Mrs. Hebert every penny and we did purchase the adjacent lot from **SEV-A TEL** Builders.

NOTE: Go back to the beginning of the Battles story, and you will better understand why Ralph is in my memory every single day.

A little additional information about our builders is that they had built two beautiful ranch homes adjacent to each other, also on Bridge Street, only a quarter mile from the state line.

COMING HOME to start a private practice wasn't as easy as I had anticipated, especially starting from scratch, with three children and Claire expecting our fourth, without a penny to our name and trying to project the image of a doctor.

When we got to know the Sevigny's and Tellier's better, we were on a first name basis, but they always respected my title and when being introduced, it was always "Doctor" Plomaritis.

They worked overtime to get us into the living portion of the house, which in retrospect wasn't fast enough as I had to sell my Graflex camera to help pay our living expenses. I also took on a couple of side jobs to make ends meet.

NEW JOB TO THE RESCUE

DR. MARVIN WEISBERG, who graduated two years ahead of me, became quite an entrepreneur. He started a business called **WARNER DAVIS, INC.,** in New York, consisting of only natural organic vitamin products, manufactured exclusively for the Chiropractic Profession.

He called to ask if I would be interested in being his New England Distributor. He explained the details, that there would be no out-of- pocket expenses, a gas allowance, a list of Chiropractors in New England to call on once monthly, and that payment would come to me twice monthly, based on the consignment orders. I told Marvin that I would discuss it with Claire and get back to him in a few days.

Well, once I explained the call to Claire, we analyzed the benefits of an immediate income. Knowing that it would take a couple of years to establish a private practice, and also that I would be able to meet most of the successful practitioners in New England, I called him back in fifteen minutes before he changed his mind, or found someone else.

This was a blessing in disguise, as I will explain a little later. At first I allocated three days a week with the following schedule: I would get up at 5:00 A.M. and drive to the most distant locations in Connecticut, Vermont and Maine, and work my way back toward home, so my last call for that day would be closest to home. The following week I would cover Rhode Island, Massachusetts and New Hampshire, being considerably closer, which allowed for twice as many stops per day. It was a great experience meeting all the so-called pioneers of that era.

DEVELOPING NEW FRIENDSHIPS

Wow!! Would you believe I actually remember the names of the first few accounts in Connecticut, from over fifty years ago? Dr. Michael Barone in New Haven, Dr. Louis Labbadia in Middletown, and Dr. George Paul in Hartford were my first accounts and friends for several years.

Our friendships continued, even after I departed from Warner Davis. We established golf and dinner outings, one date a month during the summer, for a round of golf and dinner, alternating golf courses in New Haven, Middlebury, Hartford and Vesper C.C., my course in Tyngsboro, Massachusetts.

Dr. Richard Vincent from Beverly, Mass. was my best account and become one of my best friends in the Chiropractic circles. He was very helpful in guiding me toward my ultimate goal of strengthening our RSA (state chiropractic law), becoming an accredited state, and protecting the consumers from graduates of non-accredited Chiropractic colleges.

We attended the annual New England conventions together and remain friends to this day. His office was only forty minutes from my home in Pelham, and I made it a point to see him every two weeks for the two years I was the Warner Davis distributor. We made it a social visit, going to the bowling alley for lunch and to bowl a couple of strings. I was constantly picking his brain to apply some of his political skills toward enhancing our state RSA.

Dr. Marvin Weisberg, using his entrepreneurial skills, expanded his business to include a travel agency in conjunction with Warner Davis. He put a package together that guided instructors from accredited Chiropractic colleges to lecture in popular European cities like Lisbon, Rome or Athens. He called the excursions **"GRADUATE STUDY SEMINARS"** and that satisfied the annual continuing education requirements for State License renewal.

As a distributor, Marvin included the entire package for both me and Claire for a total of $250. We attended the first two, Portugal and Spain, Paris and Rome. They were both much needed vacations for Claire, to get a break from the four children. Her mother babysat; otherwise, our financial situation at that time wouldn't have allowed us that luxury.

NOTE: One day early on, I called Marvin's office and asked to speak to Dr. Weisberg. The gal answering the phone said, with a terrible New York accent, "Yes, may I ask who is calling?" I said, "Dr.Titus Plomaritis." Her next comment was **"NO SHIT, WHAT'S YOUR REAL NAME?"**

WORKING TO ESTABLISH
ACCREDITATION IN N.H.

It was sad to see what a bad reputation my profession was getting from the five other Chiropractors in Pelham, who would treat busloads of patients within minutes, giving no physical examinations, no x-rays, and no diagnosis. All patients would lie on a table, get a quick upper cervical adjustment (HIO), and with no set fee, only a donation box at their pleasure on the way out the door.

I decided then and there that the only way to cure that ailment was to devote my time and energy to elevating the standards for licensure in the state of New Hampshire.

Over the next eight years I established a very good private practice in Pelham, and taking into consideration that our children had established friendships from within the school system and our town's community, we decided to expand our home/office and remain in Pelham, N.H.

CHIROPRACTIC ONGOING

PCO OFFICE

100 Bridge St
Pelham, New Hampshire

1. Plomaritis Chiropractic Office
2. Lowell, MA
3. Lawrence, MA
4. Haverhill, MA
5. Nashua, NH
6. Salem, NH
7. Methuen, MA
8. Andover, MA
9. Tyngsboro, MA
10. Westford, MA
11. Billerica, MA
12. Windham, NH
13. Chelmsford, MA
14. Tewksbury, MA

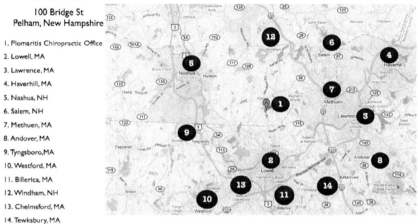

Plomaritis Chiropractic Office (PCO)

PLOMARITIS CHIROPRACTIC OFFICE (PCO), 100 Bridge Street, Pelham, New Hampshire, is in the number (1) spot on the map above. I created the map to give you some idea of where the majority of my patients came from and how far they had to travel.

When I first started my private practice, the majority of my patients came from Lowell, Massachusetts, which was only five miles down the road on Bridge Street (also Route 38). The farthest distances on the map from the PCO were Andover, Westford and Haverhill, which were about ten miles.

I had three distant traveling patients who are worth mentioning because of the unusual circumstances.

The **FIRST** was a gentleman from New York. I do especially remember his occupation. You see, he was the only one out of approximately 20,000 patients over my career who was a **SULKY SALESMAN.**

I remember his first call to my office, in the mid 60's. He asked if I could see him immediately because he strained his back removing a sulky from the roof of his station wagon. My office policy was never to refuse a patient in distress, so I told him to come on over and as I attempted to give him the directions, he interrupted me and said, "I have the directions, from the sulky drivers at Rockingham Park who referred you."

Well, Mr. Thibodeau was a regular patient for the next twenty years.

He would call me a couple of days prior to leaving New York to set up an appointment schedule for that particular trip.

His regular trips were through Rockingham Park in Salem, N.H and would then continue on to Scarborough Downs in Scarborough, Maine.

They always included two treatments heading North and two when returning South. His station wagon, with a couple of sulkies on the roof, would always be in my parking lot at 6:00 AM.

The **SECOND** patient was also unusual in that he was a businessman (owner of some mills) from Biddeford, Maine. He also was the owner of sulky racehorses and was referred to me by Mr. Thibodeau.

After a few adjustments, his acute low back problem dissipated, and I then suggested that he would be less apt to have a recurrence if he received monthly maintenance adjustments.

I tried to refer him to a Chiropractor in Biddeford who was very professional and had great credentials, whom I had met in my earlier Warner Davis distributor travel days. Relating to him, as I had previously, that the Chiropractor in Biddeford used similar chiropractic techniques and stated he wouldn't have to travel so far.

I couldn't convince him, so for the next five years he never missed his monthly maintenance full spine adjustments. What's interesting about this patient is that, like Mr. Thibodeau, you would always see his vehicle in my parking lot at 6:00 AM. The big difference was that his automobile was a **CHAUFFEUR-DRIVEN ROLLS ROYCE.**

The **THIRD** patient, Ryan, was referred by his brother, Patrick O'Brien, from Lowell, MA. Patrick had described his brother's symptoms as, "low back pain, that travels down one leg and he leans to one side." Patrick also stated that, "Ryan had already been to an orthopedic surgeon, who told him he had all the symptoms of a ruptured disc, and suggested surgery."

Ryan's thinking was that his brother had a similar condition a few years earlier and made a total recovery. He said to me, "I would like to have you treat me as you did my brother, and if it doesn't get better in three months, I will go back to the surgeon and have surgery."

Now, the kicker here was that Ryan didn't drive and his brother Patrick didn't get home from work until 7:00 PM, so I scheduled him for 8:00 PM, three times weekly for six weeks, plus home care of moist heat and corrective therapeutic exercises three times daily.

NOTE: The only case I ever treated that was worse than his was one of my dear friends from the Vesper Country Club, Dr. Robert Lawlor, who was an Ophthalmologist. On one occasion he even had an ambulance take him to my office directly from a Lowell Hospital, when he had one of his severe recurrences while performing eye surgery.

Well, as luck would have it, Ryan also made a slow, but full recovery within his time frame. **OH!!**, I forgot to mention, what was peculiar about this case was that **RYAN CAME IN FROM IRELAND.**

NOTE: On his last visit, scheduled on a Friday, he brought his **FIDDLE,** as planned. Patrick had informed me to have a bottle of Irish whiskey on hand as he related, "Ryan gets a little thirsty when he plays his fiddle in the evening."

It was an evening that my children never forgot. They were allowed to stay up late for the show, and they applauded wildly after each tune, as Ryan would take a healthy swig from the bottle of Irish whiskey, and continued on until the bottle was empty. His flight back to Ireland was scheduled for the following week.

CLOSE CALLS—FIFTH INCIDENT

I remember one Sunday morning in the middle of winter, about six a.m., while driving up to Canon Mountain for a ski day with my son Steven, about thirteen years old at the time, in my newly purchased Porsche.

I've never really been a person who gets excited about high speed automobiles and only bought the Porsche because I received a good deal— and my boys talked me into it. It was a two-seater and was supposed to be our (Claire's and my) "date car" for our evenings at the movies or dining out without the kids.

Anyway, as we were driving up to Canon and getting closer to our destination, a Chevrolet passed us at a high speed and Steven started with his comments, "Dad, you don't let a Chevy pass a Porsche", and "Come on, Dad, blow out the engine."

Steven with me & Porsche 911

Being the agreeable Dad, I started accelerating and Steven further encouraged me, "That's more like it" and "Can't wait to get home and tell Buddy" as I was going close to eighty mph, when I hit an ice patch going around a curve. I hit the brakes and immediately started spinning out of control, and when I came to a halt I was facing a thousand foot drop down a canyon.

Then, I started to wonder if it was my Bible reading punishment sessions early at the barber shop that might have had something to do with THE GOOD LORD protecting me from these close calls.

DR WILLIAM J. GARRITY, FIRST ASSOCIATE AT PLOMARITIS CHIROPRACTIC OFFICE

I remember the very first day, when **DR. WILLIAM J. GARRITY** came to Pelham, New Hampshire. It had snowed all night and my parking lot was being plowed. I had been on the phone rescheduling patients when the office doorbell rang as the plow was leaving.

I said to myself, it must be a patient in distress, I went downstairs and opened the entrance door that led into the office waiting room, and there he was, Dr. Garrity, making his first impression toward becoming my first associate at the PCO.

I had submitted an advertisement for an associate position in the New England Chiropractic Journal. Dr. Garrity had been one of three applicants responding and I had forgotten that I had set up an interview for that particular morning.

Again, I should mention that before interviewing candidates for my first associate, I conferred with my friend, Dr. Vincent, who had experience with associates and contractual agreements. Having had no experience with associates in the past, I had a basic set of questions to ask and was to pay attention to their reactions as well as their answers. My initial plan was to take notes and then evaluate each candidate with my office manager (Claire Plomaritis) before making a decision.

I hadn't planned on spending too much time interviewing each of the candidates, however, under the circumstances, and being aware that Dr. Garrity had traveled a good distance for this interview, I invited him in and informed Claire that it was Dr. Garrity at the door. We chatted for quite a while, when Claire came downstairs, introduced herself and invited him to stay for lunch.

Our daughter, Lyn, was home at the time which actually gave us three perspectives of Dr. Garrity's personality, intelligence and presentation. Our major concerns were that his Chevy Chevette was leaking oil and he was planning to commute 115 miles each way three times weekly.

Well, let me tell you, Dr. Garrity was a tremendous addition to the PCO. His

In this, patient with autonomic dysfunction a subluxation between T-5 and T-6 is found resulting in systemic symptoms and pain. I am demonstrating the diagnostic procedure "motion palpation" before proceeding with treatment.

presence allowed the office to be open six days weekly. I worked Mondays, Wednesdays and Fridays. Bill worked Tuesdays, Thursdays and Saturdays. He had a great work ethic and never missed a day in the five years he worked as my associate.

Bill and I were recently reminiscing, and he related that when he was my associate, he and Dawn, his wife, had two children, Steven and Lauren. They have doubled their clan since, with two additional children, Doug and Heather.

Dr. Garrity also played a major part in designing my 2,500 square foot **PLOMARITIS CHIROPRACTIC OFFICE** floor plan. He used his experience as clinic director at National Chiropractic Colleges prior to moving east, in selecting state of the art equipment and the Transworld X-Ray unit for our new suite of rooms in the newly built Plomaritis Professional Center.

OUR NEW EQUIPMENT

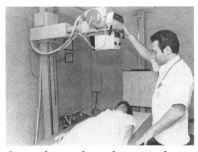

Optimal central ray placement during patient positioning was accomplished by using the state-of-the-art floating x-ray table top. This required only finger tip pressure.

TRANSWORLD X-RAY UNIT:

To reduce radiation, we obtained a three phase 325v x 125 kVp model which allowed for shorter radiation exposure to the patients. The three-phase X-ray generators allowed for higher mA than the same one using a single-phase X-ray generator. Both had a moveable bucky, which reduced distortion. The cassettes were rare earth and reduced the amount of X-ray exposure.

Weight bearing studies for spine/pelvis were obtained using the vertical table system. To maximize central ray accuracy, we used a free-floating flat table top requiring only finger tip pressure positioning. In short, this configuration was the best system available to maximize optimal plain films at minimal exposure. The X-ray suite was designed by Dr. Garrity and myself.

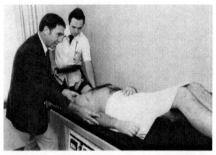

To decompress a very painful right lateral C-5/C-6 disc protrusion resulting in cervical radiculopathy, Dr. Garrity focuses on the clinical impact of distractive vector forces, using traction while I, more assuredly gently stabilized the patient for maximal clinical benefit.

HILL ANATOMOTOR ROLLER MASSAGE TABLE: with the Lumbar and Cervical traction attachments. Traction is created as the gliding top pulls against the controlled resistance of the traction unit. At the same time, two sets of adjustable-height massage rollers straddle the spine and rhythmically loosen taught muscles.

Dr. Garrity is now a DO, in Suffield, Connecticut, having graduated from the University Of New England Osteopathic Medicine, in 1996.

An interesting tidbit about Dr. Garrity, that still brings a smile to my face, occurred in 1981. He was employed at the time as clinic director of the National College of Chiropractic in Lombard, Illinois, and had decided to leave that position and return to the East Coast. He had scheduled taking the New Hampshire and Massachusetts State Licensing Examinations on the same trip, as they were administered only two weeks apart.

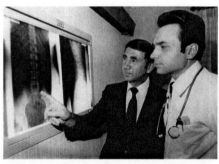

Before treating a patient, Dr. Plomaritis asks Dr. Garrity his opinion on whether the vertebrate of interest is an L-5 or L-6, namely a congenital anomaly resulting in this instance of iliolumbar ligament instability causing pain during the orthopedic exam.

Well, only a couple of days after the release of the scores to the candidates, Floris Lannigan from the Secretary of States office called me with the most bizarre request. She said "Dr. Plomaritis, one of the newly licensed examinees called and requested a review of his exam".

The board members were in agreement, and Dr. Garrity came to the Secretary of State's office, reviewed the exam and departed. Within a week the board received a letter from Dr. Garrity with documentation from a clinical diagnostic text book, that, in fact, left little doubt that his answer was partially correct. The board agreed to give him credit for that question and to change his score from 99% to 100%.

PLOMARITIS PROFESSIONAL CENTER (PPC)

Let's fast forward to 1983, when we decided to expand once more, only this time we combined the two one-acre lots. And, with **LEE BERARD'S** design, we converted our residence into the first professional building in Pelham. It was a masterpiece of designing as he attached the 9,000 square foot addition to the existing three bedroom ranch, with a fire door passageway connecting the two structures.

Designer Lee Berard's sketch of the Plomaritis Professional Center

Dr. Titus Plomaritis with Lee Berard, the designer of the Plomaritis Professional Center, Pelham's first professional office building.

Envirovac Sewer System

State of the art, two pint toilet flush system that conserved water. It was transported from Illinois in a flatbed truck and required a crane to lift it and place into the PPC's designated service area before completion of the construction around it. It was the first of it's kind in the state of N.H. It had 850 gallon capacity that only required drainage once every two weeks by just opening the valve, close to my right hand in the attached photo. It drained into two septic tanks that would automatically pump its waste into the leach fields. Built in 1982, engineers came along with the unit to assure of its proper installation.

September 21, 1983, The Observer: Officially Open—there were no halfway measures about the ribbon cutting at the new PLOMARITIS PROFESSIONAL CENTER on 100 Bridge Street here Saturday afternoon. The ribbon was cut in three places, as can be seen. Dr. Titus Plomaritis (l.) stands by as scissors are wielded by (l. To r.) Executive Council Louis Georgopoulos, US Congressman Norman D'Amours and State Senator Vance Kelly. With them are Chairman Alice kirby of Pelham's Board of Selectman and Claire Plomaritis. Salem Observer photo.

CHIROPRACTORS OVERCOME THE AMA; PRACTICE NOW LEGAL IN MASSACHUSETTS

BOSTON—October 16, 1966—Chiropractic is now a legal profession in the state of Massachusetts.

The practice has been officially authorized by the State Legislature after many years of bitter debate, and **GOVERNOR JOHN VOLPE** signed the bill, to bring some 200 to 300 practitioners out of limbo and into public view and regulation.

The Governor's office received 50,000 letters from citizens urging that the bill be signed—despite the objections of medical doctors (**AMA**).

AMA PLANNED TO ELIMINATE CHIROPRACTIC

On November 2, 1963, the AMA Board of Regents created the "Committee on Quackery," with the goals of first containing, and then eliminating chiropractic. The steps needed were as follows:—

1—To ensure that Medicare should not cover chiropractic.

2—To ensure that the U.S. Office of Education should not recognize or list a chiropractic accrediting agency.

3—To encourage continued separation of the two national associations.

4—To encourage state medical societies to take the initiative in their state legislatures regarding legislation that might affect the practice of chiropractic.

THE LONGSTANDING FEUD between chiropractors and medical doctors continued for decades. The AMA labeled chiropractic as an "unscientific cult" in 1966, and until 1980 held that it was unethical for medical doctors to associate with "unscientific practitioners."

"WHISTLEBLOWER" TURNS THE TIDE

HOWEVER, in 1975 an anonymous AMA insider describing himself as a disgruntled AMA staffer and identifying himself as "Sore Throat" released information to the press concerning the "Committee on Quackery" and its proposed methods to eliminate chiropractic.

These papers were the basis of Wilk et al. vs. AMA, the suit brought by Chester Wilk, D.C., of Illinois and five co-plaintiffs against the AMA and several co-defendants.

The hearings' judge issued her opinion that the **AMA HAD VIOLATED** Section 1, but not 2, of the Sherman Act, and that it had engaged in an **UNLAWFUL CONSPIRACY** in restraint of trade "to contain and eliminate the chiropractic profession."

INTEREST IN CHIROPRACTIC GROWS

By the mid-1990's there was a growing scholarly interest in chiropractic, which helped efforts to improve service quality and establish clinical guidelines that recommended manual therapies for acute low back pain.

TITUS AMONG THE HIGHLIGHTS DURING CONVENTION AT THE BELMONT HOTEL

WEST HARWICH, MASS.—While attending the 1966 convention of the Massachusetts Chiropractic Association, held here at the fabulous **BELMONT HOTEL,** Dr, Titus Plomaritis turned out to be the featured figure both on the golf course and on the ocean.

DR. PLOMARITIS, from Pelham, N.H., and **PAUL CORNING,** from Topsfield, Mass., tied for first place in the fourth annual Warner Davis Golf tournament, and there was an 18-hole playoff for the title—which Titus won.

Dr. Patrick Labbadia of Middletown, Conn., was runner-up in the gross division, and net runner-up was Dr. James Reese of Chicopee Falls, Mass.

DR. MARVIN WEISBERG, President of tournament sponsor Warner Davis, presented the awards.

Dr. Titus Plomaritis receiving his award from his former employer, Dr. Marvin Weisberg, President of Warner Davis

One of the highlights of the convention was the presence of Governor John Volpe, who proudly presented a copy of Chapter 409 of the General Laws of Massachusetts—which **LEGALIZED THE PRACTICE OF CHIROPRACTIC** in the Commonwealth.

The then-fabulous Belmont Hotel, located right on the Harwich town line with neighboring Dennisport, was the summertime resort for famous politicians, business tycoons and show-business personalities. The Belmont even had a ticker-tape machine, which flashed the latest stock market reports, on its mammoth front porch that overlooked one of the top beaches on Cape Cod.

Radio and television star comedian **FRED ALLEN** spent his summers at the Belmont, writing his radio scripts and books on the porch there.

The Belmont, an all-wooden structure, suffered its death knell in the 1970's when it was the victim of a mammoth fire.

TITUS IN NEAR DISASTROUS BOAT RIDE

ANOTHER HIGHLIGHT of the convention's weekend gathering took place when Dr. Plomaritis and **DR. JOHN MARKEY** decided to rent a sailboat to show their wives how great they were with the sails.

"Dr. Markey and his wife, Eileen, were close friends with Claire and I, especially in the chiropractic circles," commented Titus. "John was also an Executive Governors Councilor in the state of Massachusetts.

What a combination!! I had never been in a sailboat and John is as non-athletic as they come,

Off we go, about 50 yards off the shoreline, waiving to the girls—when the wind picked up. As we attempted to set the sails to take us ashore, we kept going further out. John is yelling instructions to me. I don't remember the names, something like tacking, and before I knew what happened, the sailboat tilted and John fell off the boat. Then, when I helped him back into the boat, it tilted again and he fell out the other side.

We ended up swimming ashore, and the entertainment for the crowd at the shoreline was over. However, we are never going further offshore again!!" summed up the Pelham chiropractor.

—AND SO ENDED A MEMORABLE WEEKEND AT THE FABULOUS BELMONT HOTEL!!

CLAIRE PLOMARITIS MAKES POLITICAL HISTORY
The Lowell Sun
Circa 1976-77

PELHAM, N.H.—On November 2, 1976, Pelham elected its first woman legislator in the town's 230 year history.

CLAIRE PLOMARITIS of Bridge Street tallied the second highest vote total among the six candidates running for the town's three state representative seats, with 1595 votes—only 65 behind the top vote-getter, Philip Currier. Also elected was incumbent Henry Seamons, Sr., with 1395 of the 3000-plus votes cast in this historic election.

"I'm so very excited, delighted and thrilled," said Mrs. Plomaritis, mother of four, after she had learned of her sure victory, "and I'll work very hard to justify the people's faith in me."

She called her husband, **DR. TITUS PLOMARITIS**, "the greatest campaign manager anyone could have," and credited her children as "motivators" behind her candidacy and eventual victory.

WON ON HER FIRST TRY

Rep. Plomaritis stated that she began to think seriously about entering the field of politics less than two years previously, and was elected to the legislative body after her first campaign.

The petite and energetic Pelham mother says she plans to be a full time representative of her constituents, and hopes to do her bit to try to change some of the antiquated laws in the Granite State.

"We have a very unique set-up in New Hampshire," said Rep. Plomaritis. "We have the third-largest legislative body in the English speaking world. With its 400 legislators, New Hampshire is outnumbered only by the

British House of Commons and the U.S. House of Representatives. Yet New Hampshire has the fourth-smallest Senate body in the country, with just 24 members."

With a glint of pride in her eyes, Mrs. Plomaritis noted that four of the State Senators are women.

Though Claire Plomaritis is the initial female representative from Pelham, the Granite State does have a total of 105 women legislators.

HOPING FOR SOME CHANGES

One of the things she hopes would change in New Hampshire's unique legislative set-up is its custom of meeting 90 days biennially. This she says dates back to 1889 when the salary of legislators was set at $100 a year.

"IT'S STILL THAT—PLUS MILEAGE," the representative commented.

According to the state constitution, the legislative body meets only during odd-numbered years, beginning its three-times-a-week sessions on the first Tuesday in January. Business must be completed by July 1. As a result of this schedule, designed to accommodate the 19th century farmers, who needed their weekends to do their chores. Today's legislature must call several special sessions to complete unfinished business.

"I'm in favor of remaining in session and not rushing bills through at the last minute," Rep. Plomaritis said. "There are so many challenging issues to deal with." One of her chief concerns is energy conservation, and she deplores the fact that there is no sound energy conservation policy.

Rep. Plomaritis says people should think more of using solar and wind energy, which are inexhaustible sources. She terms nuclear energy exhaustible, expensive, unsafe—and hazardous to human life and destructive to marine life.

CASINO GAMBLING, she predicts, will be a big issue in New Hampshire in the coming years. "You can't make Las Vegas out of New Hampshire, and an attempt to do so could spell disaster and definitely affect the quality of life that we have," she said, adding that she plans to give that particular bill a lot of thought and study.

She also plans to find out what happened to funds appropriated for an access road into Pelham off Interstate Route 93.

BRINGING UP THE TAX ISSUES

"New Hampshire **IS THE ONLY STATE** without a sales or personal income tax—and that's **ONE OF THE LAWS WE WANT TO RETAIN**," said the lady rep. "I think it's silly to make a big deal about Massachusetts people crossing the state border to buy liquor here. What's sillier is to spy on them. Let Massachusetts reduce its taxes and its consumers will buy in their home state."

She noted that there is a plaque in Governor Thompson's office which reads: "Remember, low taxation is the result of low spending."

RELISHES BEING HOMEMAKER

Claire Plomaritis is not a women's libber. She believes that women should get equal pay for equal work, but she also believes that a woman's most important role is being a wife and mother.

"I played those roles and that of homemaker by choice. I feel that the family is the backbone of society, and that the more time parents invest in their children the less problems they will have to expect from them," she said.

"When my children were small, I spent most of my time with them and had a full schedule driving them to their tennis, golf and swimming lessons—every minute of which I enjoyed," she commented.

A SOLID BACKGROUND

A native of Lowell, Mass., Claire is the daughter of the late Frank Hebert and Mrs. Laurier Hebert of Merrimack Street. Her father was a New England professional flyweight boxing champion, a veteran of 105 fights. She is a graduate of St. Louis de France and Lowell High School.

Claire interrupted her studies to marry Titus Plomaritis 25 years ago, and she worked as a private secretary at the Paris Shoe Company while her husband continued his career in physical education and the chiropractic field in New York and California after he earned a B.S. degree at Boston University. The couple now has four children—sons Titus, Jr. and Stephen, and daughters, Lyn and Diane.

In addition to her household duties, Rep. Plomaritis has always devoted at least 15 hours a week doing all the "third party" work for her husband. She makes out all his reports, including those to lawyers, insurance companies, Medicare and welfare agencies. Though he has an assistant, "I do all his paper work," Mrs. Plomaritis said, adding that she just wouldn't have it any other way.

A WOMAN OF MANY TALENTS, Rep. Plomaritis is also a licensed real estate broker in New Hampshire and Massachusetts.

REMEMBERING THE CAMPAIGN

"My husband was my campaign manager—and he conducted a good one," she said, adding that there were as many men as women working for her. Many of the Pelham town's most influential people were among her campaign workers.

"I received much encouragement from Pelham's 86-year-old former representative, Arthur Peabody, who told me just where I should go to solicit votes," she said.

THE WELL-KNOWN COUPLE

Dr. and Mrs. Plomaritis are widely known in the Greater-Lowell area. They hold membership at the Vesper Country Club where they headed the entertainment committee and organized the first winter carnival. They are also members of the Boston University Century Club, B.U. Alumni Association, American Chiropractic Association and the newly-formed Friends of the Pelham Library.

SPECIAL RECOGNITION was given to the couple at the Concord, N.H. State House when Mrs. Plomaritis was sworn in, and Senator Delbert Downing of Salem, N.H., presented them with a resolution of congratulations on the occasion of their 25th wedding anniversary.

HER FUTURE POLITICAL SUCCESS

During the next four years, Claire Plomaritis was labeled as an INDEPENDENT THINKER, and she remained opposed to sales and income taxes for the state.

She served on the following committees:

Member of Commerce and Consumer Affairs,

To study solid waste management; mandatory recycling throughout the state,

To establish a Division of Occupational and Professional Licensing and Registration,

To regulate the advertising policies of utilities companies,

Blue Ribbon Committee to study salaries of elected Hillsboro County officials,

To amend the law to better protect landlord tenant rights,

To license and regulate plumbers statewide,

To license social workers,

To include Pastoral Counselors under Blue Cross -Blue Shield,

To outlaw C.W.I.P., eliminating $12-million from residents' electric bills,

To revise investment laws of savings banks,

To study the feasibility of a direct access to I-93 from Pelham and

To study the refund policies of retail establishments in N.H.

DIDN'T FORGET HER HOME TOWN

Rep. Claire Plomaritis, despite her busy work in the legislature, also kept busy in Pelham. She continued her services as a member of the Pelham League of Women Voters, the Pelham Council on Aging, the Pelham Ambulance Study Committee (vice-president), the Pelham Forest Committee, and the Democratic 100 Club.

NEW HAMPSHIRE STATE RESOLUTION

FOLLOWING is the State of New Hampshire, Concord, New Hampshire "Resolution", honoring Claire and Titus Plomaritis:—

Whereas the institution of marriage is the most beautiful when lived in love and mutual concern, and

Whereas the family is the nucleus for a successful society, and

Whereas our American Heritage is based on a monogamous union, and

Whereas Titus Plomaritis and Claire Hebert made their personal commitment, on December 1, 1951, when they were united in matrimony in Lowell, Massachusetts, and

Whereas that commitment, being blessed with four children, Titus Jr., Steven, Lyn and Diane, has provided the basis for a good family life, and

Whereas Titus and Claire Plomaritis have further made a commitment to the Town of Pelham for the last 18 years, having conducted a successful Chiropractic practice, and

Whereas Titus' long proficiency in and enthusiasm for sports, he has served as a model for not only his own children but for the youth of the community, and

Whereas on November 2, of this year, Claire received the well deserved honor of being elected as the first woman member of the New Hampshire House of Representatives from Pelham, and

Whereas Titus and Claire are celebrating their silver wedding anniversary on this December 1,1976. By participating in Claire's swearing in ceremony, for the one hundred and forty fifth session of the New Hampshire General Court, a true milestone in their lives, be it therefore

Resolved that the Senate of the State of New Hampshire extends congratulations and wishes them good health, good luck and a long and happy life together.

Alf Jacobson-President of the Senate
Delbert F Downing, Minority Leader
Date: December 1, 1976

PELHAM DEMOCRATIC PICNIC PLANNED

The Lowell Sun

PELHAM, N.H.—June 16, 1978—Up to 500 people are expected at the biggest Democratic political fund raising event to hit the town in recent years.

It is being planned by the Pelham Democratic Town Committee, which re-elected Chairman Gerald Bourque, named Carol Giglio secretary, and nominated three state representative contenders during an informal mid-week meeting.

This major event, scheduled for August 6th, is being billed as the **"DEMOCRATIC TOWN FAMILY PICNIC,"** or **"A DAY FOR TOM,"** as it will have as its special guest and main attraction **U.S. SENATOR THOMAS McINTYRE** of Laconia.

The affair will take place at the home of Dr. and Mrs. Titus Plomaritis, from 1-6 p.m. Dr. Plomaritis is the chairman and George Mason the vice chairman of the special event.

Senator McIntyre is expected to be joined by **U.S. SENATOR JOHN DURKIN,** as well as the Democratic gubernatorial contenders—state senator Delbert Downing and Hugh Gallen—plus all the Democratic candidates for the state senate and legislature.

STATE REPRESENTATIVES NOMINATED

The Town Committee also nominated three to carry the Democratic state representative honors here in the fall, including incumbents Claire Plomaritis and Peter Flynn, as well as newcomer Augustine Messineo, the town's plumbing inspector. Each will seek a two year seat, running as a "ticket".

Meanwhile, the candidate filing deadline is fast approaching, and thus far not a single Republican has turned in papers for state representative. That in itself would be phenomenal, as Pelham has for years carried a "safe Republican" label. No less than two years ago, the state representative slate was all Republican.

GALA AFFAIR IS PLANNED

The picnic event tickets will be sold at $10 for a family, and children will be free. There will be unlimited food available and adults will be able to have beer consumed, and all will be served in a picnic atmosphere. All proceeds will go toward election needs.

"Quite a few door prizes will be given out during the course of the day," said Anita Greenhalgh, the Committee's publicity chairman, "including prizes and games for the children, along with pony rides."

CLAIRE PLOMARITIS will handle ticket sales, and **ROBERT ALLEN** is mailing out invitations.

"We want to get all the Democrats in town—along with out-of-towners—to this picnic," added Anita Greenhalgh. "We hope to get about 400-500 people. Titus told us anybody who can fit in his back yard can get in."

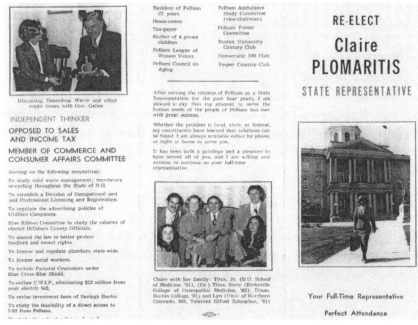

Re-elect Claire Plomaritis State Representative
Your full time Representative with Perfect Attendance—walking in front of the New Hampshire State Capitol—The cover of a six column triple fold brochure.
Top Left—She is discussing Hazardous Waste and other major issues with Gov. Gallen.
Bottom center photo:—Claire with her family: Titus, Jr. (B.U. School of Medicine, '81). (Dr.) Titus, Steven (Kirksville College of Osteopathic Medicine, '82), Diane, (Boston College, '81) and Lyn (Univ. Of Northern Colorado, MS, Talented Gifted Education, '81)"

THREE STRIKES FOR THE PICNIC BANNER

The Salem Observer

PELHAM, N.H.—August 2, 1978—The Pelham Democratic Committee's Family Picnic is scheduled to be held on the **PLOMARITIS GROUNDS** here on Sunday, August 6, and the event is being boosted by the controversial banner floating over Route 38.

THE BANNER'S FIRST STRIKE

The Committee, which has been working diligently to make this event successful, designed a colorful banner—which read **"PELHAM DEM. COMMITTEE PICNIC AUGUST 6th"**—and erected it across Route 38, near the shopping plaza, on July 24th.

The banner, to say the least, has had its ups and downs. It has been up and down three times in four days.

The Pelham Democratic Picnic banner was first erected by Committee members on Monday, July 24th. On Wednesday, July 26th, this 24-foot banner mysteriously disappeared.

Democratic State Representative **CLAIRE PLOMARITIS**, after several telephone calls, was able to piece together what happened.

It seems that a complaint had been called into the state highway department and a crew was sent to Route 38 to remove the banner. However, this turned out to be a misdirected order and the state highway department re-erected the banner on Thursday morning, July 27th.

THE BANNER'S SECOND STRIKE

Shortly thereafter, another complaint was received by Granite State Electric in Salem. A few hours later, a crew from Granite State proceeded to remove the banner from its now famous location.

THE BANNER'S THIRD—AND HOPEFUL—FINAL STRIKE

However, the **"PELHAM DEM. COMMITTEE PICNIC AUGUST 6th"** banner is up again over Route 38, near the shopping plaza, hopefully to stay until the August 6th extravaganza at the Plomaritis residence.

It seems that Granite State Electric eventually reconsidered its action and re-erected the now-famous banner.

PELHAM DEMOCRATS

Pelham Democrats
August 6, 1978: U S Senator Tom McIntyre with the Plomaritis family Left to right—
Steven, Titus Sr., State Representative Claire Plomaritis,, Diane, Lyn and Titus Jr.

The Pelham Democratic Picnic was held at the home of Dr. Titus & Hon. Claire Plomaritis, with United States Senators, Thomas McIntyre and John Durkin along with US Representative Norman D'Amours attending. This was the first and only Pelham Democratic Picnic. It was here that we had to make a decision on whom to support for Governor.

We had to make a decision between Sen. Del Downing, our District State Senator, or an unknown car dealer, Hugh Gallen from Littleton, New Hampshire.

PICKING CORRECT CANDIDATE

Senator Del Downing or Car Dealer Hugh Gallen?

Both Candidates had heavily recruited me for support for the upcoming New Hampshire Gubernatorial election, as I was the C-Pac (Chiropractic Political Action Committee) Chairman.

They both attended the first-ever Pelham, N.H., Democratic Picnic, held at my home/office site, 100 Bridge Street.

The picnic was a tremendous success, but surrounded by controversies from the beginning, starting with the up-down-up Democratic banner strung across Route 38 (also Bridge St.).

Only recently was I informed that the editor of this book, Sam Weisberg, was in attendance with his two children for the food and pony rides in our back yard. (Yes, he purchased a family ticket.)

DEL DOWNING was our District State Senator, and the N.H. Senate Minority Leader. He had been very friendly to us. He even had a **RESOLUTION** drafted in the State Senate, recognizing Representative Claire's and my 25th wedding anniversary.

I remember distinctly, when Del cornered me at the picnic and asked me for our C-Pac support, relating to the Resolution and our friendship. My reply was that we could not support him because he had supported the "Straight Chiropractic" movement. Over the two years prior, he had supported the legislation to allow students from non-accredited Chiropractic Schools to be allowed into New Hampshire, making us a dumping ground for unqualified practitioners.

Del continued that he would disassociate himself with the "Straights" and support our "New Hampshire Chiropractic Association" (NHCA).

However, I had already been aware of the heavy financial and physical support he received from Straight Chiropractors, and felt that he was trying to play both sides. It was difficult, but I did tell him we could not support him.

GALLEN VS DOWNING

INTERESTING STATISTICS

HUGH GALLEN

Lost	1972 House of Representative
Won	1973 Special election House of Representatives
Lost	1974 Governor
Lost	1976 Governor

DEL DOWNING

Won	1969-1970 State Senate
Won	1971-1972 State Senate
Won	1973-1974 State Senate
Won	1975-1976 State Senate
Won	1977-1978 State Senate

MY CHOICE? HUGH GALLEN, FOR GOVERNOR.

WHY GALLEN?

1. His strong belief in the Accreditation Process.
2. Having no previous ties with the straight organization.
3. The sincerity in his voice, when we were standing facing each other (actually, I was on the first step to be at his eye level) he said, "Dr. Plomaritis, even if you don't support me and I should become Governor, I will support Accreditation, however, if you do support me, and I'm the Governor, I'll hand carry that sucker (Accreditation Bill) through the Senate". Those words from Hugh Gallen were so pronounced, they were implanted in my brain, so much so, that to this day they have never been erased.

I had plenty of opposition from within the Chiropractic ranks, primarily because seventy-five to eighty percent of the Chiropractors were Republicans as were their patients.

My contention was that we had supported Governor Meldrim Thomson (R) in the two previous elections and he then went back on his word to Dr. Herman Olsen, our previous C-Pac Chairman. Governor Thomson had promised to support Dr. Olson's designee to the Chiropractic Board of Examiners, a major step toward bringing accreditation to the state of New Hampshire. Not only did he ignore Dr. Olson's designee, he appointed one of the radical demonstrators apposing accreditation. I repeated this over and over to my Chiropractic colleagues, throughout the campaign.

NOTE: As I was writing this story, I could actually reflect going into the upcoming NHCA convention so pumped up and preparing to rile up my troops with the following information:

A) The decision to Support Hugh Gallen for Governor and

B) The consummation with Park Haggerty for the Gallen-Mobile.

I never expected the Great Honor that my fellow Chiropractors had planned for me.

HONORS FOR TITUS

NAMED CHIROPRACTOR OF YEAR

By Manchester Union Leader

PELHAM, N.H.—August 9, 1978—The New Hampshire Chiropractic Association, at its annual convention, honored Dr. Titus Plomaritis by naming him **CHIROPRACTOR OF THE YEAR.**

Dr. Plomaritis, who resides and practices here at Bridge Street, is an active member of the N.H.C.A., serving as its vice-president.

As an active Democratic supporter, he is involved in many state and political functions, and he is a director of the Pelham Bank and Trust.

RECEIVING AWARDS this weekend at the N.H. Chiropractors Convention were Dr. Titus Plomaritis, Pelham chiropractor who was selected chiropractor of the year, and Clifton Noyes, vice president of the Manchester Union Leader. The Manchester newspaper was awarded a certificate of appreciation for the space it has provided the chiropractic profession for 12 years. Mr. Noyes accepted the award for publisher William Loeb.

HOLDS A HOST OF MAJOR MEMBERSHIPS

DR. PLOMARITIS holds active memberships in the American Chiropractic Association, Massachusetts Chiropractic Society, Maine Chiropractic Association, Florida Chiropractic Association, American Corrective Therapy Association, N.E. Association for Physical and Mental Rehabilitation, National College Alumni Association, Foundation for Chiropractic

461

Education and Research, Council on Roentgenology of the A.C.A., Boston University Varsity Club, Boston University Century Club, Lowell Rotary Club, Past President of the Lowell High School Boosters Club, University of Lowell Alumni Association, St. John's Hospital Men's Guild and president of the Raymond E. Riddick Memorial Scholarship Foundation.

He is also a Diplomat of the National Board of Chiropractic Examiners and a certified chiropractic orthopedist of the A.C.A.

GAINED FAME FROM THE SPORT OF FOOTBALL

DR. PLOMARITIS is also no stranger to the limelight of athletic fame.

The name, **"TITUS PLOMARITIS,"** is well-known in the New England area among high school and college football fans. It was a common sound to hear the loudspeaker system blaring his name as he ran for another touchdown and kicked extra points and field goals during the Lowell High School and Boston University football games of the late 1940's and early 1950's.

In fact, it is these years as a football hero that brought Dr. Plomaritis national fame recently as the famous country comedian, Jerry Clower, recalls his days on the gridiron at Mississippi State University playing against Titus and this is included in his latest comedy album.

SEVERAL COLLEGIATE ACCOMPLISHMENTS

DR. PLOMARITIS is a graduate of Boston University, class of 1953, where he received his B.S. Degree. He received his Doctorate in Chiropractic from the Chiropractic Institute of New York in 1957 and is now enrolled at the University of Bridgeport, where he will soon earn his Master's Degree in Bio-Nutrition.

As a member of the N.H.C.A., and as part of his personal philosophy, Dr. Plomaritis is an avid supporter of the continuing education program as an avenue of personal and professional growth.

A PROUD FAMILY MAN

Dr. Plomaritis is married to Claire (Hebert) Plomaritis, the first woman state representative from Pelham. They have four children—Titus, Jr., now enrolled in medical school; Steven, attending Kirksville College of Osteopathic Medicine; Lyn, a Special Education teacher working on a Navajo Reservation in Arizona, and Diane, a sophomore at Boston College, majoring in political science.

DELIVERING FOR GALLEN
GALLEN-MOBILE, ALL THE WAY TO THE CORNER OFFICE

The **GALLEN-MOBILE** looks like a Volkswagen, drives like a Volkswagen and it is a Volkswagen. However, it gave us 15,000 miles of Mercedes Benz-like performance.

I went to the Park-Haggerty Porsche-Audi-Volkswagen dealership in Lawrence, Massachusetts, and convinced Richard (Dick) Haggerty, to donate one of his used Volkswagen buses for Hugh Gallen's campaign for Governor of New Hampshire.

My pitch was that it could be classified as free advertising because I planned to drive it throughout the entire state of New Hampshire to deliver signs and literature to my fellow Chiropractors. Dick discussed it with his partner and they even agreed to have their sign painter do the professional lettering. I mounted loud speakers on the roof and within one week of the Pelham picnic I was at Gallen Headquarters picking up signs for delivery.

GALLEN-MOBILE, L to R—First Lady of New Hampshire Irene Gallen, Dr. Titus Plomaritis, and NH State Representative Claire Plomaritis.

I drove the Gallen-Mobile on Tuesdays, Thursdays, Saturdays and Sundays, right up to election day. **FRANK ELLIOTT** rode shotgun most of the time, and was in his wheelhouse with the microphone in his hands. Frank had a great voice and the wit of a comedian, and when he couldn't make it, I'd either have Dr. Ed O'Malley, Dr. David Letellier or Dr. Vincent Greco travel up to the North Country with me.

JOINING THE COMMITTEE

It was about two weeks into my commitment to the "Gallen for Governor" campaign when Walter Dunfey asked me to become a member of the "Gallen for Governor Finance Committee". It was made up of about ten businessmen who had regular meetings to discuss every aspect of the campaign as well as make a financial commitment.

Walter and I had many discussions of our football playing days on the North Common in Lowell, Mass., on sandlot football teams—he and his brothers with the **"IRISH SHAMROCKS"** and my brother George and I with the **"GREEK BLACKHAWKS"**. He also told me about the greatest football game he ever saw.

YEP! You guessed it—the Lowell-Lawrence 1948 Thanksgiving game.

Now, back to my colleagues. When I first approached a chiropractor's office in Nashua, Frank Elliott, on the microphone, bellowed over the loudspeakers: "Dr. Hulslander, Governor Gallen appreciates your support!!" as I pounded a sign on his front lawn.

Dr. Hulslander then said, "Titus, I'm a Republican, as are most of my patients. Are you trying to put me out of business?" I then gave him a pep talk, repeating Hugh Gallen's pledge to support Accreditation. The doctor replied, **"OK, OK"**.

When I came back the following week the sign was gone, and I pounded in another sign. With Frank Hulslander's office, it took five weekly visits, pounding in five new signs. It was a little frustrating at first, but eventually the signs remained in place.

DISTRIBUTING THE LITERATURE

Especially helpful were the explanatory brochures for the various Chiropractors' offices waiting rooms that were provided by the American Chiropractic Association.

They were brief and easy reading with great pictorial explanations that related to properly trained Chiropractors from the Accredited Chiropractic Colleges, recognized by the United States Department of Education, to protect consumers from unqualified practitioners.

Directly next to that stack was a stack of Hugh Gallen's flyers with his handsome face on the cover and in bold print was printed his **SUPPORT OF ACCREDITATION.**

The doctors were amazed how quickly the literature—two stacks, one with the ACA information and the other with Hugh Gallen for Governor (Supporting Accreditation) were devoured from week to week.

We had about a hundred Chiropractors from our NHCA, but believe me, we made such an impact that it appeared as though we had thousands. The Gallen headquarters had to rerun the presses to provide me with additional brochures.

THE GALLEN-MOBILE PROVED BIG HIT

The Gallen-Mobile was the talk of the campaign. I had driven it just over 15,000 miles to every county in the state of New Hampshire, and even some of the Gallen staffers thought we had more than one vehicle because of the vast territory that was covered.

One of the comical moments of the campaign occurred on the Sunday just prior to election day. The Gallen-Mobile was the lead vehicle in the caravan parade of vehicles, moving at about five miles per hour, traveling all the main streets and bridges throughout Manchester.

I was driving, with Frank Elliott by my side with the microphone in hand, and my wife Claire as our passenger in charge of the **"SPIKED"** orange juice. Frank was entertaining, with a sundry of comical remarks directed at the pedestrians as we drove. The more orange juice he consumed, the better he performed.

One incident in particular was when we were crossing the Merrimack River, and Frank directed his remarks to two guys below, who were in a boat with fishing poles. "Say hello to the next Governor of New Hampshire!!" he shouted. They were showing approval by standing up and waving their arms, when one of them fell out of the boat.

When we got to the final stop, we were all in a happy mood, when Hugh Gallen, with his wife Irene by his side, came over to the Gallen-Mobile and asked, "Can we have some of that orange juice?"

THE BIG PUSH THAT GALLEN SAID, "DID IT"

We had each of our NHCA members address envelopes in their own handwriting go to 100 of their best patients with a very short message directed to each patient by name. It stated, **"VOTING FOR GALLEN IS VOTING FOR ACCREDITATION".**

We had each of the doctors put stamps on their envelopes, with the handwritten letters inserted. The envelopes were not to be sealed, rather, we inserted a Gallen pamphlet prior to sealing them.

With the help of our C-Pac captains, we collected, stuffed and sealed all the letters one week prior to the election, using Dr. O'Malley's house in Manchester for this huge project.

I remember the day that we—Doctors O'Malley, Letellier, Greco and myself—drove to Gallen Headquarters in the Gallen-Mobile with 10,000 stamped envelopes, and I said to Hugh, "These last-minute mailings to ten thousand loyal and dedicated Chiropractic patients is what will be the deciding factor in getting you elected as our next **GOVERNOR**."

FROM DISAPPOINTMENT
TO SUDDEN HAPPINESS

We invited our Pelham campaigners to our home to watch the election results, with hopes of some high fives and champagne toasts. The early numbers were devastating, so much so that all three of the major networks declared Mel Thompson the winner. Needless to say, we all were very discouraged and wondering what else we could have done.

Then, all of a sudden, the numbers on the screen started to change favorably, and a short while later the phone rang. It was Walter Dunfey, who said, "Titus, the late numbers coming in are all favorable. Bring your gang up in the Gallen-Mobile and celebrate with us".

Celebrating at Gallen Victory Party
Back row, L-R: Dr. Titus Plomaritis, Anita Greenhalge, Hal Lynde, Governor Gallen, Al Greenhalge. Front row, L-R: Irene Gallen, Frank Elliott, Terry Elliott, Diane Plomaritis, Frank Hebert, Rep. Claire Plomaritis, Carol Giglio.

Packing the bus with our dedicated Pelham volunteers, we drove to Gallen Headquarters with the loudspeakers blasting away. When we got there, the parking lot was jammed. However, a State Trooper who was expecting the Gallen-Mobile cleared a pathway directly to the door. We were escorted to Walter Dunfey's suite and were greeted with a great big hug, and Walter stated, "Titus, we did it, and we all know how hard you worked to make it happen."

Celebrating at the State House
Governor Gallen's victory party, Left to Right—Dr.Titus Plomaritis, Barbara Dunfey, Walter Dunfey, Chief Justice Richard P. Dunfey and his Wife. Front—State Representative Claire Plomaritis

Shortly thereafter was the victory celebration at the State Capitol. Here, Claire and I met another member of the thirteen Dunfey siblings from Lowell, Mass. The Honorable Chief Justice Richard P. Dunfey said in jest, "Titus, you better keep your nose clean, or I'll throw the book at you, for all the bloody noses I got when trying to tackle you on the North Common." He then related how he followed my career and complimented me for all my accomplishments.

I remember how Walter, three-timed married hotel tycoon, always had a happy face. At one of the Governor's fund-raisers, at Walter's Rye, NH, residence, he was commenting on how fortunate he was that his wife's name was Barbara. He explained, "I can't get in trouble if I talk in my sleep, because all three of my wives names are **BARBARA**".

GALLEN BENEFIT RAISES $5,000

PELHAM, N.H.—Jan. 24,1979—As a member of Governor Gallen's Finance Committee and Chairman of the New Hampshire Political Action Committee, I felt it was imperative to have a fundraiser here at the Pelham Inn to help decrease the Governor's campaign debt.

Frank and Terry Elliott served as Co-Chairman, along with Claire and myself for this very successful affair that included big band and traditional songs sung by the twenty-member Franco-American Chorale.

The Chorale, under the direction of Robert Gaudette of Salem, N.H., sang "God Bless America", "I'll Walk With God", "I Believe" and "The Battle Hymn of the Republic." Because of encore requests, the group also sang "Winter Wonderland."

The big band was provided by the Jack Keefe Orchestra. It played a number of nostalgic pieces, as well as some newer tunes.

More than 300 people paid $50 per couple to have dinner with Governor Gallen and his wife, Irene.

The party was held to give people who had not met the new Governor that opportunity, and to give his friends in this area the chance to help him eliminate some of his campaign debt.

ENTERTAINMENT was provided during dinner by Terry Elliott, who sang the Governor's favorite song, "Green Eyes". She was joined in a duet by her husband, Frank, in "You'll Never Walk Alone," followed by the Franco-American Chorale. Music was provided for dancing. Among the many paying tribute to the state's new chief executive were New Hampshire U.S. Senator John Durkin and Mass. State Senator B. Joseph Tully, resulting in a $5000 fundraiser toward the statewide goal of $50,000.

The Governor and Mrs. Gallen received guests from 9 to 11 PM, and the highlight of the evening was a souvenir photograph of every guest with Governor Gallen.

When we were promoting this fundraiser, we assured each ticket holder that they would have a picture taken with the Governor and the First Lady. Also, that I would have the Governor autograph each photo and then have it mounted on a beautiful walnut plaque.

GEORGE PORIER, a professional photographer from Lowell, who had always been supportive of my charitable endeavors processed my negatives and made 8x10 prints of each, at cost.

I then took them to the governor's office for his personalized notation and signature. I remember the look on his face when I brought over 100 photos with a paper clip attaching each of the donors' names.

At first he started to say it would take him forever, when I interrupted him with something like, **"YOUR EXCELLENCY, THESE ARE YOUR SUPPORTERS, YOU'LL NEED THEM FOR YOUR RE-ELECTION".** As usual, he followed up with, **"OK, OK, DR. TITUS PLOMARITIS,"** and, being a smart ass, added, "I suppose you want them today". I responded, "No, no, take your time, I'll pick them up tomorrow".

He then proceeded to personalize each photo exactly as the notes attached and then some, once he realized the efforts put into this fund-raiser. It took him about a week to complete this portion of the photo saga.

I then took them to a professional laminator in Everett, Massachusetts, who mounted them on beautiful walnut plaques, at special wholesale prices, of which Frank and I absorbed the cost. The finished products were then delivered in our **GALLEN-MOBILE**, with Frank on the microphone. I'd pull up in the parking lot of one of my Chiropractic colleagues or someone's small business and you'd hear over the loud speaker something like, **"GOOD MORNING, DR. GRECO. GOVERNOR GALLEN THANKS YOU FOR YOUR SUPPORT. WE'RE HERE TO DELIVER YOUR PERSONALIZED PHOTOGRAPH WITH THE GOVERNOR".**

Frank and I had oodles of fun delivering the autographed photos. It took us about one month, on Tuesdays and Thursdays, to complete the deliveries. We observed a multitude of different expressions and reactions from my Chiropractic colleagues and small businesses, mostly that we were deranged! While Frank was blasting away on the microphone in the parking lots with the mention of the Doctor's name or business, you could see people looking out of windows only to see the **GALLEN-MOBILE** smack in the middle of the parking lot.

YEAH! I can hear some of you readers in the background mumbling to yourselves, **"NO WAY!"** Well, let me briefly explain how we did it:

1— Pre set my camera on a tripod fifteen feet from the fireplace background, with a floor mark three feet closer, to stand on.

2—Al Greenhalge and Frank Elliott saw to it that couples were in line ready to quickly move into position with the Governor and Mrs. Gallen.

3—Terry Elliott would quickly move the next couple into place with the Governor and Mrs. Gallen and instruct them to look into the camera.

4—I would get their attention and take one picture.

5—Anita would quickly escort them to Claire's little table.

6—Claire would have a pre-numbered book of exposures to place names and phone numbers next to each designated number. She gave me the designated number to identify each negative and photo with the correct names for the Governor to personalize his inscription.

Another Celebration for the Victor!!!
NEW HAMPSHIRE C-PAC Members sharing victory with Governor Gallen and U.S. Senator John Glenn.
Left to right—Dr. David Letellier, C-Pac Chairman Dr.Titus Plomaritis, Governor Hugh Gallen, U S Senator John Glenn, Dr. Gerald Pierce, Dr. Vincent Greco, and in front—NH State Representative Claire Plomaritis."

GOVERNOR'S VERY FIRST APPOINTMENT

The sequence of events leading up to my appointment to the NHCBE were not only interesting but somewhat comical.

The procedure was that the Governor nominated a person and the Governor's Council elected or rejected that nominee. However, a nominee could not be elected on the same day. He had to wait for the next Governor-Council Meeting to act on the nominee's election, normally in two weeks.

Governor Hugh Gallen informed me that he wanted to nominate me to the NHBCE at his first meeting as Governor. However, there was no vacancy on the board.

The New Hampshire Chiropractic Association (NHCA), being the strong force behind getting the Governor elected, immediately set the wheels in motion, convincing one of the current board members to resign. His resignation letter had to be in the Secretary of State's office prior to the next Executive Council meeting, scheduled for January 9, 1979, the day I was to be officially nominated.

DR. EDWARD O'MALLEY and I drove up to Berlin, N.H.—seven hours round trip—to pick up Dr. Russell Wood's resignation letter, dated January 9, 1979.

As soon as the Governor's Council Meeting was called to order, Governor Gallen's attention was set on nominations to the various boards, of which there were more than fifty vacancies.

He immediately opened with, "I nominate Dr. Titus Plomaritis, Chairman of the Chiropractic Board of Examiners".

The Secretary of State whispered to the governor that the position of Chairman must be voted on by the Board Members. Then the Governor said, "I move to elect Dr. Titus Plomaritis to the board of Chiropractic Examiners".

The Secretary of State again leaned over to the Governor and informed him that you could not nominate and elect a person to a board at the same meeting, and that he must wait until the next executive Council Meeting.

Then the Governor said, **"ALL NOMINATIONS ARE CLOSED!"** The Council then went on to other business.

SUCCESSFUL DRIVE IN GAINING PROPER LICENSING OF N.H. CHIROPRACTORS

On January 17, 1979, the NEW HAMPSHIRE BOARD OF CHIROPRACTIC EXAMINERS met to elect officers and conduct the pending business of preparing the next licensing examination.

Dr. Titus Plomaritis was elected Chairman and Dr. Frank Hulslander was elected Secretary-Treasurer. Dr. Plomaritis ordered an immediate 30 minute recess.

NOTE: Following was the line of progression in New Hampshire successfully gaining only accredited chiropractors.

GOVERNOR HUGH GALLEN, swearing me in as his very first appointment, to the—New Hampshire Board of Chiropractic Examiners.

"Please pay attention to the minor details of this story, because I've been told this **INCIDENT SET A PRECEDENT**"—Dr. Plomaritis.

As pre-arranged by Governor Hugh Gallen, I went directly to his office and was cordially greeted by the New Hampshire Attorney General and the Director of Education. Governor Gallen had apparently prepped them on the purpose of our meeting. They were prepared to assist me in closing the flood gates of applicants from non-accredited Chiropractic schools as a means of protecting the consuming public from unqualified practitioners.

I made just two requests.

FIRST was to draft a letter, addressed to **STUDENT GUIDANCE COUNCILORS** and sent to every high school student guidance councilor in the state, making them aware of the **non-accredited** Chiropractic Schools that were soliciting students from New Hampshire. Meanwhile, at the same time, providing them with a list of the **Accredited Chiropractic Colleges** that were recognized by the United States Department of Education.— **REQUEST GRANTED!!.**

SECOND was to provide the NHBCE with an Assistant Attorney General to sit in at all our upcoming NHBCE meetings, as we would prepare and administer the next licensing examination.—**REQUEST GRANTED!!**

NOTE: It had been over a year since the previous NBCE licensing examination took place, and normally there were five or six applicants for each exam. However, this time there were thirty-eight candidates!!

It should also be noted that at that time the National Board of Chiropractic Examiners had not developed a Written Clinical Competency Examination (WCCE), or Part III.

Atty. Andrew Grainger, the N.H. Assistant Attorney General, accompanied me to the Secretary of State's office, and then into the conference room where the NHBCE held its meetings.

My opening remarks to the Board Members were, "With thirty-eight candidates waiting to take the N.H. Licensing Examination, we must be certain that they are clinically competent before issuing them licenses".

I continued with, "Therefore, I am proposing a Written Clinical Competency Examination to be prepared and administered by this Board".

Following a lengthy discussion, a motion was made and duly seconded, to prepare and administer a WCCE examination.—**MOTION PASSED, 3-2!!**

I then laid out the procedures that would follow, to assure all candidates a fair and equal consideration.

THE PROCEDURES TO BE FOLLOWED

1)—Have a representative of the Secretary of State's office assigned to the board. Floris Lannigan, Assistant Secretary of State, was assigned.

2)—Floris would issue I.D. numbers to each of the thirty-eight candidates, removing their names and school affiliations from the examination papers.

3)—Floris would write and send letters to the schools of these thirty-eight candidates, requesting a list of their clinical diagnostic text books.

4)—Have each Board Member write twenty-five questions, using those text books as reference, to verify correct answers.

5)—Have the full Board, with Floris and Assistant Attorney General Grainger present, when all 125 questions and answers were reviewed. Then we would mutually select the 100 multiple choice questions to be administered for that examination.

6)—Floris would then prepare thirty-eight copies of the WCCE examination and keep them in the Secretary of State's office safe, for safekeeping, until the date of examination.

FAST FORWARD: The exam was given, with Assistant Attorney General Grainger present, and all the exams were collected by Floris Lannigan, with no names of the candidates on them, only I.D. numbers. She kept them in her office safe until the following week, which was scheduled as a special meeting for the purpose of correcting the examination test papers.

Assistant Attorney General Grainger was again present as Floris distributed the examination test papers to the Board Members for correcting, again with no names, only I.D. numbers. Floris gave each of the Board Members an examination paper and read the correct answer for each question. When five were completed, she collected them and issued five more, until all thirty-eight papers were corrected.

NOW, THE FIREWORKS!!!

For the first time throughout the entire process, the names and school affiliations were associated with the I.D. numbers. **ONLY TWO** of the thirty-eight candidates received a passing grade, and one was from an Accredited Chiropractic College with a score in the mid-80's. The other had a score in the mid-70's.

While the Board was having a discussion on the high percentage of failures, Dr. Hulslander was reviewing the two examinations with passing grades, when he interrupted our dialogue rather harshly, with, "Whoever corrected this test paper made several mistakes!!" He was referring to the mid-70's test paper.

Re-evaluation of that test paper came up with twenty incorrect answers that were marked correct. Therefore, the only person to pass the exam was the **ONLY PERSON** from an Accredited Chiropractic College.

HOLD THE FORT, WE'RE NOT DONE

Now, to find out who corrected that test paper. With Andrew Grainger present, the Assistant Attorney General was concerned that one of the five examiners falsified a Licensing Examination.

Floris was able to help, as she explained that she issued the exams to the Board Members, starting with 1,2,3,4,5 and reversing 10,9,8,7,6 and before going any further, Doctor (?) admitted that he was the accused person. He tried to justify his action by trashing the Accreditation Process.

NOTE: Following due process, Dr. (?) was removed from the NHBCE by the Governors Executive Council.

Governor Gallen informed me that Dr.(?) was the **FIRST EVER** to be removed from any of the examining boards in the history of record keeping!! I will not mention his name to save him embarrassment. However, he is the same radical Chiropractor who spoke against the Accreditation Bill every time it was introduced, and the same Chiropractor who Governor Mel Thompson nominated just prior to leaving office.

THE SAGA CONTINUES WITH GREAT RESULTS

The board was sued by both the students who failed and the schools they attended on the grounds that the New Hampshire RSA316 only required passage of the National Board Parts I & II, proficiency in adjusting skills, and that WCCE was not a requirement.

FAST FORWARD AGAIN: Atty. Andrew Grainger, defending the Board's position, allocated several days in preparing me to take the stand on behalf of the NHBCE. It was like one of my football coaches running the same plays over and over, until able to run it to perfection.

Andrew, when prepping me, said, "We are going up against one of the best defense attorneys in the state, and whatever happens that may disturb you, **DO NOT PANIC—REMAIN CALM**".

The trial lasted two days in the N.H. Superior Court. **WE WON** and it was appealed to the Supreme Court, where Atty. Grainger presented the case on behalf of the Board—**AGAIN WITH SUCCESS!!**

That decision helped several other states in New England and throughout District III, and the friendships I established with the decision were instrumental in getting elected by my peers as District III Director to the National Board of Chiropractic Examiners.

AMERICAN CHIROPRACTIC ASSOCIATION (ACA)

Chiropractors Attend Workshop

Chiropractors from New Hampshire were among those in attendance for an American Chiropractic Association Workshop in Boston for officers and directors of state associations. Participants included, left to right: Dr. Titus Plomaritis, Director, New Hampshire Chiropractic Association and Chairman of Political Action Committee: Dr. Harold Keiffer of St. Paul, Minn. Moderator; N.H. State Rep. Claire Plomaritis of Pelham; Dr. Bromley of Audubon, New Jersey; Dr. Richard Vincent, Secretary, Mass. Board of Chiropractic Examiners; and Eloi Hamre, executive director, Minnesota Chiropractic Association.

The American Chiropractic Association has been my guiding light, and has never let me down when looking for assistance, going way back as a student member in the 1950's and then throughout my active professional (PCO) and political (NH-PAC) career, to my current status as a senior retired member. I thank the ACA for the betterment of the Chiropractic profession and for the benefit and protection of the millions of chiropractic patients in the USA.

I have many great memories of my earlier years, including those of my dear friend, **DR. RICHARD VINCENT**. I would like to share a couple with you. One in particular was in the mid-1960's when Massachusetts was on the verge of Chiropractic recognition.

It was exciting to listen to Dr. Vincent, representing the Chiropractic profession, debating the President of the Mass. Medical Association on the radio, practically weekly, relevant to the pros and cons of New Chiropractic Legislation to recognize chiropractors by establishing a chiropractic licensing board. He represented our profession extremely well, and I must say that he articulated considerably better than his bowling or golfing skills.

On several occasions we traveled together when attending a New England Convention, especially the open farm areas in Maine and Vermont. His favorite phrase when we would see an old broken down barn that looked over a hundred years old was, "Titus, that would make a great Chiropractic Clinic".

Another function that we attended together was an ACA workshop in Boston, which we attended as Officers and Directors of our respective states of Massachusetts and New Hampshire.

THE ACA AT WORK

The American Chiropractic Association (ACA), based in Arlington, Virginia, is the largest professional association in the United States representing doctors of chiropractic. ACA promotes the highest standards of ethics and patient care, contributing to the health and well-being of millions of chiropractic patients.

On behalf of its members, ACA lobbies for pro-chiropractic legislation and policies, promotes a positive public image of chiropractic, supports research, provides professional and educational opportunities for doctors of chiropractic, and offers leadership for the advancement of the profession.

The mission of the ACA is to preserve, protect, improve and promote the services of Doctors of Chiropractic for the benefits of patients they serve. Its purpose is also to provide leadership in health care and a positive vision for the chiropractic profession and its natural approach to health and wellness.

The ACA and its members seek to transform health care from focus on disease to a focus on wellness. This transformation results in positive outcomes for public health, including reduced morbidity, increased functional capacity, increased longevity of the U.S. population and significant reductions in health care costs.

EXPLAINING THE WORK OF CHIROPRACTIC

Chiropractic is a health care profession that focuses on disorders of the musculoskeletal system and the nervous system, and the effects of these disorders on general health.

Chiropractic care is used most often to treat neuromusculoskeletal complaints, including but not limited to back pain, pain in the joints of the arms or legs, and headaches.

Chiropractors practice a drug-free, hands-on approach to health care that includes patient examination, diagnosis and treatment. Chiropractors have broad diagnostic skills and are also trained to recommend therapeutic and rehabilitative exercises, as well as to provide nutritional, dietary and lifestyle counseling.

CHIROPRACTIC RESEARCH

A growing list of research studies demonstrate that chiropractic care is both safe and effective. Following are excerpts and summaries that shows that evidence strongly supports the natural, whole-body and cost-effective approach of chiropractic care for a variety of conditions:

FOR ACUTE AND CHRONIC PAIN—Patients with chronic low-back pain treated by chiropractors showed greater improvement and satisfaction at one month than patients treated by family physicians.

COMPARISON TO OTHER TREATMENT ALTERNATIVES— Acute and chronic chiropractic patients experienced better outcomes in pain, functional disability, and patient satisfaction. Clinically important differences in pain and disability improvement were found for chronic patients.

FOR HEADACHES—Cervical spine manipulation was associated with significant improvement in headache outcomes in trials involving patients with neck pain and/or neck dysfunction and headache.

FOR NECK PAIN—In a study to test the effectiveness of different approaches for treating mechanical neck pain, after one year approximately 53 percent of drug-free groups continued to report at least a 75 percent reduction in pain, compared to just 38 percent pain reduction among those who took medication.

COST EFFECTIVENESS—Low back pain initiated with a chiropractor saves 40 percent on health care costs when compared with care initiated through a medical doctor, according to a study that analyzed data from 85,000 Blue Cross-Blue Shield beneficiaries in Tennessee over a two-year span.

PATIENT SATISFACTION—Chiropractic patients were found to be more satisfied with their back care providers after four weeks of treatment than were medical patients.

POPULARITY OF CHIROPRACTIC—Chiropractic is the largest, most regulated, and best recognized of the complementary and alternative medicine professions. There is steadily increasing patient use of chiropractic in the United States, which has tripled in the past two decades.

CHIROPRACTIC EDUCATION—Educational requirements for the doctors of chiropractic are among the most stringent of any of the health care professions.

The typical applicant at a chiropractic college has already acquired nearly four years of pre-medical undergraduate college education, including courses in biology, inorganic and organic chemistry, physics, psychology and related lab work.

Once accepted into an accredited chiropractic college, the requirements become even more demanding—four to five academic years of professional study, and a significant portion of time is spent in clinical training.

DOCTORS OF CHIROPRACTIC who are licensed to practice in all 50 states, the District of Columbia, and in many nations around the world, undergo a rigorous education in the healing sciences, similar to that of medical doctors. In some areas, such as anatomy, physiology, and rehabilitation, they receive more intensive education than most medical doctors or physical therapists.

As part of their professional training, they must complete a minimum of a one-year clinical-based program dealing with actual patient care. The curriculum includes a minimum of 4,200 hours of classroom, laboratory and clinical experience.

Before they are allowed to practice, doctors of chiropractic must pass national board examinations and become state-licensed.

This extensive education prepares doctors of chiropractic to diagnose health care problems, treat the problems when they are within their scope of practice and refer patients to other health care practitioners when appropriate.

DR. BRASSARD INSPIRES AT N.H. CONVENTION

Dr. Gerald Brassard, President of the American Chiropractic Association, came to N.H., and gave an inspiring presentation at our annual NHCA Convention. He then expounded on how the New Hampshire Political Action Committee (NH-CPAC) could play a vital role in the **FIRST IN THE NATION 1980 PRESIDENTIAL PRIMARY.**

NH-CPAC's Vital Roll in Carter's Win Over Kennedy
L to R: Sitting—Dr.Joseph Horan, Dr. Titus Plomaritis, Chairman of C-Pac, Dr. Lorna Fuller, President of New Hampshire Chiropractic Association, Dr. David Letellier. Standing—Dr. Edward O'Malley, Dr. Gerald Pierce, Dr. Daniel Sullivan, Dr. Gerald Brassard, President of American Chiropractic Association, Dr. Douglas Nicoletti, Dr. Peter Bosen.

Dr. Brassard praised the NHCA and its affiliate, the NH-CPAC, for its role in the successful campaigning that played an instrumental role in Governor Gallen's election to the corner office of the state capitol. He continued with his praise and added that it is a must to support a candidate at every level of government who is a friend of the Chiropractic Accreditation

Process, which is the primary means of protecting the unsuspecting consumers from unqualified practitioners.

PRESIDENT CARTER—SUMMARY OF EVENTS

The following sequence of events explains my interaction with Hugh Gallen, the Governor of New Hampshire and Jimmy Carter, The President of the United States of America. These events were instrumental in the President removing the "**mandate**" in the Medicare Bill, "**ordered by a medical doctor**"; that allowed over 40 million chiropractic patients chiropractic services by choice, and without a medical prescription.

April 25,1979— White house (security lapel pin) allowing me to work side by side with president Carter's photographer, when in New Hampshire.

Oct.17, 1979—Talking to Pres. Carter on Gov. Gallen's hotline.

Oct. 20, 1979—Meeting with Chip Carter in Manchester, NH.

Oct. 21, 1979—Letter to Chip Carter, explaining the Medicare mandate and why I couldn't activate Chiropractic support for his dad's Primary re-election (requested by Chip and mailed to his coded address).

Nov. 29, 1979—First Lady, Rosalynn Carter, at our home for a coffee with over 500 loyal supporters. Additional info hand carried to the President.

Dec. 27, 1979—White House acknowledgment of correspondence.

Dec. 27, 1979—Additional White house correspondence.

Jan. 2, 1980—Eizenstat's letter, informing me of the removal of the mandate.

Jan. 8, 1980—Letter to Chip Carter, acknowledging with extreme gratitude, Stu Eizenstat's letter relating to the removal of the mandate "ordered by a medical physician".

Jan.8, 1980— Sample Letter, sent to Chiropractors throughout the United States by the American Chiropractic Association. **"WHY YOU SHOULD VOTE FOR JIMMY CARTER"** in the upcoming primaries.

Feb. 26, 1980—Wins New Hampshire Primary.

Aug. 14, 1980—Wins the nomination at DNC as **"TEDDY QUITS"**.

THE WHITE HOUSE

WASHINGTON

25 April 1979

Titus —

Guard this pin well. Notify
any Secret Service agent
immediately if it's lost.
I'll be looking for you
during the Sponsors' Roundtable.

Anne Edwards

The White House—Letter from Ann Edwards, re: lapel security pin.

TITUS AND JIMMY TALK

PRESIDENT CARTER COMES TO TITUS' AID

I remember one day when I was at the New Hampshire State House and **GOVERNOR HUGH GALLEN** asked me to step into his office. He asked if I could organize my troops as I did for his "Governor's Campaign."

Hugh continued with his presentation and emphasized the fact that **TED KENNEDY** intended to run against President Carter in the primary although it was not customary to run against an incumbent in your own party. Being from Massachusetts, Ted Kennedy figured to win N.H., a direct neighboring state where he was very popular, wanting to embarrass Jimmy.

I explained to the Governor that I would not be able to rally my chiropractors because there was a clause in the proposed Medicare Bill that only provided chiropractic services to Medicare patients if they were referred by a medical doctor.

Hugh then picked up the phone and called Jimmy Carter's direct line, spoke to his immediate associate, who recognized Hugh's close relationship with the President, and she said, "The President is meeting with members of his cabinet, but I'll notify him and he will call you back during a break".

About two minutes later the phone rang and the President said, "Hugh, what can I do for you?" Gov. Gallen answered, "Titus is here in my office and he said that he cannot rally his troops because of a clause in the proposed Medicare Bill. Let me put him on the phone to explain." He handed me the phone and before I could say anything, the President said, "Titus, we already have chiropractors included in the Medicare Bill."

Then, I was able to explain what the problem was, **DIRECTLY TO THE PRESIDENT OF THE UNITED STATES**. "Yes, Jimmy, we are included. However, there is a catch clause that says provided the patient is referred by a medical doctor".

Then, the President stated that he was only told that the chiropractors were included in the Medicare Bill. He then asked me to get together with his son, Chip, that weekend, as he would be up in New Hampshire for Hugh's fund raiser. He suggested that I, "explain to Chip the language that would correct the problem." I thanked him for his sincere interest and said I would see Chip on Saturday evening.

Left to right: Governor Hugh Gallen, Chip Carter, (President Jimmy Carter's son) and Dr. Titus Plomaritis.

Then came Saturday evening and I was all excited because I thought all I had to do was talk to Chip Carter and it would be all resolved. Well, there is a little more to this episode, which I will explain.

THE PRESIDENT MAKES A PROMISE

First of all, the function was a fundraiser for Governor Hugh Gallen's re-election. It was held at Dunfey's Wayfarer Banquet/Convention Center, in Bedford, N.H. The place was packed and everyone there was anxious to see and shake hands with **CHIP CARTER**, President Jimmy Carter's son, as well as the Governor. This didn't provide for a quiet, one-to-one explanation of the Chiropractic Medicare Bill.

I felt a little disappointed, and wondered if they were playing games with me, when suddenly the Governor, with Chip by his side, walked over to me and Chip said, "Titus, Dad told me to talk with you and to assure you that whatever the problem is with that Medicare Bill, **HE WILL FIX IT.**"

He then proceeded to tell me that with all the commotion in New Hampshire, and with his scheduled additional appearances, he would not return to Washington until the middle of the following week. With that said, he suggested that I send him a one page letter, with a brief explanation of how the bill was currently worded and what it would take to correct the problem. He gave me his address and told me to be sure and include the little code number on the right lower corner of the envelope so my letter would go directly to his desk for immediate attention.

NEW HAMPSHIRE CHIROPRACTIC POLITICAL ACTION COMMITTEE

NHCPAC

October 21, 1979

Mr. Chip Carter
White House
Washington, D.C.

Dear Chip,

It was a pleasure seeing you and talking with you again at Mary Louise's "Roast."

Your interest in my concern over the chiropractor's role in the Administration's proposed National Health Insurance Plan was heart-warming and encouraging.

As I discussed with you, under Title I, Part A, Section 1801 of the NHI proposal, "chiropractic services" would be covered if "ordered by a physician."

This provision is unacceptable to the chiropractic profession since in all proba- bility, a medical doctor will not refer or. order a patient to a chiropractor. The American people will be denied the right and freedom to "choose" a chiropractor. Some forty million Americans freely and intelli- gently seek chiropractic care presently in all fifty states without a mandatory referral from a physician.

The chiropractor merely wants parity in treating patients within his scope of practice.

As chairman of NHCPAC I have been unable to rally my forces to support your dad here in New Hampshire in view of his Administration's proposal. We would like to play as vital a role in your dad's campaign as we did in Gover- nor Gallen's.

Letter to Chip Carter, explaining the Medicare mandate and why I couldn't activate Chiropractic support for his Dad's Primary re-election. (requested by Chip and mailed to his coded address)

TITUS

Chip Carter, Oct. 21, 1979   p.2

    Governor Gallen was the guest of honor
at the Annual New England Council Chiropractic
Convention in Bedford on Saturday, October 20th.
He electrified the audience with his positive
and stimulating remarks about involvement in
government and his sincere interest in conveying
our profession's concerns to the President.

    The removal by your dad of the mandate
"ordered by a physician" would surely generate
chiropractic support throughout the nation,
beginning most emphatically here in New Hampshire.

    I thank you, Chip, for taking the time to
share the concerns of the chiropractic profession
with your dad, our President.

    Looking forward to seeing you next time
you're in New Hampshire, I remain

        Sincerely,

        Titus Plomaritis, D.C.
        Chairman

Letter to Chip Carter, explaining the Medicare mandate and why I couldn't activate
Chiropractic support for his Dad's Primary re-election. (requested by Chip and mailed
to his coded address)

PLOMARITIS FAMILY HOSTS FIRST LADY

EVENTS THAT LED UP TO THIS PELHAM FUNCTION

1—Ted Kennedy (D) in unprecedented run against an incumbent Democratic President
2—Governor Hugh Gallen asking for my help, from the New Hampshire C-PAC, as President Jimmy Carter's N.H. campaign chairman
3—The phone call from Governor Gallen's office to President Carter, relative to Chiropractic inclusion in Medicare.
4—Explaining the mandate of a medical referral.
5—Having me talk to Chip Carter on his forthcoming visit to New Hampshire for "Hugh's Fundraiser" weekend.

PELHAM, N.H.—November 29, 1979—All Pelham Democrats registered on the town's voter checklist were invited to a coffee hour, beginning at 6 P.M. at the Plomaritis' single-level ranch style home on Bridge Street, to greet First Lady Rosalynn Carter.

According to **MRS. CLAIRE PLOMARITIS**, the excitement had brought on the feeling of an early Christmas to her household.

ROSALYNN CARTER
Requests Your Presence for Coffee
at the home of

State Representative Claire Plomaritis and
Dr. Titus Plomaritis
Bridge Street, Pelham

Thursday, November 29, 1979
6 P.M.

Paid for/Authorized by Carter/Mondale Presidential Committee, Inc.
Lee Kling, National Treasurer

Invitation from the White House to attend a coffee at the home of State Representative Claire and Dr. Titus Plomaritis

Mrs. Plomaritis is one of Pelham's three state representatives, and she and her husband, **DR. TITUS PLOMARITIS**, are hosting Mrs. Carter as part of a daylong campaign blitz throughout New Hampshire.

Mrs. Carter, along with the President's mother (Miss Lillian), Vice-President Walter Mondale's wife (Joan), and the President's daughter-in-law (June), wife of son Jack, will be traversing the state in behalf of drumming up support for the President's re-election.

GOVERNOR HUGH GALLEN, the President's re-election campaign chairman in New Hampshire, will accompany Mrs. Carter here to Pelham.

WHY THE PLOMARITIS SPOTLIGHT?

The Plomaritis home was chosen as one of the stops because of its close proximity to challenger **SENATOR EDWARD M. KENNEDY'S** own home state, "in his backyard where many former Massachusetts residents have resettled," according to Mrs. Plomaritis.

Also, the Plomaritis' well-known reputation as "hard-working Democrats" earned them the honor of the First Lady's visit here.

Mrs. Carter will stay in Pelham for about 90 minutes, before moving on to Salem, N.H.

TITUS AND CLAIRE met the President and First Lady six weeks prior, when they were invited to Washington as guests of the Carters.

Rep. Plomaritis described Mrs. Carter as a "very gracious woman," and the President as a "great man."

When asked how a family gets through this kind of an important event. Mrs. Plomaritis noted **"WITH GREAT HELPERS,"** many of whom have aided the State Representative in her own successful bid for re-election.

ANOTHER IMPORTANT purpose to host such a major event in their Pelham home was to receive the Chiropractic support for the President, and also **"TO DEFEAT TED KENNEDY** in the first presidential primary in the U.S.A. (1980)," commented Dr. Plomaritis.

FOLLOWING ARE DR. PLOMARITIS' RECOLLECTIONS OF THE PREPARATION FOR THE FIRST LADY'S VISIT

About three weeks prior to Rosalynn Carter's scheduled visit to our home in Pelham, we received a request from the White House for a list of our Democratic supporters and friends whom we would like to invite to our home to meet the First Lady.

Prior to the First Lady of the United States coming to our home, a barrage of Secret Service agents came to Pelham. They scanned our property, front and back, and informed Claire and I not to receive any packages from anyone, including the UPS and our local post office, without their initial inspection.

BRINGING IN THE POLICE CHIEF

The security personnel asked us a bundle of questions, mostly related to if we had seen any strangers in the neighborhood or received any phone calls from strangers.

The agents apparently had already visited the local police station, because our Chief of Police, **RALPH BOUTWELL**, who also served on the Pelham Bank and Trust with me, kind of quietly discussed the big event coming to Pelham.

Chief Boutwell, a staunch Republican, hadn't got over the last two big political events in town—referring to Pelham's first Democratic Picnic in 1978, and then when the Governor came in by helicopter and landed in our backyard to attend my surprise fiftieth birthday party, in September, 1979.

He said, jokingly, "Titus, you screwed up the traffic bad enough with those two events, and now I'll have to put the entire police force on Bridge Street to address the traffic for this event."

Ralph and I were both incorporators of the Pelham Bank and Trust, and we sat next to each other at our weekly Bank Committee and Directors meetings. We did concentrate on bank business. However, during the coffee breaks it was **ALL POLITICAL!**

SETTING UP THE BIG EVENT

The day before Mrs. Carter's arrival in Pelham, her staff came to our home for last-minute instructions and a dry run of what we were to expect, where to stand and how to greet the First Lady when she stepped out of the vehicle. Most importantly, they gave us special identification pins to wear, with instructions to place them in a visible location—apparently for the benefit of the Secret Service agents.

Several Secret Service agents had visited our home a few days earlier, in order to familiarize themselves with all facets of the house, especially the entrances, and some of the family's furniture was cleared and removed.

Finally, several gallons of coffee and dozens of pastries arrived in advance of Mrs. Carter's entourage.

It was a cold evening, and our home was already packed shoulder-to-shoulder—way over the fire code limit—45 minutes prior to her arrival. The crowd outside on the front lawn extended out onto Route 38, which created a huge outdoor theatre. The traffic had been detoured by the Pelham patrolmen.

We had well over 500 people, standing out in the cold, just to get a glimpse and listen to Mrs. Carter's presentation.

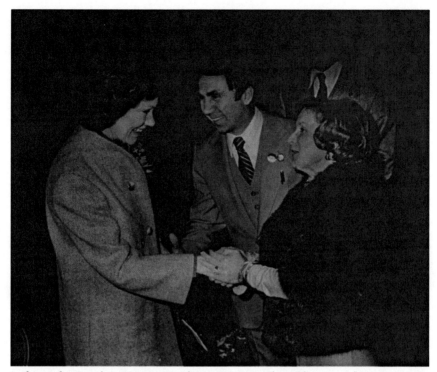

Left to right: Rosalynn Carter, Dr. Plomaritis, Rep. Claire Plomaritis. "Titus assisting Mrs. Carter as she was stepping out of the secret service driven vehicle in front of our home in Pelham, New Hampshire."

Anticipating this type of crowd, I had installed loud speakers and flood lights on the front of the house so the people outside would be able to listen to her presentation.

Now, inside, due to the huge crowd, they only allowed one camera man at a time alternating with the other two waiting in the wings.(ABC,CBS,NBC)

When Mrs. Carter concluded her presentation, she was made aware of the large crowd that was still out in front of the house. She then informed the Secret Service agents that she felt obliged to have them come through the house in some organized manner so that she could thank them on behalf of her husband, the President.

Now the comedy here was that everyone currently in the house, including our committee workers, had their coats and hats stored in one of the bedrooms, and once they were escorted out, the agents would not allow them to re-enter. My children had to throw the clothing out of the bedroom windows, which refreshes laughter every time the incident is discussed.

Mrs. Carter was very gracious in shaking hands and thanking each one individually as they were allowed into the house in an orderly manner.

Even though the affair extended an hour longer than they planned, she again was very gracious to accommodate Claire and me with a few photos and conversation. She thanked us several times for our help and loyalty to her husband, Jimmy, and to Governor Gallen.

First Lady of the United States, Rosalynn Carter, relaxing following a two hour coffee and presentation, with over 500 in attendance, at the home of Representative Claire Plomaritis and Dr. Titus Plomaritis.

SIDE NOTE: One of our neighbors who had received an invitation, had decided to take a shortcut and walk through our backyard, only to have one of the Secret Service agents, who had been stationed among the large shrubs at the rear of the house, startle him with a sudden grab from behind, in total darkness. He later related the incident to us, and stated how he had to rush home to change his stained underpants.

All in all, it turned out to be a highly-successful affair!!

THE WHITE HOUSE

WASHINGTON

December 27, 1979

Dear Dr. Plomaritis:

Thank you for the material which you gave to Mrs. Carter
during her visit to your home.

Since we understand that the previous information you sent
through Chip Carter is being handled by Stuart Eizenstat's
office, we have taken the liberty of transmitting this
additional material to his staff. They will be in contact
with you shortly.

With our warm regards,

Sincerely,

Rhonda Bush

Rhonda Bush
Director of Correspondence
for Mrs. Carter

Titus Plomaritis, D.C.
Chairman
New Hampshire Chiropractic
  Political Action Committee
Bridge Street
Pelham, NH 03076

White House letter from Rhonda Bush, acknowledging receipt of additional material
hand delivered by the first Lady.

THE WHITE HOUSE

WASHINGTON

January 2, 1980

Dear Mr. Plomaritis:

Chip Carter has asked me to respond to your concern about the Administration's policy on chiropractic benefits in the proposed National Health Plan. A number of Administration officials have met with representatives of the chiropractic profession over the past year to explore the appropriate role of chiropractic care in a National Health Plan. Based on those discussions, the initial specifications for the Administration's legislation were altered to provide a definite role for chiropractors. The intent was certainly not to severely limit public access to chiropractors.

Based on your comments and those of the American Chiropractic Association and the International Chiropractors Association, we have reviewed the actual legislative language of the NHP bill and have found that the original intent was not met. The Department of Health, Education, and Welfare very soon will provide a technical amendment to the Administration's bill which would delete the requirement that reimbursable chiropractic services can be provided only on referral from a physician, as you have requested.

I hope that this letter clarifies the Administration's position and will be helpful to you.

Sincerely,

Stuart E. Eizenstat
Assistant to the President
for Domestic Affairs and Policy

Titus Plomaritis, D.C.
Chairman
New Hampshire Chiropractic Political
  Action Committee
Bridge Street
Pelham, New Hampshire 03076

cc: Chip Carter

Eizenstat letter from White House Letter to Titus announcing the removal of the mandate, "on order of a medical doctor", from the medicare bill.

Jan. 7 or 8—Calls from all three major TV networks, wanting interviews. They said, "When word got out that President Carter had Intervened in the removal of that controversial clause in the National Health Bill, we called the ACA Headquarters, and were told that it was orchestrated by a Chiropractor in New Hampshire by the name of **DR. TITUS PLOMARITIS.**"

TITUS ON MAJOR T.V. NETWORKS

Well, one of the three networks—I don't remember which one—came to Pelham with a camera crew and taped me in action for over an hour. It was edited down to about three or four minutes and appeared on **NATIONAL TELEVISION** the next evening.

Let me try to describe how it appeared on TV.

THE CAMERA ZOOMED IN on a Carter/Mondale poster that was in your face as soon as you enter the waiting room in my office. The commentator's voice said, **"NO!** This is not the Carter/Mondale Headquarters," and as he was still talking the camera began to focus on my exterior roadside sign, as he continued, "It's the office of Dr. Titus Plomaritis, Chiropractor, in Pelham, N.H."

Not wanting to bore you with every little detail, just let me enlighten you on a couple of somewhat comical incidents.

REMEMBER, the camera was running and following my every footstep. As we walked into the treatment room, I made a few notes on the patient's progress chart. As I prepared to give the patient a cervical adjustment—with my strong hands on her defenseless neck—I said to the patient, "Would it be okay to put a Carter/Mondale bumper sticker on your car?" Nine out of ten would say, "Yes, doctor," with a little fear in their voices.

NOTE: We asked the patients ahead of time for their consent to film our patient/doctor interaction.

I then walked out into the parking lot with the patient, cleaned the area with a cloth, and applied the bumper sticker. Then, back into the office for the next patient.

During the time that the camera was running, I received three phone calls from chiropractic members of the NHCA C-PAC (captains for those areas). Dr. Letellier from Manchester said, "Titus, I need another twenty-five signs," and I replied, "Okay, David, I'll have them on your doorstep tomorrow morning at 8 A.M."

Dr. Pierce from Exeter followed with, "Titus, we're running low on waiting room pamphlets," and I chipped in with, "Okay, Jerry, I'll be in your area Thursday".

And then it was Dr. Greco's turn, "Titus, what time will you be picking me up?"—It was his turn to ride shot-gun on my next trip up into North Country, to deliver signs and literature. I answered, "Vinnie, I'm making a quick stop at David's, should be there about 8:30."

Following the national T.V. showing, my phone was ringing off the hook for the next two days, from chiropractors across the U.S.A., my relatives, and friends, which made me feel real proud.

NEW HAMPSHIRE CHIROPRACTIC POLITICAL ACTION COMMITTEE

NHCPAC

January 8, 1980

Chip Carter
White House
Washington, D.C.

Dear Chip,

Where and how do we begin to thank you for your assistance in getting our message to your dad relative to the role of chiropractors in The National Health Plan?

I cannot express the overwhelming joy experienced upon receipt of the Jan. 2, 1980 communique from Stu Eizenstat relative to the Administration's amendment to the National Health Plan, deleting the requirement that reimbursable chiropractic services can be provided only on referral from a physician.

NHCPAC has embarked on a drive to re-elect Jimmy Carter President of the United States. We will make all our friends and patients aware of the President's concern for public accessibility to chiropractic health services.

Enclosed is a copy of a letter which is being circulated nationwide, beginning here in New Hampshire, in support of your dad's re-election.

Thanking you again for your wholehearted assistance and support, I remain

Sincerely yours,

Titus

(Dr.) Titus Plomaritis, D.C.
Chairman

PS Did you find my pictures on your bedroom chair yet??

cc: Stu Eizenstat

Letter to Chip Carter, acknowledging with extreme gratitude, Stu Eizenstat's letter relating to the removal of the mandate "ordered by a medical physician".

Dr. Titus Plomaritis, B.S., D.C.

Diplomate
National Board of Chiropractic Examiners

Member
American Chiropractic Association
New Hampshire Chiropractic Association, Inc.

Telephone 603 635-7763
BRIDGE STREET (RTE. 38)
PELHAM, NEW HAMPSHIRE 03076

January 8, 1980

WHY YOU SHOULD VOTE FOR JIMMY CARTER

On January 2, 1980 the Carter Administration removed from
the National Health Insurance Plan the requirement that
chiropractic services would be available only "on order of
a medical doctor."

By removing this requirement, President Carter is assuring
you of continued chiropractic health services under the
National Health Plan.

I am urging each and every Democrat and Independent voter
to thank Jimmy Carter by voting for his re-election as President
of the United States on February 26, 1980.

Thank you for your support.

Titus Plomaritis D.C.

(Dr.) Titus Plomaritis, D.C.

PLEASE RETYPE THIS "SAMPLE LETTER" ON YOUR OFFICE STATIONARY AND SEND TO YOUR PATIENTS IMMEDIATELY. CHANGE PRIMARY DATES TO COMPLY WITH YOUR RESPECTIVE STATES

A Sample Letter, sent to Chiropractors throughout the Unites States by the American
Chiropractic Association. **"WHY YOU SHOULD VOTE FOR JIMMY CARTER"**
in the upcoming primaries.

YEP! That's me under that hat, standing at the polls in Pelham, NH for 12 straight hours on the first in the nation primary. February 26, 1980.

FEB. 26, 1980— NEW HAMPSHIRE PRIMARY ELECTION—

We had 100 chiropractors and their families covering the polls in their respective communities. They would provide transportation, when needed, and would make phone calls to their patients to remind them to get to the polls, with a friendly message of, "Jimmy needs your vote."

RESULTS OF STATE-WIDE PRIMARY—

**CARTER—52,648,
KENNEDY—41,687.**

NEXT STEP

NATIONAL DEMOCRATIC CONVENTION
at Madison Square Garden,
August 11-14, 1980

NOTE: At the request of Governor Gallen, I ran for, and won, a N.H. delegate seat to the D.N.C.. It was a delegate vote, available to the Governor, in the event he needed it for President Carter.

THE HELLENIC CHRONICLE (FRONT PAGE) "AUGUST 14, 1980—**"HEADLINE— TEDDY QUITS"**—"Titus Plomaritis of Pelham, N.H., Holds Up New York Newspaper Showing Front Page Headline on the Democratic National Convention in New York."—Dr. Plomaritis is a native of Lowell and former grid star at Boston University. His wife is a New Hampshire state legislator".

THE FINAL OUTCOME The Democratic re-election nomination of President Carter was greatly aided by our Chiropractic support in New Hampshire and across the United States, when he instructed Stuart Eizenstat to remove the mandate in the Medicare Bill, that only provided chiropractic care to medicare patients when **"referred by a medical doctor."**

PLOMARITIS MADE AN ICC FELLOW; BLASTS UNACCREDITED SCHOOLS

Dr. Titus Plomaritis, left, receiving from Dr. Herman Olsen, immediate past president of the American Chiropractic Association, (ACA), the International College of Chiropractic award.

PELHAM, N.H.—January 6, 1981—Dr. Titus Plomaritis, a Pelham chiropractor and chairman of the New Hampshire Board of Chiropractic Examiners, has been received into the International College of Chiropractic (ACA) as a Fellow—the highest honor bestowed by his profession.

In honoring Dr. Plomaritis recently, **DR. HERMAN OLSEN**, past president of the American Chiropractic Association, made special note of the many personal sacrifices made by the Pelham doctor in his efforts to keep New Hampshire a progressive state and protect the consumer from unqualified applicants of unaccredited colleges.

COMING UNDER HEAVY ATTACK

DR. PLOMARITIS has recently been the victim of heavy attacks from members of his profession who have philosophical ties to several unaccredited chiropractic schools in the United States.

This small, but vocal group of chiropractors is trying to have Dr. Plomaritis removed as chairman of the Board of Examiners because of his stand in not allowing New Hampshire to become a dumping ground for unaccredited colleges.

According to Dr. Plomaritis, these graduates are being barred from practicing in all but a few states, and the Pelham doctor says **HE WILL NOT ALLOW** New Hampshire to be the only state in New England admitting

505

such graduates until such time as they are capable of passing state board exams being taken and passed by candidates of accredited schools.

"No special consideration will be given simply because one has not availed himself of an accredited educational curriculum," Dr. Plomaritis said.

"The citizens of New Hampshire are entitled to the same degree of protection and professionalism as our sister states afford their citizens," he added.

AN OUTSTANDING BACKGROUND

Dr. Plomaritis, a Lowell High School football star in the late 1940's, and a veteran U.S. Army Paratrooper, also holds degrees from Boston University—where he also was a standout on the gridiron—The Chiropractic Institute of New York and the University of Bridgeport. He is the president of the Ray Riddick Memorial Scholarship Foundation, one of the founding members and a director of the Pelham Bank and Trust Co., a member of both the Vesper Country Club—where he is an outstanding golfer—and the St. John's Hospital Men's Guild, as well as numerous chiropractic and rehabilitation organizations.

He is married to New Hampshire State Representative Claire (Hebert) Plomaritis and the father of four children.

THE GOVERNOR'S PERSONAL PHOTOGRAPHER

Titus Plomaritis, Official Photographer. State of New Hampshire.

The badge shown at left was issued to me as my identification as the **OFFICIAL PHOTOGRAPHER** for the State of New Hampshire.

The badge allowed me to penetrate the extensive security when **PRESIDENT JIMMY CARTER** came into New Hampshire, and after working side-by-side with the President's photographer and Secret Service agents a few times they knew me as **TITUS**, and allowed me to penetrate the roped area where the media was not allowed.

I overheard New Hampshire **GOVERNOR**

HUGH GALLEN, on several occasions, tell President Carter how we, Titus and his N.H. Chiropractic-PAC, were responsible for getting him elected.

I used my personal Nikon F2 camera with the power pack attachment when serving as the Governor's personal photographer for four years. I took over 2000 photos at a multitude of functions and activities in and around the State House and whenever the Governor had a special presentation to make (all at my expense).

I also was a Delegate at the **1980 DEMOCRATIC NATIONAL CONVENTION,** August 11-14, at Madison Square Garden in New York City. I spent time with Gov. Gallen and dignitaries at a number of fundraisers by the high-rollers in NYC and at the White House.

After the Governor passed away, I prepared a beautiful picture album, consisting of Governor Gallen's best photos and presented it to Mrs. Irene Gallen as a picture story of Hugh's **GREAT FOUR YEARS.**

Note: That album was the end of Titus the photographer, however the **BADGE** remains in my glove compartment with fond memories of **HUGH!**

My energies were next directed toward:
THE NATIONAL BOARD OF CHIROPRACTIC EXAMINERS

ELECTED TO NATIONAL BOARD

Dr. Titus Plomaritis

PELHAM, N.H.—March 18, 1982—Dr. Titus Plomaritis, a practicing chiropractor here for the past 23 years, has been elected to the position of director of District 3 of the National Board of Chiropractic Examiners.

District 3 consists of Connecticut, Delaware, District of Columbia, Maine, Maryland, Massachusetts, New Hampshire, New Jersey, New York, Pennsylvania, Rhode Island, Vermont.

Dr. Plomaritis, who will serve the three-year district director term, received a B.S. degree from Boston University in 1953, a D.C. degree from the Chiropractic Institute of New York in 1957, and an M.S. degree from the University of Bridgeport in 1979.

In 1978, Dr. Plomaritis was named New Hampshire Chiropractor of

507

the Year and has served as vice-president and chairman of the Political Action Committee of the New Hampshire Chiropractic Association. He is also a member of the state chiropractic associations of Florida, Maine and Massachusetts.

Dr. Plomaritis is also a member of the American Corrective Therapy Association and the New England Association for Physical and Mental Retardation. He has been chairman of the New Hampshire Board of Chiropractic Examiners since 1979.

NBCE DISTRICT III ELECTION

TITUS ELECTED NBCE DISTRICT III DIRECTOR

It is interesting **HOW, WHEN & WHERE** a District Director for the NBCE is elected.

Running for the position of Director of District III is no different than running for a legislative seat on the state or national level. The only difference is that the campaigning doesn't require Obama's or Romney's campaign budget. The winner is usually voted in by his or her peers at the annual NBCE Conference.

Remember, now that I had been the Chairman of the New Hampshire State Board of Chiropractic Examiners for three years. I had been sharing the results of our N.H. accomplishments with all my colleagues throughout my district and especially all of New England. This included a favorable N.H. Supreme Court Decision that allowed the NHBCE to administer **CLINICAL COMPETENCY** examinations to protect the consumers from unqualified practitioners. I was well known to all my colleagues throughout New England.

It should be noted that the delegates to the annual meetings are usually the Chairpeople of their respective state boards or their designee.

THE ELECTION PROVES SUCCESSFUL

DR. RICHARD VINCENT announced that he was not running for re-election, and he had informed me of that a few months earlier, so I could lobby for the necessary votes.

DR. VERNON WEBSTER, President of the NBCE, was conducting the meeting which included the election of Dr. Vincent's vacated Director's seat. It was a known factor that **DR. PAUL TULLIO** of Chicago was considered the **"GODFATHER"**, and it was impossible to get elected without his blessing.

I remember the election like it was yesterday.

Before heading to Atlanta for the annual NBCE meeting, I took Claire's advice and called all the delegates in my district and was assured of a slam-dunk victory.

Claire's experience as a State Legislator was very helpful because she could see all the lobbying going on by Dr. Tullio and some of his soldiers.

DICK VINCENT had just remarried and was on his honeymoon, and had assured me that his designee would vote for me, but it didn't happen. Then, another from Vermont switched under pressure. It all depended on the alternate delegate from Maine, who was told by Dr. Reader, Chairman of Maine's Board, "No matter how much pressure is put upon you, cast Maine's vote for Titus."

I WON THE ELECTION as District III Director, but did not win the confidence of Dr. Tullio, Chairman of the Board. I was on his shit list for the next two years, and was assigned to meaningless committees.

DR. JAY PERRETEN, Chairman of the WCCE committee, asked Paul to put me on his committee, being aware of my interest in the Written Clinical Competency Examination, especially with all the excitement that was generated by the New Hampshire Supreme Court Decision. Paul agreed.

When I got home from that first meeting, I contacted the same four board members that were responsible for my victory, Dr. Brent Owens of Maryland, Dr. George Paul of Connecticut, Dr. Louis Latimer of Pennsylvania, and Dr. Reeder of Maine, to apprise them of my committee assignment. We all had problems dealing with the same unaccredited schools, so we worked together to create and share a pool of WCCE questions, that came from diagnostic text books utilized by all schools, even if they were not accredited.

TITUS READS THE REPORT

Following two years of documented data, I prepared a forty-page committee report for the full board, making copies for each board member with a cover page that was presented by Chairman Jay Perreten.

When Jay, with a real **Texas accent**, stood up to give his report, he kind of chuckled, as the board members were mumbling about the contents and quality of the report they were thumbing through. He said, "Ah didn't do one page of that report. '**TAWTUS**' did the whole **GALDANG THANG** , so I want him to give the report!!"

That, my friends, was the beginning of what is now a more professionally created Written Clinical Competency Examination (WCCE), now called Part III and is either used, or required, in all fifty states.

The new NBCE International headquarters in Greeley, Colorado

A SALUTE TO GROWTH

May 18, 1991, marked the beginning of a new era for the National Board of Chiropractic Examiners. On that date, the cramped quarters of its previous facility officially became a thing of the past with the dedication of a new 25,000 square-foot international headquarters.

The National Board of the 1990s bears little resemblance to the one that was created almost three decades ago—on the surface, at least.

One can see the distinctively angular lines of the brick and smoked-glass NBCE headquarters even from a distance. It sits on one of the area's highest knolls, the U.S. and Colorado flags almost always held aloft by robust air currents. It overlooks a pond and fountain, and, farther to the west, the Rocky Mountains, whose summits remain snow-capped year 'round.

Upon arrival at the facility, a visitor ordinarily pauses to contemplate the brushed stainless steel sculpture that rises from the front plaza. Once inside, they speak to the receptionist in hushed tones, and allow their gaze to take in the spacious, serene and uncluttered atmosphere — so sharply in contrast to the cramped and increasingly inadequate quarters of the previous facility.

A closer look by the visitor would reveal that the switchboard continually flashes with incoming calls, many of them queries from the upcoming exam's 5,000-or-so applicants. A closer look would reveal the NBCE operations in full swing, bustling behind closed mahogany doors that provide an illusion of inactivity.

Behind each polished door, within each National Board director and employee, can be found something of that same staunch, almost compulsive, commitment to the National Board that its founders demonstrated so well back in 1963. This is the foundation upon which the National Board was built, and the standard it still maintains.

As it enters a new era in its impressive new facility, today's National Board is undoubtedly on organization of enterprise, dedication and substance, and so much more than just another pretty face.

ALTHOUGH THE NBCE HAS SCANNED, SCORED, AND ANALYZED ITS EXAMINATIONS ENTIRELY IN-HOUSE SINCE 1987, THESE OPERATIONS WERE ONCE PERFORMED AT THE UNIVERSITY OF NORTHERN COLORADO.

THE NBCE'S FIRST PERMANENT HOME WAS LOCATED IN CHEYENNE, WYOMING.

IN 1987, THE NATIONAL BOARD MOVED ITS HEADQUARTERS TO GREELEY, COLORADO. THE DECADE THAT FOLLOWED BROUGHT MANY NEW NBCE SERVICES TO THE PROFESSION—AS WELL AS OVERCROWDED CONDITIONS.

IN 1991 THE PRESENT NBCE FACILITY WAS DEDICATED.

DESIGNED BY THE AWARD-WINNING ARCHITECTURAL FIRM OF LARRY STEEL ASSOCIATES AND BUILT BY HENSEL PHELPS CONSTRUCTION COMPANY (BOTH BASED IN GREELEY, COLORADO). THE NEW NBCE INTERNATIONAL HEADQUARTERS OFFERS OPERATIONAL SPACE GEARED SPECIFICALLY TO THE UNIQUE REQUIREMENTS OF A SECURE TESTING ORGANIZATION.

SHOULD IT EVER BE NEEDED, THE BUILDING AND SITE OFFER ROOM FOR EXPANSION.

NBCE PRESIDENT PRESIDES OVER FACILITY DEDICATION

NBCE President Dr. Titus Plomaritis, serving as master of ceremonies of the NBCE's dedication ceremonies, created the National Board's growth

A 24-FOOT STAINLESS STEEL SCULPTURE WAS SET IN PLACE ON THE DAY OF THE SPRING EQUI-NOX, MARCH 22, 1991. ENTITLED "EQUINOX", MEANING THE PAS-SAGE FROM A TIME OF DARK-NESS INTO A TIME OF LIGHT, THE SCULPTURE SYMBOLIZES THE JOURNEY OF CHIROPRACTIC INTO THE ILLUMINATION OF KNOWL-EDGE. THE ORIGINAL WORK WAS CREATED BY COLORADO SCULP-TOR DON GREEN.

efforts throughout the profession, and to those present in spirit and lasting memory.

"We dedicate this facility to all who are present". He said, "to our fore-bearers who sacrificed uncounted personal hours and immeasurable resources to create an independent institution that specializes in the production of valid academic testing for the profession. And we dedicate this building to every other individual—past present and future— who gave and who gives undaunted and inspired pursuit to attaining superior chiropractic health care for all the world".

After recognizing by name each former director of the NBCE, Dr. Plomaritis told those assembled, "This structure is symbolic of 30 years of hard work by dedicated National Board people and their colleagues. These individuals met challenge followed by challenge to learn, to grow, and to succeed. These individuals satisfied the demands of the profession to keep advancing."

CHAIRMAN SEES IMPORTANT MESSAGE IN NBCE PROGRESS

The words of Paul M. Tullio, D.C., NBCE Chairman of the Board, were brief but meaningful as he addressed the dedication audience May 18th.

"We are proud of this building — proud of what it represents, a great profession and its people. We are proud of the teamwork it displays, between the board of directors, the administration, the staff and the profession itself, people who worked together to fulfill a great need.

"We are proud of the stewardship that it signifies, for without that stewardship, the funds would not have been available. And because of that stewardship, the building will be free of indebtedness, a significant accomplishment.

"We are proud that the board of directors allowed a dream to come true — a dream that someday we would be proud of."

"We are proud because this structure sends a message, and that message is **THAT CHIROPRACTIC MUST BE TAKEN SERIOUSLY, THAT CHIROPRACTIC IS AN IMPORTANT PART OF SOCIETY, THAT CHIROPRACTIC IS NECESSARY, AND THAT CHIROPRACTIC IS HERE TO STAY!"**

BRENT OWENS, D.C. President, Federation of Chiropractic Licensing Boards (FCLB) made an official announcement to the profession. "On this day, we mark the dedication of our first corporate headquarters". What makes this day so significant is that, for the first time in 58 years, we have a permanent home".

Dr. Owens spoke of the 1,200 square feet of office space designed into the NBCE facility for lease to the Federation as its national headquarters. The furnished and fully-equipped offices have their own outside entrance, reception and conference areas.

"Yes, we are home at last", said Dr. Owens over hearty handshakes. "It is a day when dreams and visions are realized in the form of brick and mortar. Through the stewardship and sacrifices of our volunteers and staff, we have moved into a new era of service to chiropractic regulatory boards."

Following Dr. Owens' presentation, Dr. Plomaritis took the podium, and compared the assistance provided by the National Board to that of a young athlete who had attained success.

"What do they do to share a part of their success and show their appreciation for a lifetime of support? If the parents have no resources other than their strong belief in them, they help those parents. They may provide those parents with a new home. It's a dream every prodigy has," Dr. Plomaritis told those present.

"We now have an opportunity to show our appreciation of support and guidance from our parent organization by providing them with a home", he added. "And now on May 18, 1991 ... we mark and celebrate another milestone— another achievement for the profession".

ANDRE AUDETTE, D.C., chairman of the board of the Quebec Chiropractic Licensing Board and immediate past president of the Canadian Federation of Chiropractic Regulatory Boards, was on hand at the dedication of the NBCE headquarters.

Dr. Audette expressed his Board's appreciation for the NBCE's cooperation for the past 17 years. "The National Board even went so far as to have our exams translated into French at the University of Colorado," he said. This helped us tremendously, since our experience in conducting examinations was very limited following our legalization in 1973".

U.S.SENATOR HANK BROWN was among the speakers at the dedication. His opening remarks, "Dr. Plomaritis just stole my thunder, because I was prepared to speak on the history of the **EQUINOX**".

Senator Brown graciously switched gears and praised the NBCE for it's accomplishments and for building it's headquarters in Colorado.

The management staff was comprised of Janet Booth, Manager of finance and computer operations; Pamela Kurtz, Administrator; Sharon Crowell, Executive Assistant; Mark G. Christensen, PH.D., Assistant Executive Director and Director of Testing; and Horace C. Elliott, Executive Director.

A LEGACY OF DEDICATION

The National Board of Chiropractic Examiners extended its sincere appreciation to the following former officers and directors for their years of dedicated service to the NBCE and the chiropractic profession.

JEROME AUERBACH, D.C., DEVERE E. BISER, D.C., M. E. CALHOUN, D.C., M.B. DEJARNETTE, D.C., HOWARD FENTON, D.C., JACOB A. FISCHMAN, D.C., ARNOLD M. GOLDSCHMIDT, D.C., C. ROBERT HASTINGS, D.C., GORDON HOLMAN, D.C., WILLIAM KALAS, D.C., MARTIN LAWRENCE, D.C., GARY LEDOUX, D.C., KENNETH LUEDTKE, D.C., CHARLES LYNCH, D.C., DONALD MCKELVEY, D.C., VICTOR MARTY, D.C., JAMES MERTZ, D.C., S.N. OLSON, D.C., JAY H. PERRETEN, D.C., JAMES C. PLOCH, D.C., J.N. RIGGS, D.C., ROBERT RUNNELLS, D.C., EDWARD M, SAUNDERS,

D.C., S.H. SCHICK, D.C., LEWIS TAWNEY, D.C., RICHARD E.
VINCENT, D.C., PAU VOGEL, D.C., VERN WEBSTER, D.C., HENRY
G. WEST, D.C., TOM L. WORKMAN, D.C., REX A. WRIGHT, D.C.

NATIONAL BOARD OF CHIROPRACTIC EXAMINERS

The ❦ **Lamp**

SUMMER /FALL 1992   NATIONAL BOARD NEWSLETTER

Election of officers held at annual meeting

Dr. Frank Hideg, Jr., succeeds NBCE President Titus Plomaritis

The Election of officers highlighted the order of business at the 1992
annual meeting as Dr. Plomaritis handed the gavel over to Dr. Hideg who
had been working side by side with Titus for the past six years.

Brady & Belichick?

Dr. Belichick, **OPS!!** Dr. Tullio went to the podium and related that
"Dr. Latimer had a special presentation to make before Dr. Brady, **OPS!!**
Dr. Plomaritis steps down".

Not quite, it's **PLOMARITIS & TULLIO**, that teamed up as Titus
Plomaritis the Player/President, and Paul Tullio the coach/Chairman of the

Board, for an unprecedented run of six years,1986-1992, in the leadership positions at NBCE.

As a team they won more academic Super Bowls for the Chiropractic Profession, than Brady/Belichick won athletically for the New England Patriots.

COMPUTERIZATION

In 1986, a comprehensive study of the NBCE's computer capabilities was undertaken. This resulted in the hiring of a full time computer programmer, and marked the beginning of a major office automation upgrade at National Board headquarters. The NBCE now scores and analyzes its examinations entirely in-house, thus optimizing exam security and analytical capabilities. The NBCE now utilizes a forty-station computer network for data/word processing, information exchange and test item storage/editing. Additionally, desktop publishing is utilized by the Communication Department.

A state of the art mark reflex scanner was purchased for scanning of exam sheets, survey booklets and forms. The exam application is one of several items currently being redesigned in order to be submitted via the internet.

INTERNATIONAL ASSISTANCE

I was instrumental in administering a battery of exams similar to our state exam service in the fall of 1986 to twenty-four practitioners in Belgium who were seeking a means of recognition in that country. I also administered a retake exam in the spring of 1987.

THE PART III EXAM

In the fall of 1987, the part III (Written Clinical Competency Examination) was administered for the first time. The development of this exam was a large-scale project that called upon every National Board director, staff member and consultant. Now utilized by all fifty state boards, the part III exam joined the NBCE Parts I and II in making reliable, defensible test scores available in the chiropractic licensing process.

November, 1988 Board of Directors meeting in Fort Lauderdale, Florida. **THUMBS UP** was the celebratory sign for our Executive Director, Mr Horace Elliott, to proceed with finding a suitable location in Greeley, Colorado to build our new National Board of Chiropractic Examiners International Headquarters Building.

Board of Directors Meeting, November—1988
From left to right: seated, Ms. Sharon Crowell, Executive Assistant, Dr. Tom Workman, Dr. Paul Tullio. Dr. Titus Plomaritis, Dr. Frank Hideg Jr., Ms. Pamela Kurtz, Administrator. From left to right: standing, Dr. Louis Latimer, Carol Bailey, Dr. Jay Perreten, Dr. George Arvidson, Dr. James Badge, Dr. Donald Ross, Dr. Arnold Goldschmidt, Dr. Richard Carnival, Mr. Horace Elliott, Executive Director, Dr. Mark Christensen, Assistant Executive Director and Director of Testing and Evaluation.

SILVER ANNIVERSARY

The year 1988 marked the twenty-fifth anniversary of the National Board. That year I had a particularly full speaking agenda, including a presentation at the International Chiropractic Congress in Sydney, Australia.

A NEW HEADQUARTERS

In 1989 came the purchase of ten acres of land for a new NBCE facility. Ground was broken in early 1990, and the new office building was completed by the end of that year, nearly 200 guests from throughout the profession gathered on May 18, 1991, to dedicate the new international headquarters.

We also provided the Federation of Chiropractic Licensing Boards with their first ever permanent headquarters, in the headquarters building in Greeley, Colorado.

THE PRACTICAL EXAM AND JOB ANALYSIS SURVEY

Also in 1989, the NBCE began the Practical Exam Feasibility Study. As part of that study, we thoroughly researched the subject and completed the foundation of a full-scale Job Analysis.

1991 saw the distribution of a Survey of Chiropractic Practice questionnaire to over 9,000 practitioners as one stage in the Job Analysis and Practical Exam Feasibility Study.

PRACTICAL EXAM AND SPEC STUDIES

In 1992, a demonstration of a possible format for a national practical examination for the profession, was conducted and a presentation on the status of the Special Purposes Examination for Chiropractic (Spec) project was made before the annual conference of FCLB & NBCE.

SUMMARY

As you can see, the years spanning the **PLOMARITIS/TULLIO** leadership were indeed ones of **SUPER BOWL** heroics for the National Board. During those six years, the NBCE's services and capabilities grew significantly, while full-time staff increased from nineteen in 1986 to twenty-four in 1991. One very welcome addition was Dr. Paul Townsend as a second on-staff chiropractic consultant. The entire chiropractic community can be proud of the accomplishments which came about.

Dr. Belichick, **OPS!!**, Dr. Tullio went to the podium and related that it was Dr. Louis Latimer who chose this artist's rendition of **"THE DRIVE"** for this presentation.

Dr. Tullio, first made a few comments relative to when I was first elected to the National Board of Chiropractic Examiners in 1982. Stating that he had supported a different candidate in District III, because at that time, "I was not aware of the energetic, dedicated, non-stop, hands on work ethic that Titus would bring to the table". He then continued, "I was so impressed with his unselfish contributions, especially with the initial development of the **CLINICAL COMPETENCY EXAMINATION,** that I not only submitted his name, but also campaigned for him to be our next president".

Another short tale that brought laughter to the large gathering of FCLB and NBCE delegates, was when I, in typical up-beat tempo, made my first visit to the NBCE headquarters, as president. Dr. Tullio said, "It went something like this, my phone rang, it awakened me, it was about 6 o'clock in the morning, with Titus on the other end, rambling non-stop, 'There isn't anybody here at the NBCE, I've been sitting in my car for over an hour, we got to do something about these guys not being on the job and it's after 8:00 AM.' I said, '**TITUS, RESET YOUR WATCH, IT'S ONLY 6 O'CLOCK.'**"

Dr. Louis Latimer was then called upon to make the presentation. He related that his first contact with **DR. TITUS PLOMARITIS**, was back in 1979, when I called looking for information about an unaccredited chiropractic school in Pennsylvania. Dr. Latimer related, "I asked, "who did you say you were?' Titus repeated his name and I then said, '**NO SHIT, WHO AM I TALKING TO?'** thinking it was Paul Mazzoni or one of my friends playing a joke on me".

Lou continued to inform the gathering, stating, "that call by Titus was the beginning of a great relationship that Beverly (his wife) and I have, with Titus and Claire, and is ongoing".

Note: Lou passed on in 1999, however, Claire and I have made it a policy to share time with Beverly twice yearly.

Dr. Titus Plomaritis and Dr. Louis Latimer, with his contagious smile.

Dr. Tullio, Chairman of the Board of Directors of the NBCE had granted Lou the authority of selecting a gift, for the outgoing president. Dr. Latimer, with the assistance of Bev, went on a search and came across this beautiful creation of **"THE DRIVE"** by **DOUG LEW** a famous artist, who immigrated from China at age 16 (1948), specializing in **WATER COLORS AND ACRYLICS.**

Dr. Latimer in making the presentation stated, "'**THE DRIVE**' is so becoming of Titus, the dynamo, who never downshifted his gears in his six years as President and was the **DRIVING FORCE** in bringing the **NBCE PART III** to fruition and our new **NBCE INTERNATIONAL HEADQUARTERS** to completion."

The Drive

Note: I have the photo with Lou and I, with our expressions of happiness, placed directly next to **THE DRIVE,** in my home office, so I will never forget this fun loving human being, who hated absolutely no one.

SPEAKING TO THE PROFESSION AS PRESIDENT OF THE NBCE

SPEAKING IN AUSTRALIA

SYDNEY, AUSTRALIA—October 13, 1988—Dr.Titus Plomaritis, president of the National Board of Chiropractic Examiners (NBCE), addressed the 1988 International Chiropractic Congress here on October 6.

The Congress, sponsored by the Australian Chiropractors Association, was held October 2-9 in conjunction with the Spine and Low Back Pain Symposium. Both events were part of Australia's bicentennial and coincided with the World Expo '88.

DR. PLOMARITIS spoke on the role of standardized testing in helping chiropractic educators and credentialing boards maintain the integrity of the profession. He shared some of the history of the NBCE, which recently completed its 25th year of service to the chiropractic profession.

UNDERGOING A BUSY SCHEDULE

Dr. Plomaritis, a most active NBCE president, has in the course of his six-year tenure of office, amassed over a quarter million air miles during more than 50 public appearances.

He has visited with students and faculties at nearly every chiropractic college, and has administered the first international NBCE exam in Belgium, which resulted in 24 Belgium chiropractors attaining an NBCE International Certificate of Academic Proficiency.

Dr. Plomaritis has attended FCLB meetings throughout the five districts of United States and Canada, hosted test committee meetings, chaired NBCE Executive Committee meetings, and observed exam administrations at various test sites.

Dr. Plomaritis spoke at the inaugurations of Dr. Donald P. Kern as president of Palmer College and Dr. James F. Winterstein of National College, and at the annual meetings of the Council on Chiropractic Education, the Federation of Chiropractic Licensing Boards (FCLB), and the American Chiropractic Association.

In addition, he hosted the Chiropractic College Council of Academic Officers during the National Board Day Forum, held in Davenport, Iowa.

FUTURE SCHEDULE ON TAP

On Dr. Plomaritis' upcoming agenda is a presentation at the joint FCLB-NBCE conference in Las Vegas, and he will also preside over the annual NBCE Board of Directors meeting in Fort Lauderdale, Florida.

Next month he is slated to travel to Colorado for NBCE Test Committee meetings, and to Illinois for the FCLB District 3 annual meeting.

"It is an extreme honor to represent the National Board at these various functions, and be able to observe firsthand the events that are shaping our profession," said Dr. Plomaritis.

MORE MAJOR ACCOMPLISHMENTS

Prior to serving as NBCE president, Dr. Plomaritis served two terms as NBCE District 3 director, and his efforts as co-chairman of the NBCE Clinical Competency Committee were instrumental to the development of the Written Clinical Competency Examination (WCCE), which recently saw its third national administration.

AS PRESIDENT OF THE NATIONAL BOARD OF CHIROPRACTIC EXAMINERS, I MADE OVER FIFTY PRESENTATIONS, MANY WITH A WRITTEN SCRIPT, PREPARED BY STAFF.

Two very special Presentations that were prepared by me and spoken from the heart with no written notes:

1. **HONORING DR. PADGETT**, HIS INVESTITURE AS PRESIDENT OF THE NEW YORK CHIROPRACTIC COLLEGE

2. **COMMENCEMENT ADDRESS** AT NORTHWESTERN
   CHIROPRACTIC COLLEGE

HONORING DR. PADGETT

Dr. Titus Plomaritis, President NBCE's Presentation at **DR. KEN PADGETT**'s Investiture as President of the New York Chiropractic College.

"Thank you Mr. Chairman, Ken Padgett, family, Invited guests and fellow colleagues.

"It is my privilege to be here today representing the National Board of Chiropractic Examiners, and also to highly congratulate the New York Chiropractic College on the occasion of Dr. Ken Padgett's investiture as President.

"Over my thirty-year career as a chiropractor, I've had many an opportunity to observe Dr. Padgett in action, and he has continuously impressed me with his bubbling personality and leadership qualities.

"As co-chairmen of the National Board of Written Clinical Competency Examination Committee, I had the distinct pleasure of working closely with Dr. Padgett when he was selected to be on the inaugural test committee.

"Through his expertise and efforts we were able to produce a Part III examination of high quality.

"Positions of authority, such as the Presidency of a Chiropractic College, carry a tremendous responsibility, therefore individuals chosen for those positions must be of high intelligence, credibility and dedication, because, you see, it's their example that sets our professional standards, and it's their lead that inspires and challenges the rest of us.

"Many good leaders, such as Dr. Padgett, pose such a compelling presence that they really draw us into their path of distinction, rather than prodding us into it.

"I remember a story of a sales manager who was listening to a disgruntled trainee complaining to his supervisor over a lost sale. The trainee, in disgust, leaned forward and said, 'I guess you can lead a horse to water but you can't make him drink.' Just then the supervisor jumped to his feet and said in a louder tone, '**DAMN IT, FRANK!**'

(**NOTE**—at that time in my presentation, I was looking out into the large gathering and looking directly at my friend and VP of the NBCE, Dr. Hideg, and got a chuckle from our NBCE delegation).

"'WHO TOLD YOU TO MAKE HIM DRINK? IT'S YOUR JOB TO MAKE HIM THIRSTY!'

"Dr. Padgett, as President of New York Chiropractic College, has the ability to inspire a thirst in the Faculty, the Administration, and the Students—a thirst for knowledge, for proficiency, for pride of one's profession and for the pursuit of one's ultimate goal in life.

"Just remember, people, the most distinguished leaders in history were able to instill a thirst in those around them. We recognize this as ambition for a full life, rich in dignity and courage.

NOTE—A long pause while scanning the standing-only gathering, then I turned to face Dr. Padgett, with my closing.

"Dr. Padgett, on behalf of the entire National Board of Chiropractic Examiners, our officers, directors and staff, I wish you the very very best as President of New York Chiropractic College.

"And to you, your committee and your family, I would like to thank you very much for allowing me to be part of this very special occasion."

NOTE—as I turned to go back to my seat on the podium, Dr. Padgett jumped up from his seat nearby and gave me the biggest hug and thank you, as if I was his long lost child, which erupted the audience to a standing and howling ovation that seemed to go on forever.

NORTHWESTERN COLLEGE OF CHIROPRACTIC COMMENCEMENT ADDRESS

APRIL14, 1990

Introduction of Guest Speaker
Dr. Titus Plomaritis
by NWCC President
Dr. Donald M. Cassata, Ph. D.

"It is my pleasure to introduce our speaker for today. He has a very unusual name, **DOCTOR TITUS PLOMARITIS**, and I would venture that if the graduates don't remember anything else about what he has to say, they will say, 'Do you remember that Dr. Titus Plomaritis?' That's a very special Greek name, and he's well known throughout the chiropractic profession.

"The students have all seen his name before as well, when they were taking their National Board Examinations. Though Dr. Plomaritis has been with the National Board of Chiropractic Examiners for the past eight years, he's been a 30-year proponent of standardized testing, school accreditation and self regulation within the chiropractic profession.

"For the past four years, he has served as President of the National Board of Chiropractic Examiners. One of his biggest achievements has been his help in developing the Board's Part III, Written Clinical Competency Examination.

"Some of you may know that of today's graduates, they have not only survived the grueling five-year academic program, but they have also sat for the three parts of the national board examinations, before graduating today.

"Dr. Plomaritis's link to higher education began when he graduated from Boston University in 1953 with a Bachelor of Science Degree in Physical Education, and Testing and Measurements. As a student athlete at Boston University, Dr. Plomaritis suffered a severe back injury during a football game and he was able to bypass medically prescribed back surgery after a series of chiropractic treatments. He even has a song that is named after him, from his football days. He must be a famous person out in Massachusetts and Boston from his football days.

"By 1957, Titus Plomaritis had graduated from The Chiropractic Institute of New York and later received a Master's Degree in Nutrition, from the University of Bridgeport in Connecticut.

"After graduation as a Doctor of Chiropractic, Dr. Plomaritis opened a private practice in Pelham, New Hampshire, in 1958. He has subsequently taught several of our students in our Preceptorship Program.

"He is also one of the founders of the Raymond E. Riddick Foundation, which grants scholarships to students from his hometown of Lowell, Massachusetts, and currently serves as its president. Coach Riddick was Dr. Plomaritis's high school football coach and good friend.

"He is a member of the American Chiropractic Association, Massachusetts Chiropractic Association, Florida Chiropractic Association, and Boston University Varsity Club, among others.

"He was singled out by the New Hampshire Chiropractic Association, as the New Hampshire Chiropractor of the year in 1978, and has served as chairman of the New Hampshire Board of Chiropractic Examiners for five years.

"Dr. Plomaritis and his wife, Claire, who is a former Representative with the New Hampshire Legislature, have four children.

"Let's give Dr. Plomaritis a warm welcome."

COMMENCEMENT: "EXCELLENCE VERSUS MEDIOCRITY"

By DR. TITUS PLOMARITIS

"Thank you Doctor Cassata, for the great introduction.—"

(First recognizing Dr. Cassata and distinguished guests on the stage, then turning to address the graduates, faculty members, parents and friends, with standing room only at the back of the auditorium.)

DR. TITUS PLOMARITIS (at left), NBCE president, addresses the spring graduating class at Northwestern College of Chiropractic. Following the commencement exercises (below), Dr. Plomaritis chats with a graduate and member of the audience.

Photos courtesy of Northwestern College of Chiropractic

NBCE President Titus Plomaritis
speaks at college functions

"I am deeply honored by the invitation extended to me today, and it is a pleasure to address you. In accepting such an invitation, It's my pleasure, on behalf of the National Board of Chiropractic Examiners, officers, directors and staff, and chiropractic physicians everywhere, to heartily congratulate the 52 members of this graduating class. It's also my pleasure on behalf of your peers, to officially welcome you as Doctors of Chiropractic, as you enter the threshold of your career.

"To receive a Doctor of Chiropractic Degree from the Northwestern College of Chiropractic is indeed an honor and a privilege. Its alumni have achieved some of the most distinguished positions of leadership in our profession. That is a record of which you should well be proud. Your claim to it will serve you well throughout your career.

"Today begins the path of what will be sometimes frustrating, often challenging, but ultimately highly rewarding.

"Years ago, like you, I sat at my own graduating class, I listened to a speaker whose message stayed in my memory. It is just as relevant now, as it was then, and I would like to pass that message on to you today. I don't remember the exact words but the general idea surrounded our freedom, even our obligations to choose **EXCELLENCE OVER MEDIOCRITY**.

"Yes, the concept of freedom does imply, freedom to fail as well as to succeed, but it is the struggle for excellence that has elevated chiropractic to its present status within the health care professions, and it is excellence upon which our future rests. You are entering chiropractic at a time when its pulse is beating very rapidly. It sits on the very brink of discovery by the masses. In order to complete its transformation, we must individually and collectively continue to demonstrate the excellence upon which its philosophy is based.

"Off course we would all like the life of ease and comfort—if we didn't, we would not be human. But the rewards of victory are shabby indeed unless something of value is at stake, unless they are won under the risk of defeat. After all, who would go to a football game with one team on the field?

"When I became a chiropractor in 1957, many members of the medical field refused to recognize the full value in healing capacity, inherent in chiropractic. Some still refuse to do so. But a great many chiropractors applied their knowledge and their skills, and thus have oiled the gates, making passage much easier for your generation. These dedicated men and women refused mediocrity and attained excellence, and that is the excellence I speak of.

"Excellence it must be, it cannot be less. Good enough might be good enough for most people of most professions, but certainly should not be good enough for you and me. And fortunately if it hadn't been for the pioneers and the leaders of our profession, they knew that sooner or later someone invariably would come by with a better mouse trap or better health care services, and then good enough would not be good enough.

You see, good enough goes out of business, usually complaining of unfair competition. Good enough seems okay until hard times hit, and then good enough is unemployed, down on its luck. Good enough might get by in fair weather, but is troubled and sleepless when the weather turns bad.

"I once heard a story about a farmer who needed a hired hand, and one day he met a man looking for work. He said to this man, 'Do you have any references?' The man said, 'I don't have any references, but I'm a man who can sleep through a storm at night.' The farmer was somewhat puzzled by this remark, but he liked the gentleman's appearance and his demeanor and decided to hire him.

"A few weeks later the farmer was awakened, by a raging, severe thunderstorm. He jumped out of bed, put on his clothing, ran to the barn and went up to the loft where the man was sleeping. He shook his bed and shouted his name to no avail. He couldn't awaken him. He was sound asleep.

The farmer went downstairs in the barn, and there the horses were all tied to their stalls, the cows were bedded down, and the windows and doors were latched. He went in the chicken coop, the chickens were all in good order, the windows and doors were secure, and it wasn't until then that the farmer understood what the man meant, when he said he could sleep through a storm. You see, mediocrity may get us by with a crowd, but it certainly will not allow us to sleep through storms that test our courage and try our convictions.

"Sooner or later we will learn that good enough is not good enough when challenged by the consequences of mediocrity. We must stir our passion for excellence. We need men and women who will continue to make their voices heard. Our instructors taught us to think and we do not propose to surrender that freedom.

"In proclaiming that right every minute and every hour of the day, you'll be called upon to make decisions, and every decision you make will effect your life and that of your chosen profession. You alone will choose your friends, your entertainment and your hobbies. You will choose your beliefs and the level of care and commitment that you will give to your patients. Those choices will help determine how you will live each day. The ability to make up your mind, and the will to decide what you must do is one of the tests of whether you will reach the goals you wish to attain in life. It's one of the tests of greatness in men and women.

"Your years here at Northwestern have given you the basis of knowledge. You need to rise above mediocrity and attain greatness. The determination and courage to begin lies within each of you, like a turtle that must stick out his neck in order to go forward. Remember, your life is the sum total of all the decisions you have made, nothing more and nothing less.

"Our profession is the sum total of those who practice and promote its tenants, nothing more and nothing less. If you make the decision to choose excellence over mediocrity and continue to do so, you won't have to worry about your future or the future of chiropractic. Only through this decision can our numbers reach fullness, of intellect, morals and physical welfare that is justly ours.

"Before I surrender the microphone and podium to my good friend, Dr. Cassata, for his final farewell, I would like to leave you with a final message.

"I know in my heart that there are fifty-two young graduates out here who will all become very successful chiropractic physicians. There is no question in my mind. I will ask you to do **THREE THINGS**, three promises to me, to your families and to yourself.

"**FIRST**—make a promise that you will never forget your college, and you will become an active alumni of Northwestern Chiropractic College. That you will refer qualified applicants to Northwestern College, and that you will constantly be a financial contributor to the College, what ever little or whatever more you can afford. And begin today, by giving one buck. We can all afford that, and make it a policy once a year that you will send a contribution to your college, because, believe me, your tuition could no way afford to give you the education you have today.

"**THE SECOND PROMISE**—don't forget your profession. Join your National Chiropractic Association, join and become active in your State Chiropractic Association, become political at the grassroots level, know your local representative and senator, and promote chiropractic in a professional, ethical manner.

"**AND THIRD**—make the promise that you will never, ever forget your parents. They gave you the roots, they gave you their love and affection. Sometimes our parents have a very difficult time in expressing their feeling and opinions.

"With that, I would like to give you my own personal experience.

I am one of seven children. The first six were boys, and I thank God he finally gave my mother a daughter. My parents were both Greek immigrants. My father came to this country when he was thirty-five years of age, and he brought with him a very mean, stubborn, Greek disciplinary action. He married my mother, who was eighteen years younger in one of those typical old fashioned Greek marriages. He was a barber and a farmer during The Depression, when haircuts were twenty-five cents and shaves were fifteen cents. My mother worked in a factory as a stitcher for two dollars a day.

"In the typical tradition, I must say through his stubbornness, my father only read Greek newspapers and the Greek bible. He refused to speak English. In the typical tradition, when he was a boy and became thirteen or fourteen years of age he had to go to work and help support the family. And when I was fourteen years of age, I was a tough little Greek kid and was blessed with speed and football ability, and the football coach, the athletic director, the headmaster and the superintendent of schools of one of the largest schools in Massachusetts went to my father's barber shop, with an interpreter because he didn't speak English, and they said to my father, 'Your son has an opportunity to get a free education some day and you should not make him leave school to go to work.'

"They came to a compromise, and that compromise was that I could stay in school as long as I milked the cows twice a day, took care of the chickens and took care of the farm. So I opted to take that compromise and stay in school.

"The second tradition was marriage, I had to marry a Greek girl of the same religious belief. But when I was a senior in high school, I fell madly in love with a young girl who was French Canadian. Needless to say, when I saw this girl I said to myself, I want this girl to be my wife and be the mother of my children. So when we got married my dad never went to the our wedding, which was a very blessed day, and we were at arm's length for the rest of his life.

"I was fortunate and did get a free college education at Boston University. Sometimes I wonder if it was free, as I broke my wrist, cracked four ribs and broke my nose six times while playing football. However, it did give me the basic education, to give me the stepping stone to chiropractic —which is a most fantastic career in my life and it will be in your life.

"God blessed me with four wonderful children, two boys and two girls, and, you see, he looked over us. We have two boys who are orthopedic surgeons and two daughters who are educators. All four went to graduate school. They had to make a decision, too, but their decision wasn't are you going to work or are you going to school? It's what college are you going to? That was the difference.

"Now, I would be remiss if I didn't tell you, that I have the most beautiful, the most gorgeous wife in the world. There is nobody better. There may be someone equal, but I don't think there is anyone better.

She has been a great wife, a great mother, a mistress, a nurse, a legislator and, most recently, my business manager. If anybody questions my wife's integrity, please speak to Doctor Duquette, (one of the graduates) who just completed her **PRECEPTORSHIP** (equivalent to an internship) at my office.

"And finally, ten years ago my mom and dad celebrated their 55th anniversary, and we decided—the seven children—to finally have a family reunion after these many years of absence, and on my dad's deathbed, he said to me in Greek, '**Titos pee-thee-moo** (Titus my boy)' and continued 'I am proud of you and **tha-sah ghah-pow** (I love you). You have a very nice woman. She has been a good wife and a good mother, and you have four fine children.'

"With that, I want to say to you here today, as soon as this ceremony is over, I want to look out there, and I want to see a lot of hugs and kisses and hear, 'I love you and a lot of I'm proud of you.'

"THANK YOU FOR ALLOWING ME TO BE A PART OF THIS VERY SPECIAL DAY IN YOUR LIFE—I LOVE YOU ALL!!!"

CLOSE CALLS—SIXTH INCIDENT

The most recent incident occurred three or four years ago, when Lyn, our older daughter, was visiting from Alaska.

I was driving with my wife Claire and Lyn, both in the back seat, to our home in Pelham, N.H. from our younger daughter's house on Cape Cod, Massachusetts. The setting was heavy rain and slippery roads. It was approximately eight o'clock in the evening.

As we approached the Greater-Boston area the rain intensified and the traffic conditions worsened. I was driving in the middle lane and attempting to reduce my speed, but vehicles were passing me on both sides. I had nowhere to go but I had to cope with the situation as the rain was coming down so heavily that the windshield wipers were running at maximum and the visibility was terrible.

Although I was traveling at about fifty-five miles per hour, it felt like I was going 100. I was looking in the rearview and side mirrors to see if I could move over to the right lane to get off the highway until the storm let up.

When I refocused in front of me I noticed the car in the left lane just a little ahead of me had hit the guard rail, spun, and was heading directly at me with its headlights practically blinding my vision. It was an act of God, that rather than brake I accelerated and went through a small opening between the second and third lanes, avoiding what could have been a disastrous collision.

Lyn did well to comfort a screaming Claire, who was anticipating a major crash, of which several cars in back of us could not avoid. When we finally arrived home and watched the eleven o'clock news with all the police cars and ambulances at the scene, I realized that I had just dodged another bullet.

TEN STAR MEMORY OF THE NBCE

November 5, 2010:—What a great memory, as I drift off into the twilight zone. Being invited, as a past Director of the NBCE, to share in the

DEDICATION of the Horace C. Elliott Center, (a new addition to the NBCE International Headquarters) and with my dear friend, Dr. Richard Vincent on the microphone introducing me as a **PAST PRESIDENT** of this great organization sent chills up and down my spine.Twenty years of my life to the NBCE was a small price to pay, to a profession that has provided a great life to me and my family.

Officers and Directors

The above Plaque listing the Officers and Directors of the NBCE at the time of building completion of the International Chiropractic Licensing Board Headquarters, in Greeley, Colorado, in 1990. The Plaque has been permanently installed at the front entrance.

TIDBIT: It was 1990 when we dedicated the new **NBCE INTERNATIONAL HEADQUARTERS** with a plaque listing the officers and directors. It was permanently installed at the entrance of the front door. Dr. Paul Tullio had quite often said that he, "was so hard-nosed on Horace's performance that he knew deep down that as soon as he departed the plaque would be removed." Well, the first thing I did when arriving for Horace's dedication—as promised to Paul before his demise—was to visit the front entrance.

I then went out in the open air, looked up in the sky, and as loud as I could speak, said, **"PAUL, YOU CAN REST IN PEACE, THE PLAQUE IS STILL IN IT'S ORIGINAL LOCATION AT THE FRONT DOOR!!"**

FROM THE STARTING GATE TO THE FINISH LINE

Titus & Claire in 1949   Titus & Claire in 2009

WOW! Now can you understand why I consider myself the luckiest guy in the world, going from my 1949 senior prom to my 60th class reunion with the same, one and only love of my life. That, my friend, is why this book is dedicated to **"CLAIRE (HEBERT) PLOMARITIS"**!

MEMORIAL STADIUM 1948

LOWELL,, MASSACHUSETTS

LATER CHANGED TO CAWLEY STADIUM

CPSIA information can be obtained at www.ICGtesting.com
Printed in the USA
LVOW130745120413

328784LV00003B/8/P